D1523651

PREVENTIVE
APPROACHES
IN COUPLES
THERAPY

PREVENTIVE APPROACHES IN COUPLES THERAPY

edited by
Rony Berger, Psy.D.
Mo Therese Hannah, Ph.D.

BRUNNER/MAZEL
Taylor & Francis Group

USA	Publishing Office:	BRUNNER/MAZEL
		A member of the Taylor & Francis Group
		325 Chestnut Street
		Philadelphia, PA 19106
		Tel: (215) 625-8900
		Fax: (215) 625-2940
	Distribution Center:	BRUNNER/MAZEL
		A member of the Taylor & Francis Group
		47 Runway Road, Suite G
		Levittown, PA 19057
		Tel: (215) 269-0400
		Fax: (215) 269-0363
UK		BRUNNER/MAZEL
		A member of the Taylor & Francis Group
		1 Gunpowder Square
		London EC4A 3DE
		Tel: +44 171 583 0490
		Fax: +44 171 583 0581

PREVENTIVE APPROACHES IN COUPLES THERAPY

1 2 3 4 5 6 7 8 9 0

Printed by Edwards Brothers, Lillington, NC, 1999.

A CIP catalog record for this book is available from the British Library.
   The paper in this publication meets the requirements of the ANSI Standard Z39.48-1984 (Permanence of Paper).

Library of Congress Cataloging-in-Publication Data

Preventive approaches in couples therapy / edited by Rony Berger, Mo
   Therese Hannah.
        p. cm.
   Includes bibliographical references and index.
   ISBN 0-87630-876-0 (casebound)
      1. Marital psychotherapy Handbooks, manuals, etc.   2. Family
psychotherapy Handbooks, manuals, etc.   3. Marriage counseling
Handbooks, manuals, etc.   I. Berger, Rony.   II. Hannah, Mo Therese.
RC488.5.P74 1999
616.89′156—dc21   99-14074
                                                                         CIP

ISBN 0-87630-876-0

CONTENTS

ABOUT THE EDITORS

Rony Berger, Psy.D., is a clinical psychologist and a family therapist who is on the faculty of the Martin Buber Center, the Hebrew University of Jerusalem and a researcher at the Harry Truman Center for the Advancement of Peace, the Hebrew University of Jerusalem. He is Co-Editor of *The Journal of Imago Relationship Therapy.*

Mo Therese Hannah, Ph.D., is an Associate Professor of Psychology at Siena College, Loudonville, NY, and a clinical psychologist practicing with couples and families. An Imago Relationship Therapist, she is a Co-Editor of *The Journal of Imago Relationship Therapy* and of the recently released *Healing in the Relational Paradigm: The Imago Relationship Therapy Casebook* also from Brunner/Mazel.

ABOUT THE CONTRIBUTORS

Rony Berger, Psy.D., is a Professor of Psychology and Behavioral Medicine at the Medical School of Al-Quds University, Jerusalem, Israel and the Clinical Director of the Palestinian Center for Traumatic Stress Studies at Al-Quds University. He is also on the faculty of the Martin Buber Center, the Hebrew University of Jerusalem, and the Harry S. Truman Research Institute for the Advancement of Peace at the Hebrew University of Jerusalem. Dr. Berger is a clinical psychologist and family therapist practicing with individuals, couples, and families. He shares with Dr. Hannah the editorship of *The Journal of Imago Relationship Therapy.*

Susan L. Blumberg, Ph.D., is a clinical psychologist working with couples, children, and families in Denver, Colorado. She is coauthor of *Fighting for Your Marriage* and has worked on the Prevention and Relationship Enhancement Program (PREP) approach for 14 years.

Thomas N. Bradbury, Ph.D., is a professor in the Department of Psychology, University of California, Los Angeles. Dr. Bradbury's laboratory conducts basic and applied research on the longitudinal course of newlywed marriages. He is the editor of *The Developmental Course of Marital Dysfunction* and the recipient of the American Psychological Association's 1997 Distinguished Scientific Award for Early Career Contributions to Psychology.

Jon Carlson, Psy.D., Ed.D., is Professor of Psychology and Counseling at Governors State University, University Park, Illinois, and a psychologist at the Lake Geneva, Wisconsin, Wellness Clinic. He is past president of the International Association of Marriage and Family Counselors and is the editor of *The Family Journal: Counseling and Therapy for Couples and Families.* Dr. Carlson is a diplomate in family psychology and in marital and family therapy and has authored 25 books and 120 articles.

Clay Cavedo, Ph.D., is a clinical psychologist and certified Relationship Enhancement® (RE) therapist whose experience with the RE program includes supervision of therapists in training and experimental small group work. With Bernard Guerney, Jr., she has conducted investigations of the reasons for the effectiveness of the RE approach.

Rita DeMaria, Ph.D., is a marriage and family therapist and is director of The Relationship Center in Spring House, Pennsylvania. She is an active master teacher and trainer of the Practical Application of Intimate Relationship Skills (PAIRS) program, as well as a PREPARE/ENRICH trainer. She is also a coauthor of *Marriage Enrichment: Preparation, Outreach, and Mentoring* and senior author of *Focused Genograms: Intergenerational Assessment of Individuals, Couples and Families,* both published by Brunner/Mazel.

Don Dinkmeyer, Sr., Ph.D., is president of the Communication and Motivation Training Institute of Coral Springs, Florida. A diplomate of the American Board of Family Psychology, he coauthored, among others, the well-known Systematic Training for Effective Parenting (STEP) program as well as numerous professional books and articles.

Carlos Durana, Ph.D., M.Ac., is a clinical psychologist who works with individuals, couples, and groups. He is a researcher and writer who has authored articles on psychoeducation, intimacy, the use of touch, and emotionally focused approaches in psychoeducation and psychotherapy. He is a Practical Application of Intimate Relationship Skills (PAIRS) trainer who conducted the first published research on the PAIRS program.

Genie H. Dyer, Ph.D., is a certified family life educator and a lecturer at Baylor University, Waco, Texas. Along with her husband, Preston, she has published a number of professional articles and two books, *The Language of Married Love* and *Growing Together: Transition to Marriage.*

Preston M. Dyer, Ph.D., is, along with his wife, Genie, a marriage and family specialist with 30 years of experience in enrichment, therapy, education, and research. The Dyers are former presidents of the Association for Couples in Marriage Enrichment (A.C.M.E.) and are certified A.C.M.E. trainers. Preston is professor of sociology and social work at Baylor University, Waco, Texas, where he has been director of the Social Work Division since 1969. He is a diplomate in clinical social work.

Rhoderick J. Elin, Ph.D., is chief of staff at Catholic Community Services of Western Washington/Northwest in Bellingham, Washington. He is a clinical member of the American Association of Marriage and Family Therapists. He has been active in National Marriage Encounter for over 20 years (along with his wife, Andrea), serving as a presenter for over 35 Encounter weekends and sitting on the National Board of Directors and on regional boards.

Frank D. Fincham, Ph.D., is professor of psychology at the State University of New York at Buffalo. He has been a governor of the United Kingdom College of Family Mediators and previously served as director of clinical training at the University of Illinois. He was the recipient of the President's Award for Distinguished Contributions to Psychological Knowledge from the British Psychological Society.

Lori Heyman Gordon, Ph.D., is founder and president of the Family Relations Institute of the PAIRS Foundation, Pembroke Pines, Florida, and of PAIRS INTERNATIONAL, Inc. A diplomate of the Academy of Certified Social Workers, Dr. Gordon is the creator of the PAIRS (Practical Application of Intimate Relationship Skills) program for adults and of PAIRS FOR PEERS, an adaptation of PAIRS for teenagers. She has authored three books, *Love Knots, Passage to Intimacy,* and *If You Really Loved Me.*

John Mordechai Gottman, Ph.D., is professor of psychology at the University of Washington, Seattle. Having held a National Institute of Mental Health Research Scientist Award since 1979, Dr. Gottman has spent the past 20 years studying couples to discover the factors that contribute to marital success or failure. He is the author of *Why Marriages Succeed or Fail* and *The Heart of Parenting: Raising an Emotionally Intelligent Child.*

Julie Schwartz Gottman, Ph.D., is a clinical psychologist who works with couples. With Dr. John Gottman, she conducts research on factors contributing to marital success or failure at The Gottman Institute, University of Washington.

Bernard G. Guerney, Jr., Ph.D., is director of the National Institute of Relationship Enhancement®, Bethesda, Maryland. He is professor emeritus of counseling psychology and of human development/family studies at Pennsylvania State University, where he founded and directed the Individual and Family Consultation Center. A Fellow of five American Psychological Association divisions, Dr. Guerney holds diplomates in clinical psychology, marital/family therapy, behavioral medicine, and counseling/psychotherapy. He serves on the editorial boards of many major journals and has published, alone or collaboratively, scores of articles and chapters, four books, and numerous training manuals, audiotapes, and videotapes.

Mo Therese Hannah, Ph.D., is associate professor of psychology at Siena College, Loudonville, New York, and is a couples therapist in private practice. Having coauthored or authored over 25 articles and book chapters, she is coeditor of *The Journal of Imago Relationship Therapy* and of *Healing in the Relational Paradigm: The Imago Relationship Therapy Casebook.*

Harville Hendrix, Ph.D., and Helen Hunt, M.A., are husband and wife, cocreators of Imago Relationship Therapy, and cofounders of the Institute for Imago Relationship Therapy, Winter Park, Florida. Together they have authored four books on marriage and two on parenting. Three of their books, *Getting the Love You Want, Keeping the Love You Find,* and *Giving the Love That Heals,* have been on bestseller lists, including the New York Times list. Dr. Hendrix has been a couples therapist for over 30 years; Ms. Hunt is a community activist and a founder of several women's organizations, including the Sister Fund, which is committed to empowering women and girls.

Richard A. Hunt, Ph.D., and Joan A. Hunt, M.A., are husband and wife and coauthors of the *Caring Couples Network Handbook* and the official guide to marriage of the United Methodist Church, *Growing Love in Christian Marriage.* Dr. Hunt is senior professor of psychology at the Graduate School of Psychology, Fuller Theological Seminary, Pasadena, California. He is the author (with Larry Hof and Rita DeMaria) of *Marriage Enrichment: Preparation, Mentoring, and Outreach* (Taylor & Francis, 1998), among other books. Dr. Hunt is an ordained elder in the Central Texas Annual Conference of the United Methodist Church.

Adrian B. Kelly, M.Clin.Psych., is a lecturer in clinical psychology at Griffith University, Gold Coast, Australia. Dr. Kelly's interests lie in the association between couple relationship problems and individual health and in process issues in marital therapy.

Luciano L'Abate, Ph.D., is professor emeritus of psychology at Georgia State University, Atlanta. He is cofounder of the International Academy of Family Psychology and the president of the Institute for Life Empowerment, dedicated to producing mental health workbooks. He has published 29 books, including his most recent one, *Family Psychopathology: The Relational Roots of Dysfunctional Behavior,* and over 200 book chapters and journal articles.

Howard J. Markman, Ph.D., is director of the Center for Marital and Family Studies and professor of psychology at the University of Denver, Colorado. He is a nationally known researcher, speaker, and therapist in the areas of understanding, treating, and preventing marital conflict, marital distress, and divorce. He developed and evaluated the Prevention and Relationship Enhancement Program (PREP), a divorce prevention program. He is author of over 100 journal articles and book chapters and is coauthor of four books: *The Couple's Guide to Communication, We Can Work It Out: Making Sense of Marital Conflict, Fighting for Your Marriage,* and *The Clinical Handbook of Marriage and Marital Therapy.*

Sherod Miller, Ph.D., a social psychologist, is chairman of Interpersonal Communication Programs, Inc. and is the author of the COUPLE COM-MUNICATION program as well as of four published books. Dr. Miller's award-winning work on the COUPLE COMMUNICATION program at the University of Minnesota has generated over 65 independent research studies. Over 500,000 people have participated in the business and family communication programs that he developed.

Amy K. Olson, B.A., is a research associate at Life Innovations, Minneapolis, MN.

David H. Olson, Ph.D., is professor of family social science, University of Minnesota, and is president of Life Innovations, St. Paul, Minneapolis. A fellow and a clinical member of both the American Psychological Association and the American Association for Marriage and Family Therapy, Dr. Olson developed the PREPARE/ENRICH inventories, which more than 30,000 counselors have been trained to administer, and the Circumplex Model of Marital and Family Systems, which has been used in over 500 studies of families. He has written 20 books and over 100 articles on marriage and family therapy.

Les Parrott III, Ph.D., and Leslie Parrott, Ed.D., are founders and codirectors of the Center for Relationship Development on the campus of Seattle Pacific University, Washington, where Les is also a professor of psychology. The Parrotts are authors of several books on marriage, including *Getting Ready for the Wedding, Questions Couples Ask; Mentoring Engaged and Newlywed Couples;* and *Saving Your Marriage Before It Starts.*

Ronald M. Rogge, M.A., is an advanced graduate student in clinical psychology at the University of California, Los Angeles. He works with Dr. Thomas Bradbury in studying the early stages of marriage. A National Science Foundation Graduate Fellow, he has authored eight articles.

Peter A. D. Sherrard, Ed.D., is associate professor of Counselor Education at the University of Florida. A marriage and family therapist, he is an

American Psychological Association diplomate in Counseling Psychology and was the American Mental Health Counselors Association's "Researcher of the Year" in 1992.

Scott M. Stanley, Ph.D., is a clinical psychologist specializing in research on marital and relationship commitment and on the prediction and prevention of marital distress and divorce. He is codirector of the Center for Marital and Family Studies at the University of Denver, Colorado. Along with Dr. Howard Markman and colleagues, Dr. Stanley has been involved in the research, development, and refinement of the Prevention and Relationship Enhancement Program (PREP) for over 20 years. Dr. Stanley is the author of *The Heart of Commitment* and coauthor of *A Lasting Promise* and of the bestseller *Fighting for Your Marriage*.

FOREWORD

It is a distinct pleasure to have this opportunity to write the foreword to an outstanding, timely book on approaches to preventing marital distress and divorce. While divorce rates are no longer rising in the United States, they have stabilized at an alarmingly high rate. Rates of marital dissolution continue to rise in Europe and are starting to climb in Asia. Despite important contributions in the area of treatment of marital distress, studies indicate that it is an extremely hard task to start with a distressed couple and help them become nondistressed and truly happy in their relationship. For too long, it has seemed as though the field of marital therapy were sending interventionists to the bottom of a cliff to wait for couples to fall off, rather than working on building edifices to keep happy couples from toppling over as they struggle with the challenges associated with the contemporary marriage.

The editors of this book have attracted the leading contributors to the field of prevention with couples. Readers will be treated to up-to-date reports on the most important programs available for interventionists who want to help couples maintain a happy relationship or enrich relationships that have grown stale. In addition, therapists who continue to work with distressed couples will gain new insights as they read the contributions of researchers and program developers who have developed innovative tools for helping couples. For example, many of the programs in this state-of-the-art book represent a psychoeducational approach to working with couples. Here the emphasis is on providing information and teaching skills to couples, rather than on understanding and resolving unconscious conflicts. The editors also provide an outstanding introduction to, and, in their epilogue, a superb summary of, the field of prevention of marital and family distress and divorce. The chapters follow a common framework that enhances the readability of the book and enables the reader to compare programs easily. Moreover, the chapters represent a refreshing blend of research results and clinical illustrations of the importance of research. The case example provided by the editors helps bring to life the principles underlying the prevention programs and serves to highlight the differences between them.

The timing of this handbook is important because the field of marital and family therapy is undergoing a revolution. It is moving from the use of approaches that emphasize treating distressed couples with insight-oriented models to seeking ways to keep happy couples happy and/or to intervene with couples at predictable transition periods through teaching skills and providing information. The excellent research reviews in the current volume indicate that, while clearly more work needs to be done, we can be optimistic about the potential for preventing marital distress and divorce through short-term, skills-oriented, psychoeducational programs.

Readers are about to embark on a journey that will be educational, interesting, and beneficial. The editors have planned a marvelous trip through these programs; sit back and enjoy the experience.

Howard J. Markman

PREFACE

The issue of "family values" gained precedence in the late 1980s and early 1990s, due to the ongoing decline of the traditional American family, which in turn was reflected during the past several decades in the rising percentages of failed marriages and single-parent families. These shifts, coupled with the efforts of the Clinton administration to develop a national health plan, ushered in renewed interest by the lay and professional communities in preventive programs. Around the same time, two ground-breaking reports on prevention were issued. The first, commissioned by Congress, was the Institute of Medicine's (IOM) report entitled *Reducing Risk for Mental Disorders: Frontiers for Preventive Intervention Research* (Mrazek & Haggerty, 1994). The second was the National Institute of Mental Health's (NIMH) *The Prevention of Mental Disorders: A National Research Agenda* (NIMH Prevention Research Steering Committee, 1994). Such social, political and professional developments contributed a fresh impetus to the burgeoning field of prevention of marital distress.

Although several enrichment and preventive programs had been available since as early as the 1950s, new and more sophisticated programs, including PAIRS (Gordon; see chapter 10), PREP (Markman and colleagues; see chapter 13), Getting the Love You Want (Hendrix; see chapter 8), and the Marriage Survival Kit (Gottman; see chapter 14) gained visibility and popularity, due in part to the intense media coverage of this currently relevant topic. An additional factor influencing the development of preventive interventions for couples was the doubt cast on the efficacy of marital therapies by outcome research. For example, Jacobson and Addis (1993), in their review of the literature, raised questions regarding the efficacy of couple therapy intervention models while pointing out the more promising results of distress prevention programs. They concluded that "the success of these brief enrichment and prevention programs, combined with somewhat equivocal results obtained from existing therapies for distressed couples, suggests that it may be easier to prevent relationship problems than treat them once they emerged" (p. 86).

It is not surprising, therefore, that many couples and family therapists began to show interest in preventive programs. Many either incorporated such programs into their therapeutic approach (tertiary prevention) or used them for targeted at-risk populations (secondary prevention).

As academicians who teach and do research in the area of marital interventions, and as practicing family and couple therapists who are interested in prevention, we decided to explore the available texts in this arena. To our surprise, we found only a few books, several of them outdated and most failing to cover the newer, more empirically based approaches. We decided, therefore, to assemble the major contributors within the field, asking them to present their preventive approach in a structured format (see chapter 1 for details) similar to that used by Gurman and Kniskern (1981). For each approach, the contributor described the underlying theoretical assumptions, the rationale for the intervention model, and associated clinical strategies. To further enhance comparison of the various models, we asked contributors to apply their approach to the same clinical case, which we provided (see "Case Study: Ben and Alyssa, A Couple at Risk," in chapter 1).

The book is divided into four parts: "Introduction" (chapter 1), "Programs" (chapters 2–14), "Research" (chapters 15 and 16), and "Summary" (epilogue). Reflecting our emphasis (or perhaps our bias) regarding the importance of empirical findings, we included two chapters (chapters 15 and 16) that review the major research issues. In choosing the term "preventive" for our title, we opted for a broader definition that combines the reduction of dysfunctional behaviors by couples with the promotion of wellness behaviors. We believe that this more inclusive perspective reflects the current trends in the field of prevention of couples' distress.

The paradoxical nature of the title *Preventive Approaches in Couples Therapy* does not escape us. Using both "preventive" and "therapy" in the same title appears contradictory; indeed, we would have preferred to name the book *Preventive Approaches to Couples' Distress*—a more congruent but unfortunately awkward title. Furthermore, many couples therapists incorporate into their therapeutic armamentarium elements of preventive models, and many preventive approaches attract distressed couples to their program. Given that we could not avoid the blurring of preventive interventions with remedial ones, we chose to conceptualize the various intervention strategies as falling on the same continuum (see chapter 1).

This book is geared toward mental health professionals (e.g., psychologists, psychiatrists, social workers, family and couple therapists) and other interested professionals (e.g., clergy, nurses, teachers) who design, implement, and evaluate preventive programs for couples or who use preventive strategies as part of their therapeutic framework. The book could also serve as a textbook for undergraduate- and graduate-level courses on couple relationships, marriage enrichment, marriage education, and couples therapy. Finally, we believe that this text will be useful for paraprofessionals (e.g., community leaders, enriched couples) who typically carry the bulk of the responsibility of providing such programming to their communities.

We wish to thank, first and foremost, our esteemed contributors. Despite their universally demanding schedules and the exacting chapter structure we imposed on them, all were willing to put aside other priorities and work within our confines. Special thanks is accorded to the "grandfather of family prevention," Lu L'Abate, who enthusiastically supported this project, as well as to Howie Markman for his enthusiastic Foreword. We also acknowledge the generous contributions of our initial editor at Brunner/Mazel, Suzi Tucker, along with her assistant editor, Caroline Levachuck. Thanks is due also to our editor, Mark Tracton, who has supported us throughout the project. Last but not least, we offer our deep appreciation to our current Brunner/Mazel acquisitions editor, Toby Wahl, and to our copy editor, Beth Gallagher, for their tireless patience and encouragement.

Finally, we hope this volume will encourage the development of more effective, empirically based, less costly, and widely applicable approaches to couples' distress, thereby contributing to the prevention of couples' discord and to the strengthening and empowerment of families in our society.

☐ References

Gurman, A. S., & Kniskern, D. P. (1981). *Handbook of family therapy.* New York: Brunner/Mazel.

Jacobson, N. S., & Addis, M. E. (1993). Research on couples and couple therapy: What do we know? *Journal of Consulting and Clinical Psychology, 61*, 85–93.

Mrazek, P. J., & Haggerty, R. J. (Eds.). (1994). *Reducing the risks for mental disorders: Frontiers for preventing intervention research.* Washington, DC: National Academy Press.

NIMH Prevention Research Steering Committee. (1994). *The Prevention of Mental Disorders: A National Research Agenda.* Washington, DC: Author.

ACKNOWLEDGMENTS

This volume has been overdue for the past year and a half. I would like to express my gratitude to all my friends, colleagues, and family members for their unconditional love and support throughout this period. My deepest thanks, however, goes to my soul mate, Ilana, who epitomizes for me the ideal of a "modern woman": strong, independent, professional, and yet, at the same time, supportive and nurturing. I would like to share this gratitude also with my beloved twins, who have always given me strength and energy, even when they demand the same from me. My deep appreciation goes to my parents and my in-laws, holocaust survivors who exemplify how marital relationships can conquer the worst of human adversities. I would also like to thank Esty Rot, my "personal librarian," for being so efficient and generous with her time. Finally, I would also like to thank my coeditor, Mo, who has shared with me both her friendship and her professional talents.

Rony Berger

The finalizing of this volume dovetails with some daunting personal challenges in the lives of both coeditors. I, too, would like to gratefully acknowledge many people: first and foremost, my coeditor, Rony, the faithful friends who have been my "support group": Susan Paul and my best colleague and friend, Dr. Joe Marrone who, along with Joan McCormick, my untiring assistant editor, and Wade Luquet, the "slave of the slave of the world," tolerated my many long, often long-overdue phone calls. And I'd like to especially thank my four children, Monique, Willy, Alex, and Jesse, who serve as my constant inspiration to do whatever I can to change my little corner of the world.

Mo Therese Hannah

Rony Berger, Psy.D.
Mo Therese Hannah, Ph.D.

Introduction

In this chapter, we will define the arena of preventive approaches to couple distress, illuminating the importance of this field and offering a conceptual framework for comparing the various approaches. We will also outline the guidelines used by the book's contributors in writing their chapters. Finally, we will end this introduction with the case study that the chapter authors used in applying their particular preventive approaches.

☐ Demarcation of the Field

During the last few decades, there has been a proliferation of new prevention and couple enrichment training programs (Floyd, Markman, Kelly, Blumberg, & Stanley, 1995). Due to the keen interest in such programs among mental health professionals, paraprofessionals, and the general public, we saw the need for an up-to-date, comprehensive summary of current approaches.

In the past, when they were included in volumes on marital and couples therapy, preventive approaches were classified as "emerging models of marital therapy" or "group models" of couples interventions (Jacobson & Gurman, 1986, 1995). But, as will become apparent from what is presented in this volume, preventive approaches have a long history; they began to emerge long before their inclusion in volumes on couples therapy. Nor have all prevention approaches been group oriented. Even more important, as noted by many prominent theoreticians, there are meaningful differences between preventive and remedial approaches to marital and couple distress (e.g., Guerney, Brock, & Coufal, 1986; L'Abate, 1981; Mace, 1983; Markman, Floyd, Stanley, & Lewis, 1986).

In structuring this volume, therefore, one of our main challenges was devising an appropriate title, one that would encompass the diversity of preventive approaches while retaining their distinction from remedial models. We recognized that our choice of a title would reflect a deeper conceptual issue, that is, the demarcation of the field. What, in fact, should be included within the rubric of preventive approaches to couples interventions?

Preventive programs for couples, married or nonmarried, have appeared under different titles throughout the years. They have been termed "family life education" (Groves & Groves, 1947), "marriage enrichment" (Mace & Mace, 1975), "relationship enhancement" (Guerney, 1977), "skill/competence training" (L'Abate, 1986), and, more generically, "psychoeducational programs" (Leveat, 1986). Though there are clearly some differences among these programs (for further discussion, see L'Abate, 1977), they all share one pertinent commonality: They are identified as preventive rather than remedial. However, as L'Abate (1990) noted, marital and couples therapists may also claim to engage in prevention, that is, prevention of "crisis and breakdown" (p. 20).

Thus, our dilemma involves deciding whether remedial approaches should be included among the preventive approaches in the area of marital and couple distress. To make this determination, it is important to illuminate the differences between preventive and therapeutic models.

☐ Preventive Versus Remedial Approaches to Couple Distress

Preventive approaches are geared toward relatively functional couples who have not yet experienced significant relationship problems. Couples therapy models, or remedial interventions, usually target "dysfunctional couples," that is, couples who have already experienced interactional problems that have comprised relationship satisfaction, relationship stability, or both. Preventive programs are based on psychoeducational, skill- or competence-based models; therefore, such programs focus on the strengths and well-being of the couple. Though these approaches do not ignore risk factors, such as dysfunctional communication styles, destructive interactional patterns, and negative attitudes, they place greater stress on developing positive and mutually satisfying attitudes, communication styles, and intimacy patterns. On the other hand, remedial approaches are often based on the medical model and thus typically underscore the couple's pathology (Denton, 1986; Guerney et al., 1986).

Additionally, most preventive programs have in common the following ingredients: They are didactic, experiential, structured, programmatic, time limited, affirmative, usually economical, and primarily group oriented. In contrast, most remedial models are less structured, nonprogrammatic, minimally didactic, partially affirmative, not time limited, and much more expensive (L'Abate, 1977).

A more detailed differentiation between preventive and remedial interventions was proposed in the report of the Institute of Medicine's (IOM's) prevention committee (Mrazek & Haggerty, 1994). The IOM's committee divided all mental health interventions into three basic categories: prevention, treatment, and maintenance. According to Munoz, Mrazek, and Haggerty (1996), prevention is relegated to "those interventions that occur before the initial onset of a clinically diagnosable disorder" (p. 1118), while treatment (remedial) starts when a diagnosable criterion has been reached. Maintenance, on the other hand, can be either preventive or remedial, though it also occurs after the acute episode of mental disorder. These interventions are geared either toward preventing relapse or recurrence of disorder or toward rehabilitation.

Despite such important differences between prevention and remediation, during the last decade or two, there has been a gradual blurring of these two types of interventions. The influence of psychoeducational models in the medical and mental health fields, the focus by managed care on cost-effective interventions, and the growing prominence of the brief therapy movement have coalesced in the merging of the two classes of interventions. It is now common to see therapeutic models for couples that incorporate preventive ingredients (as an example, see Hendrix & Hunt, chapter 8 of this volume) and preventive models modified for use in the context of couple therapy (see Stanley, Blumberg, & Markman, chapter 13, and L'Abate, chapter 5). Thus, we agree with Guerney and Maxson's (1990) observation that "sharp demarcation between problem prevention, enrichment, and therapy have not, and perhaps cannot and should not, be made" (p. 1127).

Another way to view the commonalities among preventive and remedial approaches is to view them as falling at different points along a continuum of interventions.

☐ Three Levels of Preventive Programs

Prevention is defined as "the act of anticipating before hindering or preventing" (Webster's Unabridged Dictionary, 1983). This focus on the temporal aspect (anticipation) rather than on the nature of the intervention or the targeted group was emphasized by many preventionists (Coie et al., 1993; Heller, 1996; Mrazek & Haggerty, 1994; Price, Cowen, Lorion, & Ramos-McKay, 1989; Riess & Price, 1996). The National Institute of Mental Health's (NIMH) panel, in its report to the National Prevention Conference (Coie et al., 1993), stated that "preventive efforts occur, by definition, before illness is fully manifested" (p. 1013).

L'Abate's definition is more descriptive: "Prevention consists of any approach, procedure, or method designed to improve interpersonal competence and functioning for people as individuals, as partners in intimate relationships, and as parents" (1990, p. 7).

Historically, preventive approaches have been grouped into one of three levels of intervention: primary, secondary, and tertiary. Primary prevention with couples is considered "true" prevention in that it intervenes with couples before they are experiencing difficulties; it is "prevention before it happens" (L'Abate, 1983). Catalano and Dooley (1980) focused on the proactive nature of such services.

Secondary prevention involves interventions with "at-risk" couples, those who are experiencing some degree of relationship impairment. Secondary prevention thus provides semi-proactive services to intervene with couples "before they get worse," to borrow L'Abate's (1983) terminology.

Finally, tertiary prevention applies to couples experiencing significant problems in which the relationship itself is at stake. Here, services are provided "before it is too late," and are thus considered reactive as opposed to proactive. Couples therapy is a prime example of tertiary prevention.

It is important to note that these distinctions are somewhat artificial. As Mace (1983) indicated, "these preventive processes overlap and cannot be precisely distinguished from each other" (p. 19). Moreover, several authors use similar programs for both primary and secondary prevention, and even, more rarely, for tertiary prevention.

In identifying the preventive nature of the programs presented in this volume, one needs to clarify their primary goals. In other words, what is the program designed to prevent? The following list offers three characteristics of preventive couples therapy.

1. Primary: The program is geared toward helping couples deal with normative problems, such as life transitions (e.g., parenthood, geographical moves, job changes).
2. Secondary: The program is designed to prevent future dissatisfaction or the loss of desirable relationship characteristics, such as passion and intimacy.
3. Tertiary: The program aims to keep serious couple problems from leading to further deterioration of the relationship and marital separation.

Items 1 and 2 describe most of the programs in this volume, which therefore could be considered primary or secondary preventive models. However, some contributors suggest that their programs also address couples' more significant difficulties and can thus be viewed as tertiary models.[1] Others point out that, with some modifications, their interventions can also be used for tertiary prevention.

If couple intervention models are conceptualized as lying along a preventive continuum (L'Abate, 1990), with family education on one side and couples therapy on the other, then we have resolved the polarization between prevention and remediation, thus permitting the application of marital and couple interventions to the varying levels of prevention.

A similar view was reached by the IOM's prevention committee, which stated: "The committee agreed on the usefulness of viewing treatment and prevention as part of a spectrum of interventions of mental health disorders, instead of seeing them in opposition to each other" (Munoz et al., 1996, p. 1120).

☐ The IOM's Categorization of Preventive Interventions

Another way to classify the various preventive strategies was suggested by the IOM's committee (Munoz et al., 1996), which subdivided the field of prevention into universal, selective, and indicated interventions. This categorization is based on the presence and severity of risk factors for developing a mental disorder. Hence, preventive universal strategies are geared toward an entire population group not considered to be at risk. Selective preventive strategies are directed toward individuals or groups who demonstrate relatively significant risk for developing a mental disorder. Finally, indicated preventive strategies address those individuals or groups who have already developed some symptoms (although not a full-blown disorder) or those who manifest a biological predisposition for a mental disorder.

Using the concept of levels of prevention, *universal* interventions are clearly primary prevention, *selective* interventions would be considered secondary prevention, and *indicated* interventions would appear to be either secondary or tertiary prevention.

---

[1]A notable exception is chapter 7 on Imago Relationship Therapy, which originated more as a tertiary preventive model. However, due to the fact that the model has many ingredients common to primary and secondary prevention models, we decided to include it in this volume. Furthermore, the application of Imago Relationship Therapy in a workshop format could be considered either a primary or secondary prevention approach.

In using the above strategy to evaluate the programs described in this volume, most would appear to be universal programs geared to the general public. However, the self-selection of participants into such programs could qualify the programs as selective strategies.

Preliminary evidence for this consideration was provided by Hogan, Hunt, Emersson, Hayes, & Ketterer (1996), who showed that highly distressed couples enroll in the Imago Relationship Therapy couples workshop (see Hendrix and Hunt, chap. 8 of this volume). In addition, DeMaria's (1998) survey of married participants in the PAIRS program (see Gordon and Durana, chapter 10 of this volume) demonstrated that most of these couples were of the highly distressed "devitalized" type, according to the ENRICH typology (see Olson and Olson, chapter 9 of this volume). This phenomenon is believed to apply to participants in other interventions besides those just mentioned, although further research is needed.

Finally, some programs (for example, SE; see L'Abate, chapter 5 of this volume) fall into the category of selective interventions in targeting a particular individual or group at risk. A few programs fit the label of indicated programs, due to their application to specific groups who demonstrate some degree of symptomatology.

☐ Preventing Dysfunction Versus Promoting Wellness

As suggested above, the murky differentiation between prevention and remediation in the field of couples' distress has not proven helpful in the task of demarcating the field of prevention. Another dilemma relates to the goal of preventive interventions. While some practitioners focus on the narrow objective of preventing psychological disorders, as defined by the DSM-IV (American Psychiatric Association, 1994), others add to it the enhancement of wellness.

This more inclusive definition was articulated in the Prevention Task Panel Report for then-President Carter's Commission on Mental Health (Albee, 1996). However, this definition has recently been replaced by a more concise definition which maintains that "the goal of prevention science is to prevent or moderate major human dysfunctions" (Coie et al., 1993, p. 1013). The predominance of this definition was demonstrated in the recent IOM and NIMH reports. The IOM report (Mrazek & Haggerty, 1996) went so far as to exclude mental health promotion from its view of prevention, stating that "health promotion is not driven by a focus on illness, but rather a focus on the enhancement of well-being" (p. 27).

The most ardent and outspoken critique of the "narrow definition" and its "new preventionists" has been Albee (1996), who challenged the notion that promotion of well-being is geared toward achieving optimal states of wellness by asking: "Does not a feeling of well-being, of positive self-esteem, of enhanced social competence strengthen resistance to stress?" (p. 1131). He asks, "Are these not protective factors in another guise?" This position is supported by other prominent preventionists in the field of couple distress (e.g., Guerney, 1986; L'Abate, 1977).

Albee also suggests that underlying these seemingly polarized definitions lie very different views of human dysfunction: the disease model versus the stress-learning model. According to Albee (1996), the disease model stresses "genetic, biochemical, or other physical defects and [the] environment for causes that trigger these internal defects" (p. 1131). On the other hand, the stress-learning model "focuses the search on environmental factors such as poverty, exploitation, and prejudice that produce augmented stress" (p. 1131). The implication in espousing the later model is that prevention should include social and political activities geared toward social change.

Albee's polarization of the field into preventionists who support the promotion of wellness and those who do not seems to us misguided. Since there is almost a concensus in the prevention field regarding the importance of dealing with both risk factors and protective factors, addressing the latter ought to include wellness promotion strategies. Furthermore, not all preventionists who share the IOM or NIMH definitions of prevention necessarily support the disease model.

Nevertheless, we agree with Albee's emphasis on wellness promotion, especially in the field of couple relationships. We concur also with his recommendation (Perry & Albee, 1994) that a "[prevention] agenda should be developed independently of a model already committed to individual defect over social injustice, biogenetic causes over social learning, micro-over macro-interventions, and traditional processes over positive outcomes" (p. 1088).

☐ The Case for Prevention

Though divorce rates in the United States have slightly, yet steadily, declined since the late 1980s (National Center for Health Statistics, 1996), at least 4 out of 10 newlywed couples face an eventual divorce (Norton & Miller, 1992). The proportion of couples who end their relationship through separation or divorce is high (e.g., about 42% of marriages in the United Kingdom, 55% of marriages in the United States, 35% of Australian marriages, and 37% of German marriages end in divorce). More disconcerting is the fact that, of those couples who remain together, a significant proportion live in an unhappy or abusive relationship (Mace

& Mace, 1980; O'Leary, Barling, Arias, & Rosenbaum, 1989; Olson & Olson, chapter 9 of this volume). These statistics are underscored by those indicating a slow but significant decline in marital quality during the 1970s and 1980s (Glenn, 1991).

The combined economic, social, and psychological effects of marital disruption are astounding. A recent NIMH report suggests that marital distress and destructive couple relationships have been linked to higher rates of depression, mental disorders, alcoholism, conduct disorders in children, health problems, and decreases in work productivity (Coie et al., 1993). The impact on children and adolescents is particularly alarming. The all-time-high rates of depression and suicide in youngsters have been linked to the high rate of marital dissolution (Klerman & Weissman, 1990). Similarly, the relationship between various adult psychopathologies and couple distress has been documented (Beach, Sandeen, & O'Leary, 1990; Heiman, Epps, & Ellis, 1995; Jacobson, Holzworth-Munro, & Schmaling, 1989; McCrady & Epstein, 1995). Furthermore, couples' conflictual relationships have been associated with a decline in physical health, as measured by compromised immune functioning (Kiecolt-Glaser, Fisher, Ogrocki, Stout, Speicher, & Glaser, 1987).

In sum, marital dysfunction is undoubtedly one of the major social, psychological, and health risk contributors to the deterioration of our society, costing us, according to some estimates, billions of dollars yearly (Markman, Renick, Floyd, Stanley, & Clements, 1993).

The prevalence, durability, and enormity of this problem, as indicated by the above data, testify to the need for comprehensive approaches to intervening in couple and marital distress. Traditionally, the mental health establishment has provided couples and marital therapy for treating couple dysfunction. Indeed, there is evidence that at least 40 percent of all mental health patients attribute their problems, at least in part, to couple issues (Veroff, Kulka, & Douvan, 1981). The steep increase in the number (which has more than doubled) of marital and family counselors over the past decade (Gurman & Kniskern, 1991) suggests a growing demand for services in this area. Yet, despite the growth in accessibility and acceptability of these services, the dismal rates of marital stability and dissatisfaction have not improved significantly. More far-reaching and economically viable approaches are needed. Preventive programs for couples, such as the approaches described in this volume, might very well be the solution.

L'Abate, one of the strongest advocates of prevention in the area of marital and family distress, outlines five arguments in favor of preventive approaches as opposed to remedial ones. For L'Abate, "prevention is cheaper, more innovative, easier, happier and cleaner" (for further discussion, see L'Abate, 1983, pp. 51–53).

Bradbury and Fincham (1990) provide a more detailed rationale for the use of prevention with couples, focusing on the deficits of remedial models as well as the assets of preventive approaches. The most potent deficit associated with remedial models, according to these authors, is that remedial approaches "have not been shown to produce clinically significant change in reliable fashion" (p. 378). On the other hand, the strengths of preventive approaches include their preventing couples' suffering and relationship deterioration before they fully emerge, enabling couples to deal with relationship difficulties on their own, reaching a far wider audience, and providing more economically viable interventions.

Another strong argument in favor of preventive approaches comes from several longitudinal studies demonstrating that early destructive premarital and marital conflict is a major risk factor for future marital dysfunction and divorce (Gottman, 1994; Kelly & Fincham, chapter 16 of this volume; Markman & Hahlweg, 1993; Olson & Olson, chapter 9 of this volume). Furthermore, there is evidence that, once destructive patterns characterize the couple relationship, it is difficult to eradicate them (Raush, Barry, Hertel, & Swain, 1974).

☐ Barriers to Prevention

Though most of us accept the adage that an ounce of prevention is worth a pound of cure, several authors (Bradbury & Fincham, 1990; L'Abate, 1983) suggest that a more critical and perhaps empirical evaluation is warranted. Indeed, if common sense dictates that prevention is far superior to remediation, why has prevention not attained a popularity equal to that of couples and marital therapy?

Several experts in the field of marital distress and divorce prevention (Bradbury and Fincham, 1990; Guerney et al., 1986; L'Abate, 1983) have described psychological, sociocultural, and professional barriers to the use of preventive approaches. The most obvious and perhaps formidable barrier involves the couple's motivation to change. Attempting to prevent future distress in nondistressed couples creates an inherent paradox: Because preventive programs are geared toward at-risk couples who have not yet developed significant relationship problems, what would motivate such couples to pursue and invest in preventive programs? Although the notion of preventing problems seems intuitively appealing, Bradbury and Fincham (1990) observed that, realistically, many couples live by the motto, "If it ain't broke, don't fix it." Indeed, this issue was addressed by Floyd et al. (1995), who recommend that preventive programs "incorporate mechanisms for inducing couples to learn and practice new ways of relating as well as marketing strategies for reaching potential consumers of prevention" (p. 213).

A sociocultural barrier to the use of preventive approaches, particularly in the 1980s but also in the 1990s, reflects this society's emphasis on open-market ideology along with its recent preoccupation with corporate restructuring and downsizing. We believe that such trends, besides shaping the economic agenda, have made an impact on the sociocultural features of many of our institutions, including the mental health community, with its current domination by managed care, brief therapies, and cost-effective interventions. Although some observers (L'Abate, 1981) suggested that these developments could strengthen the prevention movement, we view them instead as a barrier. In an era in which managers and politicians are required to demonstrate productivity via short-term gains, it is hard to engender support for prevention, which is, by definition, a long-term investment.

Other sociocultural factors impeding the growth of preventive approaches to couple and marital distress were noted by Vincent (1973) and Mace (1983). The myth of "naturalism," which suggests that marital happiness comes naturally and effortlessly, and the "intermarital taboo," which calls for couples to deal with their dirty laundry in private, are still prevalent today, leading many couples to shy away from preventive programs. Unfortunately, these same couples are likely to find themselves eventually in need of remedial interventions, which, ironically, are associated with similar barriers.

More recently, Bradbury and Fincham (1990) discussed pessimism about the institution of marriage as a barrier to the utilization of preventive approaches. They suggest that such pessimism "results in people being less likely to request and take part in prevention services" (p. 379).

Finally, even if all the barriers to using preventive approaches with couples were overcome, the question regarding whether such approaches are actually effective would remain unanswered. Although prevention proponents have declared the efficacy issue settled (see Guerney & Maxson, 1990), Bradbury and Fincham (1990), drawing conclusions from their excellent review, were much more tentative. They noted "a slight tendency for prevention programs to improve premarital and marital relationships from immediately before to immediately after the intervention, relative to no-treatment controls and, to a lesser degree, relative to attention-only controls" (p. 386). Further, they point to the paucity of studies documenting the longer term outcomes of preventive programs, and they join previous reviewers (Gurman & Kniskern,1977; Hof & Miller, 1980; L'Abate, 1981; Mace & Mace, 1975) in recommending longitudinal research to demonstrate the durability of effects. Although some of the contributors to this volume (see chapters 4, 10, and 13) report such findings, Hawley & Olson (1995), in a recent study, concluded that "longitudinal research is needed to ascertain whether there are any long-term effects of marital enrichment with newlywed couples" (p. 146). The lack of unequivocal empirical evidence could be viewed, therefore, as an additional barrier to the proliferation of preventive couples programs.

☐ Comparison of the Preventive Approaches

We have attempted to organize and present the major preventive approaches to couple and marital distress in a structured manner in this book (see the guidelines for authors, discussed in the "Structure of the Handbook" section, below). To encourage comparison and contrast of the models, we instructed the authors to apply their model to the identical case of an at-risk couple (see the case study of Ben and Alyssa, later in this chapter). So that readers can engage in their own comparative analysis, we adopted three of L'Abate's (1981) comparative dimensions and added several of our own.

Table 1.1 compares the prevention programs discussed in this handbook along the following seven dimensions: theoretical underpinnings, major ingredients, degree of structure, format, facilitation modality, facilitators, and targeted population.

As can be seen in Table 1.1, although there is variability among theoretical approaches to prevention of couple distress, there is even greater similarity, particularly in terms of the therapeutic ingredients, facilitation modalities, and targeted population. Most of the approaches utilize a combination of cognitive, behavioral, and affective aspects, but with different emphases. Some add spiritual ingredients as well. The approaches vary in the degree of structure they employ, with Marriage Encounter (ME) being the most loose and structured enrichment (SE) the most structured.

In terms of format, the programs are roughly divided into intensive programs, which run as 2-day workshops, and a period of weekly sessions, ranging from 6 to 10 sessions. Most preventive programs in this volume offer 10–20 hours of training (including workshops), but some are as brief as 6 hours (COUPLE COMMUNICATION [CC] and SE), whereas others provide many more hours of training, like the 120-hour Practical Application of Intimate Relationship Skills (PAIRS) program. Such a difference is extremely important, particularly if one gets similar preventive effects from short-term programs and long-term programs.

☐ Structure of the Handbook

We provided the authors of the chapters with a fairly succinct topical outline for two reasons: first, to impose some degree of structure and

(text continues on p. 15)

TABLE 1.1. Comparison of the preventive approaches

Program	Theoretical Bases	Major Ingredients	Degree of Structure	Format	Facilitation Model	Facilitator	Population
A.C.M.E (Dyer & Dyer)	Eclectic-humanistic, social learning, cognitive-behavioral	Communication group process, modeling, behavioral contracts, exploring belief system	Low	Weekend retreat, on-going groups, sometimes follow-up	Didactic, experiential	Certified couples	Functional couples, unscreened
ME (Elin)	Religious-reflective-sacramental	Modeling, giving information communication skills, spiritual reflection	Low	Weekend retreat	Didactic, experiential	Clergy and/or encountered couples	Married couples, unscreened
RE (Cavedo & Guerney)	Rogerian, learning interpersonal	Communication, negotiation and conflict-resolution skills, modeling, positive reinforcement, behavioral contracts, practice sessions	Medium	Marathon (1–2 days) or mini-marathon (4 hours)	Didactic, home study with phone coaching, experiential, audiotapes & text	Para-professionals with training	Married couples
SE & DW (L'Abate)	Eclectic-systems, social learning, cognitive-behavioral	Communication skills, conflict resolution, problem-solving, behavioral tasks and contracts, paradoxes	High	6 weekly 1-hour sessions	Didactic, individualistic, written assignments	Master's level students trained in SE	Functional couples, carefully screened

Program (Author)	Theoretical base	Content/skills	Level	Format	Methods	Leader qualifications	Population
CC (Miller & Sherrard)	Communication-systems theory	Communication skills, behavioral contracts, raising self-awareness, behavioral practice and modeling	Medium	Conjoint or group (varies)	Experiential, small group, didactic, manuals	Professionals, structured training & certification	Premarried and married couples, unscreened
TIME (Carlson & Dinkmeyer)	Adlerian theory	Communication, conflict-resolution and choice-making skills, positive reinforcement behavioral contracts, role-playing	High	10 sessions, group or various other	Didactic, experiential, audiotapes, text	Professionals preferred but not required	Married couples, unscreened
IRT (Hendrix & Hunt)	Eclectic-humanistic, object relations, self-psychology, cognitive-behavioral	Communication skills, giving information, commitment, understanding family of origin, self-awareness, behavioral rehearsals, fun enhancement	Medium	2-day workshop (20 hours)	Didactic, group/individuals, audio/videotapes, ongoing therapy, written assignments, regressive exercises	Master's-level certified therapists	All couples
PREPARE/ENRICH (Olson & Olson)	Eclectic, empirically based	Self and couple assessment, communication, conflict-resolution and goal-setting skills	High	2 hours with feedback or four 2-hour sessions	Written questionnaires, didactic-experiential, workbooks, videos	Professionals, clergy, and lay couples, with 1-day training	Premarried and married couples, unscreened
PAIRS (Gordon & Durana)	Eclectic-humanistic systems, object relations, social learning, cognitive-behavioral	Communication skills, understanding family of origin, clarifying expectations, negotiation skills, role-playing, behavioral contracts	Medium	Intensive 120-hour skills-training program	Experiential, group, "regressive" exercises, written assignments	Professionals with training	All couples

Continued

TABLE 1.1. *Continued*

Program	Theoretical Bases	Major Ingredients	Degree of Structure	Format	Facilitation Model	Facilitator	Population
SYMBIS (Parrott & Parrott)	Bowenian systems, cognitive-behavioral	Understanding family of origin, communication and conflict-resolution skills, mentoring, restructuring expectations	Medium	10 sessions, counseling, 1:1 mentoring, prescheduled follow-up	Didactic, experiential	Master's-level therapists or pastoral counselors	Premarried couples
CCN (Hunt & Hunt)	Religious, mentoring, sacramental, cognitive-behavioral	Mentoring, spirtual emphasis, commitment, modeling, role-playing, giving information, nurturing and support	Low	1-day retreat, personal booster sessions, 1:1 contact with CCN team per couple's needs	Team: experiential, readings, individualistic	Caring couples, pastors, & professional consultants	All couples
PREP (Stanley, Blumberg, & Markman)	Social learning, cognitive-behavioral	Communication, conflict-resolution, negotiation skills, restructuring expectations, fun enhancement	Medium	Six 2-hour sessions, week-end workshop, 1-day workshop, with 2 evenings	Didactic, experiential, group/individual, videotapes & text, written assignments	Professionals, clergy (pref. familiar with PREP)	All couples
SMH (Gottman & Gottman)	Eclectic-empiricistic, social learning, cognitive-behavioral	Communication, conflict-resolution and problem-solving skills, cognitive restructuring, self-instruction, behavioral tasks	Medium	2-day workshop with 6-month follow-up	Didactic, experiential, videotapes & text	Experienced clinicians	Functional couples, currently unscreened

uniformity on the material, and second, to allow for comparison and con-trast of relevant dimensions of the approaches. Given the common theo-retical roots and overlapping strategies of many programs, as well as the clear advantages of some along certain dimensions, we believed it impor-tant to design a chapter format that would allow such commonalities and differences to emerge.

Outline of Chapter Structure

1. Introduction
   (a) Historical background of the theory underlying your approach.
   (b) Discussion of what the theory has added to the understanding of couples' relationships.
   (c) Personal and historical factors and other theories influencing the development of your approach.
2. Theoretical Underpinnings
   (a) Description of the couple/marital theory (developmental stages, purpose of committed relationships, etc.).
   (b) Philosophical, religious, psychological, and social assumptions that underlie the view of couples/marriage.
   (c) How the preventive interventions stem from these assumptions.
3. Intervention Model
   (a) How the model of intervention follows from the theory described in part 2, above.
   (b) Specific goals outlined by your approach.
   (c) Tasks associated with those goals.
   (d) Skills for preventing couple/marital distress and enhancing com-mitted relationships.
4. Specific Methods and Strategies for Intervention
   (a) Activities, exercises, readings and other techniques, including infor-mation on frequency and length of interventions.
   (b) Brief rationales for the interventions.
5. Format of Application
   (a) How couples are recruited for the program.
   (b) How screening and assessment (if any) are done.
   (c) Population(s) for which the approach is appropriate.
   (d) Step-by-step description of the main format of the program.
6. Qualities and Role of the Leader, Facilitator, or Therapist
   (a) Education, training and background of leaders, with rationale.
   (b) Role of the leader vis-a-vis participants (leader-participant or non-participant; authoritative vs. egalitarian; self-disclosure, etc.).
7. Application of the Preventive Model to a Couple at Risk.

8. Empirical Evaluation and Research
   (a) Brief review of any empirical findings, anecdotal reports, and informal research on your approach.
   (b) Description of any research that is being planned.
9. Summary, Conclusions, or Final Comments
   (a) Limitations, strengths, and contraindications of the approach.
   (b) How the approach might be enhanced theoretically and clinically.

☐ Case Study: Ben and Alyssa, A Couple at Risk

When Ben and Alyssa show up for the first meeting of your program, they don't stand out among the other couples there. Like most, they indicate on your information form that they're attending because they want "to make a good marriage better." The couple is well dressed and they arrive on time. They are holding hands. They have no problems.

Ben and Alyssa are the kind of neighbors with whom you'd feel comfortable leaving a set of your house keys, so that they could feed your cat while you're out of town. They're the sympathetic parents who're glad to pick up your kid from the childcare center when you get stuck working late. Now thirty-ish (Ben is 3 years older than Alyssa), married for 5 years, and the parents of a toddler, the two radiate intelligence and stability. Ben earned his law degree from Columbia; Alyssa got her teaching credentials from Columbia's Teachers College. They're nice young people with a future ahead of them.

Ben and Alyssa were, from their first date, the "perfect match": "identical twins" who were "meant for each other." They met and fell in love the summer after Alyssa's high school graduation. By summer's end, Alyssa's older boyfriend told her that he wanted to get married; could they set a wedding date? Alyssa's delight yielded to embarassment as she realized that she now had to reveal one of the few details of her life she'd been withholding from the man of her dreams: Her father, Jack, had Alyssa's next four years mapped out for her. It took several hours to persuade her incredulous boyfriend ("We're going to wait until you graduate to get married? We're not even going to *live together*, either?") that they ought to go along with Jack's plans ("Demands, you mean," Ben corrected her). It was in everyone's best interests, Alyssa assured him—especially theirs. Ben, sobered by the information about his future father-in-law, agreed to these parental directives with bemused tolerance. "No way we could have moved in together, like our friends were doing," Alyssa related. "My father would've disowned me. Lots of parents threaten to do that; mine would *do* it."

The long-delayed wedding was held the weekend after Ben graduated from law school. Alyssa had just completed her teaching degree; Ben, near the top of his law school class, had received two solid job offers even before his diploma had arrived in the mail. With the generous consent of his wife, Ben accepted the highest salary offer, the one from a large legal firm in a distant midwestern city. Although Alyssa, like most new brides, wasn't quite sure what she was in for, she agreed to move halfway across the country, far from her family, to a city where she didn't know a soul.

The couple bought a spacious three-bedroom home in the city's suburbs. Alyssa's parents cosigned the couple's mortgage application and, as a wedding gift, gave them the money they needed for the downpayment on their home. Free at last, as free as they'd ever be, the couple began their future.

Although Ben and Alyssa shared important similarities, they could hardly have had more dissimilar upbringings. Ben had been raised in the inner city, the only child of a divorced single mother. Alyssa, the eldest of three girls, was raised in a tony New York suburb by parents who were married once, to one another, and who were still married after 25 years.

Ben's mother, Sarah, had divorced Ben's father shortly after Ben was born. Sam had, as Sarah put it, "a pair of constantly wandering eyes that followed every skirt that walked by." A couple of months after Sarah had discovered that she was pregnant with their first child, she made another, less-welcome discovery: evidence of yet one more of her husband's affairs. "I think this gal was about the fourth one he'd had during our 3 years of marriage," Sarah commented. "I was fed up. I'd told Sam, the last time this had happened, 'Just once more, Sam, and that's it.' So, *that was it.*" Having been raised in a tough Jewish neighborhood in Brooklyn, Sarah wasn't one to shrink from a challenge: She left the unfaithful Sam when she was 3 months pregnant. The divorce became final when Ben was a few months old; Sam quickly married his latest flame, moved out of state, and became a deadbeat dad. Sarah then invested her considerable energy into figuring out how to raise Ben as a single parent. She and her infant son moved in with her parents ("Just until I get on my own two feet," she assured them), and while her mother watched the baby, Sarah worked toward the nursing degree she'd started years ago, before she'd met Sam and become more interested in him than in nursing. Barely 30, Sarah was disinclined toward remarrying ("I'd had enough of that so-called institution," she'd comment to anyone who wondered), bestowing on her the permanent role of father as well as mother to young Ben. ("I'll bet she was a better father than Sam would've ever been," Ben observed.) Having finished her R.N. degree by the time Ben was 2, Sarah immediately took on a full-time nursing job at the local hospital. After receiving her first paycheck, she thanked her parents and moved Ben and herself into a comfortable two-bedroom apartment in the safest area of Manhattan they could afford. She was Ben's only support and his primary champion until, and after, the day he graduated from law school at the age of 25. "The proudest day of my life," Sarah beamed.

Sarah had invested every available gram of energy into raising her only child but, by comparison, Alyssa's father made Sarah look negligent. Alyssa's dad, Jack, and her mother, Caroline, were nearing their 21st anniversary when Ben and Alyssa met; they were the "'till death do us part' type," Sarah noted. From the day he'd married his childhood sweetheart, Jack planned to clone the family his parents had produced: three boys, upper middle class, devout Methodists, moral and productive citizens. Jack got three girls instead; nonetheless, he saw no reason why his girls couldn't be fashioned into the same mold he'd planned for his never-to-materialize boys. Caroline was a peaceful woman, as unassuming as one would have to be to get married and stay married to the likes of Jack. Her keenest interest, aside from making sure that everyone was getting along with one another, was in pleasing God; to a good Christian wife, pleasing one's husband is included in that package. Caroline developed a workable modus operandi in her marriage: She agreed, almost on reflex, with whatever Jack said. Scripture and the pastor (and Jack) had stated, after all, that a Christian woman should be subservient to her husband, not to mention the fact that arguing with Jack was like kicking a broken washing machine: pointless and painful.

Prior to meeting the love of her life, Alyssa, their oldest, had incited little controversy in the family. She'd inherited her mother's amiable nature and a streak of her father's perfectionism. As she was finishing up an admirable high school record, she fantasized about rooming at Columbia, earning one of its prestigious teaching degrees while enjoying her first hint of adulthood's freedom. Columbia did, in fact, award Alyssa a coveted admission ticket but failed to accompany it with an adequate funding package. Jack, to whom higher education was just slightly lower in priority than Bible study, agreed to pay the pricey college's tuition, but under one condition, the same contingency Jack's own father had applied to him: Alyssa was to live at home throughout college, following her parents' rules and remaining accountable to them. The amenable Alyssa, with no better alternatives—at least, not at that point—gave in.

Thus, when Jack and Caroline's precious first-born, barely out of high school, became mesmerized by an older Jewish college man from a broken home, the two parents reacted, in unison, with predictable horror. Would Alyssa abandon her Christian faith? Would she give up going to college and move in with "that boy?" Would she have a child out of wedlock? Would she get involved in radical politics? Fortunately, despite her anomalous choice of a mate, Alyssa was a typical eldest child: Since all first-borns of families have spent at least some time, during their child-hood, at the center of their parents' world, they tend to develop parentlike characteristics—ambitiousness, hypermaturity, a strong sense of moral-ity—that make them resemble a miniature composite of their parents. Since Alyssa had agreed to remain under her parents' roof and their au-thority, despite her fascination with "that boy," Jack concluded that his daughter had chosen the moral high road, indicating that her virtue re-mained intact. Both parents breathed easier and subsequently monitored Alyssa a little less closely.

Still, Alyssa's parents remained unenthused about Alyssa's choice of a marital partner. Although, as Caroline would comment, Ben seemed to be a "polite young man" who would be an "adequate provider" for a wife and children, Jack had lots of misgivings. Alyssa was raised as an obser-vant Christian; Ben was a nonpracticing Jew. Ben had grown up without a father; what could he possibly know about fathering children? And Ben's mother seemed awfully liberal, like one of those women's-lib types. Still, as long as Alyssa continued living at home, finished college, and kept her virtue, Jack saw no reason to interfere with the relationship.

Meanwhile, Alyssa, irrevocably in love, hadn't been as successful at resisting Ben's sexual advances as her parents had been imagining. In fact, she hadn't been successful at all. However, she and Ben were care-ful, very careful. They limited their intimate liaisons to parking spots no-where near Alyssa's neighborhood. More to satisfy her parents and to ward off guilt than to pray, Alyssa showed up for Sunday services, but for her, the spiritual fire had long since died out.

Sarah's opinion of her daughter-in-law, in contrast, was wholehearted: She applauded Ben's choice of a mate; Alyssa was the adoring wife her son deserved. Equally as important, Sarah felt, was Alyssa's having a strong enough sense of herself to love a man without desperately needing him. In this way, Sarah concluded, Alyssa was the sort of woman Sarah had always fancied herself to be. "I can't stomach those women who get mar-ried just to have a man take care of them the rest of their lives," Sarah would comment to Ben, particularly when he'd started dating a girl whom Sarah thought to be of that ilk. To Sarah, Alyssa was a woman after her own heart: Alyssa would put Ben first, as Sarah always had. Alyssa seemed to understand what Ben needed in a wife: a faithful guardian of home and hearth so that he could slave away his days, evenings, and weekends for the law firm. When the time was right—when Ben's legal career was well-enough established—Alyssa could return to her teaching career. Sarah's vision of the family picture was perfectly fulfilled: Ben would have the devoted and supportive partner of which Sarah herself had al-ways been deprived.

Sarah's estimation of her daughter-in-law was close to the mark: Alyssa was, in fact, thoroughly dedicated to Ben. She'd also learned something about dealing with men, for better or for worse, from watching her mother interact with her father. Although Alyssa hadn't agreed with many of her mother's tactics, she'd been impressed by how effectively her mom had defused the many landmines in her marriage to Jack. That, Alyssa had to admit, took talent. And Alyssa, indeed, had no objections to putting Ben's career first. Ben had, after all, labored long and hard to get his law degree, longer and harder than Alyssa had worked to get her teaching credentials. Now Ben was studying, seemingly endlessly, to pass the bar. Getting her teaching credentials, by comparison, had been a cinch. Besides, that high starting salary Ben had been offered by the firm had given him such a thrill; salary didn't mean nearly as much to Alyssa, who'd take a teaching job just about anywhere, for any amount, if it would make Ben happier and more successful. It was no surprise to Sarah or anyone, then, when Alyssa happily agreed to move with Ben to an area where she, herself, hadn't yet found any career prospects.

Ben's mother had raised him in the Reformed Jewish tradition, but Ben's interest faded after his bar mitzvah, and he had been nonpracticing since his late adolescence. He lightheartedly describes his attitude toward religion as "benign indifference; like Woody Allen says, 'As far as God's concerned, I'm the loyal opposition.'" Despite Alyssa's religious upbringing and her father's impressions of her, Alyssa was not particularly devout, either, when she and Ben first met and throughout the first few years of their marriage. "Once I got out of high school, I figured it was about time I made up my own mind about religion and morality and such stuff," Alyssa commented, "rather than just believing what my parents had taught me. The things I was hearing in church, and that my Dad was always talking about, just didn't fit for me anymore." Throughout those early years, Ben and Alyssa shared a common creed: Faith is fine, but it's no substitute for using your God-given brain to get through life.

The couple enjoyed 3 years of emancipated bliss, parent-free, childless, and responsible only to one another. They were earning good money. They worked hard during the week and partied hard on the weekends, either alone or with friends. If they had a few drinks too many on Saturday night, no problem; they could sleep in on Sunday morning. Talking over late dinners, after Ben's long workdays, they shared similar visions: They wanted to travel all over the world; they wanted two children, a boy and a girl; they'd always put their marriage first and keep the romance going. They made love frequently. They hardly fought at all; there wasn't much to fight about.

But the couple made the same discovery that many couples do after the first child comes along: There's more to fight about once you have kids. For Ben and Alyssa, the onset of parenthood had been particularly unsettling. Midpregnancy, Alyssa had developed high blood pressure, like her mother had during her own pregnancies. Next, toxemia followed; despite close medical monitoring, 8 weeks before the baby was due, Alyssa started premature labor. Often, premature labor can be stopped, but when Alyssa's baby showed signs of distress, a quick delivery became crucial. As the medical team rushed her into the operating room for an emergency C-section, everyone, including the doctor, wondered whether the baby would make it through the birth without some type of mental or physical damage. Some wondered whether the baby would make it at all.

Meanwhile, Alyssa's parents had responded to the crisis in their usual style: They prayed for a miracle. They got their friends, neighbors, co-workers, and fellow church members praying as well.

Whether miraculously or not, baby Benny emerged from his premature birth journey very much alive. Although his first few moments in the world were tense ones, after he'd been whisked away to the neonatal intensive care unit and had spent several weeks there, he was finally pronounced out of danger, healthy, and ready to go home. Ben chalked it all up to good luck and the wonders of modern medicine. Alyssa, understandably frantic throughout the ordeal, had slowly calmed down and had gradually become transformed. She was, in fact, a changed person: She was convinced that she, and her child, had been touched by God. Benny's health was no fluke, nor was it merely a result of medical intervention; it was a miracle, attributable, no doubt, to the prayers of her parents and others. The ever-agnostic Ben was too relieved to care about who was responsible for his son's rescue, and he was too tired to engage in a debate over his wife's spiritual convictions. He poured a celebratory glass of champagne the day they brought Benny home from the hospital and proposed a toast to Benny's good health. Ben was puzzled when Alyssa declined to share a glass with him, but he figured that nursing mothers weren't supposed to drink, anyway.

Although Alyssa had originally planned on a 6-month maternity leave from her third-grade teaching job, Benny's birth had inspired not only a reawakening of her long-abandoned religious fervor, but also a shift in her career plans. Having almost lost her baby, Alyssa had concluded that the primary purpose of her life was to raise the child God had given back to her. "Children need a mother at home more than the school needs a teacher, Ben," she pointed out. Ben, stunned at first ("You want to *quit teaching*?"), eventually figured that his otherwise nontraditional wife would, sooner or later, get bored staying home, change her mind, and return to the classroom. He'd go along with Alyssa's plans—for now, anyway.

Meanwhile, Ben had been having mixed feelings about his own job. The 6 years he'd been at the law firm seemed more like 12. He'd started to chide himself for getting into law in the first place. It had been his maternal uncle, a sometimes–father figure and attorney in private practice, who'd taken the adolescent Ben under his wing and persuaded Ben that he, too, could do very well in law. Flattered by his uncle's attention and endorsement, Ben had followed the uncle's lead. However, back when Ben's uncle had started law school, lawyers weren't being caricatured as the money-grubbing ambulance-chasers that they're often depicted as nowadays. Back then, the legal profession had symbolized independence, wealth, and status. So far, in Ben's on-the-job experience, he had encountered none of these. Although Ben made a good living, particularly for a man his age, he paid dearly for it: He was chained to a desk for 50 hours a week and got assigned what must have been the firm's most boring cases. Ben's dissatisfaction with the firm became stronger as his tenure there grew longer. He often daydreamed about doing something else, anything else—maybe starting his own business and being his own boss. There was just one problem: What job or what business would pay enough to support his growing family? Ben was now his family's sole breadwinner, after all.

Meanwhile, Ben and Alyssa stumbled under the weight of first-time parenthood. For most new parents, uninterrupted sleep seems unattainable, eventually becoming a distant memory. One walks around in a haze. Ben and Alyssa's first few months with Benny weren't much different; in fact, they were much worse. Benny was apparently healthy, but with his history of prematurity, he had to be monitored more closely than other babies, especially at night. Having been born 8 weeks early, the 8-week-old Benny was, on certain developmental dimensions, a newborn. Both parents, realizing that they would either swim together or sink en masse, mustered all of their mutual sympathy and divided the parenting chores equitably. They alternated the nighttime baby checks. Ben took the 5 a.m. shift with the baby so that Alyssa could sleep until Ben left for work. Ben did the dinner dishes while Alyssa rocked the baby to sleep. Alyssa would take the sleepless and screaming Benny for a car ride around the neighborhood at midnight, so that Ben could get some sleep. It wasn't easy, but at least it seemed fair.

One evening, an exhausted Alyssa, who'd been wearing a milk-stained nightgown when she'd greeted her equally exhausted husband at the end of his workday, noticed that Ben seemed especially tense that night. He looked, in fact, downright depressed. Alyssa put the baby down and, rubbing Ben's shoulders, asked him what was wrong. Ben, sullen at first, finally began to talk. He talked, without stopping, for a half-hour, which was about 25 minutes longer than he would usually spend talking to Alyssa those days. He talked about his disappointment with his work, with his life, with *their* life. His wife didn't interrupt. She listened without commenting. She nodded her head in agreement. After a while, Ben, looking relieved and relaxed, became quiet. Alyssa said she understood. She promised to pay more attention to him. The couple made love that night for the first time in weeks.

For several weeks afterwards, Alyssa remembered, each evening, to change into something sexy before Ben arrived home. Although she was too nervous to leave the baby with a sitter, she took Ben out, with the baby, to dinner at a family restaurant. Instead of ignoring Ben when he was grouchy, she tried to cheer him up. Sometimes she reminded herself of her mother.

Ben appreciated Alyssa's efforts, and his spirits lifted somewhat. But many evenings, sleepy yet desperate for a little time without legal briefs or a crying baby, Ben would sit in his living room late at night and ponder the path his life was taking. He'd begun to wonder if any of the fun and good times of his old life would ever return.

By the time Benny turned 6 months old, a full night's sleep was at last within his father's reach. But by then, Ben had begun to question whether he'd ever get his old *wife* back. Alyssa, he mused, had invested herself 100 percent in Ben before the baby came along; now Ben got, at best, the leftovers at the end of Alyssa's day. Time was in shorter supply than ever: Aside from devoting most of her waking moments to Benny, Ben's newly converted wife went to church on Sundays, Bible study on Wednesdays, and prayer meeting on Fridays. It seemed like every time Ben looked for her, Alyssa was communing with the Almighty. And, like many devout Christians, she no longer drank, which explained her declining the glass of champagne the day Benny came home from the hospital.

Still, Ben acknowledged, at least Alyssa hadn't turned into the nagging proselytizer her father was. In fact, as much as she wanted him to join her for church, she had never yet preached to Ben. Alyssa had, thus far, fulfilled her vow to never become like her father, who had constantly exhorted his family to be better Christians, better workers, better people— just plain better. Alyssa tolerated, without comment, Ben's nightcaps and occasional weekend six-packs. A few drinks wouldn't do any harm, she figured.

Then, one Saturday afternoon, Alyssa made a startling announcement: She was pregnant again. She related this to Ben with a big smile on her face. She'd just found out. No big deal; everyone says it gets easier with the second one: You already know what to expect.

Watching his fading dreams of leaving the law firm vanish entirely,

Ben took the news the best he could; he hugged and congratulated his wife. But inside, he felt a stirring of familiar feelings, feelings similar to those he'd felt that long-ago summer, when he'd learned that Alyssa's father had her life—and therefore Ben's life—planned out for the next 4 years.

That evening, one of Ben and Alyssa's still-infrequent arguments erupted. This one was a little longer and louder than any they'd had so far.

Ben later related, "It's hard to admit this, but my whole family situation was starting to get to me. The baby was finally sleeping through the night. I was just beginning to get a full night's sleep after being sleep deprived for 6 months. Alyssa and I had just started to spend a little bit of time alone together, without one of us holding a crying baby. I was beginning to hope that, maybe in a few years, Alyssa could go back to teaching and I could find a new job. *And then she gets pregnant again!* Look, I don't mind her staying home with the kids for a while. But it'll be 6 years before our second kid is in grade school. So, maybe Alyssa could start teaching and I could get into a new field then. But that's *if* this is our last child. Can you believe that, a few times, Alyssa's mentioned having *three*? Does she have any idea what that would mean? It would mean my staying at the law firm for at least *10 more years*. I'd be over 40 by the time I could get out of law and into something else. I guess, when it comes to working, women have choices. Men don't."

Alyssa, meanwhile, had been thinking about her own marital disappointments. For example, Ben wasn't much of a listener anymore. In the past, he'd always paid attention to her when she was upset, and he would at least listen long enough to understand what she was going through. Now, whenever Alyssa brought up problems, Ben would typically offer a quick solution or two and then move on to another subject, just like her father used to. This tendency was becoming particularly bothersome as Alyssa's pregnancy progressed. She'd begun to feel, despite her faith in God, more anxious about the outcome of the pregnancy. She'd think: What if this baby is born too soon, like Benny was? What if this one dies? Alyssa had been having nightmares about the baby's birth more and more frequently. The few times she'd come to Ben with her worries, he'd said something like, "Don't worry; it'll just makes matters worse," or "Don't worry; things will work out just fine," or "You should trust in God, like your religion says to." His advice left Alyssa feeling cold. Doesn't Ben understand that she's not asking him to solve her problems? She just wants him to listen to her and to understand how she feels, that's all. Why doesn't he do that anymore, the way he used to?

☐ References

Albee, G. W. (1996). Revolution and counterrevolutions in prevention. *American Psychologist, 51,* 1130–1133.

American Psychiatric Association. (1994). *Diagnostic and statistical manual of mental disorders* (4th ed.). Washington, DC: Author.

Bradbury, T. N., & Fincham, F. D. (1990). Preventing marital dysfunction: Review and analysis. In F. D. Fincham & T. N. Bradbury (Eds.), *The Psychology of Marriage: Basic Issues and Applications* (pp. 375–401). New York: Guilford.

Beach, S. R. H., Sandeen, E. E., & O'Leary, K. D. (1990). *Depression in marriage: A model for etiology and treatment.* New York: Guilford.

Catalano, R., & Dooley, P. (1980). Economic changes in primary prevention. In R. H. Price et al. (Eds.), *Prevention in mental health: Research, policy and practice* (pp. 21–40). Beverly Hills, CA: Sage.

Coie, J., Watt, N., Ewst, S., Hawkins, J., Asarnow, J., Markman, H., Ramey, S., Shure, S., & Long, B. (1993). The science of prevention: A conceptual framework and some directions for a national research program. *American Psychologist, 48*(10), 1013–1022.

DeMaria, R. (1998). *A national survey of married couples who participate in marriage enrichment.* Ann Arbor, MI: UMI Dissertation Services, No. 983-3080.

Denton, W. (1986). Starting a local marriage enrichment group. In W. Denton (Ed.), *Marriage and family enrichment* (pp. 69–77). New York: Haworth.

Floyd, F., Markman, H., Kelly, S., Blumberg, S. L., & Stanley, S. (1995). Preventive intervention and relationship enhancement. In N. S. Jacobson & A. S. Gurman (Eds.), *Clinical handbook of couple therapy* (pp. 212–226). New York: Guilford.

Glenn, N. D. (1991). The recent trend in marital success in the United States. *Journal of Marriage and the Family, 53,* 261–270.

Gottman, J. M. (1994). *Why marriages succeed of fail.* New York: Simon & Schuster.

Groves, E. R., & Groves, G. H. (1947). *The contemporary American family.* Chicago: Lippincott.

Guerney, B. G., Jr. (1977). *Relationship enhancement: Skill training programs for therapy, problem prevention, and enrichment.* San Francisco: Jossey-Bass.

Guerney, B. G., Jr., Brock, G., & Coufal, J. (1986). Integrating marital therapy and enrichment: The relationship enhancement approach. In N. S. Jacobson & A. S. Gurman (Eds.), *Clinical handbook of marital therapy* (pp. 151–172). New York: Guilford.

Guerney, B. G., Jr., & Maxson, P. (1990). Marital and family enrichment research: A decade review and a look ahead. *Journal of Marriage and the Family, 52*(4), 1127–1135.

Gurman, A. S., & Kniskern, D. P. (1977). Enriching research on marital enrichment programs. *Journal of Marriage and Family Counseling, 3,* 3–10.

Gurman, A. S., & Kniskern, D. P. (Eds.). (1991). *Handbook of family therapy, Vol. II.* New York: Brunner/Mazel.

Hawley, D. R., & Olson, D. H. (1995). Enriching newlyweds: An evaluation of three enrichment programs. *The American Journal of Family Therapy, 23*(2), 129–147.

Heiman, J. R., Epps, P. H., & Ellis, B. (1995). Treating sexual desire disorders in couples. In N. S. Jacoboson & A. S. Gurman (Eds.), *Clinical handbook of couple therapy* (pp. 471–495). New York: Guilford.

Heller, K. (1996). Coming of age of prevention science. *American Psychologist, 51,* 1123–1127.

Hof, L., & Miller, W. (1981). *Marriage enrichment: Philosophy, process, and program.* Bowie, MD: Brady.

Hogan, T. F., Hunt, R., Emersson, D., Hayes, R., & Ketterer, K. (1996). An evaluation of client satisfaction with "Getting the Love You Want" weekend workshop. *The Journal of Imago Relationship Therapy, 1*(2), 57–66.

Jacobson, N. S., & Gurman, A. S. (Eds.). (1986). *Clinical handbook of marital therapy.* New York: Guilford.

Jacobson, N. S., & Gurman, A.S. (Eds.). (1995) Clinical handbook of couple therapy. New York: Guilford.

Jacobson, N. S., Holzworth-Munro, A., & Schmaling, K. B. (1989). Marital therapy and involvement in the treatment of depression, agoraphobia and alcoholism. *Journal of Consulting Clinical Psychology, 57,* 5–10.

Kiecolt-Glaser, J. K., Fisher, B. S., Ogrochi, P., Stout, J. C., Speicher, C. E., & Glaser, R. (1987). Marital quality, marital disruption, and immune function. *Psychosomatic Medicine, 49,* 13–33.

Klerman, G. L., & Weissman, M. M. (1990). Increasing rates of depression. *Journal of American Medical Association, 61,* 2229–2235.

L'Abate, L. (1977). *Enrichment: Structured interventions with couples, families, and groups.* Washington, DC: University Press of America.

L'Abate, L. (1981). Skill training programs for couples and families. In A. S. Gurman & D. P. Kniskern (Eds.), *Handbook of family therapy* (pp. 631–661). New York: Brunner/Mazel.

L'Abate, L. (1983). Prevention as a profession: Toward a new conceptual frame of reference. In D. R. Mace (Ed.), *Prevention in family services* (pp 49–62). Beverly Hills, CA: Sage.

L'Abate, L. (1986). *Systematic family therapy.* New York: Brunner/Mazel.

L'Abate, L. (1990). *Building family competence: Primary and secondary prevention strategies.* Newbury Park, CA: Sage.

Leveat, R. F. (Ed.). (1986). *Psychoeducational approaches to family therapy and counseling.* New York: Springer-Verlag.

Mace, D. (Ed.). (1983). *Prevention in family services: Approaches to family wellness.* Beverly Hills, CA: Sage.

Mace, D., & Mace, V. (1975). Marriage enrichment - Wave of the future? *The Family Coordinator, 24,* 171–173.

Mace, D., & Mace, V. (1980). Enriching marriages: The foundation stone of family strength. In N. Stinnett, B. Chesser, J. DeFrain, & P. Knaub (Eds.), *Family strengths: Positive models for family life.* Lincoln, NE: University of Nebraska Press.

Markman, H. J., Floyd, F. J., Stanley, S. M., & Lewis, H. (1986). Prevention. In N. Jacobson & A. Gurman (Eds.), *Clinical handbook of marital therapy* (pp. 173–195). New York: Guilford.

Markman, H. J., & Hahlweg, K. (1993). The prediction and prevention of marital distress: An international perspective. *Clinical Psychology Review, 13,* 29–43.

Markman, H. J., Renick, M. J., Floyd, F., Stanley, S., & Clements, M. (1993). Preventing marital distress through communication and conflict management training: A four and five year follow-up. *Journal of Consulting and Clinical Psychology, 62,* 1–8.

McCrady, B. S., & Epstein, E. E. (1995). Marital therapy in the treatment of alcohol problems. In N. S. Jacboson & A. S. Gurman (Eds.), *Clinical handbook of couple therapy* (pp. 369–393). New York: Guilford.

Mrazek, P. J., & Haggerty, R. J. (Eds.). (1994). *Reducing risks for mental disorders: Frontiers for preventive intervention research.* Washington, DC: National Academy Press.

Munoz, R. F., Mrazek, P. J., & Haggerty, R. J. (1996). Institute of Medicine report on prevention of mental disorders. *American Psychologist, 51,* 1116–1122.

National Center for Health Statistics. (1996). *Advance report of final divorce statistics, 1989 and 1990.* Hyattsville, MD: National Center for Health Statistics.

Norton, A. J., & Miller, L. F. (1992). *Marriage, divorce and remarriage in the 1990's.* Washington, DC: U.S. Dept. of Commerce.

Notarius, C., & Markman, H. J. (1993). *We can work it out: Making sense of marital conflict.* New York: Putnam.

O'Leary, K. D., Barling, J., Arias, I., & Rosenbaum, A. (1989). Prevalence and stability of physical aggression between spouses: A longitudinal analysis. *Journal of Consulting and Clinical Psychology, 57,* 263–268.

Perry, M., & Albee, G. W. (1994). On "The Science of Prevention." *American Psychologist, 49,* 1087–1088.

Price, R. H., Cower, E. L., Lorion, R. P., & Ramos-McKay, J. (1989). The search for effective prevention programs: What we learned along the way. *American Journal of Orthopsychiatry, 59*(1), 45–58.

Raush, H. L., Barry, W. A., Hertel, R. K., & Swain, M. A. (1974). *Communication, conflict and marriage.* San Francisco: Jossey-Bass.

Riess, D., & Price, R. H. (1996). National research agenda for prevention research. *American Psychologist, 51,* 1109–1111.

Veroff, J., Kulka, R. A., & Douvan, E. (1981). *Mental health in America: Patterns of help-seeking from 1957–1976.* New York: Basic Books.

Vincent, C. E. (1973). *Sexual and marital health.* New York: Basic Books.

Webster's new universal unabridged dictionary (2nd ed.). (1983). New York: New World Dictionaries/Simon & Schuster.

2

CHAPTER

Preston M. Dyer, Ph.D.
Genie H. Dyer, Ph.D.

Marriage Enrichment, A.C.M.E.-Style

☐ Introduction

The marriage enrichment movement, born in the social upheavals of the 1960s, emerged from several sources. At about the same time that Father Gabriel Calvo, a Catholic priest in Barcelona, Spain, led the weekend couples retreat that marked the beginning of Marriage Encounter, Herbert Otto, the founder of the human potential movement, was working with couples in California.

In October 1962, David and Vera Mace led a retreat for a group of Quaker couples at Kirkridge, a retreat center in western Pennsylvania. David Mace was a pioneer in the development of marriage counseling in Great Britain and the United States. On their 40th wedding anniversary, in 1973, the Maces founded the Association for Couples in Marriage Enrichment (A.C.M.E.).

The marriage enrichment model that the Maces developed at Kirkridge become the prototype for A.C.M.E.-style marriage enrichment. By the mid-1960s, Leon and Antoinette Smith of the United Methodist Church had designed Marriage Communication Labs for couples. Upon A.C.M.E.'s founding in the early 1970s, the Maces and Smiths merged their programs. The programs founded by these pioneers differed in format and style, but held two central beliefs in common: (a) that the marital relationship itself was the key to successful family life, and (b) that preventive interventions were more efficient and more effective than treatment.

From these beginnings, the marriage enrichment movement embraced the new approaches to interpersonal skills training of the late 1960s and early 1970s. These included the work of Sherod Miller and his associates at the University of Minnesota, which led to the development of the COUPLE COMMUNICATION (CC) program; Bernard Guerney, Jr., and his associates, who developed Relationship Enhancement in Pennsylvania; and Winifred Coulton of the Family Communication Center in California, who worked with the National YMCA.

Although marriage enrichment has become a generic term in our culture, no one is sure of its origin. Whether or not he coined the term, David Mace certainly did much to place it into popular usage. This chapter focuses on the approach to marriage enrichment pioneered by David and Vera Mace and promoted by A.C.M.E.

Marriage Enrichment

Even after 30 years, the term "marriage enrichment" is far from precise, and no standard definition has emerged in the literature. Most who work in the field would agree that in its simplest sense, marriage enrichment refers to programs designed for couples who have fairly well functioning relationships but wish to make them more satisfying.

The Maces clearly did not use the term to mean the provision of additives from the outside, as in "vitamin-enriched" bread. For them, enrichment came from within the relationship. Growth and potential better define enrichment, "the idea being that in each marital dyad there exists an inherent capacity for mutual fulfillment and development which in most instances remains largely unappropriated" (Mace, 1976, p. 323). They believed that marriages fail in many cases because couples are unable to capitalize on their resources. It followed, therefore, that programs developed to help couples unlock their potential, "could not only prevent some marriages from failing, but also improve the quality of many mediocre but stable unions in which interpersonal relationships never reach more than a superficial level" (Mace, 1976, p. 323).

David Catron (1984) has used the diagram below to further illuminate this concept. Imagine life's experiences distributed along a continuum from treatment to enrichment. Most people have needed treatment for a medical, emotional, or marital problem. At that time they were functioning in the treatment sphere. The goal of treatment is to move the patient or client out of the realm of treatment into the area of normal functioning. The normal sphere of functioning includes being able to cope with

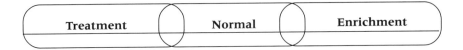

| Treatment | | Normal | | Enrichment |

the ebb and flow of daily challenges, to meet the demands of the day, to cope. Prevention would also fall into this sphere because it is designed to prevent someone or some couple from slipping back into the need for treatment.

Most people experience the first two spheres. Therefore, these two spheres are generally understood. If you are not in the normal sphere, then you are in treatment. So it is understandable that when a couple says they are going to a marriage enrichment event, people assume they have a troubled marriage. Catron (1984) argues that there is more to the continuum than treatment or merely coping. Enrichment, as it applies to marriage, moves to the dimension of marital growth. Marital growth involves being intentional about developing the marital relationship by setting goals and directions for the marriage. In this sphere marriage is more than "just settling down" or just coping.

Recently David & Sarah Catron, executive directors of A.C.M.E., had the opportunity to confirm this idea by asking a group of marriage enrichment couples in Australia to complete the sentence "Marriage enrichment is. . . . " Some of the responses were: "a life time process in which couples have an opportunity to develop their marriage potential"; "an experience where exploration of growth replaces complacency"; "a powerful experience where I can learn more about myself and my spouse"; "a time to celebrate our relationship with others" (Catron & Catron, 1996, p.5). Such statements would seem to support the view of marriage enrichment held by the Maces and Catrons.

A.C.M.E.

After nearly 40 years doing marriage counseling, David Mace came to the conclusion that marriage treatment was not the answer to the increasing dissatisfaction in marriage and the booming growth in the divorce rate. His and Vera's work with couples groups had convinced them that couples need help long before their marriages have severe problems and they have done real damage to their relationship. Acting on this belief, on their 40th wedding anniversary, they formed A.C.M.E. "Our purpose was to create an organization that married couples could join as a way of expressing their support for successful marriage. . . . We took for A.C.M.E.'s slogan 'To work for better marriages, beginning with our own' " (Mace & Mace, 1974, p. 159). The Maces hoped that the association would give shape and direction to the developing marriage enrichment movement, especially in the areas of standard-setting and the training and certification of leaders (Mace, 1983).

Though it never grew to the size and international status the Maces had envisioned, A.C.M.E. today is a strong nonprofit, nonsectarian organization with members throughout the United States and Canada, and with affiliated associations in other countries. It is essentially a network of persons working for better marriages through national, regional, and state organizations and local chapters. "The mission of the Association for Couples in Marriage Enrichment is to promote enrichment opportunities and resources that strengthen couple relationships and enhance personal growth, mutual fulfillment and family wellness" (A.C.M.E., 1993, p. 9). In the 1993 strategic plan, the association's board of directors identified 10 operating principles for the association (A.C.M.E., 1993):

1. Healthy families promote healthy communities and lead to world peace. The best way to produce healthy families is to promote healthy marriages.
2. Healthy marriages foster ongoing personal growth and mutual fulfillment.
3. Relationship skills can be taught and learned.
4. People and relationships can grow, change, and benefit from relationship skill training.
5. Our primary emphasis is experiential education for and continuing development of healthy relationships.
6. We encourage therapy when appropriate.
7. Marriage enrichment is a lifelong process.
8. A.C.M.E. provides valuable prevention-oriented services in ways that are sensitive, responsive, and flexible.
9. We want to have an impact on as many relationships as we can.
10. We encourage and will participate in research in marriage and family enrichment.

A.C.M.E. supports a wide variety of marriage enrichment activities, from weekend retreats for couples to basic and advanced training for leader couples. These events differ in their structure, setting, and format. Once leader couples meet the requirements of certification, they are free to use their own creativity in the development and presentation of events within the parameters above.

☐ Theoretical Underpinnings

Although the earliest phase of the marriage enrichment movement was affected by Otto's human potential movement, encounter groups, and humanistic psychology, today's practitioners are more strongly influenced by social learning theory, cognitive-behavioral theory, family systems theory, and communications theory.

Companionship Marriage

Burgess' (Burgess, Locke, & Thomas, 1971) concept of the companionship family had a major influence on the Maces' thinking about marriage. Studying the family after World War II, Burgess, a family sociologist at the University of Chicago, identified a new model of the family emerging in the United States. He called the new form the "companionship model," in comparison with the traditional structure, which he termed the "institutional model." He saw the companionship model as an adaptation to social changes in our society, such as industrialization, urbanization, high mobility, and broadening concepts of democracy. The institutional model has a structural emphasis and is patriarchal, authoritarian, and legalistic, with a rigid hierarchical role structure supported by a strong emphasis on family. Unity is derived primarily from traditional rules and regulations, specified duties and obligations, and other external social pressures affecting the family. The companionship model is egalitarian and democratic, with a flexible role structure. Unity in the companionship model depends on internal cohesion from interpersonal relationships rather than external coercion exerted by custom and community opinion. Personal happiness and individual achievement are valued over familism.

Strong believers in egalitarian relationships, the Maces saw potential for more satisfying marriages in the companionship model. They also saw that, unfortunately, factors inherent in the model made it more unstable and eventuated in the increasing divorce rate. Many people in companionship marriages lack the interpersonal skills necessary to sustain a marriage based solely on relational characteristics such as mutual affection, intimacy, sympathetic understanding, comradeship, and mutual respect. As much as couples might want a marriage based on a loving, companionate relationship, many couples simply lack the tools to make it work. In addition, people's expectations of marital happiness have been expanded by the potential offered by the companionship model. Further complicating the situation, outside forces that held marriages together in the past have been greatly weakened. The Maces saw their task in marriage enrichment to be helping couples capture the promise of companionship marriage.

The Myth of Naturalism, Privatism, and the Intermarital Taboo

The Maces used two additional concepts to explain the difficulties couples experience in developing satisfying, long-lasting companionship marriages. The "myth of naturalism" (Vincent, 1973) asserts that successful marital relationships should come naturally and effortlessly to normal adults. Anyone who has difficulties in relationships, therefore, is considered to be inadequate. The assumption is that, having grown up in a family, everyone should know how to function in family relationships. Even if this had been true in the institutional model of the family, it would not be true in the companionship model because of the new skills necessary to maintain a relationship-oriented marriage.

The second concept, privatism, reinforces the first. This concept refers to cultural attitudes that hold that anything that occurs within the family is too private to be shared with non-family members. This belief may have been functional in the institutional model, when extended family members were around to discuss family issues. But for the more isolated companionship marriage, it was like shutting the couple in a box and leaving them with little preparation and even less help for figuring out how to relate to each other in mutually satisfying ways. David Mace later referred to the effects of privatism as the "inter-marital taboo," which says, "As a married couple, you shall not reveal to other married couples what is going on inside your marriage" (Mace & Mace, 1976, p. 329).

The Maces saw these two restraining factors as obstacles to successful companionship marriages. They believed that marriage enrichment programs had to be designed to overcome the myth of naturalism and the intermarital taboo, if they were to be successful.

Group Interaction for Couples

The Maces believed strongly that couples could help each other by sharing their relationship experiences. This is the underlying principle for A.C.M.E.'s focus on couples interacting with each other in couple-led groups. These interactions are of three kinds: between the leader couple and the total group; among couples in the total group; and between the husband and wife, either in the group or in a separate place.

A unique technique that promotes interaction in A.C.M.E.-style events is the use of open couple dialogue. The members of the leader couple, or of any participating couple, face each other and discuss an issue, with the rest of the group quietly listening. This technique is discussed more fully in a later section.

The Primary Coping System and Intentional Marriage

What are the essentials needed to succeed at companionship marriage? "In marriage I believe that the central question is whether or not the couple possess what I call a primary coping system. . . . If they do . . . the couple can handle their marriage in such a way that it will grow and flourish" (Mace, 1982a, pp. 27–28). Mace's primary coping system consists of three essentials:

1. a commitment to growth,
2. an effectively functioning communication system,
3. the ability to resolve conflict creatively.

The primary coping system has become central to A.C.M.E.'s approach to marriage enrichment. The first essential focuses on the concepts of growth and intentional marriage. Change is inevitable, but marital growth requires planning. Being intentional about marriage requires setting goals and contracting for specific behavior changes. Planning for growth is an essential element in all A.C.M.E.-style marriage enrichment, and so, near the end of each event, participants develop a "growth plan" for the next 6 months. This essential also acknowledges the balance that must be maintained in individual and couple growth. A growing, flexible, mutually satisfying relationship requires simultaneous growth and development of the individual partners and of the marital relationship, with each supporting the other. The other three essentials focus on the development of specific relational skills.

Communication is a basic tool for relational growth. Couples can tolerate considerable disagreement but little misunderstanding. A basic goal of A.C.M.E.-style marriage enrichment is for couples to learn to communicate with each other in a way that leads to understanding. A.C.M.E. leader training has relied heavily on the work of Miller and his associates (Miller, Nunnally, & Wackerman, 1975). Many leaders are also certified CC leaders. Use of specific Interpersonal Communications, Inc. material was discontinued in 1995 with the publication of "Communicating for Understanding" (Dyer, Dyer, Wood, & Wood, 1995). This new chapter in the A.C.M.E. leader training manual (Michael & Michael, 1992) incorporates basic communication principles from Miller et al. (1975) and other communication theorists' work, emphasizing the building of a communication bridge of understanding between partners.

David Mace's book, *Love and Anger in Marriage* (1982b), provides a strong foundation for understanding and managing anger in marital relationships. Trainers and leaders added a variety of newer approaches to Mace's work. A.C.M.E.-style programs stress the inevitability of conflict in relationships and teach anger management and conflict resolution skills.

To the Maces' original three, a fourth essential has been added in contemporary practice: the ability to develop and maintain intimacy (P. M. Dyer & G. H. Dyer, 1989). The fourth essential was added in recognition of the importance of emotional and sexual intimacy in companionship marriages. Couples cannot always rely on spontaneous intimacy, but they can learn how to avoid obstacles to intimacy and to build bridges between their separateness.

Focus on Strengths and Growth

In A.C.M.E.-style events, couples identify issues that need improvement, but the focus is on strengths and growth rather than on problems. The assumption is that each couple has strengths on which to build and that couples can be trusted to determine their own areas and rate of growth. Identifying and celebrating strengths is an essential element of events. Growth plans and agreements for specific action by each partner help couples make step-by-step progress toward goals they set for their marriages.

☐ Intervention Model

The theoretical concepts discussed thus far are evident in the characteristics of marriage enrichment activities promoted by A.C.M.E., as stated below:

1. Marriage enrichment events are for couples who have a "healthy" marriage. In practice, this translates to couples who are not in immediate marital crisis and not seeking couple therapy for marital problems.
2. The event is led by one or more A.C.M.E.-trained and -certified couples, whose leadership reflects an interactive, participatory style.
3. The method is basically experiential and dynamic rather than didactic and intellectual.
4. Participants have an opportunity for couple interaction in private couple dialogue and within the context of the group.
5. Use may be made of structured experiential exercises.

6. Participant couples usually have some voice in determining the agenda for the event (A.C.M.E., 1995).

Leader training sponsored by A.C.M.E. is designed to teach leader couples a process for enriching marriages, rather than a specific program, event, or format. Consequently, there is variation in the way individual leader couples design and lead events. This process (see the section on "Specific Methods") also incorporates the theoretical concepts just listed.

Structure

A.C.M.E.-style marriage enrichment events vary in degree of structure. The "miniretreat," often used as an introduction to marriage enrichment, has a standard agenda and is highly structured. The Growth in Marriage for Newlyweds is structured to the point of having a manual to follow. The full weekend retreat is generally the least structured and allows the participants the greatest voice in determining the agenda. In any of these, however, the leader couples are free to change the agenda and structure to fit the situation or their preference, within the parameters of the characteristics stated above. Consequently, the degree of structure will always vary by leader couple.

Objectives

The following objectives for marriage enrichment events are generally accepted by A.C.M.E. leader couples, although wording may vary and additional objectives may be added to fit a specific situation:

1. to increase each partner's awareness of self and partner, with an emphasis on the positive aspects, strengths, and growth potential of the individuals and the relationship;
2. to identify within the relationship directions for relationship growth;
3. to develop and encourage the use of effective communication, problem-solving, and conflict-resolution skills;
4. to learn skills and discover ways in which positive growth can take place;
5. to increase mutual intimacy and empathy (P. M. Dyer & G. H. Dyer, 1989, p. 9).

Interaction within groups is structured by a set of ground rules that facilitate achievement of the objectives. Most leaders use ground rules similar to the following.

1. There is no confrontation. All participation in activities is voluntary. Everything done in the group is voluntary. Each person decides to what extent he or she wishes to participate. It is acceptable if a couple decides not to do an exercise or dialogue as long as they do not interfere with other couples. The leaders even avoid going around the circle having couples take turns, as this might be considered confrontation by some.

2. We are here to share experiences, not to exchange opinions. Intellectualizing, diagnosing, analyzing, and advice giving should be avoided. Sharing experiences from relationships increases options and reduces isolation.

3. Speak for self. Each individual speaks for himself or herself. "I" statements are used rather than "you" statements, which assume that the speaker knows what another person is feeling, thinking, or wanting. Each person takes responsibility only for his or her own perceptions, thoughts, feelings, and wants.

4. Everything shared in the group is confidential. Confidentiality is expected. Perhaps nothing will be said that the speaker would not want shared outside the group, but if confidentiality is not assured, people might feel uncomfortable about sharing their relationship experiences. It is a privilege to hear another couple discuss something personal in their relationship. To preserve this privilege, it is essential that such sharing be treated with respect and confidence.

5. Concerns come first. A concern is a worry or preoccupation that interferes with a person's full participation within the group. It may be sickness, the need for a bathroom break, room temperature, digression from the ground rules, or anything else that inhibits full participation. When someone has a concern, it takes precedence within the group. The individual need only say, "I have a concern," and the group action stops to allow that person to share the concern (P. M. Dyer & G. H. Dyer, 1989, pp. 9–10).

Experience has shown that establishing ground rules is an effective way to both build structure and initiate a group contract. Knowing what behavior is expected reduces anxiety and helps to overcome fear of the unknown.

Skills

Because A.C.M.E.'s style depends on couple leadership, skills required for leading enrichment activities are both individual and relational. Skills in both areas are represented in the following qualities, on which potential leader couples are evaluated:

1. demonstrates ability to contribute positively to a healthy, growing marriage relationship;
2. demonstrates cooperative teamwork with partner;
3. demonstrates warmth and caring;
4. effectively communicates understanding and insights to others;
5. shares marital experiences openly;
6. demonstrates sensitivity to needs of others in the group;
7. demonstrates ability to cope effectively with a difficult situation in the group.
8. demonstrates effective planning and design skills (A.C.M.E., 1995).

Experience has shown that, in general, couples who are secure enough in their marital relationship to open up about their marriage to the group make the best A.C.M.E.-style leaders.

☐ Specific Methods and Strategies for Intervention

As stated earlier, A.C.M.E. marriage enrichment leaders are trained to direct a marriage enrichment process rather than an event. Process refers to the underlying flow or direction that guides an enrichment activity from beginning to end. It is the "thinking, knowing" element that designers and leaders bring to the practice of enrichment. It tells them where they are going and how to get there. In highly structured models, the process may be built into the design so that leaders can follow a step-by-step manual. In such models, the designers take responsibility for the flow and direction of the event. In less structured models where participants have more input into the content of the event, individual leaders must take responsibility for the process. The process should be evident whether the event is a workshop for 100 couples, a retreat for 6 couples, or an individual couple working to enrich their marriage in the privacy of their own home. The five stages of the process model used by A.C.M.E. will be discussed later in this section.

Methods

As noted previously, A.C.M.E leaders depend on two methods or procedures to maintain the flow and accomplish the tasks of the marriage enrichment process. These methods are experiential learning and group process. The dynamic, experiential educational model used in enrichment provides a successful structure for increasing interpersonal functioning (Harrell & Guerney, 1976).

The focus of any event is each couple's own marriage, and couples use their own experience for learning. When other material is used in an event, couples are encouraged to take the information and apply it to their own experience. The leaders present a relational concept or skill and then model that concept. Participant couples are given an opportunity to apply the concept to their own relationships.

Group process provides the context within which experiential learning will occur. Group process can encourage the learners as they venture into new avenues of learning. The group process can give support and affirmation as couples discover new ways to relate, and it can provide immediate reinforcement for changes in behavior (P. M. Dyer & G. H. Dyer, 1990).

Groups of couples are different from groups of individuals. Mace (1975) refers to the couples in marriage enrichment groups as subgroups, "each of which is a pre-existing and ongoing social unit" (p. 171). This makes the dynamics of couples groups different from that of groups of individuals. The marital partners are connected to one another in a systemic arrangement that makes it inevitable that change in one will require a change in the other.

The focus of enrichment groups is on the relationship, but individuals must not get lost in this focus. It is important to maintain a balance, since relationships cannot grow without the growth of the individual partners. Leaders must therefore use techniques that focus attention on the relationship without losing sight of the individuals (P. M. Dyer & G. H. Dyer, 1989).

Techniques

A.C.M.E. marriage enrichment leaders use a variety of activities and techniques associated with experiential learning and group process. However, they focus primarily on structured exercises, modeling, couple dialogue, and group discussion.

Structured exercises are part of most marriage enrichment activities. The Maces often quoted a Chinese proverb to explain the use of exercises:

> When I hear, I forget.
> When I see, I remember.
> When I do, I understand

Effective exercises provide for all three of these experiences. The primary role of exercises in a marriage enrichment event is to demonstrate what is taught, to allow for practice, and to have the couple incorporate the learning into their relationship (A.C.M.E., 1992).

The learning goal of an exercise should always be clear to both the leader and the participants. In structured exercises, participants are asked to participate in an activity that is suggested by a leader, who takes responsibility for setting up the situation and adequately processing it after its completion. In the marriage enrichment group, individuals generally are asked to consider some aspect of their relationship and then to share their perspective with their partner. As a couple, they may discuss their insights with the group (P. M. Dyer & G. H. Dyer, 1989).

Exercises have a variety of purposes. Exercises are helpful when new material is introduced, giving the couple a vehicle for using the information. They are also useful in allowing couples to practice new skills or to help a couple or group when they are stuck on an issue or topic and need help in moving on (P. M. Dyer & G. H. Dyer, 1990). Exercises should be chosen carefully to fit the purpose and should be couple oriented, non-competitive, not anxiety producing, and neither too time-consuming nor complicated (A.C.M.E., 1992). Inexperienced leaders sometimes become too dependent on exercises. As a result, the group may become dependent on the leader to produce exercises, which decreases the effectiveness of group interaction.

Modeling has long been recognized as a key factor in learning new behavior. The A.C.M.E.-style marriage enrichment process relies heavily on the concept of couple modeling. From the beginning, the Maces emphasized couple modeling as a primary technique for leader couples. Leaders often use modeling to demonstrate a skill or exercise that they ask the couples to do. Moreover, effective married couple leaders become models for the group in relating, communicating, and resolving issues.

In A.C.M.E.-style marriage enrichment, the leaders serve as the primary models for the group. As the interactive process moves along, however, and as other couples begin to share their marital experiences, any of the other participant couples may become models. Mace (1982a) states that this is the means by which the "intermarital taboo," the belief that what goes on in a marriage should never be shared with others, is broken down, allowing couples to learn from one another's successes and problems (pp. 138–139).

Couple dialogue is the essence of A.C.M.E.-style marriage enrichment. It is considered to be a fundamental element in any marriage enrichment event promoted by A.C.M.E. Couple dialogue is a technique in which members of a couple face each other and talk about an agreed-upon topic, using communication skills to the best of their ability. Couple dialogue achieves five purposes in enrichment groups: It is a representation of the "social unit" structure of the group; it maintains the relationship emphasis; it maintains the experiential emphasis; it provides an atmosphere of support and restraint; and it fosters learning through cross-identification and modeling (A.C.M.E., 1992).

Dialogue is used in several ways in A.C.M.E.-style enrichment groups. The three most frequently used forms are private couple dialogue, simultaneous dialogue, and open couple dialogue.

Private couple dialogue is the most frequently used form. Participants may be asked to individually complete an exercise or set of dialogue questions while sitting in the group and then to leave to discuss the questions or exercise privately for a specified period of time.

The difference between private dialogue and simultaneous dialogue is that, in the latter, the partners talk to each other within the group. They are asked to turn to one another within the group and talk quietly, all at the same time. The quiet sound of voices around the couple provides the sense of privacy that allows them to feel comfortable talking to one another. Quiet music is sometimes used to provide additional privacy. Private dialogue is usually used for longer, more involved assignments, whereas simultaneous dialogue is better for shorter time periods.

Open couple dialogue is widely used by leader couples trained by A.C.M.E. This technique involves one couple in dialogue while the other couples in the group listen. The Maces developed this technique as a part of their Quaker Retreat Model (Mace, 1982a). This method is usually used in small groups of six to eight couples. The leader couple generally models open couple dialogue and then encourages other couples to participate. Mace describes the method as follows:

> Couple dialogue in the group [is] the most effective way of sharing experiences. The couple's private dialogue gains a new validity when they can relax the intermarital taboo and share their communication with the group. Again and again, things begin to happen when couples dialogue aloud so that the others can hear them. As long as the couple are describing their situation, they can only be partially heard. When they begin to dialogue together, the authentic situation comes through. For us, everything else that happens in the couple group—discussion, teaching, exercises—is secondary. It is when the couples are able to dialogue in each other's presence that the real experience, the real sharing, the real learning happens. (Mace & Mace, 1976, p. 10)

Mace argues that this technique allows the marriage to speak for itself, rather than having one or both of the partners speak for the relationship. In terms of group dynamics, it very effectively keeps the focus on the relationship. However, overdependence on open dialogue and placing excessive pressure on couples to dialogue in front of the group is detrimental to the group process.

Group discussion is a technique used by both participants and leaders. Skilled leaders seek to balance group discussion with exercises and couple dialogue in ways that allow variety and vitality for the group. It is essential to keep the focus on relationships and sharing experiences, rather than to theorize, advise, analyze, or diagnose. The ground rules identified earlier are an effective way to minimize the possibility of intellectualizing.

☐ Format of Application

Recruitment for marriage enrichment events occurs through A.C.M.E. organizations and local chapters, churches and synagogues, social service agencies, colleges and universities, and referrals from counselors who do marriage and family work. The "intermarital taboo" often makes couples hesitant or fearful of enrichment groups. To overcome this, recruitment efforts are designed to assure couples that marriage enrichment is for couples with healthy relationships who want to build on strengths they already possess. Potential participants are assured that there will be an opportunity to learn new skills, that participation is voluntary, and that they will be allowed to move at their own pace (A.C.M.E., 1992).

Experience has shown that the most successful method of recruitment is through those who have experienced a marriage event themselves. An invitation by someone the couple knows and trusts reassures the couple that the experience has merit and provides an opportunity for marital growth.

Local A.C.M.E. chapters coordinate, sponsor, and recruit for enrichment activities in local communities. Chapter meetings held a few times per year may allow couples to experience marriage enrichment in a brief activity and encourage participants to become involved in other types of enrichment activities sponsored by the chapter. These may include retreats, workshops, a marriage enrichment festival or rally, and ongoing marriage enrichment groups.

Churches and synagogues recruit for marriage enrichment events to be held for their members or for members of nearby communities. Church or synagogue recruitment is most successful when the church leaders are involved and enthusiastic about marriage enrichment in their own relationships.

Universities and colleges offer opportunities for recruitment. In these settings, particular groups may be targeted, such as parents of freshmen at orientation, engaged couples, newlywed couples, faculty, and staff. Continuing education programs are excellent sources for recruitment. These programs may be one- or two-session workshops or even semester-long groups.

Social service agencies and counseling centers may target specific groups for enrichment activities. Remarried couples, parents of teenagers, couples in prepared childbirth training, or couples in retirement may be the focus of recruitment for workshops or ongoing marriage enrichment groups (A.C.M.E., 1992).

A.C.M.E.-style marriage enrichment takes place in four different formats. The A.C.M.E. style originated with the retreat format, as did most marriage enrichment programs. A retreat usually takes place in a retreat setting over a weekend with six to eight couples participating. A marriage enrichment workshop (a miniretreat) is held in a local setting for a day and a half, with six to one hundred couples. A marriage enrichment series involves five to six couples meeting weekly for four to six weeks to focus on a particular topic. Ongoing marriage enrichment groups (MEGs) meet regularly for a year or more and have five to six couples. A MEG serves as a support group for marital growth.

Although for many years the retreat was the premiere event, A.C.M.E. currently puts greater emphasis on MEGs. Retreats often result in attitudinal changes and increased motivation for behavioral change (often it is hard to convince couples at a retreat to limit their growth plan goals to three). It is doubtful that much sustained behavioral change occurs at a weekend retreat. Such change is more likely to occur when attitudes and motivation are reinforced through meetings with other couples who have had similar experiences and are serious enough about their relationships to meet monthly. These monthly meetings follow the same process and use the same methods and techniques as are used in the retreat.

Dynamic, Experiential Learning

With their emphasis on skills development and the acquisition of new knowledge about relationships, A.C.M.E.-style events rely on experiential rather than didactic learning. In a position paper in 1975, the Maces asserted: "What achieves change and growth in persons and especially in relationships is the opportunity to experience new ways of functioning and the discovery that they are more satisfying and more effective than the old ways" (Hopkins, Hopkins, Mace, & Mace, 1978, pp. 9–10).

Experiential learning is based on the assumption that people learn best by doing. The belief that experience precedes learning and that involved learning is more potent than vicarious learning forms the basis for experiential learning. Behavior change in interpersonal relationships is more likely to occur when learning is dynamic and learners are engaged as active participants in the process (Harrell & Guerney, 1976). Thus, leaders must use techniques that allow couples to actively experience new methods of interaction and to practice skills designed to improve their interpersonal relationships (P. M. Dyer & G. H. Dyer, 1990).

The Process Stages of A.C.M.E.-Style Marriage Enrichment

It was noted earlier that leaders trained in the A.C.M.E. style are taught a process that can be used with any format. This process has five stages: (a) security and community building, (b) development of awareness, (c) development of knowledge and skills, (d) planning for growth, and (e) celebration and closure (P. M. Dyer & G. H. Dyer, 1989).

In the security and community building stage, the process begins with the recognition that people come to any marriage enrichment activity with some degree of ambivalence, anxiety, and resistance. If the experience is to be positive, this anxiety and resistance must be reduced as early as possible. Only after people become comfortable with the situation can they become participants and begin to connect with their spouses and with the other couples in the group. Three tasks need be accomplished at this stage to move the attender to become a full participant: (a) a sense of structure must be provided to reduce anxiety and increase a sense of security; (b) connections must be made among participants, their spouses, and the group; and (c) a contract must be initiated between spouses and among group members. These tasks do not follow in sequence and seem to need to be accomplished at once.

Leaders who communicate a sense of knowing where they are going and how to get there by identifying objectives and schedules help to achieve the first task. Exercises identifying individual hopes and fears for the event, imagery such as a memory journey of the positive aspects of one's relationship, and ice breaker exercises that introduce the individual partners and their relationship to the group help achieve connection. Encouraging couples to identify information not to be shared in the group, discussing ground rules, and securing commitment initiates couple and group contracts.

When couples feel a sense of security in the situation and have developed a degree of connectedness with each other and with the group, they are ready to move into the developing awareness stage. At this stage, couples are encouraged to evaluate how they are currently functioning in their relationship. This phase should help couples identify which areas in their relationship produce satisfaction and which areas require some change to make the relationship more fulfilling. This stage is successfully completed when it has stimulated a positive attitude toward growth, a recognition of the potential for change, and a desire for tools and new ideas with which to accomplish change. Two tasks of this stage are (a) for couples to evaluate their relationship as it currently exists, and (b) to create a need for new ideas and for acquiring or enhancing relationship skills.

A variety of assessment-type exercises that emphasize strengths and growth are used to accomplish these tasks. One popular exercise asks each partner to identify what she or he likes about the marriage, what could be better in the relationship, and what he or she is willing to do to make the marriage better. After the leader couple has shared their responses to the exercise in an open dialogue, participant couples share their responses with each other in a private dialogue.

Once this readiness for learning exists, the process moves into the skill and knowledge development stage. If growth is to occur, participating couples must discover some skills for relationship building and maintenance, alternatives to old ways of thinking and acting, and new options for handling troublesome issues. The three tasks of this stage are (a) maintaining a positive attitude toward change, (b) developing competence in relationship skills, and (c) exploring new ways of thinking and behaving. Communication skills, skills to handle anger and conflict, and ways to develop and maintain intimacy are emphasized at this stage. Couples have the opportunity to practice and develop identified skills. Practicing skills with partners and open couple dialogue provide effective means of skill development. Open dialogue in the group makes couples more conscious of using skills; their efforts are reinforced when they find their verbal interaction more effective and they receive affirmation from the other couples.

The fourth stage, planning for growth, gives the couple an opportunity to develop a specific plan of action for changing their marital interaction. The focus of this stage is on intentionality. This concept asserts that married couples can assume responsibility for the outcomes of their relationships. They can do this by identifying together particular directions in which they want their marriage to move and by contracting together for the specific actions necessary for the desired change to occur. The tasks of this stage are (a) committing to intentional relationship growth and (b) developing a specific plan for individual and relationship growth.

Couples have seen intentionality modeled throughout the event. In this stage they are encouraged to explore the possibility for planned growth for their relationships. They are encouraged to create and commit to a concrete plan for continual growth. The plan might include change in one or several relationship areas. Couples know from the beginning of the event that this activity is coming. They are directed to review assessment exercises from the awareness stage and to think about their work together throughout the event. From these data, they are asked to establish no more than three goals for relationship growth. Next, they are instructed to identify specific ways in which each can help move the relationship toward the designated goals. From these options they select two or three specific actions and commit to work on them. Leaders suggest that couples write out their goals and contracts so that they can be seen daily, reviewed weekly, and revised as needed.

The final stage, celebration and closure, brings the process to an end. Its purpose is to reinforce commitment, celebrate relationship, convey appreciation and affection, and close the process. The tasks of this stage are (a) to reinforce commitment and (b) to celebrate and affirm the enrichment experience, one's spouse, and the other couples who share the experience with them.

To reinforce commitment, some leaders ask couples to share parts of their growth plan with the other couples, so that the group becomes a part of the commitment. A variety of techniques are used to bring closure to the event, such as renewal of marriage vows and exercises in which the couples affirm each other, as partners, as well as the other couples in the group.

All five stages are present to a greater or lesser degree in every event, regardless of the number of participants, degree of structure, or time frame. For example, in a weekend retreat, all of Friday evening may be given to community building, in order to create a sense of connectedness in the group of eight couples who are going to spend 15 to 18 hours together. In a support group of couples who meet every 3 or 4 weeks, the couples might take 20 to 30 minutes at the beginning of each meeting to share "concerns and celebrations" as a means of reconnecting with each other. In a very large group, a dialogue by the leader couple, or a brief introduction by one leader followed by a brief simultaneous couple dialogue, may be all that is needed to complete the first stage. In long events, such as retreats or workshops, the process not only governs the overall flow from beginning to end but may even repeat itself in ministages in each session of the event. Awareness of these stages makes it easier to lead, design, and evaluate events.

☐ Qualities and Role of the Leader or Facilitator

Married Couple Leadership

Experiential learning is facilitated in A.C.M.E.-style events by the use of married leader couples. A.C.M.E. leader training is open only to couples. This may be the most distinctive characteristic of this marriage enrichment style. This is not surprising, considering that the Maces began their work with couples groups as couple leaders themselves. Married couple leaders provide a living laboratory of marriage as they share from their marriage experience. They provide models and establish the climate of safety, openness, support, and sharing within the group. With married couple leaders, everything the couple does represents a model for the participants: the way they share leadership, the way they demonstrate respect and caring for the other, and especially the way they make themselves open and vulnerable to each other and to the group. The open couple dialogue technique is a major vehicle for this modeling.

A.C.M.E. leaders are expected to possess the following characteristics:

1. having a commitment to marital growth and currently working effectively on their own marriage;
2. having the ability to function well as a team, cooperating smoothly, and not competing or getting in each other's way;
3. possessing the ability to communicate a warm and caring attitude to other couples in the group;
4. having a willingness to share their own experiences, to be open, and to make themselves vulnerable, if necessary, in order to help other couples;
5. having sensitivity to group members and group process;
6. having a basic knowledge of human development, marital interaction, and group process; and
7. valuing marriage enrichment as a process best continued through A.C.M.E. membership and participation in an ongoing enrichment group (A.C.M.E., 1995).

A.C.M.E.-certified leader couples must successfully complete a 40-hour A.C.M.E. Basic Training Workshop, lead two events that meet A.C.M.E. standards, and receive favorable evaluations from the couples in the groups they lead.

The Maces considered the leaders' role as one of "participating facilitators." The participating facilitator role is most effective when the leader couple sincerely identifies their intention to enrich their own marriage during the event. The following defines the objectives of the participating facilitators: to participate fully in the experience; to provide direction by giving short lectures and suggesting exercises and activities; to share their marital experiences with the group; and to intervene only to maintain ground rules and time agreements (P. M. Dyer & G. H. Dyer, 1989; P. M. Dyer & G. H. Dyer, 1990). The leadership style is egalitarian and is modeled by the leader couple, who share the leader role equally. Leader couples do not present themselves as experts, but rather as another couple in pursuit of enrichment. They demonstrate this by fully participating in every activity that they suggest to the group. As participating facilitators, leader couples use much more self-disclosure than would be used in a therapy context.

☐ Application of the Preventive Model to a Couple at Risk

Alyssa and Ben came to an A.C.M.E. marriage enrichment retreat with some anxiety and ambivalence. They had attended a local chapter meeting of A.C.M.E. and liked what had happened there. The husband/wife leader couple had talked about positive conflict resolution. In front of the group, they had discussed with each other their own struggles with resolving conflict and how they had begun to see conflict as a positive force in their relationship. When the leader couple finished, the other couples in the group had the opportunity to talk privately about the use of conflict in their marriage.

Alyssa and Ben approached the subject cautiously. Certainly, conflict had not been a positive force in their relationship. They noticed other couples engaging in conversation and the leader couple continuing their dialogue privately. This had given them courage to begin to explore how they each approached conflict in their marriage.

They had never discussed how each of them felt about conflict and the ways they handled it. They reflected on the leader couple's discussion of how they had moved toward making conflict a positive force in their relationship. Alyssa and Ben wondered if they could do the same. Both were amazed at how calmly they discussed such a hot topic. They agreed to continue their discussion at home, but never did because they feared that the discussion might get out of hand.

They heard about the retreat at the chapter meeting, and after talking about it for several days, decided to attend. Alyssa's mother quickly agreed to stay with Benny while they were at the retreat.

The chapter meeting had been their only previous experience in marriage enrichment, and they were still somewhat uncertain about what might happen at the retreat. They began to feel a little more comfortable as the group gathered and began visiting together. As the session began, the leader couple explained the agenda for the weekend. They outlined the objectives and ground rules and the leaders' role. Both Alyssa and Ben began to relax. The explanation of activities fit what they expected.

The leaders suggested that they close their eyes, relax, and participate in a memory journey. They were led to remember their history together, focusing on the joys and celebrations of their relationship and the good feelings they had shared in their dating days and earlier on in their marriage. As they neared the end, Alyssa felt Ben reach for her hand. Later, when they talked together about their memories, they felt close to one another in a way they had not experienced in a while.

When they were asked to introduce their marriage to the group, they found themselves identifying strengths they had ignored. As they listened to others introduce their relationships, they were comforted to hear that others had experienced some of the same issues and concerns they had. They both began to think that their problems might not be as severe as they had feared. When the last couple finished, Ben and Alyssa felt a sense of connectedness and security with the group.

The leaders then asked them to do a final exercise for the evening. Each person was to identify three things they really liked about their marriage, three things that could be better in their marriage, and three things they were willing to do to make their marriage better.

After the interaction of the last few hours, it was easy for Alyssa to identify three things that she really liked about their marriage, but she felt some anxiety about identifying three things that could be better. How would Ben react? She puzzled over what she could do to make things better. She could quickly identify a whole list of things Ben could do better, but what about her? She listened as the leaders, using open dialogue, modeled how they had completed the exercise. When it was their turn to privately share their responses, Alyssa and Ben tried to follow the leader couple's example by being open, listening carefully, not interrupting, and trying to avoid defensiveness. They weren't totally successful, but nonetheless went to their room feeling a sense of hope for having shared their pleasures in being a couple and their ideas about some possible changes.

Saturday morning, Alyssa and Ben were asked to complete an exercise about how they talked to one another. As they spoke about the exercise, they realized that they needed to find some new ways to talk so that they each felt understood. They remembered the leaders saying that the goal of communication was understanding, not just exchanging information.

Later they paid close attention as the leaders demonstrated interpersonal speaking and listening skills. Ben thought about how often he only half-listened to Alyssa and disregarded much of what she said. He also wondered about the leaders' comments about the contribution of emotions to understanding. He had always felt uncomfortable when Alyssa had talked about her feelings or asked about his. Alyssa was impressed with how the wife was able to ask for changes in a positive way and how her husband had not become defensive. She wished Ben would not get so defensive when she tried to tell him what was bothering her or how important her faith was to her. Then she contrasted the way she normally approached Ben with the way the leader had communicated with her husband. She suddenly became aware of how critical and blaming she was in her approach. No wonder Ben reacted defensively.

In the exercise that followed, they were asked to each create a wish list of things they would like their partner to do or to do more often. They then shared their list, practicing the speaking and listening skills they had seen demonstrated. They worked diligently to follow the modeling. The skills seemed very artificial at first, but when time was called, each felt a little more comfortable using them. By lunch, they felt that they had some new ideas and skills that would be helpful to them as they tried to better understand one another.

After lunch, they returned to explore the creative use of conflict. They discussed the things that create anger for each of them, what the underlying feelings are, and how they act when they are angry. Both learned new things about themselves as well as about each other as they spoke. They agreed that neither of them liked the way anger was handled in their relationship and were excited about using some new techniques for containing anger.

The discussion moved to resolving differences that lead to conflict in the first place. Although they had been introduced to the "creative use of conflict" concept in the chapter meeting before the retreat, they found the discussion surprising and enlightening. Was it really possible to handle conflicts in a way that strengthened the relationship? They certainly had not experienced that, even in the weeks since the chapter meeting. They wondered if it really were possible. Yet the leader couple and some other couples in the group described their experiences with conflict as positive.

The leader couple demonstrated a three-step model for resolving conflict, using a real issue in their relationship. As they worked through each step, the leader couple used the communication skills demonstrated earlier. They frequently checked back with each other to see if they understood the other; they respected the other's feelings and affirmed the other's ideas.

Now it was Alyssa and Ben's turn. The leader couple asked them to agree on an issue they were willing to discuss. Alyssa wanted to talk about religion, particularly her wish for Ben to attend church with her. Ben wanted to talk about the number of children they were going to have. After a short discussion, they agreed to tackle Ben's issue.

Before they began, they talked about how much they appreciated the way the leaders had communicated while using the conflict resolution model, and so agreed to use the communication skills they had practiced earlier. As they began, they both noticed that the skills seemed less artificial than before. When time was called, they really had not totally resolved the issue, but felt they had a better understanding of each other's underlying issues and had generated a number of options they were both willing to explore. The discussion had been difficult, but neither of them had become defensive or withdrawn from the interaction. Before they rejoined the rest of the group, they made an appointment to continue their discussion, as the leaders had suggested. Ben and Alyssa left the session feeling a sense of accomplishment about the way they had communicated and worked through the model. They both felt affirmed by the other and had renewed confidence in their ability to work through their problems together.

Saturday evening was designed to think and talk about developing and maintaining intimacy in marriage. They had not experienced much intimacy lately. Ben blamed Alyssa for this, and Alyssa thought that intimacy could come only spontaneously; she had no idea that it could be intentionally created. Both wondered how to make that happen. They felt a bit of embarrassment as the discussion turned toward sexual intimacy, but soon found themselves discussing their joys and frustrations with marital sex openly before the group. They became enthusiastic in their participation and left the group that evening feeling a sense of intimacy and closeness.

Sunday morning, after identifying the concerns and celebrations of group members, the group generated a list of issues they had in their relationships. They continued to discuss, sometimes simultaneously and sometimes with a couple working openly in the group with the others listening supportively, the successes and struggles they had had with these issues. Alyssa and Ben were amazed to hear other couples express some of the same concerns they themselves had, and they were encouraged to hear about some of the successful resolutions couples had experienced. They also heard some very practical ideas that they wanted to try.

On Sunday afternoon, they were asked to make a growth plan for their relationship. They were to identify goals and contracts (what each would do to help meet that goal) for the next 6 months. The leaders suggested that they might want to join an ongoing MEG as a part of their contract.

Alyssa and Ben were serious about their growth plan. They identified three goals and a number of contracts for each goal. They agreed that a MEG would be helpful. Both were worried that, by Monday morning, the good feelings and resolve they had experienced over the weekend would be gone. Hopefully, meeting monthly with five or six other couples would keep them working with the skills they had learned during the weekend and would support them in maintaining their commitment to an intentional marriage.

Alyssa and Ben certainly did not have all their problems solved during the weekend, but they were introduced to many new ways to work with their issues. They found that they are not alone and that other couples have some of the same struggles they do. They discovered and learned to celebrate the strengths of their relationship. They also found a group that would continue to support them throughout the coming months.

☐ Empirical Evaluation and Research

Little research has been done on A.C.M.E.-style marriage enrichment. The lack of a prescribed program and the independence of leader couples is a drawback for systematic program evaluation.

At the University of North Carolina at Greensboro, Swicegood (1974) completed a dissertation that focused on marriage enrichment retreats led by David and Vera Mace. Participants consisted of 25 couples who participated in retreats led by the Maces and 18 nonmatched couples who served as a control group. Assessments were made on rankings of family values and perception of couple communication and agreement.

The study found that the A.C.M.E. retreat couples significantly increased their consensus on ranked values, while no change occurred in the control group. For the retreat group, significant change occurred in five out of thirteen communication areas from pretest to posttest; two areas showed change for the control group. The degree of husband–wife agreement showed significant change on all thirteen areas for the retreat group but no significant change for the control group.

The study participants considered the retreat a success. Twenty-five felt very satisfied with the retreat, nineteen were satisfied, and two were dissatisfied. Forty-two of the forty-six participants agreed that their marriage had been enriched by the experience.

Two masters' theses have evaluated A.C.M.E.'s Growth in Marriage for Newlyweds program. This is a structured program, led by A.C.M.E.-certified leaders, which uses the characteristic A.C.M.E. style. Michael (1983) used a pretest/posttest design with a matched control group. There were 25 participant couples in each group. She assessed trust, intimacy, and overall relationship change. The treatment group showed positive change in trust and intimacy, although not at the $p < .05$ level of statistical significance. Positive relationship change did occur at a statistically significant level in the treatment group, but not in the control group.

G. H. Dyer (1985) studied 16 couples married 6 to 24 months who were nonrandomly assigned to either a Growth in Marriage for Newlyweds group or a no-treatment group. She assessed marital communication, conflict resolution, sexual relationship, family and friends, egalitarian roles, and overall relationship change. Compared with the control group, the treatment group showed statistically significant, positive change in the conflict resolution, egalitarian roles, and positive relationship change items. In all areas measured, the treatment group showed positive change, but not at the $p < .05$ level of statistical significance.

The studies cited here suggest positive outcomes for participants of A.C.M.E.-style marriage enrichment programs, but are extremely limited in scope. Much more research is needed to document the effectiveness of this marriage enrichment approach.

☐ Summary

The style of marriage enrichment associated with A.C.M.E. is distinguished from other forms of marriage enrichment primarily by its insistence on married couple leadership and the use of the open couple dialogue technique. It shares with other marriage enrichment approaches its emphases on working with "healthy" relationships, interpersonal skills training, and experiential learning. Although the weekend retreat was its original format, A.C.M.E. now promotes a variety of formats, and its leadership views ongoing small groups of couples that meet at least monthly as the vehicle most likely to produce intentional growth.

A.C.M.E.-style marriage enrichment has been adapted to and used in several other cultures, including those in Central and South America, Thailand, and Taiwan. In the United States, it has been most successful with middle-class Caucasian couples. Data are not available on the number of minority couples that participate in individual leader couple's groups, but the difficulty in recruiting non-Caucasian couples is often a topic of concern among leader couples. Efforts on the part of A.C.M.E. to recruit and train minority leader couples have had poor results so far.

The effectiveness of A.C.M.E.-style marriage enrichment lacks empirical research documentation. Efforts to study the effectiveness of the retreat and the ongoing group formats are essentially nonexistent. Some support for the effectiveness of the style is found in systematic evaluations of specific programs that use the style, such as The Growth in Marriage for Newlyweds (A.C.M.E.) and Growing Together (PREPARE/ENRICH). Clearly, a limitation of this approach is the lack of research. Nonetheless, thousands of couples who gather for MEGs, local chapter meetings, and state and international conferences attest to what they believe A.C.M.E.-style marriage enrichment has done for their marriages.

☐ Contact References

Readers interested in learning more about A.C.M.E. can contact the Association for Couples in Marriage Enrichment, P.O. Box 10596, Winston-Salem, NC 27108; phone: 1-800-634-8325; fax: 1-336-721-4746; email: wsacme@aol.com; website: http://home.swbell.net/tgall/acme.htm

☐ References

Association for Couples in Marriage Enrichment. (1993). *Strategic plan.* Winston-Salem, NC: Author.

Association for Couples in Marriage Enrichment. (1995). *Standards for the training and certification of leader couples for Marriage Enrichment events.* Winston-Salem, NC: Author.

Burgess, E., Locke, H. J., & Thomas, M. M. (1971). *The family* (4th ed.). New York: Van Nostrand Reinhold.

Catron, D. (1984). Enrichment—Beyond merely coping. *Marriage Enrichment, 12*(5), 1.

Catron, D., & Catron, S. (1996). What is marriage enrichment? *Marriage Enrichment, 24*(6), 5.

Dyer, G. H. (1985). *The effects of marriage enrichment on neomarital relationships.* Unpublished master's thesis, Texas Woman's University, Denton.

Dyer, P. M., & Dyer, G. H. (1989). *Marriage enrichment process, methods and techniques.* Winston-Salem, NC: Association for Couples in Marriage Enrichment.

Dyer, P. M., & Dyer, G. H. (1990). *Growing together: Leader's manual.* Minneapolis, MN: PRE-PARE/ENRICH, Inc.

Dyer, P. M., Dyer, G. H., Wood, B., & Wood, B. (1995). Communicating for understanding. In *Basic training workshop: Participants guide and resource manual* (pp. 29–39). Winston-Salem, NC: Association for Couples in Marriage Enrichment.

Harrell, J., & Guerney, B. G., Jr. (1976). Training married couples in conflict negotiation skills. In D. H. L. Olson (Ed.), *Treating relationships* (pp. 151–166). Lake Mills, IO: Graphic.

Hopkins, L. D., Hopkins, P., Mace, D. R., & Mace, V. (1978). *Toward better marriages.* Winston-Salem, NC: Association for Couples in Marriage Enrichment.

Mace, D.R. (1975). Marriage enrichment concepts for research. *The Family Coordinator, 24,* 171–173.

Mace, D. R. (1976). The couple dialogue—where it all begins. *Marriage Enrichment, 3*(2), 10–11.

Mace, D. R. (1982a). *Close companions.* New York: Continuum.

Mace, D. R. (1982b). *Love and anger in marriage.* Grand Rapids, MI: Zondervan.

Mace, D. R. (1983). The marriage enrichment movement. In D. R. Mace (Ed.), *Prevention in family services* (pp. 98–109). Beverly Hills, CA: Sage.

Mace, D. R., & Mace, V. (1974). *We can have better marriages.* Nashville, TN: Abingdon.

Mace, D. R., & Mace, V. (1976). Marriage enrichment: A preventive group approach for couples. In D. H. L. Olson (Ed.), *Treating relationships* (pp. 321–338). Lake Mills, IO: Graphic.

Michael, P. (1983). *The effect of Growth in Marriage for Newlyweds on newlywed couples' perception of trust, intimacy, and overall quality of the relationship.* Unpublished master's thesis, University of Missouri-Kansas City.

Michael, P., & Michael, R. (Eds.). (1992). *Basic training workshop: Participants guide and resource manual.* Winston-Salem, NC: Association for Couples in Marriage Enrichment.

Miller, S., Nunnally, E., & Wackerman, D. (1975). *Alive and aware.* Minneapolis, MN: Interpersonal Communications.

Swicegood, M. L. (1974). *An evaluative study of one approach to marriage enrichment.* Unpublished doctoral dissertation, University of North Carolina-Greensboro.

Vincent, C. E. (1973). *Sexual and marital health.* New York: McGraw-Hill.

CHAPTER

3

Rhoderick J. Elin, Ph.D.

Marriage Encounter: A Positive Preventive Enrichment Program

☐ Introduction

The roots of Marriage Encounter (ME) can be traced to Barcelona, Spain. There, in 1952, a young Catholic priest, Father Gabriel Calvo, was confronted by two moving experiences that sparked the ME program (Calvo, 1978).

First, he found many of his parishioner couples seeking his help and guidance with the problems, conflicts, and tensions they had with each other and their families. At about the same time, Fr. Calvo met a group of couples who deeply impressed him due to the positive, trusting, and united nature of their marriages. This seemed to be what the other troubled couples were desperately seeking but couldn't find.

Fr. Calvo then sought the cooperation of this group of successful couples in developing a program to help those who were struggling to make their marriages and family lives better.

From that simple beginning, ME, which is now both a weekend experience and a movement, had its birth. Today, some 45 years later, over 2 million couples from throughout the entire United States and 23 other countries have participated in a ME weekend experience, making it one of the largest marriage enrichment programs known.

Specifically, ME is a weekend experience that emphasizes personal reflection and communication between a husband and wife. It usually begins on a Friday evening and ends the following Sunday afternoon. It is most often held in a retreat setting, hotel, or church, away from the distractions and tensions of the couples' everyday lives, so that couples can more fully concentrate on their relationships.

Usually 10 to 25 married couples attend a ME weekend. Two or three volunteer couples with a clergy person or couple make up the "team" who lead the encountering couples through the weekend process. All members of the volunteer team have experienced a ME weekend and have received training on the purpose and process of ME as well as on the writing and presentation of their talks. Fr. Calvo (1988) says that the purpose of the team is to facilitate the process and set the atmosphere. Actually, he states, "the husband and wife give the Encounter to each other" (p. 17).

There are 13 presentations on specific topics. All team members share experiences from their lives to illustrate the particular points covered by the topic as well as provide general information for insight and skill development.

After each presentation, the couples are given one or more questions on the topic presented and are asked to spend some time individually reflecting upon and writing about their personal feelings in response to the questions given. The emphasis throughout the ME experience is on feelings, not judgments or opinions. The questions and/or activities are developmental in nature to help participants put aside their judgments, assumptions, and opinions and get to their true feelings about the issues and topics presented. Listening for understanding without criticism or judgment is equally emphasized throughout the weekend process.

Following their personal reflections, the individuals are asked to get together alone with their spouses to share their written reflections with each other and to further discuss what each has written. There is no group sharing done by the encountering couples; it is a very private experience.

The weekend is enhanced by several low-key symbolic services for reconciliation and healing and culminating with a renewal of marriage vows on Sunday afternoon.

Follow-up studies and anecdotal reports indicate that the ME experience has proven effective not only as a divorce-preventive intervention, but also as a marital enrichment program.

Three National Organizations

At ME's inception in the United States, there was only one national organization, National Marriage Encounter, with many state and regional affiliates. However, due to conceptual and philosophic differences in the early 1970s, the New York National Marriage Encounter split off to form its own organization, which is now called Worldwide Marriage Encounter, under Fr. Charles Gallagher. From this, another national organization, United Marriage Encounter, was later developed. These, then, are the three ME organizations in the United States today: National, Worldwide, and United. The ME weekend is basically the same in all three organizations as far as the structure, process, and purpose. The major differences are primarily denominational.

National Marriage Encounter is interfaith and nondenominational. Worldwide Marriage Encounter is an affiliated organization representing 13 specific religious denominations that present ME weekends: Baptist, Roman Catholic, United Methodist, United Church of Christ, Episcopal, Jewish, Presbyterian, Reformed, Seventh Day Adventist, Orthodox, Mennonite, Lutheran, and United Church of Canada. United Marriage Encounter is made up primarily of Protestant denominations. Some individual churches within denominations, depending upon the region, may affiliate with or support a different national organization than other churches within that denomination. Or they may support all three national organizations and affiliate with none. The determining factor is usually the experiences of the leadership facilitating the establishment of the ME program in the region.

More information on the three national ME organizations can be obtained by contacting them directly. (Specific addresses and telephone numbers are noted at the end of this chapter.)

☐ Theoretical Underpinnings

As a process, ME has been described in many glowing and positive terms. Perhaps Demarest (Demarest, Sexton, & Sexton, 1977) describes it best when stating: "It is an unabashed affirmation of marriage, a celebration of the family" (p. 3). Its theoretical roots lie in the religious and sacramental understanding of the meaning of marriage, which includes the concepts of commitment, trust, openness, and mutuality.

Fr. Calvo's belief, as reported by Demarest et al. (1977), is that there is within each couple a divine energy of love that can be brought alive. This energy of love can be released only by deep personal sharing between a husband and a wife about their feelings regarding the issues of their life together as a couple. Fr. Calvo (1976) pointed out that this process cannot take place automatically, but requires an ongoing dialogue between marital partners.

Fr. Calvo's manual (1983) describes ME as a process designed to give couples the opportunity to examine their lives together—their weaknesses and strong points, their attitudes toward each other and toward their relationship, their hurts, desires, ambitions, disappointments, joys, and frustrations—and to do so in what he considers an open and honest, face-to-face, heart-to-heart encounter between spouses.

Essentially religious in its orientation, ME sees all relationships as going through three phases: illusion, disillusion, and joy. How a couple handles the disillusionment that comes and goes in their relationship determines not only the attainment of the third phase, joy, but whether the relationship will survive.

Fr. Calvo's process, using religious and sacramental illustrations as well as the lived experiences of couples who have weathered disillusionment storms, helps couples develop insight into and skills to grapple with the confounding issues life throws at them.

Tate-O'Brien (1982) states: "In ME we are taught how people go from here (the way we are) to there (the way we can be) by listening to stories and reflections. . . . The process becomes an exercise in adult catechesis. With none of the trappings of the academic world, Marriage Encounter fosters the kind of personal and community growth which in another context would be called 'conversion' " (p. 14).

Fr. Calvo (1988) believes that what is meant for a couple, ultimately and in a religious sense, is unity. Anything that disrupts or negatively effects the couple's unity is going to lead to dysfunction in the relationship. He describes it as "A challenge for you to develop more fully your potential for growth in love, wholeness, holiness and happiness, as you live out God's vision and plan [unity] for your marriage each day of your lives" (p. 47).

☐ Intervention Model

In an article specifically discussing the dynamics of the ME process, Fr. Calvo (1976) enumerated 10 areas that are involved in the weekend experience: discovering oneself, talking of the other, mutual trust, growth in knowledge of each other, growth in understanding each other, learning to accept each other, learning to help each other, growth in love and union, opening up to others, and transcendent love.

Discovering Oneself

Fr. Calvo believes that this is fundamental to the ME process. He feels that no one can hope to find or love another unless an honest self-discovery is made. Activities presented during the weekend seek to help the couples remove their "masks" so that understanding and acceptance of each other is enhanced.

Talking to the Other

Here, Fr. Calvo is speaking of dialogue between husband and wife not in the sense of mere communication of ideas but as a deeper, personal feeling activity.

Mutual Trust

Here, trusting means baring oneself without reservation, opening the doors of one's deepest nature without equivocation, reserve, or fear. Activities throughout the weekend are designed to develop and deepen the level of mutual trust between husband and wife.

Growth in Knowledge of Each Other

Through personal reflection and dialogues, couples gradually begin to become more open and trusting and to share more and more of themselves with each other throughout the weekend.

Learning to Accept Each Other

This, Fr. Calvo (1976) states, is the true matrimonial consent: "I accept you. Do you accept me?" (p. 47). Without such acceptance, he believes, the marriage is a lie. Again, activities of the weekend are designed to address and develop this level of acceptance between the spouses.

Learning to Help Each Other

Mutual help is felt to be an infallible sign of true friendship. Confiding in one another, Calvo feels, is an essential building block for being there for the other and helping one another.

Growth in Love and Union

For Fr. Calvo, this is where all previous steps lead. From this, he feels, springs mutual gratitude and profound joy in the couple.

Opening Up to Others

Fr. Calvo (1976) believes that this is what makes a couple's marriage a sacrament—"to unite in order to open up, to give life to the world, to 'encounter' each other in order to manifest their love to the world" (p. 47).

Love Transcendent

Without a spiritual component—a triangle made up of husband, wife, and the spiritual—true love is not possible.

☐ Specific Methods and Strategies for Intervention

McManus (1993), Bosco (1976), Cline (1987), Stedman (1982), Tate-O'Brien (1982), and others believe that the following four strategies used in the ME process make the weekend a positive experience for most couples.

Couple Presentations

Intensely personal lived experiences shared by the team couples are typically very cathartic and give the encountering couples courage to reach for deeper understanding and growth in their own marriage relationships. These presentations help couples to realize that they are not alone in their struggles to make their marriage better.

Modeling

Besides establishing an atmosphere of love and openness, the volunteer team couples provide a model of deep communication between husband and wife as the weekend progresses. The teams' presentations and modeling of skills make it easier for encountering couples to experience trust, confidence, and understanding within their relationship.

Time

Couples are provided an extended period of time alone, free from the pressures, distractions, and interruptions usually present in their lives. In an atmosphere of love and openness, with uninterrupted time together, couples have the opportunity and support to get in touch with their deep-down, "what I'm really feeling" selves. The concentration of 40 or so hours together is often a unique experience in itself for many couples.

Personal Reflection

Finally, the guided written personal reflections are an effective way for couples to get more in touch with their thoughts and feelings. Writing allows them to express feelings freely, without the inhibition that often results from assumed partner responses and interruptions. It also provides opportunities for couples to stretch past their comfort levels for risking and trusting in their relationship.

☐ Format of Application

The ME weekend is divided into 13 steps revolving around four general themes. These general themes start with the consideration and appraisal of one's self and proceed to concerns regarding the couple in relationship to spirituality within the marriage and, finally, to issues involving the couple in community.

Manuals prepared by Fr. Calvo (1983) and National Marriage Encounter (1981) describe the 13 steps and their purposes and goals, and list specific activities and questions to be used with each step. These steps are used by volunteer teams in preparing to present weekends. The steps, purposes, and goals, along with some of the activities, are as follows.

Step 1: Introduction and Orientation

The purpose and goal of this first step are not only to welcome the couples and introduce them to one another, but also to orient the encountering couples to ME and the process to be followed throughout the weekend. The orientation and the activities in this step focus on three main ideas:

1. The crisis of the modern couple: divorce and an apparent disrespect for marriage.
2. ME's offer of a way for living married life together to counteract the crisis by providing an opportunity to effect the kind of relationship that can withstand the pressures.
3. The rhythm and process of the ME weekend:
   - **Presentation:** A brief exposition of ideas and lived experiences are presented by the volunteer team couples and clergy. This is meant to motivate the couples to experience each step.
   - **Personal reflection:** A private time for each individual to write about himself or herself in relation to the questions given at the conclusion of each presentation; these reflections include feelings, attitudes, hopes, dreams, and frustrations.

- **Couple dialogue:** Husband and wife meet privately to share their personal reflections with each other and to discuss them mutually.

The activity requested of couples in this first step is for them to experience the rhythm of the weekend by reflecting on two issues: why they've decided to come to ME and what they hope to gain from the experience. They are then asked to follow the "couple dialogue" process by reading what each has written and then briefly discussing their responses.

Step 2: Encounter With Self

This step is felt to be an indispensable condition for a deep and ultimate encounter with one's spouse. It is also preparatory for the personal reflections that are to follow. The purpose of this step is to help couples look honestly at themselves as individuals within their relationships and to encourage them to remove any barriers or masks that may hinder them in knowing and accepting their spouse as he or she is.

Using the "rhythm of the weekend," one of the volunteer team couples shares their lived experiences, their "story" as it relates to the topic of an encounter with oneself. The talk illustrates the difficulty of the task, the barriers or masks we use to defend ourselves, and what the couple learned and did to overcome the barriers to openness.

The encountering couples will then be asked to personally reflect on questions designed to guide them through an honest self-appraisal.

Time usually is not provided for couple dialogue at this point, because the exercise is truly meant to be an encounter with oneself. Sharing and dialogue can come later in the weekend if and when individuals so desire.

These first two steps, then, complete the "I" or "self" phase of the ME experience. Next, the "couple" phase begins with an appraisal of the current state of one's marriage relationship.

Step 3: Symptoms of Spiritual Divorce and Subjects for Understanding

The purpose and goals of this step are threefold:

1. to help couples discover the reality of the state of their marriage;
2. to awaken couples to the existence of negative pressures and attitudes influencing their marriage; and,
3. to assist couples in discovering the topics they need to begin to discuss, in order to come to a mutual understanding and a greater sense of marital happiness.

Through the lived experiences of one of the team couples as well as through exposition, essential ideas are presented and illustrated. These central ideas include the following: All marriages are subject to stress and pressures; good marriages don't just happen, they demand work; there's a basic law of life involved in the growth of love (illusion, disillusion, and joy); and the way we deal with the basic law of life, especially disillusionment, determines the quality of our marriage.

The concept of "spiritual divorce" (a sense of strangers coexisting, a remoteness of souls) is introduced and the signs and symptoms of spiritual divorce are discussed.

For the personal reflection on this step, spouses are asked to separately review a list of symptoms of spiritual divorce and check any or all that may be present in their marriages. They are then asked to consider how they themselves contribute to the symptoms checked off. In addition, each spouse is given a list of "subjects for understanding." They are asked to choose one or two topics that they personally feel most uncomfortable discussing but which need the most understanding and attention. These subjects for understanding include issues like health, time, money, work, rest, sexual intimacy, marriage, children, relatives, relationship with God, and family atmosphere.

Each spouse is next asked to write out feelings and thoughts regarding the areas he or she checked. Then, in a couple dialogue, couples are to share their reflections with one another and to gain further insight through discussion.

Step 4: Parable of the Sower (Openness to God's Plan)

The purpose of this step is to prepare each person to be open to the word of God and to marriage in the "plan of God." First, after reading a parable (Matthew 13:1–23) aloud and sharing what it says to them personally, a team couple encourages the encountering couples to personally reflect on what the parable says to them. They are asked to consider what obstacles might hinder them from being open. Step 5 usually follows without couple dialogue.

Step 5: Marriage in God's Plan

In this step, the Biblical tenets regarding marriage and family are presented. The goal is to help each couple discover those tenets and what Calvo (1983) calls the Golden Rule: "All that promotes real marital and family unity (persons, circumstances, things) is in accordance with the

Plan of God. All that endangers or corrupts marital and family unity . . . is not in accordance with the Plan of God" (p. 22).

Drawing upon personal experiences of key moments in their married life, a team couple describes times when they lived their marriage according to God's plan and in a spirit of unity and times when they did not. To help couples understand the concept of unity, couples spend time in personal reflection and a couple dialogue in which they list and discuss three events in their married lives that united them the most.

Step 6: Confidence and Dialogue

Fr. Calvo (1983) states that the purpose of this step is to show that marital love is "an act of free will, intended to endure and grow by means of the joys and sorrows of daily life" (p. 24). The goal is to inspire couples to desire a marital relationship where all things are shared without reservation or selfishness.

The team's presentation illustrates the development of their mutual confiding and how they have benefited from it. The team also shares the difficulties they have encountered and some of the ways they have overcome them.

The personal reflection and couple dialogue at this step centers around three issues: (a) the areas in their married lives in which they're failing to show mutual confidence; (b) the steps they could take to overcome those failings; and (c) how they could improve their unity.

Step 7: Community Meditation on the Wedding at Cana

Through the Biblical story of the wedding at Cana (John 2:1–11), Step 7 seeks to demonstrate the phenomenon of sharing and receiving thoughts that arise from contemplating the Word of God. Its goal is to prepare the couples for the consideration of Step 8, the sacrament of marriage and its graces.

A team couple or clergy person usually provides the background to the Scripture reading and then reads the passage. Teams often share briefly about what the passage says to them. Others are given time to share if they so desire. There is no couple dialogue nor is there other personal reflection at this step.

Step 8: The Sacrament of Our Marriage and Its Graces

The purpose of this step is to help couples discover the sacrament (covenant) of their marriage and to resolve to live and give witness to that sacrament. A team couple shares their lived experiences that describe the sacrament of marriage and define the concept of sacramental graces. There is no personal reflection for this step; rather, the encountering couples move directly to Step 9, "Matrimonial Evaluation."

Step 9: Matrimonial Evaluation

This step is designed to prepare the couples as individuals to personally reflect on their marriage. This and the next step are viewed as the heart of the weekend experience.

After a short instructional and motivational presentation by a team couple on the marriage evaluation handout that has been distributed, the couples are asked to go off individually to complete the evaluation. The evaluation asks them to respond to a series of questions about, first, themselves, then the two of them in relationship, their spiritual development, children, relatives, neighbors, home, and community. The time allotted to personally reflect on and respond to this marriage evaluation is usually 90 minutes.

Step 10: Conjugal Dialogue

This step is the actual objective, the goal of ME. There is no presentation here; rather, brief instructions are given to the group to separate and go off to private places as couples. They are to read each other's personal reflections from Step 9 and to then discuss what they have just finished reading. This step is scheduled to last 90 minutes as well and is called by many "the great dialogue."

Step 11: Marriage Spirituality

The purpose of this step is to help each couple discover and commit themselves to a new way of living married life. The goal is to eliminate the gap between faith and married life by keeping alive the concepts developed in Step 5, "marriage in the plan of God." A secondary goal is to encourage couples to give witness to the unity and sanctity of marriage in their families and communities.

A team couple presents examples from their married life that demonstrate what "marriage spirituality" means to them and ways in which they have tried to love and understand their spouses more fully.

The personal reflection and couple dialogue that follows this presentation deal with how they can keep alive the spirit of their marriage, which they hopefully have rekindled over this weekend.

Step 12: Commitment to Marriage

This step encourages couples to reflect on their responsibility to serve as witnesses to the covenant of marriage. The goal is to urge them to put into action the ideas they learned on the ME weekend.

The presentation by a team couple is designed to give concrete examples of how couples can live out the covenant of marriage: through a commitment to each other, their family, and to the world and through continually expressing their unity as a married couple.

During the personal reflection period, each spouse is asked to develop a plan for their future together as a married couple. Then, after discussing their individual plans in couple dialogue, they are to draw up a couple plan.

Step 13: Closing Celebration

This step wraps up the ME weekend experience through a symbolic ceremony of thanksgiving, which concludes with a renewal of wedding vows and a closing prayer or blessing.

Follow-Up

Before the weekend experience ends, the couples are informed about follow-up activities. These include a renewal meeting of the couples from the weekend ME, ongoing small group meetings with other "encountered" couples, anniversary ME weekends, regional and national conferences, and volunteer opportunities.

The purpose of the follow-up activities is to keep alive the spirit of the weekend experience in the lives of the couples. The activities also provide opportunities to use the skills they've learned and to put ideas into action, so that their dialogue and marriage remain open and growing.

Recruitment

Couples are recruited for the ME weekend in a variety of ways. When there is church affiliation or sponsorship, notices in church bulletins and flyers are used. Public media are often used for announcements of upcoming weekends, information meetings, and general contact information. Since ME is a volunteer program, word-of-mouth support and referrals from encountered couples are especially helpful. The national offices of the ME organizations have publicized toll-free numbers for telephone inquiries and referrals. (See "Contact References" at the end of this chapter.)

Who Is ME For?

Marriage Encounter is appropriate for any married couple who wants to better their marriage. It is open to all persons, regardless of age or faith. Newly married couples as well as couples married over 50 years have found the ME experience to be beneficial. Organizational literature suggests that a ME weekend strengthens and improves the marriages of couples who have a good relationship. For those experiencing difficulties but who are willing to be open and to learn, the ME experience can clarify issues and provide new opportunities for growth.

Because ME is based on self-referral and is a volunteer program, no prescreening or assessment of potential participants is done.

☐ Qualities and Role of the Leader or Facilitator

As has been stated previously, the ME weekend experience is facilitated by two or three volunteer couples, usually along with a clergy person or couple. They constitute the team that leads the encountering couples through the weekend process.

The National Marriage Encounter's *Guide for Teams* (1981) states that "properly prepared couples and clergy person(s) from any area can present an authentic Marriage Encounter within the parameters of Calvo's manual" (p. 3). The guide states further that the role of the team on a ME weekend is not to provide answers; instead, they are to ask questions and allow the couples to discover their own answers. The quality of the process is not dependent on how much the team says or how well they say it, but rather on how much time and encouragement they give to the encountering couples to make their own discoveries.

Key qualities sought in team members and clergy include openness, authentic humanness, an understanding spirit, and a warm personality. In addition, all team participants must have previously participated in a ME weekend experience, must be willing to prepare their presentations according to the guides and manuals of the ME organization, and must have their own talks critiqued to insure adherence to the guidelines and philosophy of ME. Finally, they must be willing to commit sufficient time and resources to prepare for the weekend.

Central to the role of clergy is the notion of spirituality. Fr. Peter Sammon (1980) sees this to mean having a deep personal relationship with God. He states further that "the clergy person must also have the ability to share openly that relationship with the couples on the weekend" (p. 16).

Fr. Calvo (1983) emphasized that the team is to continually stress that it is the encountering couples, themselves, who are in actuality presenting the experience to each other: "[T]hey are the only persons really involved in the Marriage Encounter" (p. 4). He sees the work of the team as establishing an atmosphere of simplicity, informality, peace, and serenity, which will inspire confidence and love throughout all the talks, dialogues, and conversations.

☐ Application of the Preventive Model to a Couple at Risk

The case study of Ben and Alyssa presented by the editors provides an example of an ideal couple candidate for a ME weekend. Their differing religious and family backgrounds are fertile ground for discovery and growth in their relationship.

The weekend process, starting with the "encounter with self," should prove valuable in drawing both Ben and Alyssa into a needed examination of themselves: who they are and where they are at present as individuals. This is accomplished by both individuals personally reflecting on their principal defects or faults, the ways in which they overly center on themselves, and the listing of their positive qualities and potential. In so doing, clarity regarding themselves will help them to begin to share more of their true selves with each other.

In looking at their life together as a married couple and the current state of their marriage in the third step, "symptoms of spiritual divorce and subjects for understanding," they'll confront areas of concern for both and begin to gain a deeper understanding of each other.

The process of personal reflection and couple dialogue will hopefully help Ben and Alyssa not only to understand each other more fully but also to develop concrete skills that they can continue to use to further nurture their marital relationship long after the ME weekend is over.

Hearing the stories of the volunteer team couples can encourage them to be more open and trusting with each other as well as to see that they are not alone in their struggles with married life.

The presentations, activities, and personal reflections and their couple dialogues can be positive steps in helping them explore their disillusionments, hurts, and frustrations as well as their individual and couple strengths, thereby enabling them to develop greater couple unity.

While the issues that are problematic for them (e.g., religious differences, Ben's increased drinking, Alyssa's desire for a third child, Ben's career concerns, etc.) will not be resolved for them on their ME weekend, hopefully they'll begin to acknowledge their existence. The ME process should also assist them in becoming more open and trusting with each other about these areas so that their deeper feelings and thoughts can be mutually shared. The weekend's activities can also assist them in prioritizing their concerns and developing plans to deal with them through continued dialogue and action.

The ME experience, while emotionally intense and very structured, should leave Ben and Alyssa with an overall feeling of hope and optimism about their ability to come close together again. They'll understand themselves, each other, and their relationship at a much deeper level than they did before the weekend. But more importantly, they can leave the encounter with skills and plans that they can put into action for continued marital renewal and strengthening.

Follow-up activities are available to encourage them in their continued growth and couple development.

☐ Empirical Evaluation and Research

The National Institute for the Family (1990), in collaboration with The Center for Applied Research in the Apostolic, conducted perhaps the most comprehensive study on the effectiveness of ME in 1990.

The study involved couples who attended a ME weekend between 1965 and 1989. Using subjective measures, it sought to compare the initial effects of the ME weekend with its long-term residual effects. The results of the study indicated that 49% of the respondents rated ME's impact as "very good" for them, and 62% rated the long-term impact on intimacy and closeness as "high" or "very good." For improving communications, 46% said that the immediate impact was "high" and 37% stated that it was "very good." The long-term impact on communication was rated as "high" by 62%.

The area of sexual relationship was rated as being "highly impacted" by 62%, whereas 48% reported improved sexual relationships due to the original weekend experience. Fifteen percent of those reporting indicated an "excellent" marriage prior to ME, but 61% felt that way immediately after the weekend experience.

McManus (1993) discusses a doctoral thesis by George McIlrath which reviewed 30 academic studies on the effectiveness of ME. McIlrath concluded that there was a significant positive impact on the couples involved in the studies. McManus quotes from the study that "Marriage Encounter programs have often received affirmations of 80% to 90% in post-weekend surveys and . . . the program demonstrates clear effectiveness when its participants are involved in rigorous and controlled pre/post-weekend research" (p. 73).

The National Marriage Encounter Prison Ministry (1996) has gathered subjective evaluation data on all the 138 ME weekends given to date in federal and state prisons throughout the country. On a rating scale of 1 (low) to 10 (high), the prisoners' and their spouses' reactions to the ME experience averaged 9.6. This score was derived from averaging the scores of 1,793 couples (3,586 individuals). Anecdotal comments from the prisoners and their spouses support the program's effectiveness and attest to its impact on them as individuals and as couples.

Hessel (1985) completed a study on the long-term impact of ME on couples attending weekends in the Green Bay, Wisconsin area between May 1976 and May 1984. Her study found that over three fourths of those responding perceived a change for the better in their relationships. Over 80% attributed the perceived change to the ME experience. Two thirds reported a perceived change for the better in relationships with their children and with God. Over one third perceived a change for the better in relationships with their parents and in-laws. Three fourths of the respondents reported that the ME experience effected married life for the better. Overall, Hessel found that almost 90% indicated a favorable impression of the ME weekend. Communication and communication skills were reported as the most valuable parts of the experience for most.

Research Limitations

Research conducted thus far, while addressing long-term as well as short-term reactions and impressions, is nonetheless limited to subjective measures and is complicated by difficulties in tracking couples.

☐ Summary

With over 2 million couples worldwide having participated in a ME weekend experience, ME is one of the largest marriage enrichment programs. It has proven effective not only as a preventive intervention for marital dysfunction, but also as a valued marriage enrichment activity. Because it is so widespread as a movement, the weekend experience is readily available to couples throughout the country. And, though ME is not intended to take the place of professional counseling where that is needed, it can be a valued resource not only as an adjunct to marital therapy but as an enrichment activity for those seeking to strengthen their marriages. ME's follow-up opportunities provide a kind of "marital support group" for those couples who seek continued growth in their marriage relationships.

Scholars such as Cline (1987) and Stedman (1982) as well as national and regional studies have validated ME's effectiveness. Its strengths are many and varied. As a marriage enrichment program, it is readily available, with weekends given throughout the United States, Canada, and many foreign countries. The cost of the weekends is relatively inexpensive, making it a very cost-effective program. Opportunities for ongoing support and follow-up involvement enhance and nurture marital relationships. The multidimensional approach, including a spiritual emphasis, makes the ME experience unique as a marital enrichment program. The opportunities for communication skill development give couples tangible skills they can utilize long after the weekend is over. The atmosphere of openness and honesty created by the volunteer team is extremely helpful to the encountering couples in expressing their feelings, needs, and dreams. And, finally, the overall message of hope and optimism of the weekend experience is both inspiring and motivating.

However, ME does have its limitations. It is not marital therapy, nor is it intended to be. Professional help is still essential for extremely dysfunctional relationships or where individual psychosocial maladjustment and/or personality issues are prevalent. These situations, however, are not screened out, due to the self-referral nature of the program. While these individuals and couples may gain some benefit from the weekend experience, referrals for professional help are given by the volunteer team members and clergy as situations present themselves on the weekends.

☐ Contact References

All three national ME organizations can be contacted through toll-free telephone numbers. Their addresses and phone numbers are:

National Marriage Encounter
4704 Jamerson Place
Orlando, Florida 32807
800-828-3351

Worldwide Marriage Encounter
1908 E. Highland, #A
San Bernardino, California 92404
800-795-5683

United Marriage Encounter
P. O. Box 209
Muscatine, Iowa 52761
800-334-8920

☐ References

Bosco, A. (1976). *Marriage encounter: The rediscovery of love.* St. Meinrad, IN: Abbey.

Calvo, G. (1976, August). *The dynamics of the process of marriage encounter.* Minneapolis, MN: International Marriage Encounter, pp. 2–4.

Calvo, G. (1978, January). *Ten years of marriage encounter in the U.S.* Minneapolis, MN: International Marriage Encounter, pp. 6–8.

Calvo, G. (1983). *Marriage encounter manual.* Orlando, FL: National Marriage Encounter. (Original work published 1969)

Calvo, G. (1988). *Face to face: Becoming a happier married couple.* Minneapolis, MN: International Marriage Encounter.

Cline, V. B. (1987). *How to make a good marriage great.* New York: Walker and Company.

Demarest, D., Sexton, J., & Sexton, M. (1977). *Marriage encounter: A guide to sharing.* Minneapolis, MN: Carillon Books.

Hessel, P. L. (1985). Report on long-term impact of the Green Bay marriage encounter. An unpublished report to Marriage Encounter, Green Bay, WI.

McManus, M. J. (1993). *Marriage savers.* Grand Rapids, MI: Zondervan.

National Institute for the Family. (1990). *Worldwide marriage encounter: National survey and assessment.* Washington, DC: Author.

National Marriage Encounter. (1981). *Guide for teams.* Orlando, FL: Author.

National Marriage Encounter Prison Ministry. (1996). Unpublished evaluations of 138 prison ME weekends, National Marriage Encounter Prison Ministry, Cincinnati, OH.

Sammon, P. J. (1980). Why have clergy on the weekend. *Marriage Encounter, 10,* 16–17.

Stedman, J. M. (1982). Marriage encounter: An insider's consideration of recent critiques. *Family Relations, 31,* 123–129.

Tate-O'Brien, J. (1982). Through storytelling, the marriage encounter prompts conversion. *Marriage Encounter, 2*(3), 14–15.

Clay Cavedo, Ph.D.
Bernard G. Guerney, Jr., Ph.D.

4
CHAPTER

Relationship Enhancement® Enrichment and Problem-Prevention Programs: Therapy-Derived, Powerful, Versatile

☐ Introduction

Relationship Enhancement® (RE) traces its roots to the early 1950s (see Guerney, 1990) when the second author of this chapter noticed difficulty with retaining parents in an otherwise effective child-therapy program. He reasoned (Guerney, 1964) this might be due to parents' "jealousy" of the therapist's special healing role with the child, and/or to a perceived threat to the parents' self-esteem from feeling placed in the role of "bad" parents who had "messed up" their child. It seemed likely that both of these factors could be dealt with by enlisting the parents as the therapist's helpers or "psychotherapeutic agents" (see Guerney, 1977). It was reasoned that if parents could be trained to behave in a therapeutic manner with their children, the change in the family system would greatly increase the effectiveness of the child's therapy. This led to the creation of Filial Therapy, now also called Child RE Family Therapy, or Filial Family Therapy, in which parents are taught to conduct play sessions, identical to Rogerian Child-Centered Play Therapy, with their children. They then learn to transfer and generalize these skills to use in daily life when it is appropriate to do so. They also learn behavior modification skills to use at home. They work through their own emotional difficulties as these are related to their attempts to use and transfer the therapeutic methods into the play sessions and into their daily interactions with their children. The method can be employed with single families or with groups of families.

The initial 3-year NIMH research project indicated that the approach was highly effective (Guerney, 1976; Guerney & Stover, 1971; Oxman, 1971). This lent impetus to the creation of RE therapies based on the same philosophy, principles, and methods (albeit not Play Therapy per se) for couples and for families with older children. Since RE therapy was largely based on skill training, it was a logical step to do as our clients kept urging us to do: create programs to teach the skills to couples and families *before* they get into trouble. These became the RE enrichment and problem-prevention programs.

☐ Theoretical Underpinnings

The theory that forms the base on which RE approaches stand is a unique synthesis of what the second author believes to be the strongest elements of the four major schools of psychotherapy: psychodynamic, behavioral, humanistic, and interpersonal. Based on his interpretation of psychological research, particularly in the area of psychotherapy and behavior modification, on his clinical and field experience, and on informal observations over time, certain elements were selected and others rejected from each school. What remained was integrated into a unified, systemically oriented, skill-training-based, theoretical perspective. Limiting ourselves here to some of the major elements accepted from each school, and not covering what was rejected from each, we can very briefly describe the major elements underlying RE as follows. From psychodynamic theory were drawn the concepts of the importance of the unconscious and the power of defense mechanisms. Also included were the concepts of the necessity for psychological growth of promoting self-understanding (insight) and the healing power of catharsis, or the powerful experiencing or re-experiencing of formerly repressed or suppressed emotions (Guerney, 1994b). From Adler was drawn the concept that human behavior is best understood in terms of seeking goals and an understanding of the power of the drive to mastery that is activated when humans seek a goal.

From humanistic theory, Rogerian theory in particular, was drawn the concept that defense mechanisms (and the resulting distortions of reality) are triggered primarily by threats to a person's self-concept. Also drawn from Rogers is the concept that consistently demonstrating acceptance, respect, and empathy is the most effective way to promote a strong positive relationship and to reduce another's need to employ defense mechanisms, and therefore is also the most effective way to help another to explore his or her thoughts and feelings openly and honestly and to achieve catharsis and insight.

From learning theory in all its dimensions—social, behavioral, and cognitive—was taken the concept that useful, life-enhancing behaviors can be taught and learned in a systematic manner. It is believed that teaching participants appropriate skills greatly enhances and speeds growth and positive relationship change. Methods drawn from learning theory and used in behavior therapy are deemed extremely useful not only for the professional who teaches RE skills, but also for the participants themselves, in order to help bring about changes desired by both themselves and their partners.

From interpersonal theory, as originated by Sullivan (1947) and elaborated by Leary (1957), was drawn the concept that important people around us train us to act as we do. All people unconsciously act in certain ways to get responses from others that feel comfortable and that reduce anxiety. Many habitual ways of behaving—often ones that had their purposes earlier in life—become so unconscious and automatic that Leary (1957) calls them "reflexes." Some of these may quite consistently draw undesired responses from others. RE theory holds that bringing a wide range of interpersonal behaviors into the realm of conscious choice is the key to efficient, cost-effective methods of improving personal and interpersonal satisfaction (or "health" to those who prefer medical terminology).

Therefore, RE trains participants to recognize that every action or inaction of another person provides an opportunity to consciously influence the nature of the other's next response, and consequently all the ones that follow. Except in captive relationships, and usually even there as well, one is not powerless.

One always has the choice to behave in ways that are likely to elicit more rather than less desired responses from another. In the realm of any interpersonal relationship, but especially marital and family relationships, it is the goal of RE to teach the participants how to make such choices consciously. Personality, interpersonal theory holds, is best viewed as one's internal and external pattern of interpersonal behavioral predispositions and reactions. Increasing people's ability to make flexible, conscious choices in the service of achieving their positive personal and social goals is viewed as the fastest and surest route to strengthening adjustment as well as relationships and, of course, therapeutic efficiency and effectiveness.

From the RE perspective, therapy, prevention, and enrichment are seen primarily as different points on the same continuum. The goals of prevention, therapy, and enrichment can each be seen as *helping people change in positive directions*. Whether it is prevention or therapy is often merely a function of time, for example, whether you see the couple early in marriage or late in marriage. If you do not train couples in skills early, you may very well have to do it later if the decay of the relationship or its dissolution is to be halted. If you do not do it early, the consequent build-up of various forms of psychic scar tissue likely will make the learning of new patterns more complicated and difficult. In that case, therapy rather than prevention is called for.

☐ Intervention Model

The skills built into RE are those we viewed as most likely to help satisfy the strongest desires of families in this and almost all other cultures; love, compassion, belonging, trust, loyalty, security, and pleasure are seen as major among these. Each partner's fulfillment of these desires for the other and for other family members, if any, is viewed as the key psychosocial function of committed romantic relationships. Providing a stable, caring atmosphere of love and intimacy nourishes each member's self-esteem and personal psychological growth. Compassionate responsiveness may be the most important single factor in promoting secure and reliable pair bonding, constructive intimate relationships, and an atmosphere for personal growth. At a somewhat more specific level, factors that RE holds to be important for long-lasting, healthy couple relationships are the ability to resolve problems in ways that are perceived as mutually fair; the ability to retain a caring atmosphere during problem-solving discussions; the ability to take the other's perspective *and* to communicate to one's partner that you have done so; the ability to see self and other clearly (without negative distortions such as those found in the phenomenon of negative sentiment override); the ability to prevent, or failing that, to break out of, negative–negative communication exchange cycles and anger escalation; the ability to make the changes in behavior patterns one wishes to make and to help one's partner make the changes he or she wishes to make. These, too, are abilities that come with mastering the skills in RE programs and therapy.

Another aspect of building and maintaining satisfying and enduring relationships involves the ability to include the full picture when discussing a conflict or problem. The most generally deficient aspect of this requirement is the omission of positive thoughts and feelings about one's partner. In an intimate relationship, there are always underlying positives, thoughts and feelings lying hidden beneath negative feelings. The motivation for an intimate to change is tremendously enhanced—in our therapeutic experience it almost always marks the turning point—when one partner arrives at a mixture of feelings engendered by a certain confluence of perceptions. That confluence involves perceiving the pain he or she is causing a loved one within the context, at least, of the partner's strongly expressed desire for a reciprocally positive relationship or, at best, within the context of the other's deep love and caring for him or her.

A key general principle in bringing about constructive change in a relationship is to honestly express important feelings and thoughts in a way that does not threaten the self-concept of one's partner any more than is necessary for honest expression. Doing this means learning to express oneself in a compassionate manner. It is this type of expression that enhances the partner's ability to understand and accept the speaker's feelings and thoughts, and to convey compassionate understanding back to the speaker. This in turn makes it easier for the speaker to continue to be open and compassionately honest in his of her further expressions. In fact, honesty and compassion are the two values that very directly and overtly are promoted and strengthened by RE. The consistent application of these within interpersonal relationships invariably leads intimates (and almost everyone else) to an increase in a third value, which is equity. In RE programs and therapies, couples learn nine interlocking skills that foster healthy relationships. Use of these skills changes interactions in the direction of greater mutual respect, understanding, cooperation, and caring.

Following is a brief description of the *purpose* of each skill. (Space prohibits explication here of the specific *guidelines* taught to the participants that define each skill. Those guidelines are highly specific. They are like the rules of a game. When the rules are followed, skillful behavior is the result.)

Expressive skill enables participants to better understand their own sources of stress, needs, and desires, and to express them to others in a way least likely to foster defensiveness, anxiety, hostility, and conflict and most likely to elicit sympathetic understanding, cooperation, and support. The expertise prompts its possessor to engage others in the process of conflict and problem resolution more promptly and successfully, and with less anxiety.

Empathic skill enables participants to more compassionately understand the emotional, psychological, and interpersonal needs and desires of others and, over time, to more quickly and frequently elicit open, honest, relevant, trusting, cooperative, sympathetic, supportive, and intimate behaviors from others.

Discussion and negotiation skill helps couples to preserve a more positive emotional atmosphere when discussing difficult issues, thereby avoiding anger escalation and defensive digressions, and to understand the deep feelings and root issues necessary to resolve these difficult issues most broadly and successfully.

Facilitative (coaching) skill enables participants to exit negative–negative communication spirals and begin (or resume) using the RE skills instead and, in general, to help each other to master the RE skills.

Problem or conflict resolution skill enables participants to devise creative solutions to problems—solutions that maximize *mutual* need-satisfaction and therefore are likely to prove workable and durable.

Changing-self skill enables participants to eliminate or reduce unwanted behaviors and increase desired behaviors so that they can put into practice agreements they have reached with their partner or objectives they have set for themselves.

Helping-others-change skill enables participants to help others to change their attitudes, feelings, and behaviors in order to implement their personal and interpersonal agreements and objectives.

Transfer and generalization skill enables participants to use the skills in their daily lives and with important others besides the partner, for example, children, parents, friends, and coworkers.

Maintenance skill enables participants to maintain a high level of skill over time.

We believe that the fact that the RE problem-prevention and enrichment programs were derived from RE couples therapy is responsible for the program's capacity to help couples quickly reach deep levels of feelings and often to achieve significant intrapsychic insights. We believe that a major factor in this regard is the way participants are taught to respond to their partners' self-expressive statements. In many other programs, and in the basic training of most therapists regarding the type of response to use with their clients, participants are trained to paraphrase or "mirror" what the other person has said. In RE, the first response that should be made to the person who is expressing himself or herself is called an *empathic response.* It is the same response that is taught and used by therapists doing RE couple therapy (and, for that matter, by RE therapists doing intrapsychically oriented therapy with individuals).

In an empathic response, mirroring and paraphrasing are avoided as much as possible for a great many reasons we do not have the space to enter into here. Also avoided is so-called active, or reflective, listening, along with the general rationale for using it. Generally, the rationale focuses on the separateness and differentness of the person who is expressing himself or herself from the person who is reacting to that expression. The rationale is largely cognitive: to check accuracy in light of those presumed differences. We believe that under these assumptions and goals, the risk is high that the person expressing himself or herself will perceive such responses as mechanical, formulaic, superficial, and unnecessary. It is not a powerful way of inducing intimacy and bonding.

The assumptions and rationale of the empathic responder are quite the reverse. The cognitive element is not key. What is key is creating a certain feeling within the speaker when he or she hears the empathic response: a feeling that what he or she thinks, feels, and does is vitally important to the responder, who deeply cares about, appreciates, and values the speaker and his or her thoughts, feelings, and wishes, and is giving his or her all to try to understand deeply. To bring that feeling about, the empathic responder seeks a total *identification* with the speaker while listening and responding. An erasure of a sense of differentness and separateness is sought. The empathic responder's objective is to place himself or herself inside the speaker and then to use the self, now totally identified with the other, as the major vehicle for discovering that which has *not* yet been said, but would be immediately recognized as valid by the speaker. The objective is not mirroring, but *"X-raying."* To make such discoveries, empathic responders, following the skill guidelines, look inside themselves and ask a series of questions about how they would react, given what the speaker had said and had revealed nonverbally, everything else they know about the speaker, and most of all, how the empathic responders themselves would think and feel in those circumstances. The empathizer's identified self is what is used to generate the "X-ray." In the consistent context of attempts clearly based on compassionate identification and a consistent eagerness to make any corrections necessary, making mistakes in using this process is not a problem. And when the X-ray is accurate, a great many positive things follow. These include not only the kinds of things we mentioned before, but very frequently a change of perspective, of understanding, and of heart on the part of the empathizer himself or herself.

Figure 4.1 shows how the nine RE skills can operate to bring about improvement in a couple's relationship and, when fully acquired and consistently used in a variety of situations over time, can be expected to yield improvement in physical and mental health as well. It illustrates the RE position, that in the effort to create positive, lasting changes, emotion, cognition, and behavior all should be targeted for change together, in a spiraling, synergistic fashion.

The figure shows this by diagramming the following points. In their dialogues at home, as the couple works on issues to enhance their relationship or to resolve problems, empathic skill increases their compassion, trust, openness, and respect. Expressive skill promotes catharsis and also the expression of positive emotion. Discussion and negotiation skill allows the couple to remain focused and to get down to the roots of the problem even when they discuss the most troublesome, anxiety-arousing kinds of conflicts. All the while, the partners help each other to consistently maintain skill usage and to perfect the skills by employing facilitative skill to coach one another. All of these factors, but especially the empathy, the constructive catharsis, and the ability to see the partner's pain in the context of the partner's love (through the frequent surfacing of underlying positives) creates a desire to help meet the needs of the

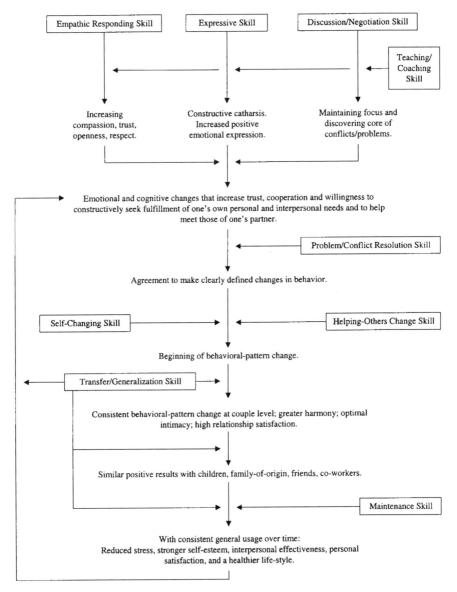

FIGURE 4.1. Copyright 1997 by IDEALS. Reproduced with permission.

partner. Sometimes the dialogue itself is all that is needed to resolve a conflict or problem because the resolution is not one that requires the development of a new behavioral pattern on the part of either or both partners.

When a new pattern of behavior is required, problem or conflict resolution skill enables a couple to develop a clear-cut agreement that comes as close as possible to meeting each partner's needs 100 percent, and to agree on who will do exactly what, when, and how often. It also helps them to develop a plan to evaluate how well the agreement is working and to make any necessary modifications over time. In such instances, further agreements are reached that allow effective deployment of changing-self and helping-others-change skills to actually bring the changes about consistently in daily life.

Where desirable, the learners can deploy new behavior with other people in other situations by using transfer and generalization skill. Such transfer and generalization is routinely applied to the use of the RE skills per se. As the couple develops and implements enhancement plans and succeeds in resolving problems and conflicts, they develop confidence in their own and their partner's willingness and ability to do so. The result is greater harmony, optimal intimacy, and high relationship satisfaction. In addition, through transfer and generalization, and their capacity to use maintenance skill to maintain the positive changes over time, participants may improve other significant relationships. This is because they are taught how to use the skills unilaterally when the others involved do not know the skills. Therefore, they know how to change the way others treat them and to resolve major sources of stress, which, after all, usually stem from, and can be resolved by, changing the way others (their boss or supervisor, for example) treat them. The generalized incorporation of the skills constitutes a significant personality change, and in general may succeed in making major mental and even physical health improvements. In the last respect it should be kept in mind that RE includes skills derived from behavior modification, and adds to them skills that better enable participants to enlist the aid of others to help them make changes in their behavior. Thus, the RE skills are fully applicable to behavioral problems such as smoking and drug or alcohol consumption.

☐ Specific Methods and Strategies For Intervention

Composition and Time Formats for RE Programs

RE enrichment and problem-prevention programs and RE therapies can be used with individuals, a couple, or a family, or with groups of individuals, couples, or families. There is no rigid time format. Enrichment and problem-prevention programs can be divided into two 1-day programs—the first day for the core skills and the second day for the advanced skills—or held on 2 consecutive days (e.g., on a weekend). They also can be conducted in a series of weekly meetings. These generally last

2 hours per week for 10 to 15 weeks. Another example of time formats is half-days, conducted once a week over 4 weeks. While the day-long formats are more convenient for many couples, that certainly is not always the case. There are very important advantages to a program that is spread out over a number of weeks. It provides more frequent opportunity for home study of the skills, and even more important, it allows couples much more opportunity to use the skills to resolve problems and develop skills at home. In addition to the direct benefits that it provides, the spacing out of sessions also affords the opportunity for more use of logs and other forms. Such home assignments permit the extremely valuable monitoring and supervision of skills as they are used in daily life.

Home Study With Coaching

This is a unique format for enrichment programs. It is a distance education program. It is unique because it includes 4 hours of coaching (and even more is available if desired) by a certified RE Couples Program. For decades, the second author of this chapter resisted the idea of trying to teach RE skills in any way except through personal contact because he is convinced of the vital importance of coaching. But not long ago, it suddenly dawned on him (and when it did he couldn't believe that he hadn't thought of it earlier) that you *can* coach a couple without being with them physically. Any couple with an extension phone or a speaker phone can be offered individual coaching. Even with 4 hours of private coaching of skills while the couple works on important issues or problems in their relationship, the cost of such a home study program is significantly less than that of a workshop. In addition, the couple avoids the financial, time, and lost-productivity costs of travel, not to mention the trouble parents might have of finding someone to look after their children. We consider this a very important breakthrough in the field of marital enrichment and problem prevention. The name of the RE home study program is *PhoneCoach®* .

RE Therapy Session Formats

RE therapy has these session formats: marathon (1 or 2 continuous days, usually on a weekend); minimarathon (3 or 4 hours); double sessions (usually 1½ hours); single sessions (50 minutes). Marathon and minimarathon sessions are particularly useful for professional clients (who might prefer to be seen for a 2-day weekend than lose 2 days of productivity and income), clients who fly in from out of town, and clients who travel a long distance by car. They also are excellent for resolving crises and making decisions about whether to reconcile. Otherwise, the same advantages accrue to spread-out therapy as were stated above for enrichment and problem-prevention programs. RE therapy also can be conducted over the phone.

RE Therapy Modes

The *crisis resolution* mode is used when there is a crisis that must be solved in 1 to 5 hours because only a limited number of therapy hours is available, or because the problem must be solved before a particular date that is being imposed externally, or because of the needs of one or more members of the family. It is a method designed to accomplish the resolution of a single conflict in 1 to 5 hours of therapy depending on the deadline, which could be concentrated into marathon sessions of a week or two, 1 day, or a half-day. The therapist assumes the roles of the clients at great length, making extensive use of certain RE therapeutic methods called *becoming* and *laundering* that are described in a later section.

The *experiential* mode (see Guerney, 1989) is used when the time limit on therapy, for one or more of the reasons cited above, is from 5 to 10 therapy hours, or the therapist or a client is unwilling to delay work on their most serious problems until such time as they have a good grasp of the RE skills. The major difference between this and the *time-designated* mode described next is that the clients begin work on their most serious problems immediately rather than waiting until they have fully mastered the core skills. This saves time but introduces the risk that clients will not learn the skills as thoroughly or reliably as in the time-designated mode.

The *time-designated* mode is one in which an estimate is made, on the basis of information gathered at intake, of how long it will take for the clients to resolve their major problems and be able to use the skills in their daily lives. The effort is made to obtain a commitment from them for that length of time. Usually the time is between 10 and 20 hours, but it may be longer if there are certain problems that generally take a long time to see through to a fully solid solution, especially if they exist in combination (e.g., the probable need for extensive catharsis of early life trauma, an affair with undecided outcome, a last-chance effort with separation already in place, alcohol or drug abuse). The couple understands that the estimate is made on the assumption that they will work outside the sessions to master the skills and, once mastered, to resolve their conflicts and problems. There is a commitment to a certain number of sessions, an awareness by therapists and clients alike that at that time there will be an evaluation of whether their most serious problems have been solved and their most important goals met. If goals are not fully met by then, a new target date will be set for another evaluation. It is believed that this procedure better maintains clients in therapy and best avoids the problems of, and secures the advantages of, both the open-ended and time-designated modes of determining the duration of therapy.

There is flexibility with respect to these modes. For example, one may start out in the time-designated mode and, for any of several reasons, decide to switch to the experiential mode; or, one might switch to the time-designated mode after resolving an initial crisis.

Methods for Intervention

One of the important things to understand about the RE process is that, once the basic skills are learned, and that is very early on, the clients are never allowed to interact unskillfully with each other. When one or both cannot be skillful, the therapist uses *troubleshooting, modeling, becoming,* and *laundering* (methods that are explained in later sections), with the therapist serving as their skill-coach. It also is important to understand that after the basic skills are acquired, interactions are almost exclusively between the partners. Discussion and negotiation skill guarantees that both partners will receive empathy whenever they express themselves. That, in turn, means that at all times when in dialogue, each partner is in either one of two modes of behavior that cannot be mixed together. One is in either the empathic mode or the expressive mode; whenever one is expresser, the other is an empathic responder. The discussion and nego-tiation guidelines show them when and how to switch from one mode to the other in a constructive and coordinated way that takes into account their emotional needs at the time.

When teaching participants an RE skill, the following steps are gener-ally used in those formats that involve more than a single day or weekend.

1. Explain the rationale for the skill and how it can help the participants reach their relationship goals.
2. Give reading assignments for study of the core RE skills: (a) from the *Relationship Enhancement® Program Manual* (Guerney, 1991b) or the *Relationship Enhancement® Auxiliary Manual* (Guerney, 1991a); and/ or (b) from the *Relationship Enhancement® Audio Program* (Guerney, 1994a); and (c) via demonstrations of unskilled vs. skilled dialogues from the *Relationship Enhancement® Demonstration Audio Tapes* (Guerney & Vogelsong, 1981).
3. Use videotaped or live role-playing within the session to further dem-onstrate the skill.
4. Explain and answer questions about the guidelines of the skill.
5. Supervise the couple in practicing the skill with each other around an issue of importance to the couple.

6. Give home assignments for practicing the skill by means of role-playing using the *Relationship Enhancement® Demonstration Audio Tapes* (Guerney & Vogelsong, 1981) at home.

7. Give home assignments to practice the skills at home in progressively more difficult areas while discussing real topics, issues, and enhancement plans and problems or conflicts.

8. When applicable, have the couple complete a "relationship questionnaire," logs, and brief reports, and record audiotapes of their home problem-solving sessions, using materials from their manual (Guerney, 1991a, 1991b).

9. Closely supervise progress and skill performance by means of the above.

10. As the participants become fully proficient at skill usage, routine supervision of audiotapes may be dropped, but practice reports and other assignments continue.

Topic Sequence

Usually, in RE prevention and enrichment programs, participants are guided to discuss, first, topics that involve strong feelings that would not arouse any defensiveness, concern, or anxiety in their partner, such as highly memorable experiences or relationships in their childhood, and then positive feelings and thoughts about the partner, and enrichment suggestions, that is, ideas for improving the relationship that they believe their partner also will like (e.g., spending more time together in an enjoyable pursuit). Then they may discuss their mild or moderate relationship issues before addressing their most serious problems. In this way, the truly hot and difficult topics are not discussed until the partners are practiced enough that "staying in the skills" and proficiency in their execution has become habitual.

Leader's Role

In RE groups of five couples or more, if it is feasible, the leader works with an assistant coach for each three to five couples. These assistant coaches often are leaders or therapists in training. Or they could be volunteers, as is usually the case in premarital programs and other programs run by religious congregations. The leader first reviews and supervises home assignments. On those dates that participants have set aside to do a follow-up evaluation on the implementation of behavior changes worked out in the course of problem and conflict resolutions (usually the first two they have developed), the leader helps the couple conduct that evaluation and make necessary revisions. He or she has the couple share any good feelings generated by changes made in their partner's behavior so far. The leader supervises the development of needed plan revisions, if any. If a topic is not being continued from the previous week or from the issues being worked on at home, the leader reviews the relationship questionnaire to select a topic. Then, for most of the session, the leader and any assistants supervise (coach) the use of the RE skills on the chosen topic. If an issue is not fully resolved in the session, the leader recommends either continuing that topic at home or waiting to do so until the next session, choosing another to do at home. The leader then discusses possible additional home assignments with the couple.

Specific Leader or Therapist Responses

There are a about a dozen leader or therapist responses used in RE. Space permits describing only a few, and we will therefore concentrate mainly on those unique to RE.

Becoming

In becoming (see Snyder, 1996), rather than providing the client with the words to say, as in modeling, or making suggestions as to the type of client response that would be appropriate, as in prompting, the therapist takes on client A's persona and speaks to A's partner, B, as if the therapist were A. Becoming is used in crisis situations when a difficult issue must be addressed immediately but the couple does not yet possess the skills to do it well, in situations when a client is too overcome by emotion to speak, or when the underlying feelings and dynamics involved are simply too complex to use modeling or prompting. (It is usually extremely effective in unblocking adolescents too resistant to be willing to speak.)

Here is an example of becoming: Karen, the wife, is crying, but seems to want to say something she cannot get out. The therapist decides that becoming would be more appropriate than troubleshooting. The therapist might say to her: "Karen, if it's all right with you, I'd like to speak for you to Danny." Karen nods vigorously. The therapist turns to Danny, the husband, and says, "Danny, I love you more than I've ever loved anyone." The therapist looks over to Karen questioningly, she again shakes her head strongly, yes. The therapist continues for her, "It scares me to death when you drink and drive. When you're late coming home, I keep imagining you in the hospital." Turning to Karen: "Am I on track Karen?" Karen replies, crying harder: "Yes, or dead!" Becoming can be used for only a few sentences, or for a whole session, as needed.

Troubleshooting

Troubleshooting is used in virtually any type of troublesome situation. In troubleshooting, the leader or therapist uses the RE skills directly with the participant, whereas usually he or she is coaching the couple in the skills. For example, when a participant is unable to continue using the skills due to very strong feelings, and the participant's partner is not skilled enough to handle the situation empathically, the therapist responds empathically to the participant until the feelings are released enough for the therapy participants to continue using the skills themselves. Another example would be if a participant were unwilling to follow RE procedures. The leader would then listen to the participant and respond empathically until it was evident that the participant wanted to hear the leader's point of view, at which time the leader would use expressive skill to present his or her position on the matter, and then return to listening and being empathic toward the client. The dialogue would continue in that manner until the conflict was resolved to the satisfaction of both parties.

Laundering

Laundering is a complex method that involves the therapist continuously becoming for both partners while receiving input, usually unskilled, from both and responding empathically to both. Whenever the therapist is speaking to A, or is spoken to by A, the therapist is to be viewed and addressed as if he or she were A's partner, B, and vice versa. It is very different from other RE methods in that the clients talk to the therapist rather than to each other, and the solutions to conflicts and problems generally are first (instead of almost never) suggested by the therapist while in the persona of a client. It is used to solve extremely difficult, highly emotional problems in a short period of time, and is the central method of the crisis resolution mode of RE therapy.

☐ Format of Application

Recruitment

Couples can be recruited for RE programs in a number of ways. Local churches can be a source of premarital as well as married couples. Child welfare agencies, physicians, and mental health professionals in private practice can be referral sources. Its strong record in comparative studies is a major aid in recruitment efforts. Similarly, RE therapy has special appeal to managed care organizations because, even in its longest format, the time-designated mode (Snyder & Guerney, 1993), it is brief (highly effective in 10 hours) and far more effective than traditional marital therapy. Many well-controlled studies have demonstrated its power to improve relationships; clinical experience has shown it to be useful with a wide variety of psychiatric disorders; and it has been proven effective in a group format, which is highly cost effective.

Screening

With respect to RE or any other enrichment or problem-prevention program, it seems appropriate, when feasible, that an effort be made to educate the potential consumer about what to expect and to determine at the time of enrollment whether clients expect more help than can be delivered in the time-frame of the program. Again, this depends on feasibility: If the consumer is signing up for a short-term weekend program, we might also try to see whether a long-term RE program, or, perhaps, individual therapy, would be better options. If so, these possibilities might be discussed with the prospective participant.

With respect to RE therapy, as with any other therapy, care should be taken during the intake process to assure that clients are referred for other treatments or resources whenever that is appropriate (e.g., to someone who can prescribe medication for depression, to Alcoholics Anonymous for alcohol abuse, or to specialists in treating certain disorders, e.g., panic attacks or phobias). However, whenever couple or family treatment, or family-assisted treatment, can be used, we view RE Couple/Family Therapy as the treatment of choice. Clients who often would not be considered for active inclusion in family therapy can be included in RE family therapy. For example, even if a referred adult client has become unable to speak meaningfully because of aphasia, or has very limited intelligence, methods like becoming may well be able to overcome that obstacle. Even when the referred client cannot participate, other family members can be used as psychotherapeutic agents to help the person in need of help (Guerney, 1969). In terms of age range, Filial Family Therapy extends down to preschool ages.

Appropriate Populations

RE has been used successfully with a very wide variety of populations. It is helpful for premarital couples (Ginsberg & Vogelsong, 1977); for one-couple or group couples therapy in community health centers (Ross, Baker, & Guerney, 1985); for participants with more severe problems, such as chronic schizophrenics (H. Malone, personal communication, November 8, 1982); for psychiatric inpatients and/or their families (Vogelsong, Guerney, & Guerney, 1983; Zahniser & Falk, 1993); in community residential rehabilitation centers (Accordino & Guerney, 1994; Accordino &

Herbert, 1997); for alcoholics (N. Armenti, personal communication, March 18, 1980; Matter & McAllister, 1984; Waldo & Guerney, 1983); for spouse batterers (Guerney, Waldo, & Firestone, 1987; Waldo, 1986, 1987, 1988); in the treatment of depression (B. G. Ginsberg, personal communication, March 18, 1981); for borderline clients (Waldo & Harman, 1993); for narcissistic clients (Snyder, 1994); for severely disturbed delinquents (J. T. Welsh, personal communication, November 22,1982); and for drug addicts in rehabilitation settings (Cadigan, 1980). Experience has shown RE to be an effective approach with African-American couples, and it has been recommended as a culturally sensitive and effective therapy for this population (Moore, 1997). RE has also been used as a basis for a package designed for cross-cultural couples counseling (Ibrahim & Schroeder, 1990). Similarly, it has been deemed exceptional with respect to gender sensitivity (Snyder, 1992). RE methods and skills have also been used effectively to train paraprofessionals (Avery, 1978; Cadigan, 1980; Guerney, Vogelsong, & Glynn, 1977; Most & Guerney, 1983); elementary students (Vogelsong, 1978); high school students (Avery, Rider, & Haynes-Clements, 1981; Haynes & Avery, 1979; Rocks, 1980); elementary teachers (Guerney & Merriam, 1972; Hatch, 1973; Merriam & Guerney, 1973); and high school teachers (Haynes & Avery, 1979; Rocks, 1980).

Both RE enrichment and problem-prevention programs and RE therapy can be used with families with adolescent and preadolescent children. A RE problem-prevention program has been used with groups of public school children as low as the fifth grade (Vogelsong, 1978) and as group therapy for children even younger than that, as well as for adolescents, including those in residential treatment centers for adolescents (Guerney & Harriman, 1989). RE Family Therapy has been used successfully when including children as young as 8 whose role was central in the family's problem (G. Hardley, personal communication, Jan. 13, 1984). However, in the great majority of cases, the appropriate RE mode for children under 10 years of age is Child RE Therapy, also referred to as Filial Family Therapy, which was referenced and briefly described at the beginning of this chapter. There is also a format for RE Family Therapy for people who do not have any other family members willing to attend therapy. This is referred to as Unilateral RE Family Therapy (Guerney, 1977). This can be conducted with a single person or a small group of individuals in the same predicament. It centers around the use of the individual as the therapist's psychotherapeutic agent for changing the family system and the adjustment and behavior of other family members as well as one's own. It places heavy emphasis on role-played behavioral rehearsal to bring about systemic and psychological change in the family. RE also can be used with single persons who desire to improve their ability to establish and maintain romantic relationships.

There also is RE therapy that does not involve the family; it is called

Individual (or Personal) RE Therapy (Guerney & Snyder, 1997). This is a form of RE therapy that focuses on problems in which family members are not involved. To clarify further, RE therapy can involve families in many ways: as coclients, as psychotherapeutic agents for the client, or as the subjects of a sole client's efforts to bring about changes in other family members and the family system. In Individual (Personal) RE Therapy, they are not involved in any of those ways. Rather, although interpersonal skills invariably play a very important role both within the therapy session and in the outside world, and other people's behavior toward the client may well be changed through the client's efforts, the major purpose is self-change, and the starting point of the therapy is generally perceived by the client as an intrapsychic rather than an interpersonal problem. Personal RE Therapy can be conducted with a single person or in groups.

RE programs and RE therapy of all types are contraindicated for psychopaths and any others for whom lying has become a lifestyle (we do not include "denial" as such).

☐ Background and Role of the Leader or Therapist

RE offers training for, and distinguishes between, RE program leaders and RE therapists. RE program leaders are trained to lead RE prevention and enrichment workshops. Lay persons from any walk of life may apply for training. Since RE is so well documented and the methods are clear and systematic, it has not been difficult to train leaders from a variety of backgrounds. Large numbers of volunteer couples in religious organizations have been trained to conduct RE-based programs to strengthen marriages and to train engaged couples. Training, supervision, and/or certification as an RE program leader is available through the nonprofit National Institute of Relationship Enhancement®. The same is true for RE Couples/Family Therapy, which may also be learned at other Relationship Enhancement® institutes in various parts of the country. Videotapes (e.g., Guerney, Nordling, & Scuka, 1997; Guerney, Scuka, & Scuka, 1997; Snyder, 1996) showing how RE programs and RE Couple/Family/Filial therapies are conducted are available for rental or purchase.

Introductory workshops, live therapy demonstrations, or full-scale training also can be conducted locally for individual agencies, groups/practices, or consortiums. Advanced workshops in RE therapy are offered at least once a year. Home study programs for RE program leadership and Couple/Family Therapy are expected to be ready by the time the present book is published. Training and supervision also are available for those who wish to become "approved supervisors" to train others in RE program leadership or therapy.

The National Institute of Relationship Enhancement® acts as a clear-inghouse for materials, workshops, and training in RE. It also provides a national referral base for RE program leaders and RE therapies for access by the public and other therapists. Ways to contact the Institute are pre-sented at the end of this chapter.

To receive training in RE therapy, the trainee must hold at least a master's degree in one of the helping professions, such as clinical psychology, coun-seling, or social work, or be enrolled in such a graduate program. RE therapists are taught to train couples in the RE skills and to use all the basic RE intervention methods. In addition, they are trained in advanced methods, such as becoming, which are helpful in crisis intervention and other difficult situations. Again, since RE is so well defined and system-atic, experienced marital therapists have been able to learn the program well enough for effective utilization after a 3-day training workshop (Ross, Baker, & Guerney, 1985). However, further training and supervision, avail-able nationwide, is strongly recommended.

The role of the RE program leader or therapist is to help clients (a) learn to use the skills in such a way as to quickly reach their deepest feelings, including their positive underlying ones, about an issue or prob-lem; (b) determine, at the problem's core, what they really do and do not want; (c) develop solutions and behavioral plans to maximize mutual need-satisfaction; (d) help themselves and their partners change their attitudes, feelings, and personalities in such a way as to incorporate those new behaviors. The RE leader or therapist almost never offers an opinion that has not been specifically requested by the couple. The therapist's focus is on seeing to it that the RE *process* is followed well enough to work its magic. The fact that the therapist's focus is almost exclusively on pro-cess rather than content easily enables RE therapists, from the beginning, to be seen as very fair (not favoring one side over the other), thereby avoiding what can be a serious problem, and a major cause of drop-out, in marital therapy. This, plus their own use of the RE skills, probably accounts for the fact that RE leaders are consistently rated by clients at the highest level on scales of empathy, openness, genuineness, and trust-worthiness.

☐ Application of the Preventive Model to a Couple at Risk

To give the reader an idea of what the coaching process is like in RE, an imaginary coached dialogue as part of a 1-hour-per-week RE program will be presented. There is no reason to think that Ben (B) and Alyssa (A) would not benefit from the more economical format of a Group RE program. But to save space and to make it more comparable to most readers' experiences, which we assume involves much more experience with individuals or with single couples than with groups, we will set our clients in a single-couple RE program format. The dialogue and the coaching process would be essentially the same whether it was an individual-couple format or a group-couple format. The difference would be that sometimes in the multiple-couple format, one couple would be coaching another couple, with the leader coaching the coaching couple rather than directly coaching the primary couple (for explications of group RE approaches, see Griffin & Guerney, in press, and Guerney, 1977; to see a comparison of the dialogue process in RE Family Therapy as compared to two other types of family therapy, see Guerney, 1990). The dialogue will come from the seventh week of the program. But first it is necessary to give some additional information about some of the processes that have taken place prior to that time.

After the usual training procedures for eliciting consistent performance in home assignments, A and B had worked consistently and well at learning the skills by reading their manual and listening to the *Relationship Enhancement® Demonstration Audio Tapes* (Guerney & Vogelsong, 1981), completing report forms on their practice sessions, and taping their work on enhancement and conflict issues—tapes that were briefly supervised in-session by the leader. In this manner, A and B have already acquired high levels of empathic, expressive, discussion and negotiation, and facilitative (coaching) skills and some competence in problem or conflict resolution skill. A has read detailed explications of the other skills (Guerney, 1991a) as well, and B has listened to the same material on audiotape as he commuted to work.

As a result of their having developed some relationship enhancement plans, at least twice a month the couple now either goes out together on a "date" (in the interest of improving her relationship with B, A has overcome her fear of leaving baby Benny with a sitter) or stays at home and, after baby Benny has gone to sleep, has a romantic meal and a discussion of nonmundane, noncontroversial topics. Their sex life as well as their feelings about the relationship have significantly improved as a result. A says that B is more sensitive to her feelings and a better listener now than he has ever been. She said this is especially true during their romantic meals. It is very much the case when she tells him about her problems. She said he's very good about using his empathic skill, instead of rushing in to give advice as he used to do. Also, as they have agreed, they spend a minimum of 1½ hours a week using the skills at home at specifically scheduled and virtually inviolate times. As the leader, L, had suggested, during the initial home practice sessions, A and B practiced their skills by working jointly with the *Relationship Enhancement® Demonstration Audio*

Tapes (Guerney & Vogelsong, 1981). B would stop the tape after listening to each of the tape-wife's statements, respond empathically to it, and then turn the tape back on to hear how the skilled husband on the tape responded to the same statement. A did likewise, responding to the tape-husband. That way, they improved their empathic skill through comparing their own efforts with the statements of someone already skilled. After two such sessions, they practiced their skills in the following manner: one of them, say A, practiced expressive skill by speaking about issues and problems that were not emotionally charged for B, while B practiced empathic responding, not yet seeking the expressive mode to give his views on the issues, as he would do in future weeks in accord with the discussion and negotiation guidelines. He could become expresser, however, if A asked for his views.

Early on, the hour-long session was devoted to enhancement issues, then to minor issues, and later to major problems and conflicts that were approved for home discussion by L. Such approval is given only when the leader believes the couple could successfully work on an issue at home by continuing where they had left off in the office session. The heaviest issues were still being initiated only at the office sessions; A and B were not yet free to choose to work on any issue they wished to work on at home. L selected the topics they would be working on in the session and at home from their relationship questionnaires. They both had filled these out privately, kept a copy for themselves, and given the original to the leader.

To designate the mode the speaker is supposed to be in, that is, expresser or empathic responder, we will indicate "Ex" or "ER" after the A or B (Ben or Alyssa). Also, we will put in brackets the category of response L is using in her coaching. At times, we also point out in brackets the particular guideline A or B is following at the moment.

In RE, until the couple is fully skilled, the RE leader is extremely active in teaching and in securing adherence to the skills, but almost never, at any stage of RE, does the leader intrude on the content, i.e., on decisions concerning the couple's lives. To do so would interfere with the success that can be achieved when the process is left in the hands of the couple. The reinforcements given by L are for good performance of RE skills, not for the particular ideas or feelings expressed.

The prior issue, just resolved, was from A's list. A had wanted B to come with her to church a few times, without commitment of any kind, so that he "could experience how wonderful and how comforting" it was. The issue was resolved through the mutual belief, based on a deeper understanding of their backgrounds and of how they felt, that they should respect each other's views. They needn't refrain from discussing religion, but there should be no effort at this stage of their lives to change each other's religious behaviors. Essentially, theirs was an agreement to dis-agree. But they also decided that B would not attend church and, in light of all the other family needs, A would not increase her time commitment to the church for the foreseeable future.

So, it was now B's turn to initiate discussion about one of his major problems or conflicts. L suggested for discussion one of the topics B, on the relationship questionnaires, had originally put in the "unwilling" cat-egory (i.e., he was unwilling to discuss it), but had recently changed to being "willing" to talk about at the present time: his desire not to have a third child. B accepted L's suggestion regarding the topic, but began by talking to L instead of to A, as would have been expected.

B: [to L] *This is very difficult for me to talk about because I believe Alyssa very much wants to continue to have children beyond the one we are going to have now. I also think she has very strong feelings about it, so this is really tough.*

L: [L] briefly contemplates troubleshooting, but decides that B is really sharing his feelings rather than resisting the idea of going ahead. L also believes that even if he is resisting, A was able to provide empa-thy, and that in this instance, such empathy, especially from her, would allow B to proceed with greater ease and confidence. L says: *I think it would be good to say that to Alyssa.*

B: [Ex, to A] *It's very hard for me to talk about my not wanting to have any more children beyond this one.*

A: [ER] *You're very worried about my reaction. You believe I want to continue to have children, and it's kind of scary to even think about telling me that you don't. It feels to you like you would be challenging me or criticizing me.* [As A pauses here and sees B nodding his head in strong assent, letting her know she is on the right track, she continues.] *You're afraid my feelings will be hurt, and that maybe I will be very upset, perhaps resentful* [and as she sees him continue to shake his head in assent, she continues], *or maybe even angry.*

L: [Reinforcing] *Excellent, Alyssa. Beautiful.*

B: [ER] *That's right.* [B spoke at some length about his deep concern that this and future pregnancies might jeopardize A's health, and how dev-astated he would feel if anything happened to her. With the help of the therapist, this was expanded to an expression of his love for her. His expression of love deeply moved A, and she quietly cried as he spoke of it. Despite this, she was able to provide excellent empathy to B. Then B proceeded.] *Another problem here is, I don't really like my job. Not at all. Its really getting me down. I don't think I'm cut out for it. I'm not even sure I ever really wanted to be a lawyer in the first place. Or it may be the particular things I'm doing, because lawyers have all kinds of things they* *can do. Part of my problem is that I really don't know what it is I want to do. But the thought of staying where I am for even the 6 years until this baby gets into school really, really gets me down. And to think about yet another baby and maybe years beyond that* [shaking his head in a "no" gesture and pursing his lips] *gee! And besides the time, the more children we have, the more money we will need to take care of them, and just think of the money we'll need to send them through college!* [Continues shaking his head.]

A: [ER] *You're burned out at your job. It has really become a great burden for you. And although you really don't have any clear vision of what you would like to do, you're not sure that being a lawyer would be the right thing to equip you for it. You fear you might have to do some retraining or reeducation, and I guess it looks to you like you might well be making less money, at least at first, if you changed jobs. My wanting additional children would just pile another heavy weight on a burden that is already weighing too heavily on you.*

L: [Reinforcing] *That was really great, Alyssa.* [Modeling] *You might add something like, "It feels like you are being caught in a trap."*

A: *Yes. It's not that you feel I'm deliberately trying to work against you, you're not saying that, but nevertheless, with this baby coming, you feel like you are already sort of trapped, and having still another baby in the future makes you think you may never be able to get out of it. Like then there surely would be no escape. And that's truly very depressing for you, and perhaps frightening too.*

B: *That's it exactly. Trapped. Depressed. Worried, very worried. That's it.* (Pause.) [Using the type of phrase that, as part of discussion and negotiation skill, signals to one's partner the invitation to become Ex. In an exchange of Ex and ER modes, B continues,] *I'd very much like to know your reactions to what I've said.*

A: [ER] [Beginning her statement with the last empathic response before switching modes] *You'd like to know what I . . .*

L: [Interrupting A] *I'm sorry, Alyssa. I'd like to coach Ben here and see if he'd be willing to be the expresser for one more statement. I'm wondering if that's O.K. with you.*

A: *O.K.*

L: [to A] *Thanks.* [to B] *If it is feasible for you at this point, I'd like to have you include some underlying positives again, to complete this part of the picture.* [The timely inclusion of underlying positives is one of the most important of the expressive guideline skills, and one that is the most difficult for both participants and leaders to learn. Believing that B would have trouble thinking of many possibilities on his own, L continues,] *I mean things like: what Benny means to you; what you think the new baby will mean to you; what you value about Alyssa as a wife and as a mother; about her motives, with respect to you as a husband and what you* *think her wishes are for you in terms of your happiness in life, and also the other way around. Tell her again now where your relationship with her and with the children fits into your life and your priorities. All, of course, as they relate to this job issue. Can you do some of that at this point?*

B: [to L] *Absolutely.* [Ex, to A] *You and the children are by far the most important thing in my life. In fact, I can stand this job only because of what I want for you and Benny. And any job, whatever it might be, could not be more important than you and him. And there isn't any doubt in my mind that will be equally true for the new baby. And I appreciate tremendously that just as I love and care about you and your happiness, you care about mine. And I greatly appreciate it that you somehow manage to show it more on a day-to-day basis than I do. And I admire enormously how committed you are to the children, and how well you take care of them and look after their needs. I also understand how much being a mother means to you and I admire that too. I really don't want to deprive you of any of that.* [Deliberately or not, B next is following another expressive skill guideline, that of the interpersonal message, in his next statement.] *I just think that if there is a balance which allows me also to find satisfaction in my work, then that in the long run will benefit all of us, you and the children as much as me, because if I'm happy in my work, I think I will be a lot more upbeat and have a much better attitude and more energy for the family all around.*

L: [Reinforcing] *That was beautifully done, Ben—the interpersonal message at the end as well as the underlying positive.*

A: [ER] *You deeply love me and Benny and know you will also love the new baby. And you know that I love you deeply as well, and that I care a lot about your happiness, just as you do mine. You appreciate my values about being a good mother, and you appreciate the way I mother Benny. And it is not at all that you want to deprive me of being able to make mothering a key factor in my life. What you want is to be able to afford to get a job that you can get some real satisfaction out of, and you think that if you could afford to do that, it couldn't help but benefit all of us, not just you.* [Seeing B's nodding vigorously to her empathy, pausing to see if he was going to add or correct anything, not finding that, and recalling B's prior invitation for her to become Ex, A continues,] *And now you'd like to get my reactions to what you've said.* [Switching now, by B's prior invitation, to Ex.] *Well, let me say first that it was gratifying and touching to hear what you said. Despite the complaints I have heard you make, I hadn't realized, not at all, just how trying and difficult you are finding your job. I just thought it was the kind of upset that was, well, kind of routine for such a job. So seeing your pain here, as also was the case with the pain of your worry about my health, was very revealing, very important, to me. It has had a big impact. One thing I think it is important for you to understand before I give you the rest of my reaction is* *that I can't think only of what I want. I have not just me to please, and you to please, and not only the children either. I have to go by what God wants me to do. God wants* . . . [KABOOM! That is the sound of L's heart falling down into the pit of her stomach. So the cue for what L needs to do now is, in this instance, not at all subtle. Usually, it might be just a little tightening of L's stomach, or the sense that a bead of sweat might be about to form on L's forehead, or that one's eye or lip may be on the verge of twitching; most frequently the cue is simply a muffled voice from the inside of one's head saying, "Uh, oh!" These are a leader's cues to immediately begin to Troubleshoot. So she does.]

L: [Coaching/troubleshooting] [Coaching, which is the only therapist response that permits interruption,] *Sorry to interrupt you, Alyssa, but I think it is important for me to do some coaching here.* [Troubleshooting, which begins, whenever feasible, with empathy,] *God is a central force in your life. It's extremely important to you that your decisions and actions be in accord with God's will.*

A: *Yes, it would be impossible for me to knowingly do otherwise.*

The space that can be allotted to this section forces us to switch to narrative style here to complete this case episode. Once L perceived that A felt her relationship and obligations to God were fully understood and accepted by L, L continued to coach, but used the troubleshooting mode to do it. This obligated L to "own" the RE guidelines, that is, to state them subjectively, and it permitted L to ask A to empathize with L's views about the guidelines, which could be expected to increase A's understanding and acceptance of how they applied even to what God wanted her to do. L explained, "It would not matter whether God joined us in the office and stated the pertinent wishes directly to us all—well, let me step back from that particular ledge, let me say instead, a large, powerful angel with huge wings, who informed us in a very deep and loud voice that he was telling us *exactly* what God wanted. From my point of view, it would still be desirable for you to state God's wishes subjectively. I would still want you to say what *your* views, *your* beliefs, *your* perceptions, of God's views were, or of what the angel said they were. The idea is to give your partner room to perceive the exact same information, whatever the source, in a way that is different from your understanding. The idea is to dialogue in a way that I believe allows you not to engage in a battle over the 'truth,' but instead to stay with the goal of each best meeting your own needs in light of the other person's perceptions and needs." A empathized well. And when she expressed her views, it was clear that she had been influenced by her positive experiences in making use of the RE skills. She expressed her willingness to continue to use them consistently. She could still talk about and respond to what she believed God wanted her to do.

She felt comfortable, she said, not demanding that anyone else bow to or cave in to her point of view, even though it did reflect God's wishes.

Ironically, it turned out that what she was going to say when L interrupted her was that she believed that God wanted her to serve her entire family, and that being a mother was a clear mission given to her by God. But God never indicated that this mission was best served by having as many children as possible. Rather, she (A) thought of it as being best served by creating the best *family* environment possible for her children, and that this very much included helping B lead a life that was fulfilling. And that, in turn, included B having a job that at least was not a large burden, and hopefully would be one that was truly satisfying. After a discussion that ran through the eighth session, they reached the decision that, before deciding such issues as when B might leave his job, or whether A should consider going back to work, or indeed, whether or not they could afford to have a third child, it would make sense for B to find out what he wanted to do vocationally, and whether or not he could do it without further training or a reduction in income. They asked for and received a referral from L to a vocational counselor.

L had no regrets about not simply suggesting vocational counseling when the issue came up, despite the fact that she felt it would be useful. She felt the new insights and feelings of mutual support and togetherness that emerged from the discussion were worth every second spent. She did feel annoyed with herself for experiencing the KABOOM sensation when A was about to reveal what God wanted her to do, and because she feared that A was going to say that her mission from God was to continue child-bearing as long as she was physically able, or at least to have several more. L was annoyed also that she allowed herself to predict what a client was going to decide, and doubly annoyed because she had realized that A had experienced what in RE is termed the "magic confluence of feelings": the experiencing together of the two feelings that in combination usually bring about very giving, sincere, and strong desires to make changes for the good of the relationship. That confluence involves experiencing the pain your actions are causing or might cause your partner, together with the love, concern, and caring your partner feels for you. But L did not feel too badly for underestimating the power of the magic confluence, because regardless of what might be decided by the client or God, there was no way she could let a client speak unskillfully to a partner in the session once the client had been taught the relevant skill. So she would have had to do what she did, regardless. And from the point of view of skill training, it was and would be very valuable to the couple in the future.

☐ Empirical Evaluation and Research

Research has shown RE to be an exceptionally effective approach. It has been experimentally compared with a range of other couples programs. In each of the comparisons, RE was found to be generally superior to the alternate treatment on either outcome measures or process variables.

In a comparison with a behavioral program, Wieman's Reciprocal Reinforcement Program (Wieman, 1973), and a wait list control group, both programs showed gains over controls in terms of marital communication, adjustment, and cooperativeness. The RE participants, however, rated their experience as more deep, good, worthwhile, exciting, strong, fair, important, comfortable, and professional than did the participants in the behavioral program. The Reciprocal Reinforcement participants rated their experience as more light, safe, easy, cold, and calm. In both treatments, gains were maintained 10 weeks after treatment. These were time-limited group programs of 8 weeks duration.

In another study of RE in a group format, Jessee & Guerney (1981) compared RE to Jessee's Group Gestalt Relationship Facilitation program. Both groups showed gains on all variables studied, including marital adjustment, trust and harmony, and rate of positive change in the relationship. The RE participants showed greater gains than the Gestalt participants in communication, relationship satisfaction, and ability to handle problems. The sample consisted of both distressed and nondistressed couples.

In a comparison with a traditional discussion treatment (Ridley, Jorgenson, Morgan, & Avery, 1982), RE participants showed greater improvement in satisfaction, communication, intimacy, sensitivity, openness, and understanding. Brock & Joanning (1983) compared RE to the COUPLE COMMUNICATION program using a mixed sample of distressed and nondistressed couples. RE was found to be more effective in improving marital communication and satisfaction on both behavioral and self-report measures. The RE participants still maintained greater gains at three months following treatment.

These results form a body of evidence clearly proving that the improvements gained from participation in RE group programs are treatment specific. That is, they cannot be attributed to placebo, Hawthorne, thank-you, or experimenter-demand effects. We believe that a firm conclusion in that regard is unique in the field of enrichment and problem prevention.

Griffin & Apostal (1993), working with groups, used an own-control design with a 6-week, 2½-hour-session-per-week, Marital RE Program with both distressed and nondistressed couples. They found that the RE program, in comparison to the control period, led to a significant improvement in differentiation of self for both the husbands and the wives, with a concomitant reduction in anxiety. Brooks (1997), working in a group practice setting in a rural southern town, used a time-limited 12-week, RE Couples' Group Therapy format (Griffin & Guerney, in press). She found that, in comparison to the control period, the RE treatment couples showed significantly greater gains in a variety of areas, including marital adjustment, trust, and intimacy. Gains were maintained at a 3-month follow-up.

Dyadic, as opposed to group, RE was studied by Ross et al. (1985). Five marital therapists averaging 6 years in marital and family therapy experience were given 3 days of training in RE, their first and only training in RE. Distressed couples seeking therapy at a community mental health center were then randomly assigned to receive either RE therapy or the therapist's originally preferred eclectic therapy. The therapists' preferred orientations were all eclectic, with emphases covering a wide range, including psychodynamic, behavioral, and client centered. After 10 weeks, the RE-treated couples showed significantly greater gains than the couples treated with the therapist's originally preferred method on all measures used. These included the quality of their communication, the general quality of their relationship, and their marital adjustment. With premarital couples, RE has been found to be more effective than a problem-solving program and a relationship discussion program (Avery, Ridley, Leslie, & Milholland, 1980; Ridley, Avery, Dent, & Harrell, 1981; Ridley, Avery, Harrell, Haynes-Clements, & McCunney, 1981; Ridley, Avery, Harrell, Leslie, & Dent, 1981). Another study found it to be more effective than the Engaged Encounter Program (Sams, 1983).

In an award-winning meta-analytic study that consolidated data from 85 different studies of marital enrichment and clearly structured therapy programs, RE "demonstrated by far the largest effect size" (Giblin, Sprenkle, & Sheehan, 1985). Giblin and associates compared 14 types of marital programs (some were modifications of other programs) as well as "other" and "placebo" categories. They found an average effect size of .44 among the studies. Two programs had effect sizes smaller than the placebo category (which had an effect size of .22). The other programs ranged between .22 and .58, with the exception of RE, which was found to have an effect size of .96. RE was, in fact, the only program found to produce very large positive effect sizes.

There are indications that the gains from RE are well maintained for fairly long intervals. A study (Guerney, Vogelsong, & Coufal, 1983) of Group Family RE with mothers and daughters found that RE-treated pairs not only maintained gains at 6 months, but also maintained their superiority to both the no-treatment control and the alternate discussion group treatment. This study demonstrated that the long-range as well as the immediate gains of RE are treatment specific. A study of Child RE (Guerney & Stover, 1971) with emotionally disturbed children found not only significant improvement in the treated children, but also that most children maintained or had even increased their gains 15 months later. A similar study by Sywulak (1977), and a follow-up 3 years later (Sensué, 1981), found that the RE-treated children remained at a normal level of adjustment.

☐ Summary

Both research and clinical experience have shown RE to be an exceptionally fast, effective, and enduring intervention. It has been found to impact couples positively on many important relationship, personality, and behavioral dimensions, such as couples' adjustment, satisfaction, communication, and conflict and problem resolution; individuals' self-esteem and self-differentiation; the discontinuation of wife-battering; and the maintenance of freedom from substance abuse. RE can also achieve a positive impact in an exceptionally short period of time. In a recent study with distressed and nondistressed couples, significant improvement was found in the couples' ability to resolve difficult relationship issues after only 1½ hours of working with RE (Cavedo, 1995). The potential of RE for achieving highly rapid results is very important for participant retention and when working with couples in crisis.

RE is an extremely versatile and adaptable approach. It can be used with a variety of populations, from those seeking prevention and enrichment to the severely distressed. It can be used with couples, with one member of a couple seeking to improve the relationship, with families with older or younger children, and with subunits of families. It can be given in an individual or group format, and as either time-limited or time-designated therapy. Volunteers and lay couples can be trained to give highly successful prevention and enrichment workshops, and therapists and counselors can use it within their practices to aid virtually any type of client (Fonash & Guerney, 1993; Matter & McAllister, 1984; Rose, Battjes, Leukefeld, 1984; Waldo & Guerney, 1983). It will give readers some idea of the wide range of application for RE to note that, in addition to the studies mentioned previously, RE has been used successfully to facilitate the postdivorce adjustment of both women and men (Avery & Thiessen, 1982; Thiessen, Avery, & Joanning, 1980) and to improve interpersonal relationships in industrial work teams (Rathmell, 1991).

Current and future clinical study and research is being focused on new and better ways of delivering RE training to professionals and to the public, on the briefest formats of RE, on exploring the use of Personal RE Therapy in individual and group formats, on the use of RE with populations not previously isolated for study (e.g., blended families) on the application of RE to organizational and personnel development in business and industry, and on support groups. Anyone interested in collaborating on field efforts or research in these newer areas is invited to contact the second author.

☐ Contact References

Those interested in learning more about any aspect of RE or who wish to be on our mailing list may contact the National Institute of Relationship Enhancement® (phone: 1-800-4-FAMILIES [1-800-432-6454]; fax: 301-680-3756) or visit the Institute's website: http:/www.nire.org

☐ References

Accordino, M. P., & Guerney, B. G., Jr. (1994). Effects of the Relationship Enhancement® program on community residential rehabilitation staff and clients. *Psychosocial Rehabilitation Journal, 17*(2), 131–144.

Accordino, M. P., & Herbert, J. T. (1997). Relationship Enhancement® as an intervention to facilitate rehabilitation of persons with severe mental illness. *Journal of Applied Rehabilitation Counseling, 28*(1), 47–52.

Avery, A. W. (1978). Communication skills training for paraprofessional helpers. *American Journal of Community Psychology, 6,* 583–592.

Avery, A. W., Rider, K., & Haynes-Clements, L. A. (1981). Communication skills training for adolescents: A five-month follow-up. *Adolescence, 16,* 289–298.

Avery, A. W., Ridley, C. A., Leslie, L. A., & Milholland, T. (1980). Relationship Enhancement® with premarital dyads: A six month follow-up. *American Journal of Family Therapy, 8,* 23–30.

Avery, A. W., & Thiessen, J. D. (1982). Communication skills training for divorcees. *Journal of Counseling Psychology,* 203–205.

Brock, G. W., & Joanning, H. (1983). A comparison of the Relationship Enhancement® program and the Minnesota Couple Communication Program. *Journal of Marital and Family Therapy, 9*(4), 413–421.

Brooks, L. W. (1997). *An investigation of Relationship Enhancement® therapy with rural, southern couples in a group format.* Unpublished doctoral dissertation, Florida State University, Tallahassee.

Cadigan, J. D. (1980). RETEACH program and project: Relationship Enhancement® in a therapeutic environment as clients head out (Doctoral dissertation, Pennsylvania State University, 1980). *Dissertation Abstracts International, 41*(10-B), 3881-B.

Cavedo, L. C. (1995). Efficacy of an extremely brief Relationship Enhancement® intervention format and two coaching styles (Doctoral dissertation, Pennsylvania State University, 1995). *Dissertation Abstracts International, 56,* 9600146.

Fonash, J. M., & Guerney, B. G., Jr. (1993). Relationship Enhancement® therapy for codependents. In K. R. Falk & R. R. Fry (Eds.), *Co-dependency and the dysfunctional family: A collection of papers* (pp. 19–22). Stout, WI: School of Education and Human Services, University of Wisconsin-Stout.

Giblin, P., Sprenkle, D. H., & Sheehan, R. (1985). Enrichment outcome research: A meta-analysis of premarital, marital, and family interventions. *Journal of Marital and Family Therapy, 11*(3), 257–271.

Ginsburg, B. G., & Vogelsong, E. L. (1977). Premarital relationship improvement by maximizing empathy and self-disclosure: The PRIMES Program. In B.G. Guerney, Jr. (Ed.), *Relationship Enhancement®: Skill-training programs for therapy, problem prevention and enrichment* (pp. 268–288). San Francisco: Jossey-Bass.

Griffin, J. M., Jr., & Apostal, R. A. (1993). The influence of Relationship Enhancement® training on differentiation of self. *Journal of Marital and Family Therapy, 19*(3), 267–272.

Griffin, J. M., Jr., & Guerney, B. G. Jr. (in press). Brief couples Relationship Enhancement® therapy: An extendable eight meeting format. In B.G. Guerney, Jr. (Ed.), *Relationship Enhancement® therapist's manual.* Rockville, MD: IDEALS.

Guerney, B. G., Jr. (1964). Filial therapy: Description and rationale. *Journal of Consulting Psychology, 28*(4), 303–310.

Guerney, B. G., Jr. (Ed. & Commentator). (1969). *Psychotherapeutic agents: New roles for nonprofessionals, parents, and teachers.* New York: Holt, Rinehart & Winston.

Guerney, B. G., Jr. (1976). Filial therapy used as a treatment method for disturbed children. *Evaluation, 3,* 34–35.

Guerney, B. G., Jr. (1977). *Relationship Enhancement®: Skill-training programs for therapy, problem prevention and enrichment.* San Francisco: Jossey-Bass.

Guerney, B. G., Jr. (1989). *Relationship Enhancement® family therapy: The experiential format (P-family)* [Videotapes]. Rockville, MD: IDEALS.

Guerney, B. G., Jr. (1990). Creating therapeutic and growth-inducing family systems: Personal moorings, landmarks and guiding stars. In F. Kaslow (Ed.), *Voices in family psychology* (pp. 114–138). Beverly Hills, CA: Sage.

Guerney, B. G., Jr. (1991a). *Relationship Enhancement® auxiliary manual.* Rockville, MD: IDEALS.

Guerney, B. G., Jr. (1991b). *Relationship Enhancement® program panual.* Rockville, MD: IDEALS.

Guerney, B. G., Jr., (1994a). *Relationship Enhancement® audio program* [Audio cassettes]. Rockville, MD: IDEALS.

Guerney, B. G., Jr. (1994b). The role of emotion in Relationship Enhancement® marital/family therapy. In S. M. Johnson & L. S. Greenberg (Eds.), *Emotion in marriage and marital therapy* (pp. 124–147). New York: Brunner/Mazel.

Guerney, B. G., Jr., & Harriman, M. (1989, July). *A systematic, holistic model of residential treatment.* Paper presented at the Third National Conference of the Albert E. Trieschman Center, Cambridge, MA.

Guerney, B. G., Jr., & Merriam, M. L. (1972). Toward a democratic elementary school classroom. *Elementary School Journal, 72,* 372–383.

Guerney, B. G., Jr., Nordling, W., & Scuka, R. (1997). *Relationship Enhancement® couple/family therapy: A three-day training program* [Videotapes]. Rockville, MD: IDEALS.

Guerney, B. G., Jr., Scuka, R., & Scuka, M. (1997). *The Relationship Enhancement® program: A three day training program* [Videotapes]. Rockville, MD: IDEALS.

Guerney, B. G., Jr., & Snyder, M. (1997). *Relationship Enhancement® individual therapy.* Manuscript submitted for publication.

Guerney, B. G., Jr., & Stover, L. (1971). *Filial therapy: Final report on MH 1826401.* University Park, PA: Pennsylvania State University, Department of Human Development and Family Studies.

Guerney, B. G., Jr., & Vogelsong, E. (1981). *Relationship Enhancement® demonstration audio tapes* [Audio cassettes]. Rockville, MD: IDEALS.

Guerney, B. G., Jr., Vogelsong, E., & Coufal, J. (1983). Relationship Enhancement® versus a traditional treatment: Follow-up and booster effects. In D. H. Olson & B. C. Miller (Eds.), *Family Studies Review Yearbook, Vol. I* (pp. 738–756). Beverly Hills, CA: Sage.

Guerney, B. G., Jr., Vogelsong, E., & Glynn, S. (1977). *Evaluation of the family counseling unit of the Cambria County probation bureau.* Rockville, MD: IDEALS.

Guerney, B. G., Jr., Waldo, M., & Firestone, L. (1987). Wife-battering: A theoretical construct and case report. *The American Journal of Family Therapy, 15*(1), 34–43.

Hatch, E. J. (1973). *An empirical study of a teacher training program in empathic responsiveness and democratic decision making.* Unpublished doctoral dissertation, Pennsylvania State University, University Park.

Haynes, L. A., & Avery, A. W. (1979). Training adolescents in self-disclosure and empathy skills. *Journal of Counseling Psychology, 26*(6), 526–530.

Ibrahim, F. A., & Schroeder, D. G. (1990). Cross-cultural couples counseling: A developmental, psychoeducational intervention. *Journal of Comparative Family Studies, XXI*(2), 193–205.

Jessee, R., & Guerney, B. G., Jr. (1981). A comparison of Gestalt and Relationship Enhancement® treatments with married couples. *The American Journal of Family Therapy, 9*, 31–41.

Leary, T. (1957). *Interpersonal diagnosis of personality.* New York: Ronald Press.

Matter, M., & McAllister, W. (1984). Relationship Enhancement® for the recovering couple: Working with the intangible. *Focus on Family and Chemical Dependency, 7*(5), 21–23 & 40.

Merriam, M. L., & Guerney, B. G., Jr. (1973). Creating a democratic elementary school classroom: A pilot training program involving teachers, administrators, and parents. *Contemporary Education, 45*(1), 34–42.

Moore, C. D. (1997). *Relationship Enhancement®: A culturally sensitive family therapy for African Americans.* Manuscript submitted for publication.

Most, R. K., & Guerney, B. G., Jr. (1983). An empirical evaluation of the training of lay volunteers for premarital Relationship Enhancement®. *Family Relations, 32*(2), 239–251.

Oxman, L. (1971). *The effectiveness of filial therapy: A controlled study.* Unpublished doctoral dissertation, Rutgers University, New Brunswick, NJ.

Rathmell, C. G. (1991). *The effects of the Relationship Enhancement® program with industrial work teams.* Unpublished doctoral dissertation, Pennsylvania State University, University Park.

Ridley, C. A., Avery, A. W., Dent, J., & Harrell, J. (1981). The effects of Relationship Enhancement® and problem solving programs on perceived heterosexual competence. *Family Therapy, 8*, 60–66.

Ridley, C. A., Avery, A. W., Harrell, J. E., Haynes-Clements, L. A., & McCunney, N. (1981). Mutual problem-solving skills training for premarital couples: A six-month follow-up. *Journal of Applied Developmental Psychology, 2*(2), 179–188.

Ridley, C. A., Avery, A. W., Harrell, J. E., Leslie, L., & Dent, J. A. (1981). Conflict management: A premarital training program in mutual problem solving. *American Journal of Family Therapy, 9*, 23–32.

Ridley, C. A., Jorgensen, S. R., Morgan, A. C., & Avery, A. W. (1982). Relationship Enhancement® with premarital couples: An assessment of effects on relationship quality. *The American Journal of Family Therapy, 10*, 42–48.

Rocks, T. (1980). *The effectiveness of communication skills training with underachieving, low-communicating secondary school students and their teachers.* Unpublished doctoral dissertation, Pennsylvania State University, University Park.

Rose, M., Battjes, R., & Leukefeld, C. (1984). Family skills. In *Family Life Skills Training for Drug Abuse Prevention Booklet* (pp. 15–17). Rockville, MD: National Institute on Drug Abuse.

Ross, E. R., Baker, S. B., & Guerney, B. G., Jr. (1985). Effectiveness of Relationship Enhancement® therapy versus therapist's preferred therapy. *American Journal of Family Therapy, 13*(1), 11–21.

Sams, W. P. (1983). Marriage preparation: An experimental comparison of the Premarital Relationship Enhancement® (PRE) and the Engaged Encounter (EE) programs (Doctoral dissertation, Pennsylvania State University, 1983). *Dissertation Abstracts International 44*, 3207.

Sensué, M. E. (1981). *Filial therapy follow-up study: Effects on parental acceptance and child adjustment.* Unpublished doctoral dissertation, Pennsylvania State University, University Park.

Snyder, M. A. (1992). Gender-informed model of couple and family therapy: Relationship Enhancement® therapy. *Contemporary Family Therapy 14*(1), 15–31.

Snyder, M. (1994). Couple therapy with narcissistically vulnerable clients: Using the Relationship Enhancement® model. *The Family Journal, 2*(1), 27–35.

Snyder, M. (1996). *Demonstrations of becoming and laundering in Relationship Enhancement® couple therapy* [Videotapes]. Rockville, MD: IDEALS.

Snyder, M., & Guerney, B. G., Jr. (1993). Brief couple/family therapy: The Relationship Enhancement® approach. In R. A. Wells and V. J. Giannette (Eds.), *Casebook of the brief psychotherapies* (pp. 221–234). New York: Plenum Press.

Sullivan, H. S. (1947). *Conceptions of modern psychiatry.* Washington, DC: The William Alanson White Psychiatric Foundation.

Sywulak, A. E. (1977). *The effect of Filial therapy on parental acceptance and child adjustment.* Unpublished doctoral dissertation, Pennsylvania State University, University Park.

Thiessen, J., Avery, A. W., & Joanning, H. (1980). Facilitating post-divorce adjustment in females through communication skills training. *Journal of Divorce, 4,* 35–44.

Vogelsong, E. L. (1978). Relationship Enhancement® training for children. *Elementary School Guidance and Counseling, 12*(4), 272–279.

Vogelsong, E., Guerney, B. G., Jr., & Guerney, L. (1983). Relationship Enhancement® therapy with inpatients and their families. In R. Luber & C. Anderson (Eds.), *Family intervention with psychiatric patients* (pp. 48–68). New York: Human Sciences Press.

Waldo, M. (1986). Group counseling for military personnel who battered their wives. *Journal for Specialists in Group Work, 2*(3), 132–138.

Waldo, M. (1987). Also victims: Understanding and treating men arrested for spouse abuse. *Journal of Counseling and Development, 65,* 385–388.

Waldo, M. (1988). Relationship Enhancement® counseling groups for wife abusers. *Journal of Mental Health Counseling, 10*(1), 37–45.

Waldo, M., & Guerney, B. G., Jr. (1983). Marital Relationship Enhancement therapy in the treatment of alcoholism. *Journal of Marital and Family Therapy, 9*(3), 321–323.

Waldo, M., & Harman, M. J. (1993). Relationship Enhancement® therapy with borderline personality. *The Family Journal, 1*(1), 25–30.

Wieman, R. J. (1973). Conjugal relationship modification and reciprocal reinforcement: A comparison of treatments for marital discord (Doctoral dissertation, Pennsylvania State University, 1973). *Dissertation Abstracts International, 35,* 493-B.

Zahniser, J. H., & Falk, D. R. (1993). Relationship Enhancement® marital therapy with a schizophrenic couple: A case study. *The Family Journal, 1*(2), 136–143.

CHAPTER **5**   Luciano L'Abate, Ph.D.

Structured Enrichment and Distance Writing for Couples

☐ Introduction

The purpose of this chapter is to describe the use of structured enrichment (SE) programs and distance writing (DW) with couples. These two applications developed as steps in the evolution of a laboratory method in clinical psychology (L'Abate, 1990, 1994). As approaches, SE and DW are atheoretical but, as will be discussed, both can be used to evaluate theoretical models.

A variety of factors contributed to the creation of SE for couples. With the advent of couples and family therapies, there was a demand for methods that would allow structured training in working with multirelational systems, that is, couples and families. In addition, the growing emphasis on prevention led to the development of structured interventions that enabled trainees to practice with functional and semifunctional couples before intervening with dysfunctional ones. Finally, structured programs provide a linkage between research in the field and semiclinical or preventive interventions.

☐ Theoretical Underpinnings of SE

In the last quarter century, clinical psychology has attempted to answer a question that has haunted the fields of prevention and psychotherapy since their inception: What kind of intervention will be beneficial for which problem at what cost and with what kind of therapist or trainer? This question has generated other issues, including one that is at the core of both SE and DW: How can we match problem with solution if we do not have a catalogue of available solutions? To be sure, we have a classification system that follows classical psychiatric nosology (see DSM-IV; APA, 1994). But is there a method of classifying clients and interventions that would enable the matching of problems with solutions? SE and DW offer catalogues of interventions from which a professional helper can choose specific interventions to match the specific needs of couples.

SE and DW were used in the laboratory method with couples as an attempt to (a) lower costs of mental health practices, (b) find more cost-effective ways to delivery service, (c) link clinical practice with research, and (d) develop theory on the basis of practice. One motivation for the creation of SE was strictly practical: to allow a helper to work with as many couples as possible at the lowest possible cost without sacrificing standards and criteria of responsible practice.

It was found that the most effective way to help couples at risk for personal, marital, or family breakdown was to work with them at a distance using well-defined, structured materials or programs. There are too many couples in need and too few qualified professionals to help them to allow reliance on the single-couple–one-helper format. Forthofer, Markman, Cox, Stanley, and Kessler (1996) estimated that "work loss associated with marital problems translates into a loss of approximately $6.8 billion a year" (p. 597).

To work responsibly with couples at a distance, the quality of the intervention must be controlled. Thus, SE uses a structure that includes written instructions to be read to each participating couple. SE programs, however, differ from other preventive programs in that they can be modified for the specific needs of a particular couple. While other preventive programs take a "funnel" approach (i.e., one program is designed to fit all couples), SE consists of 50 different programs, hundreds of lessons, and thousands of exercises, from which a combination can be selected to fit a couple's needs. As practical applications of SE evolved, a theory of personality development began to take shape.

The relational and contextual context of personality development that provides the rationale for preventive and clinical applications borrows from resource exchange theory. According to Foa and Foa (1974), there are six classes of resources exchanged among people: status, love, information, services, money, and possessions. I reduced these six classes to three modalities of life: (a) being or *presence*, which combines status and love; (b) doing or *performance*, which combines information and services; and (c) having or *production*, which combines money and possessions.

However, I changed status to *importance* and love to *intimacy*. Being is nonnegotiable; doing and having are negotiable. The greatest resource exchanged among intimates, especially couples, is importance. However, in intimate (close, committed, and prolonged) relationships, along with importance, intimacy is needed to cement the relationship over time. To rephrase Freud's notion of what constitutes optimal mental health, "Lieben und arbeiten," for couples, the answer is to know how to love and how to negotiate.

Love and negotiation thus can be viewed as the goals for any intervention with couples. That is, we are trying to teach couples how to love each other and how to negotiate with each other in more effective ways.

Resource exchange theory has been limited in relating to multipersonal systems like couples and families. This statement is not meant as criticism, but strictly as a comment on the monadic thinking that was pervasive at the time the theory was developed. Therefore, I added to the levels of analysis and interpretation to differentiate among (a) public, (b) private, (c) internal or intrapsychic, and (d) historical-situational levels. The public level refers to the self-presentational facade level, that is, impression formation and management: how a couple, for example, wants to be perceived outside the home, when trying to meet societal expectations of "normality." Publicly, the couple may want to convey the impression to others that they are loving and well adjusted, while that same couple might be fighting like cats and dogs when inside the home. The private level, or how a couple functions while away from public scrutiny and in private, is called the phenotypical level. This is how a couple really functions under the stress of prolonged closeness without the mask or facade of public presentation. Most couples as well as individuals and families, no matter how dysfunctional, like to think of themselves as "appearing normal," even though they may, in fact, not look very normal when in private.

Below these two visible and recordable "descriptive" levels, there are two hidden and difficult-to-observe "explanatory" levels. The intrapsychic or internal level is genotypical: It is how each member of the couple feels and thinks about himself or herself. This is the frequently used explanatory level that includes constructs like "self-esteem," "ego," or "internal working models." Many theorists use such inferred and hypothetical traits and states without relational or contextual meaning to "explain" behavior. For example, a couple fights because they both have "low self-esteem," or are "insecure." The historical-situational level explains all the levels described above, since it contains all of the past and present relationships (family of origin, family of procreation) that produced whatever intrapsychic constructs one attributes genotypically, along with functioning at public and private (phenotypical) levels.

This four-level schema helps us to understand, in part, how couple relationships start on the basis of self-presentational factors (appearance, education, ethnic origin, religion, propinquity, or similarity).

As couples become better acquainted, they will explore and expand toward the phenotypical level, learning to know each other better away from the public eye and in the privacy of the home and/or the bedroom. The inferred, hypothetical genotypical level, as far as this theory is concerned, is made up of how (a) important/unimportant one feels and thinks of himself or herself, and (b) how differentiated one is from influential figures in one's life (parents, partner, and relevant others). This differentiation is described through the likeness continuum, to be expanded upon below.

However, the nature of the couple's relationship, regardless of phenotype, will be determined by historical and situational factors. For instance, if both partners are the products of broken homes, the chance that their relationship will break up at a given time is higher than that of a couple whose parental marriages were intact and positive.

The functionality/dysfunctionality differentiation at the genotypical level is a function of a likeness continuum made up of a six-step bell-shaped curve, ranging from the extreme of (a) symbiosis ("I am you," "I am nothing without you," "You and I are one"), through (b) sameness ("If I do what you tell me and I behave like you, conforming blindly and without question to what I am told to do, I will be all right"), (c) similarity ("I may choose to be a little like you, but there is room for me to be myself"), (d) differentness ("I do not need to be like everybody else"), and (e) oppositeness ("I will do and be the opposite of what you want me to do and be"), to the other extreme, autism or alienation ("I am nothing, I want nothing, I need nothing, I like nothing").

This dialectical continuum is applicable to genotypical self-definition in that individuals and couples continuously compare themselves with important others, such as parents, partners, lovers, relatives, siblings, friends, teachers, and so on. This continuum, borrowed from social comparison theory, affects all aspects of life choices, including parenting, marital selection, thinking, clothing, and appearance, among others.

The two extremes, symbiosis and autism or alienation, are the most dysfunctional. Sameness and oppositeness fall in the middle of the functional/dysfunctional continuum, while similarity and differentness are the most functional.

From this continuum emerge three levels of functionality, as represented by the ARC model. Combining the two extremes of symbiosis and autism or alienation produces the abusive-apathetic (neglectful) style of intimate relationships (AA). This is the most dysfunctional of the three styles. Combining sameness with oppositeness produces the reactive-repetitive (RR) style, which is intermediate in functionality/dysfunctionality. Combining similarity with differentness produces the conductive-creative (CC) style, the most functional of the three. The major source of conflict in couples derives from reactivity, the thoughtless, immediate reaction of one partner to whatever the other partner says and does, without thinking about the consequences of the reaction ("I did or said this because you did or said that"). Fifty percent to 60% of all intimate relationships between partners and between parents and children are reactive, and these produce the most couple conflicts and divorces.

The developmental theory of interpersonal competence and personality socialization in the family makes *sharing presence* (combining importance and intimacy) and *negotiating power* (combining performance and production) the two fundamental abilities necessary for survival and enjoyment (L'Abate, 1994; L'Abate & Baggett, 1997b). Presence represents how importance and intimacy are manifested and shared in a relationship, that is, consistently/inconsistently, weakly/strongly, continuously/discontinuously, etc. The combination of doing and having define *power*. How information, services, money, and possessions are used by a couple determines whether power is negotiated or not. Gradations may range from "nothing is negotiable," as in a slave–master relationship, to "everything is negotiable," as in chaotic-dysfunctional couples. In functional couples, presence is shared unconditionally and is not negotiable; we do not negotiate how much we love someone. Power, on the other hand, is negotiable in democratic relationships but is negotiated unsuccessfully or is not negotiated at all in dysfunctional ones. In dysfunctional couples, there is a diminution of presence and a parallel increase in power conflicts over services, information, money, and possessions, indicating that presence has not been shared effectively. Pathology develops in couples when issues of presence are fused, confused, and diffused with issues of power ("If you loved me, you would buy me. . . ," or "If you loved me, you would do what I want you to do").

In sum, most pathological relationships are characterized by deficits in being or presence, which requires a reciprocal emotional availability, with someone considered important not only for one's survival but also for one's enjoyment of life. This attribution of importance is what is continuously exchanged in intimate relationships, either verbally, nonverbally, or in writing.

From this notion of the exchange of importance between partners emerges a model of relational and contextual self-hood. The model is defined by four personality propensities: (a) *selfulness* ("I am important; you are important"), leading to presence and cooperative problem solving and negotiation; (b) *selfishness* ("I am important; you are not"), leading to autocracy, denial of dependency, competitiveness, manipulation of partner, and conflict; (c) *selflessness* ("You are important, but I am not"), leading to overdependency, manipulation of self, heteronomy, and over-reliance on the partner; and (d) *no-self* ("Neither one of us is important"), leading to contradictory and inconsistent abuse and neglect, the cradle of pathological relationships. Selfulness is the most functional propensity among the four. No-self is the most dysfunctional, while selfishness and selflessness are intermediate between selfulness and no-self along the continuum of functionality/dysfunctionality. Selfulness is characterized by the CC style, which affirms the importance of the self and the partner. Selfishness and selflessness are characterized by the RR style.

Stereotypically, in most Western cultures including the American, and depending on the criteria used, at least 50% of men are socialized for selfishness, while at least 50% of women are socialized for selflessness. Gender ratios are equal for selful and no-self types. The latter exhibit an AA style that is pathogenic in the couple as well as in their offspring.

The model predicts that most selful individuals will be attracted to and marry a similarly selful individual, producing a harmonious and growth-oriented relationship with a CC style. Most selfish individuals will be attracted to, and attract, selfless persons, while no-self individuals will attract similar no-self individuals. While reciprocity, equality, and intimacy are the characteristics of selful couples, repetitively negative reactivity, competitiveness, manipulation, and acrimony are characteristics of selfish/selfless couples. No-self couples are characterized by contradictory and inconsistent physical, sexual, and verbal abuse and emotional neglect.

Based on these personality propensities, one can predict that selful couples will be able to love and negotiate with a minimum of conflict. Selfish/selfless couples will be characterized by the polarity of denial of dependency (selfish individuals) versus overdependency (selfless partners) and will exhibit the highest conflict and divorce rate. Although conflict is present also in no-self couples, due to their strong dependency needs, they tend to stay together, even though their conflict might be even more intense than that of selfish/selfless couples. Love and negotiation are present in selful couples, are sporadic in selfish/selfless couples, and are absent in no-self couples.

☐ SE Intervention Model

Primary prevention strategies like SE might be very beneficial to selful couples and, under certain conditions, to selfish/selfless couples. No-self couples will need tertiary prevention strategies, that is, crisis intervention and psychotherapy, plus the addition of primary and secondary prevention strategies. The goal of any intervention is to help couples learn how to love and negotiate in more effective ways.

SE includes a library of 50 programs (L'Abate & Weinstein, 1987) and accompanying case studies (L'Abate, & Stevens, 1986; L'Abate & Young, 1987). Programs were developed eclectically from different theoretical and atheoretical sources.

The goal of these interventions is to assist couples in learning how to relate to one another using a CC style rather than an RR style. The ultimate goal is to help couples differentiate presence from power.

There is no one single way to help couples to relate in a CC style and to differentiate presence from power. There are many ways to help couples make positive changes, as is attested to by the numerous approaches presented in this book. The pertinent issue thus becomes the selection of the SE program, or a set of lessons and exercises, that best matches the needs of a particular couple. For instance, a couple who wants to learn to communicate better can choose one of three possible programs: negotiation, assertiveness, and equality.

Each SE program is composed of three or more lessons, with each lesson containing five or six exercises, yielding a total of over a thousand exercises. The lessons are scored for nine dimensions of couple and family interaction (Kochalka & L'Abate, 1997): (a) description of self and partner, (b) evaluation of self and partner, (c) self-expression in the relationship, (d) ability to reflect, (e) touching each other, (f) brainstorming, (g) play, (h) role taking, and (i) negotiation. Programs relevant to prevention deal with developmental stages of the family life cycle, starting with premarital issues, marital issues, and sexuality (six programs), male–female relationships (seven programs), parenting (six programs), and later stages of the family life cycle (four programs). A second section deals with couples and families according to their level of emotional, educational, and intellectual development, from introductory (three programs) to intermediate (four programs), affective (four programs), cognitive (four programs), and relational skill building (four programs). A third section contains programs for nontraditional couples and families (divorced, single-parent, adopted, blended, and dual-employment). A fourth contains programs for dysfunctional couples and families (general, physically handicapped, mentally handicapped, alcoholic, drug-addicted, and depressed).

Through participating in SE, which involves making appointments, completing homework assignments, discussing emotionally charged issues in a relatively objective and rational fashion, and confronting issues from a new perspective, couples become capable of changing their repetitive reactions, enlarging their repertoire of responses, and hopefully adopting more of a CC style.

☐ Specific Methods and Strategies for SE Intervention

Because SE offers a wide range of programs, lessons, and exercises, a quantitative system was developed to allow a match among (a) the needs of the couple, as stated in their initial interview; (b) the couple's needs as judged by trainees and supervisor; and (c) objective test results.

After coding the over one thousand SE exercises according to the nine dimensions just described, we developed an evaluation instrument that classified couples according to the same nine categories. This instrument, the Family Profile Form (Kochalka & L'Abate, 1997), yielded scores with adequate test/retest reliability and discriminated significantly between clinical and nonclinical couples. In addition, results from this measure correlated significantly with well-established instruments, such as the Family Environment Scale and the Dyadic Adjustment Scale (Kochalka & L'Abate, 1997).

Based on a couple's responses to this Family Profile Form, we can administer SE exercises that fit the couple's area of deficit (defined by both partners agreeing about this deficit) or their area of conflict (the partners disagree about the deficit, which is acknowledged by one partner but denied by the other). For example, a couple may agree or disagree that touching is an area of deficit for them, but in either case, the exercises from all the different SE programs that deal with touching would be appropriate for this couple

☐ Format of Application of SE

In initially developing and evaluating SE, we recruited couples from the undergraduate student population. Most couples were "going steady," engaged to be married, or already married. They were primarily Caucasians from middle-class backgrounds. Couples were evaluated on a before/after treatment basis using a battery of paper-and-pencil self-report tests (see L'Abate & Young, 1987). The objective test results, in combination with the impressions of the enricher(s) and supervisor and the couple's stated needs, were used to identify three SE programs that appeared to match the couple's needs.

After the couple chose one of the three programs, the couple was typically seen for six SE sessions and were then re-evaluated using the same test battery. They also received feedback and debriefing afterwards (L'Abate & Young, 1987). Each couple received enrichment alone, with one or two trainers, in keeping with the intent of SE to tailor each couple's enrichment program to the specific needs of the couple.

Examples of the use of this approach with couples can be found in L'Abate and Young (1987).

If, upon finishing SE, the couple was found to need additional treatment, the couple was given the choice of (a) doing nothing further, (b) taking an additional SE program designed to deal with the issues that emerged during the couple's previous SE program, or (c) participating in therapy in whatever setting they desired. If the couple chose either additional SE therapy or another therapy, they were seen by an enricher or a therapist whom they had not worked with previously.

☐ Qualities and Role of the Enricher

SE leaders are referred to in the program as "enrichers." Most enrichers have been graduate students in the family psychology track of a clinical psychology graduate training program. Their educational level has varied from bachelor's to master's degrees. They have been selected on the basis of undergraduate grades, GRE scores, personality factors (empathy, warmth, and unconditional positive regard), indications of previous clinical work, and letters of recommendation. Most graduate students who have trained as enrichers have wanted to become couples or family therapists. However, before doing clinical work with dysfunctional couples or families, they have had to perform SE with at least three couples. During this experience, they were screened and supervised in their relationship and structuring skills. The success of such enrichers in conducting SE has led to the conclusion that, given a specific and clear structure, paraprofessionals with personal but no professional qualifications can successfully run couple enrichment programs.

☐ Empirical Evaluation

To date, most of the research on the outcomes of SE has been unpublished. However, quite a few case studies have been published (L'Abate & Stevens, 1986; L'Abate & Young, 1987).

Three in-house doctoral dissertations (Ganahl, 1981; Sloan, 1983; Wildman, 1976) and a consumer satisfaction survey (L'Abate & Rupp, 1981) demonstrated positive outcomes associated with SE, in comparison to contrast groups. Only a handful out of over two hundred couples dropped out. Another doctoral dissertation (Yarbrough, 1983) used the Negotiation program successfully with undergraduate couples.

Coleman (1986) studied the application of SE to low-income, black, single-parent families. Predictably, the results were questionable, as SE programs were not intended to help single parents who are in crisis and who show definite clinical symptoms.

☐ Introduction to DW in Preventive Therapy for Couples

The media through which couples can learn how to love and how to negotiate more effectively are verbal, nonverbal, and written. The written medium is the most recent addition to the full complement of approaches used to help couples change for the better. DW allows for a degree of specificity and individualization that is not available in verbally based preventive or therapeutic approaches (Esterling, L'Abate, Murray, & Pennebaker, in press; L'Abate, 1990, 1991, 1992; L'Abate & Baggett, 1997; Pennebaker, 1997).

During the past 12 years, I have requested, as a condition for entering into a therapeutic contract with me, that clients complete homework assignments in writing. Whether an individual or part of a couple or family, clients have to agree in writing to complete 1 hour of written homework for every 1 hour of therapy. DW became a standard technique in my clinical practice for at least three reasons: (a) to enable couples to assume more responsibility for changes in their relationship; (b) to save me time; and (c) to make couples therapy more cost-effective. DW programs can be used in addition to face-to-face SE or psychotherapy or as an alternative to SE or psychotherapy. It is also appropriate for couples who need a boost in their relationship, not psychotherapy.

Many therapeutic and preventive programs operate on two tracks, with one track in the professional office and the other in the home. It thus becomes our responsibility to provide, for the at-home track, specific materials that are isomorphic with the problems presented by a given couple (L'Abate, 1986, 1992, 1994).

For instance, if a group of couples attends a preventive program to increase intimacy, DW would involve assigning written homework that is specific to the different needs of each couple in the group. Each couple receives a homework assignment, which may be different from that of any other couple in the group. One couple could be assigned a program on arguing and fighting (L'Abate, 1992), while another couple could receive a program on depression, and a third couple be assigned to work on a program to learn negotiation (L'Abate, 1986). DW, therefore, would allow a match, as is done with SE, between the couple and the solutions to their problems, as opposed to the notion that one program fits all couples, regardless of individual and couple differences.

DW procedures consist of (a) open-ended diaries or journals (ODW);

(b) guided questions drawn from open-ended writing (GDW); (c) focused writing (FDW; Pennebaker, 1997), as in "Write about all your hurts received in the past"; and (d) programmed materials (PDW), such as workbooks on specific conditions or symptoms like depression, negotiation, or intimacy (L'Abate, 1986, 1990, 1992, 1994; L'Abate & Baggett, 1997a).

☐ Theoretical Underpinnings of DW

The same theoretical assumptions that underlie other psychological interventions with couples also underlie DW: to teach couples how to love and how to negotiate more effectively than they have done in the past. Indeed, the first two PDW programs were designed to help couples learn how to negotiate and be intimate (L'Abate, 1986).

Change in any philosophical, religious, or psychological system can take place when there is an external intervention. If couples want to make positive changes in their relationships, they must receive and act upon new information. By devoting time to the completion of individual and joint written homework assignments, they learn to reflect upon and process new information that was not previously available to them. This makes change possible.

☐ DW Intervention Model

DW programs were derived from theoretical models about depression, negotiation, and intimacy (L'Abate, 1986; L'Abate, Johnston, & Levis, 1987). The major theoretical contribution to the DW approach relates to *reactivity*, which is usually intense when couples begin therapy. Hence, the initial purpose of any intervention, whether preventive or therapeutic, is to lower the intensity of couple reactivity. By prescribing predetermined times for the couple to confront each other using the medium of homework assignments, it is possible to lower reactivity and increase the learning of conductive and creative skills.

An example of DW would be assigning couples to spend, between the second and the third sessions, 20 minutes a day for four consecutive days writing down all the hurts they have experienced during their lives (Esterling et al., in press; Pennebaker, 1997). After each partner completes this assignment individually, the couple meets together to discuss their lists of hurts. Both partners also complete a debriefing form, which they use to report on the process of coming together. All materials are brought to the next therapy session.

Each workbook consists of lessons varying in number, from six for the "Intimacy" workbook to more than twenty for both the "Problems in Relationships" workbook and the workbook on "Impulsivity."

☐ Specific Methods and Strategies for Intervention

PDW workbooks that have been used extensively as homework assignments in conjunction with couple therapy are those on (a) arguing and fighting, (b) depression, (c) negotiation, (d) intimacy, and (e) problems in relationships.

☐ Format of Application of DW

Following is a discussion of the format used to administer the lessons contained in one of the five workbooks.

Arguing and Fighting

After many years of frustration with my inability to effectively deal with this symptom, and after finding that depression was not always at the bottom of arguing and fighting, I developed a model of abusive behavior along with a three-lesson introduction to understanding why couples argue and fight without resolution.

The first lesson of this workbook asks each partner to describe the frequency, rate, duration, intensity, and content of their arguments or fights. The second lesson gives 10 explanations for arguing and fighting in couples, which are to be ranked according to how well they apply to the experience of each partner. If none of the explanations is acceptable, the respondent can give his or her own explanation. The third lesson prescribes arguing and fighting according to specific instructions, dictating when, how long, and in what manner the couple is to fight. The instructions include the prescription to use abusive language ("You-ing"), blaming the partner through generalizations ("You never . . . You always . . . "), bringing up the painful past, mind reading, excusing self-errors but not forgiving the partner for his or her errors, bribery and blackmail, threatening, and setting deadlines. The couple is to tape-record this fight. The couple is to bring the tape to the therapist, whom they believe will be listening to it. Instead, the therapist will tell them that he or she already knows that they fight "dirty," and that they are the ones who need to recognize that fighting in an abusive manner gets them nowhere. Consequently, each partner is given a scoring sheet on which he or she records, while listening to the fight on tape, how often he or she used any of the seven abusive fighting behaviors mentioned above. Once they have brought their scoring sheets back to the therapist, each one receives a lesson on the behavior which he or she displayed the most frequently during the fight. For instance, if one partner often said "You . . . " in a blaming fashion, he or she will be given a lesson about the destructive effects of using this pronoun. If the other partner used mind reading most often, he or she is given the lesson about the problems associated with mind reading. Once they have completed these lessons, if they are still using destructive patterns while arguing or fighting, they are administered the lesson that matches that pattern (L'Abate, 1992).

☐ Application of the Preventive Model to a Couple at Risk

The most cost-effective way to deal with Ben and Alyssa would be through a combination of SE and PDW. What follows is a description of what our hypothetical couple would have experienced had they entered a SE program.

The initial interview was conducted by a professional, who proposed that Ben and Alyssa complete a program consisting of SE and written homework assignments. A lengthy informed consent form (L'Abate & Baggett, 1997a) was read and signed by both partners. SE was to be administered by a master's level assistant enricher; PDW homework assignments would be completed under the supervision of the professional. The couple would have six sessions of SE, once every three weeks, along with one final session one month after the termination of SE and DW. They would be mailing in their weekly homework assignments.

Session 1

In the first SE session, Ben and Alyssa received the first lesson of the "conflict resolution" program (L'Abate & Weinstein, 1987, pp. 147–157), which consists of exercises on the first wedding anniversary, avoidance and denial of conflict, and conflict engagement. For homework between the first and second sessions, they received the following instructions: "For 20 minutes a day on four consecutive days, make a list of hurts you received before and during your marriage. After you have listed these hurts, compare and discuss these lists with one another." The couple was instructed to mail copies of these lists (retaining the originals for themselves) to the enricher along with written feedback about their discussion of their respective hurts.

In the feedback notes, Alyssa reported that she had broken down and cried about her past, and that when she started crying, Ben had held her tightly and also started to cry. They felt very good about this experience.

Session 2

This session opened with a discussion of the outcome of writing down and sharing all the hurts they had received in their lives. Ben reported that he had collected a lot of hurts and that he was glad that he got "this baggage off my shoulders."

The second SE lesson on conflict resolution had the couple consider the outcomes of previously used conflict resolution patterns and taught them new ways to resolve conflict. They were given a sequence of steps necessary to solve a conflict. They then completed a Conflict Resolution Form, which asked them to state a specific conflict as well as the steps they would use to handle the conflict. Once they applied the sequence of steps to their conflict, they indicated whether they were satisfied or dissatisfied with the outcome.

Ben and Alyssa brought up their difficulty with negotiating. Since their arguing and fighting style is RR, they agreed that the program on arguing and fighting would be most appropriate at this time. They were given the first three lessons, which they were to complete and mail back to the enricher once per week during the following three weeks.

During the third week, Ben and Alyssa mailed back the instructions from the third lesson, which prescribes how to fight, commenting that they could not fight the prescribed way. They reported that they had not used any of the abusive patterns outlined in this lesson; instead, they had had a very successful discussion in which neither of them had gotten angry. In addition, they had been able to solve issues related to moving to another town to find a better work situation for Ben.

Session 3

After discussing their "unsuccessful" homework assignments ("I can't believe you are not going to argue and fight again. However, if you both agree, we shall move on to the "negotiation" program. Is that OK with you?"), Alyssa and Ben agreed to use the program on negotiation as homework assignments. The third lesson of the "conflict resolution" program, on "practice makes perfect," is administered next. The exercises include constructive confrontation, resolving conflict, and learning to express feelings appropriately during conflict. Ben suggested that a hidden area of conflict was religion. Even though he was not an observant Jew, he had recently become aware of his "Jewishness," which he had denied in the past. At the same time, Alyssa continued to affirm her Christian upbringing. How could the two of them come together to share their spirituality? They discussed the possibility of finding a religious setting that would acknowledge their respective religions. Ben suggested that they join the Unitarian Universalist Church. Although Alyssa had never heard of this church, she agreed to attend one service to explore whether or not they could both feel comfortable there.

As their homework assignment, they were given the first three lessons of the "negotiation" program (L'Abate, 1986), which covers (a) the goals of marriage, (b) the law of give and take ("the Golden rule"), and (c) practicing "I" statements.

Session 4

During the discussion of their homework, Ben acknowledged his failure to follow the golden rule in his marriage. Alyssa acknowledged that she had let her true self down by trying to placate Ben and fulfill his desires. She realized that she needed to work on valuing herself to avoid letting down Ben and the children ("If I do not value myself, what will Ben think of me, and what kind of example will I give to my children?").

Next, they were given the "conflict resolution" program's third lesson, on constructive arguing. They completed a contract on how they were going to deal with a problem and come up with solutions. As homework, they received lesson 4, on styles in relationships, along with lessons 5 and 6, on options for responding to each other. These are interactive lessons in which couples practice the three styles of responding, AA, RR, and CC, to each other's purposely provocative questions. In lesson 5, they practiced differentiating among emotional, rational, and active responses to provocation. In lesson 6, they learned to respond in terms of either awareness of self or awareness of context.

Session 5

A discussion of the homework brought the pleasant realization that they were now able to identify their previous styles of relating. Ben and Alyssa learned that they had been primarily reactive in the past, not only with each other but also with their parents. Alyssa said that as a result of the practice lessons, she came to understand how emotional she was in her responding. She wanted to become more rational in her responses but also freer to express her feelings without having to go into action. Ben realized how rational he had been in the past and how much he had been avoiding his feelings. Both recognized the importance of simply acknowledging and sharing feelings without doing anything about them.

Next came the first lesson of the "working through" program (L'Abate & Weinstein, 1987, pp. 157–162), which teaches how to (a) list problems, (b) assume personal responsibility, and (c) talk about oneself. As homework, Ben and Alyssa were administered lessons 7 and 8 of the negotiation program. Lesson 7 is a long and complex lesson on priorities, including the consequences of the past choices one has made and the need for reassessment. Lesson 8, on the triangle of living, covers the exchange of resources according to the three modalities of being, doing, and having. This lesson would be especially relevant for Ben and Alyssa who, in their frenetic attempts to perform and produce, have let go of their presence and become less and less emotionally available to each other. It was important, therefore, that they reassess their resources for being (presence), doing (performance), and having (production).

In their written feedback regarding this lesson, Ben admitted that he ranked doing and having over being, while Alyssa put being and having before doing. From their discussion, they concluded that the more helpful sequence would be being, doing, and having.

Session 6

During their discussion of the homework, the couple expressed appreciation for having viewed their priorities in ways that were clarifying and exciting to them. As a result of the homework assignments and ensuing discussions, they felt much more at ease with each other, as well as clearer about what they wanted for each other and for themselves.

Next they received the second lesson of "working through," which covered their viewpoints on their individual needs, wants, likes, and personal feelings, including present and past situations, social and economic pressures, vocational pressures (if relevant), physical illness (if any), and unexpressed grief. As homework assignments, they were asked to follow guidelines in negotiating a conflict area using the ERAAwC model (L'Abate, 1986, 1994; L'Abate & Baggett, 1997): expressing feelings (*emotionality*), generating various courses of action with their respective pros and cons (*rationality*), choosing one course of action over others and applying the chosen course of action (*activity*), and consideration of the outcome (*aware-*

ness) within the context of their relationship. They were to mail written feedback about their negotiation to the enricher before the next session.

Session 7

Session 7 was a follow-up session, held one month after the previous session. Here they further discussed their negotiation assignment to determine whether they had applied the negotiation model correctly and whether the outcome was successful. In their feedback notes, they had reported that a major source of conflict was sex. They agreed upon some basic guidelines: to satisfy Alyssa, Ben would invest more time and effort in precoital caressing, touching, and warming up. Afterwards, they would spend more time reliving the experience instead of turning around and going to sleep. They had become aware of how important it was for them to be together physically and emotionally without any demands for performance, production, perfection, or problem solving.

During this session, they practiced in vivo role reversal and experimental role taking, which comprise the third and fourth lessons of the "working through" program. After they completed these lessons, the issue of intimacy was raised. Ben and Alyssa stated that, as far as sharing joys and hurts in their families of origin and in their own relationship, intimacy was no longer a problem for them. They were very satisfied with the outcomes of both SE and PDW. Consequently, as agreed upon beforehand, this became the termination session. A six-month follow-up would be done through the mail.

☐ Summary

The above discussion describes programs that match a given couple's problems with solutions that are administered verbatim through a written protocol (SE) or through written assignments (PDW). Along with other possible benefits, these methods allow one to assess whether a predesigned and structured program is successful in addressing a couple's specific set of difficulties. Rather than relying on the spoken word, as preventive programs typically do, SE and PDW ensure, through the written word, that what is said and done with couples is both reliable and effective.

☐ Contact References

For more information on SE, contact the Institute for Life Empowerment (ILE), Suite 170, 6065 Lake Forrest Drive, Atlanta, GA 30328; http://

www.mentalhealth.com. An annotated bibliography of more than 50 commercially available workbooks on clinical topics for individuals, couples, and families can be obtained from ILE.

☐ References

American Psychiatric Association. (1994). *Diagnostic and statistical manual of mental disorders* (4th ed.). Washington, DC: Author.

Beck, A. T., & Young, J. E. (1985). Depression. In D. H. Harlow (Ed.), *Clinical handbook of psychological disorders* (pp. 206–244). New York: Guilford.

Coleman, D. (1986). *Structured enrichment (SE) with low income black single parent families.* Unpublished Master's thesis, Georgia State University, Atlanta, GA.

Esterling, B. A., L'Abate, L., Murray, E. J., & Pennebaker, J. W. (in press). Empirical foundations for writing in prevention and psychotherapy: Mental and physical health outcomes. *Clinical Psychology Review.*

Foa, U., & Foa, E. (1974). *Societal structures of the mind.* Springfield, IL: C. C. Thomas.

Forthofer, M. S., Markman, H. J., Cox, M., Stanley, S., & Kessler, R. C. (1996). Association between marital distress and work loss in a national sample. *Journal of Marriage and the Family, 58,* 597–605.

Ganahl, G. F. (1981). *Effects of client, treatment, and therapist variables on the outcome of structured marital enrichment.* Unpublished doctoral dissertation, Georgia State University, Atlanta, GA.

Kochalka, J., Buzas, H., L'Abate, L., McHenry, S., & Gibson, E. (1987). Structured enrichment training and implementation with paraprofessionals. In L. L'Abate (Ed.), *Family psychology II: Theory, therapy, enrichment, and training* (pp. 278–287). Latham, MD: University Press of America.

Kochalka, J., & L'Abate, L. (1997). Linking evaluation with structured enrichment: The Family Profile Form. *American Journal of Family Therapy, 25,* 361–374.

L'Abate, L. (1986). *Systematic family therapy.* New York: Brunner/Mazel.

L'Abate, L. (1990). *Building family competence: Primary and secondary prevention strategies.* Newbury Park, CA: Sage.

L'Abate, L. (1991). The use of writing in psychotherapy. *American Journal of Psychotherapy, 45,* 87-98.

L'Abate, L. (1992). *Programmed writing: A self-administered approach for interventions with individuals, couples and families.* Pacific Grove, CA: Brooks/Cole.

L'Abate, L. (1994). *A theory of personality development.* New York: Wiley.

L'Abate, L., & Baggett, M. S. (1997a). *Distance writing and computer assisted interventions in mental health.* (Available from Institute for Life Empowerment, Suite 170, 6065 Lake Forrest Dr., Atlanta, GA 30328)

L'Abate, L., & M. S. Baggett. (1997b). *The self in the family: A classification of personality, criminality, and psychopathology.* New York: Wiley.

L'Abate, L., Johnston, T. B., & Levis, M. (1987). Treatment of depression in a couple with systematic homework assignments. *Journal of Psychotherapy and the Family, 2,* 117–128.

L'Abate, L., & Rupp, G. (1981). *Enrichment: Skill training for family life.* Washington, DC: University Press of America.

L'Abate, L., & Stevens, F. E. (1986). Structured enrichment (SE) of a couple. *Journal of Psychotherapy and the Family, 2,* 59–67.

L'Abate, L., & Weinstein, S. E. (1987). *Structured enrichment programs for couples and families.* New York: Brunner/Mazel.

L'Abate, L., & Young, L. (1987). *Casebook of structured enrichment programs for couples and families.* New York: Brunner/Mazel.

Pennebaker, J. W. (1997). *Opening up: The healing power of confiding in others*. New York: Guilford.

Sloan, S. Z. (1983). *Assessing the differential effectiveness of two enrichment formats in facilitating marital intimacy and interaction*. Unpublished doctoral dissertation, Georgia State University, Atlanta. GA.

Wildman, R. W. (1976). *Structured versus unstructured marital interventions*. Unpublished doctoral dissertation, Georgia State University, Atlanta, GA,

Yarbrough, D. M. (1983). *Effects of structured negotiation training on dyadic adjustment, satisfaction, and intimacy*. Unpublished doctoral dissertation. University of Georgia, Athens, GA.

6

CHAPTER

Sherod Miller, Ph.D.
Peter A. D. Sherrard, Ed.D.

COUPLE COMMUNICATION:
A System for Equipping Partners To Talk, Listen, and Resolve Conflicts Effectively

☐ Introduction

The roots of the COUPLE COMMUNICATION program extend back to the late 1960s at the University of Minnesota Family Study Center. There, surrounded with an outstanding faculty and a research grant from the National Institute of Mental Health, Sherod Miller, Elam Nunnally, and Daniel Wackman met as graduate students and formed a research and program development team. The team focused its initial research on the transition from engagement to early marriage and on the conditions that supported couples in establishing a successful relationship. This research led to the development of the COUPLE COMMUNICATION system.

Mentors

Several mentors had a substantial impact on the development of the program. These included Reuben Hill, Virginia Satir and her colleagues, Don Jackson and Paul Watzlawick at the Mental Research Institute in Palo Alto, California, Sidney Jourard, and William F. Hill. Reuben Hill had a passion for *family development*. Satir, Jackson, and Waltzlawick operationalized the pragmatics of *communication and interactive processes*. Jourard was the vanguard of the concept of *self-disclosure* and its role in health. William F. Hill conducted the original and seminal research on *styles of communication*. The work and personal relationships with these teachers influenced many of the frameworks and skills that are taught to partners in COUPLE COMMUNICATION for navigating the inevitable rapids that occur in any relationship. The research team was also motivated in part by the members' own clinical practices and their awareness of the limits of marriage counseling and therapy (which focused primarily on repairing relationships and not on equipping couples to become their own best problem solvers).

In the early days, the team encountered considerable resistance from well-known professionals who saw skill training as superficial and incapable of impacting a couple's interaction in an empirically measurable way. The team's early experiences indicated that specific communication skills could in fact be taught and measured, supporting the transition into marriage. As a result, they continued to identify and refine specific communication concepts and skills that partners could learn to improve their ability to focus on, discuss, and resolve day-to-day concerns in a productive manner.

As the success of the program's research and development grew, it became apparent that relationships, in addition to having been initiated, were also maintained, strengthened, and destroyed through communication. Thus, the team broadened the spectrum of couples in their program. They began to include partners in all stages of development and levels of functioning who wished to learn communication skills to improve their relationship.

Goals of COUPLE COMMUNICATION

The general goals of the COUPLE COMMUNICATION program are to help couples:

- communicate more effectively about day-to-day issues,
- manage and resolve conflicts, and
- build a more viable and satisfying relationship.

Features of COUPLE COMMUNICATION

A number of features contribute to COUPLE COMMUNICATION as an effective skill-learning program. The program equips partners with:

- conceptual maps for understanding self and partner and how they communicate effectively or ineffectively together;

- eleven specific talking and listening skills for sending and receiving messages more clearly and accurately;
- tools and strategies for processing issues and resolving conflicts;
- accelerated skill-learning technology (skills mats) to help them transfer the COUPLE COMMUNICATION concepts and skills into their everyday lives;
- awareness of both attitudinal and behavioral aspects of conflict resolution and relationship building;
- communication exercises to apply the skills with children for enriching their family communication;
- confidence that the concepts and skills taught are well grounded in theory and research specific to the program;
- a practical and complete communication system in a brief, structured, inexpensive, and efficient manner.

To date, more that 500,000 couples have participated in COUPLE COMMUNICATION throughout the United States, as well as in Canada, Europe, Scandinavia, Australia, South America, Taiwan, Korea, and Japan. The program has been translated into seven languages. In 1986, Dr. Phyllis Miller joined the three originators on the program's development and writing team. The program was redesigned and updated in 1991. Its revision was based on extensive research, feedback from instructors and couples, and new learning theory.

☐ Theoretical Underpinnings

In addition to the influence of our personal mentors, the processes and skills taught in the COUPLE COMMUNICATION program spring from the theoretical insights and application of systems-theory properties and principles. A system is any whole with interacting parts (Bertalanffy, 1950; J. G. Miller, 1978). All human relationships—self-managing-adaptive systems—can be examined and understood in terms of a common set of system properties. Systems are not static. They are dynamic, living entities, which balance stability with change. The different ways that partners play out their system properties over time constitutes the dynamics of their relationship. The behavior (verbal and nonverbal) of partners toward each other communicates the dynamics of their relationship. Systems properties and principles provide a framework for examining and understanding relationship development and dysfunction. The processes and skills taught in the COUPLE COMMUNICATION program spring from the theoretical insights and application of systems-theory properties and principles (S. L. Miller, Miller, Nunnally, & Wackman, 1992).

Consistent with systems theory, all relationships are more or less:

1. *Purposeful.* Although its mission, objectives, and goals may be rather unclear or confused at times, every relationship-system has some reason for being. Purpose contributes to the meaningfulness of a partnership.
2. *Individuated.* Each member is a unique person and brings his or her individual differences—orientation, talent, and experience—to each situation in the relationship.
3. *Interconnected.* Partners' actions influence each other. Whatever affects one partner affects the other person.
4. *Differentiated.* While interconnected, each member respects the other's experience, uniqueness, interests, and function as different from his or her own.
5. *Bounded.* Human systems have semipermeable boundaries that help a couple maintain its identity and that continuously exchange energy and information within and between the couple's inner and outer environments. These boundaries are composed of formal and informal rules and expectations that govern day-to-day activities.
6. *Information processing.* Partners generate, transmit, amplify, govern, distort, and correct information. Partners are influenced by the quality of information available to them. Since two people cannot not communicate, a pair's communication is an index reflecting the nature and quality of their relationship.
7. *Synergistic—the whole is greater than the sum of its parts.* At any point in time, the interaction between members amounts to something greater than the sum of its individual members' contributions and activities. The system's collective force or "we-ness" can have positive or negative impact both on individual members and on the well-being or output of the couple.
8. *Efficient.* Relationships strive for balance and to operate at the least "cost to success ratio" possible.
9. *Self-maintaining.* Through processes of negative and positive feedback, couples support or limit each other physically, emotionally, intellectually, spiritually, and economically.
10. *Self-directing.* Any partner can seek to initiate change for the common or individual good by setting goals, making plans, negotiating issues, or resolving issues and conflicts.
11. *Self-monitoring.* Members track their own process, progress, and outcomes (results) through mechanisms of internal and external feedback.
12. *Self-correcting and -repairing.* When the system is damaged or becomes ill, or survival of the entity itself is threatened, partners can act to correct and heal the system.
13. *Interacting subsystems.* All relationships are subsystems of larger inter-

acting social systems. Every relationship itself is influencing and being influenced by other forces.

14. *Operating in context.* All relationships operate in a contextual environment composed of physical, social, economic, political, and spiritual
factors.

These system properties, common to all social systems, are played out
in an infinite number of ways among couples and families in a variety of
cultural contexts around the world. The conceptual frameworks (maps), behavioral skills, and processes taught in COUPLE COMMUNICATION are
designed to heighten a couple's ability to enhance and enrich their functioning as a system. System properties, dynamics, and principles also have
implications for the effective teaching of COUPLE COMMUNICATION.

☐ Intervention Model

Systems theory provides grounding for the program's objectives. COUPLE
COMMUNICATION has four major objectives:

1. to increase *awareness* of self, partner, and the relationship (properties
of individuation, interconnectedness, boundaries, and synergy);
2. to teach *skills* for talking and listening together more effectively (differentiation, information processing);
3. to expand *options* (processes) for enriching the relationship (self-maintaining, directing, monitoring, and repairing);
4. to increase *satisfaction* with outcomes of issues and the relationship
(purpose and efficiency).

Delivery Context

COUPLE COMMUNICATION may be positioned as an enrichment or
therapy function. Because of the core set of skills that it teaches, the program fits into premarital, marriage enrichment, or other relationship-edu-
cation programming. The program is particularly beneficial as a component of a brief-therapy treatment plan.

Optional Formats

The program can be taught to one couple at a time or in a group format:

Conjoint format: One couple (privately) in six 50-minute sessions.
Small group: Two or four couples in four 2-hour sessions.
Large group: Five to twelve couples in four 2-hour sessions.

Detailed agendas for the various formats are provided in the *Couple Communication Instructor Manual* (S. L. Miller et al., 1992).

Each session provides practical conceptual frameworks (cognitive organizers), specific communication skills (behavioral options), and interactional processes (guidelines) for discussing and resolving issues. Learning occurs around the real-life issues couples choose to discuss during the program, with feedback and coaching on their interaction from the instructor and other participants. The following is a conceptual overview of each group-format session.

Session I: Caring for Self

Session I focuses on caring for self: self-individuation and esteem. Since every person is unique (as is every couple), how each partner in a couple relationship experiences a situation or issue differs to some extent from how the other partner does. The COUPLE COMMUNICATION program recognizes that individual differences can be the source of conflict or collaboration, and it gives partners tools for communicating their uniqueness appropriately. It embraces the differences as a positive resource for the partnership.

The Awareness Wheel® is presented in the first session to help partners self-focus. Specifically, it helps them:

- increase their self-awareness,
- understand situations and issues better, and
- use this self-information to communicate more effectively and satisfactorily.

These objectives are accomplished by:

1. identifying three basic types of issues (topical, personal, and relational);
2. practicing "self-talk" (using the Awareness Wheel for reflection and processing of issues);
3. learning six talking skills (based on the Awareness Wheel) for expressing self clearly, congruently, and responsibly.

The Awareness Wheel is the first conceptual map and practical tool introduced in the program. Theoretically, the Awareness Wheel represents the *informational structure of a situation or issue*. Similar to the way a sentence contains a grammatical structure, a situation or issue contains an informational structure.

This structure incorporates sensory data, thoughts, feelings, wants, and actions and serves to prompt and organize an individual's awareness. Once a person understands this key structure, he or she can analyze situations and process issues more efficiently and effectively.

The concept of self-individuation involves balancing (negotiating and renegotiating) the natural and ongoing tension between separateness (personal autonomy: self as an individual) and connectedness (mutuality: self in relation to significant others). Individuation is neither self-effacing nor egotistical. Self-individuation then means:

- knowing your authentic self—your life-affirming intrapsychic forces—in a situation;
- acknowledging, accepting, and acting congruently on your awareness;
- discriminating between experiences in one's relationships (especially between issues and situations involving one's spouse, family of origin, or children).

In the first session, partners learn how to nurture their own healthful self-focus and personal development (maintaining an autonomous self in a relationship system) by exercising:

- self-awareness, understanding (de-idealization), and delineation (boundaries). Participants learn how to know themselves realistically, recognizing and acknowledging the parts or aspects that constitute their experience and influence their behavior. Blind spots are reduced.
- validation and confidence. Participants are encouraged to examine the validity of their observations, thoughts, feelings, wants, and actions and to trust their experience, recognizing that it is real and has consequence for them.
- ownership and responsibility. By acknowledging and taking responsibility for their awareness, participants realize that they both contribute to and respond to situations and issues.
- assertion-agency. Partners also realize that they can direct and put their awareness to work for themselves and their relationship. They find that they can determine the quality of their communication.
- congruent disclosure. By skillfully matching and communicating what is said and done, participants develop more healthful, meaningful, satisfying, and productive relationships.
- self-esteem. In contrast to overvaluing self (narcissism) or undervaluing self (self-deprecation), self-focus and the processes of individuation—valuing and caring for self—build self-esteem.
- choice and commitment. Increased self-awareness and self-esteem help participants to act constructively on their choices.

Session II: Caring for Your Partner

Session II focuses on caring for one's partner: differentiating and building other-esteem. Expanding other-awareness and understanding is critical to building a viable relationship.

Other-focus skills are taught by:

1. reviewing the Awareness Wheel, the foundation for tracking other-awareness;
2. learning five listening skills that facilitate accurate and constructive other-focus;
3. practicing the Listening Cycle®, a skills strategy for acquiring high-quality other-information, particularly in complex and stressful situations.

Gaining competence in these areas demonstrates other-focus and facilitates other-awareness. Participants learn:

- *to follow rather than to lead.* The quickest way to connect with another person is to follow rather than to lead. The typical inclination for most people is to lead rather than to follow. Attentive listening relinquishes control to the other person in order to gain the best available other-awareness. Following usually builds trust, too.
- *to pursue understanding before agreement.* In our high-pressured, fast-paced, action-oriented world, the cultural bias is to act before—or without—understanding. The other-focused, attentive listening skills provide positive alternatives to habits that are often negative.
- *to heighten self-receptivity and responsiveness.* Actively engaging the conscious mind with listening skills reduces the potential for internal or external distraction.
- *to communicate concern and validate the partner's experience.* The act of attending, accepting, supporting, and empathizing with—but not necessarily always agreeing with—the other's awareness is an affirming, esteem-building activity. It also signals respect for one's partner and the valuing of difference. These behaviors, more than any others, strengthen a relationship.
- *to reduce resistance.* The quickest way to reduce self- and other-resistance is to listen to the other person (particularly in pressured, stressful situations).

Session III: Resolving Conflicts: Mapping Issues

Session III focuses on learning to resolve conflicts: collaborating in esteem-building ways.

Our own experience and other research (Markman, 1987; Notarius & Markman, 1993) indicate that both the level of relationship satisfaction and, frequently, the continued existence of a relationship itself depend on the quality of communication and the abilities of partners to resolve conflicts effectively.

During Session III, participants are shown specifically how to resolve conflicts more effectively by:

1. learning a framework of functional and dysfunctional options for handling conflict;
2. identifying their own patterns of conflict resolution and levels of satisfaction with those process and outcome patterns;
3. learning and applying the eight-step "mapping-an-issue" collaborative process based on the six talking and five listening skills taught in Sessions I and II.

While individuation and differentiation comprise the major theoretical concepts underlying Sessions I and II, respectively, collaboration is the major concept underlying Session III.

Collaboration means working together (combining information) as a partnership-team (whole) with a common purpose for the good of all partner-members (parts). The process of collaboration incorporates the best of individuation and differentiation.

The mapping-an-issue model operationalizes a *self–other–system focus* for collaboration around conflict-resolving and decision-making processes. The model has a number of practical features that grow out of theoretical considerations. It enables partners to:

- show respect to each other by first establishing a contract and setting up procedures to work through an issue or conflict;
- work in a systematic linear (stepwise) fashion while incorporating non-linear (associational) information;
- use the structure of issues and situations to consider, organize, and understand "soft" subjective information in a rational, objective way;
- reduce partial awareness;
- attend to process and outcome;
- identify one's own contribution (past action) and response (current action) to an issue or situation;
- incorporate both partners' concerns and wants;
- maintain focus on the central issue rather than on tangents;
- be action oriented, while restraining tendencies to pre-close on issues;
- test solutions for mutual fit;
- work collaboratively to create systemic outcomes that neither partner would probably have generated individually.

Partners within a well-differentiated relationship are able to handle conflicts and interpersonal tensions constructively. In fact, differences about various issues or situations help partners grow and develop as they renegotiate their balance of autonomy and intimacy across phases of development.

Session IV: Choosing Communication Styles

Session IV helps partners identify and distinguish between the positive and negative impacts of different styles of communication, or alternative ways of talking and listening together.

The content taught in this session encourages partners to take better charge of their lives and relationship by choosing more situationally appropriate and effective ways of communicating.

This is taught in COUPLE COMMUNICATION by:

1. presenting a map of four basic styles (styles I through IV) of talking and listening;
2. having participants identify their own typical style;
3. integrating the Awareness Wheel and specific talking and listening skills with styles III and IV;
4. practicing "straight talk" and "attentive listening" in the discussion of a real issue.

The concepts of individuation, differentiation, and collaboration are reflected most visibly in the styles of communication partners use as they relate to each other over the course of time. In this way, styles of communication serve as an index of a couple's relationship.

Less differentiated couples frequently speak for each other, assume, and use "control talk, "attempting to direct and persuade each other. As pressure increases and they do not know how to incorporate their differences functionally, partners easily slip into "fight and spite talk." Fight and spite talk are generally dysfunctional ways of signaling unresolved issues. In time, interactional dissatisfaction increases, and these couples become highly conflicted couples.

Boszormenyi-Nagy and Spark (1973) assert that "genuine dialogue" is the necessary context within which mature individuation must occur. The self–other caring attitudes operationalized through the talking and listening skills used in search talk and straight talk facilitate genuine dialogue—connecting and collaborating rather than controlling and coercing. These styles support the congruent alignment of internal experience with external expression.

The graphic on the next page summarizes the interrelationship of COUPLE COMMUNICATION sessions and theoretical concepts.

☐ Specific Methods and Strategies for Intervention

Maxicontract

The program begins with a *maxicontracting* session. Either in person or by telephone, the instructor uses an informational brochure on the program

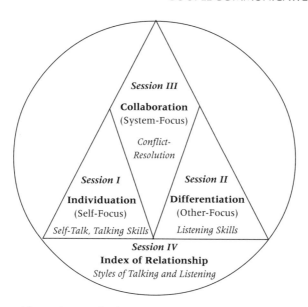

to contract with each couple for participation. The maxicontract assures that both partners understand the goals and nature of the program, and that both want to participate. Since the program is for couples, both partners must be willing to participate.

While the maxicontract only takes about 10 to 15 minutes, on average, this initial contact is worth a session in itself. Any difficulty such as poor attendance, low involvement, or unfulfilled expectations during the program can easily be traced to a poor or nonexistent maxicontract. Whether the program is taught with up to 12 couples as an enrichment event or integrated into a conjoint marriage therapy plan, establishing a maxicontract is essential.

Program Materials for Couples

When a couple decides to participate in COUPLE COMMUNICATION they also purchase a "couple packet" that includes:

- two *Talking and Listening Together* workbooks (Miller, Nunnally, Wachman, & Miller, 1991), one for each partner;
- two "skills mats" (one for talking and the other for listening): large canvas floor mats that are accelerated, kinesthetic learning tools to help partners practice and apply skills;
- two sets of pocket cards (four cards in each set) for review, reinforcement, and practice of skills.

These supports are used in preparation for sessions, as well as during and following the program.

Minicontracts

Couples learn to create *minicontracts* during the program. Minicontracting precedes any group activity in which the couples would be discussing an issue in front of other couple participants and receiving feedback from them. The minicontract puts couples in charge of their own disclosure and learning by deciding:

1. if they want to participate in a particular exercise;
2. which issue to talk about that would be appropriate in the context, respecting their privacy and individual or couple boundaries;
3. if they want feedback on their skill usage from other participants and the instructor.

The minicontract enhances partners' sense of agency—being able to choose what, when, where, and how to communicate. Outside the program, partners are also encouraged to take charge and schedule their discussions of important and stressful issues.

Session Design Activities

Both the group and conjoint COUPLE COMMUNICATION instructional designs make use of multimethod (auditory, visual, and kinesthetic) experiential learning activities. The design for each session includes the following seven teaching methods:

- *Assessments* of participants' *typical* and *desired* communication and skill behaviors. By "asking" partners to determine how they communicate before (prequestionnaire), during (action plans), and after (postquestionnaire) the program, the assessments provide them with benchmarks for setting learning goals and measuring change.
- *Presentations* of cognitive maps, processes, and skills. This "telling" is designed to organize, create, and interrelate conceptual understanding of the materials taught in COUPLE COMMUNICATION.
- *Demonstrations* of skills and processes. "Showing" partners, using either live or video examples, models the use of skills and processes for participants. Instructors themselves must be able to do accurately and appropriately anything they ask participants to do.
- *Practice exercises* of skills and processes. "Doing"—actually experimenting with and rehearsing skills with real issues—is a critical part of the experiential learning process. Research findings on the program indicate that couples highly value the skill practice time during sessions and benefit from the program proportionately to the extent that they practice and incorporate the material into their lives between sessions.

- *Feedback* and coaching on use of skills and processes. Blanchard, noted author of *The One Minute Manager* (Blanchard & Johnson, 1993), says "feedback is the breakfast of champions." Without feedback—specific, accurate, and timely—and coaching, a person has no way of knowing how well or poorly he or she is doing in the learning and application of new behaviors. Feedback and coaching are built into both the practice demonstrations and the practice exercises.
- *Application* of maps, processes, and skills. The goal of COUPLE COMMUNICATION is to have a positive impact on the day-to-day communication interaction of couples. Applying (transferring and integrating) the program materials to real issues in day-to-day situations is the ultimate test of the program's effectiveness.
- *Transfer of learning:* The program is best taught with time between sessions (a week or so) in order for partners to apply the skills, day-to-day, together.

Communication Skills Mats: Accelerated Learning Tools

A unique feature of COUPLE COMMUNICATION is the use of skills mats—one for talking and another for listening—which partners use to prompt skill practice during and between sessions. Each floor mat is a 30-inch square canvas printed with either the Awareness Wheel or the Listening Cycle frameworks on them. As partners actually step about on the mats, the tools *structure* who talks and who listens; help partners *delimit* and *focus* on a single issue; *slow down* interaction; facilitate *clear, direct,* and *congruent* talking; access *deeper* and *richer* information; reduce *defensive* listening; and substitute *concrete constructive* skills (options) for *destructive* habits.

With a mat, the left side of one's brain responds to the *digital information* of a framework (words and concepts) while the right side of the brain accesses *analogical information* (associated experience). A person may actively use all three channels—visual, auditory, and kinesthetic—simultaneously. Participants consciously link and integrate concepts with experience. For instance, by stepping about on the Awareness Wheel skills mat, a participant learns how to access and process sensate, cognitive, affective, conative, and behavioral information more clearly and accurately.

The mats also leverage learning. An instructor is able to teach more material to more people more effectively in less time. A number of couples can be working simultaneously around a large room, practicing skills and receiving feedback and coaching. Couples use the skills mats during each session and between sessions for skill practice. Then they retain them for continued use, skill review, and reinforcement.

These simple yet powerful learning tools have created a breakthrough in communication-skills training by actively engaging the whole brain and body in learning. In short, they accelerate and extend skill learning and retention.

☐ Qualities and Role of the Instructor or Facilitator

Instructors come from a variety of human service professions, including graduate study in psychology, social work, counseling, psychiatry, family life education, and pastoral studies. Most COUPLE COMMUNICATION instructors are active practitioners (therapists, counselors, ministers, or teachers) in one of a variety of settings.

Congruence and Recursiveness

Besides an instructor's professional training, the most important characteristic of an effective COUPLE COMMUNICATION instructor is his or her personal and relational congruence. As a matter of ethics, COUPLE COMMUNICATION instructors are asked "to practice what they teach." That is, the instructors are expected to use the concepts and skills in their own daily lives to build relationships and resolve conflicts. Second, the teachers must be able to recognize and use the concepts accurately. For example, they must know the difference between a thought and a feeling (emotion) and not confuse the two in their language. Personal and interpersonal congruence has its recursive effects on training. If an instructor is saying one thing and doing another, his or her effectiveness is diminished.

Leading by Example

Also, as a general rule, participants in COUPLE COMMUNICATION are not asked to do anything the instructor is unable or unwilling to do. In each session instructors are encouraged to demonstrate personally the concepts or skills using a real and current issue of their own choosing, before involving any other person or couple in the exercise.

Certified Instructors Ensure Quality

Finally, while not all professionals who attend COUPLE COMMUNICATION instructor training become certified COUPLE COMMUNICATION instructors, they are all encouraged to do so.

The benefits of certification to the instructor include couple referrals from Interpersonal Communication Programs, Inc. and discounts on quantity purchases of couple packets. Instructors are required to use couple packets with each couple they take through the program. Instructors are free to set their own fees (charges for the program) with couples. COUPLE COMMUNICATION is not franchised.

The COUPLE COMMUNICATION instructor certification is a thorough process that includes:

- study and training, including attending an instructor workshop;
- evaluation by couple participants (as well as self-evaluation);
- written examination;
- agreement to a set of ethical practices.

☐ Application of the Preventive Model to a Couple at Risk

Alyssa heard about the COUPLE COMMUNICATION program at her church. She thought the program would provide a useful activity for the two of them to do together. She picked up a COUPLE COMMUNICATION brochure and later asked Ben if he would be willing to consider participating in the program. Ben looked over the program description and had some reservations about taking any program offered at her church, but was willing to consider it when he found out that COUPLE COMMUNICATION was nonsectarian. He liked the idea that COUPLE COMMUNICATION focused on gaining practical communication skills and conflict-resolving tools to help the two of them deal more effectively with their real issues. He also thought enhancing his skills might be helpful in his law practice.

The two met with the COUPLE COMMUNICATION instructor for their maxicontract in a brief session to learn more about the program and to discuss any important questions or concerns. When they mutually agreed to participate, the instructor provided them with a "couple packet" including workbooks, skills mats, and pocket cards. The instructor also gave them directions for completing their prework, including a self-assessment questionnaire indicating how they were currently communicating with their partner and how they wished to talk, listen, and resolve conflicts as the result of the course. (Partners retake the same self-assessment at the end of COUPLE COMMUNICATION to see how their communication has changed.)

Session I

After briefly meeting the other eight couples in the group, the partners are introduced to the Awareness Wheel as a tool to help each participant work through and talk about issues more clearly. Each partner (in consultation with the other) is given the opportunity to select a current issue of his or her own choosing (but separate from the one the partner chooses to process) for practice using the Awareness Wheel.

The instructor first demonstrates how to use the Awareness Wheel skills mat, using a real issue from his or her own life. A coaching demonstration is also provided that shows couples how to coach each other using the support tools. Then couples separate into small-group foursomes (two couples each) to practice using the Awareness Wheel to process (talk about) each of their own issues.

In Ben and Alyssa's foursome, the other two partners were the first to step about the skills mat and self-talk their issues. At first, Ben thought the mats were silly, but as he observed and coached the other two, he found himself becoming engaged by the process. In fact, Ben was willing to be number three on the mat. As he stepped on the mat he identified his issue as job dissatisfaction. He began by saying that he thought he was trapped and believed his work was not challenging or personally rewarding. Then he moved to data, and gave a couple of examples to illustrate the lack of challenge. Next he stepped on the feeling zone and expressed his frustration and disappointment with his career and work. The want zone was also easy for Ben, because he wanted to make a change in his work, but he was not sure exactly what it should be. He thought it might be a career in commercial real estate (stepping tentatively to the thought zone). He also had a want for Alyssa: that she not be anxious about his career and restlessness. Ben then moved to current actions and described his current actions as mainly just dragging himself to work with low energy for his activities there. He declined to step on future action because he was not ready to do so, and was not sure what to do next. As he stepped off the mat, he commented to the group that, even though he did not know what his future action would be yet, it was helpful to talk directly about what he was experiencing.

Alyssa's issue was her apprehension about the birth of their second child. After identifying her issue, she stepped on the feeling zone and said she was scared. Then she went to data and began recalling several key events from the premature birth of their first child. She stepped next to wants and said she really hoped for a healthy baby, with no complications, but (moving to actions) said she could not help but worry and recall the difficulties of the prior birth. Alyssa then jumped to thoughts, saying she would never have gotten through the first six months with a new baby without Ben's cooperation and help. Then she stepped on feelings and expressed her appreciation briefly to Ben for the way he shared the sleepless nights. Next she stepped on "wants for other" and told Ben she hoped this next baby would not be so taxing for him or for her (as she shifted to "wants for self"). After a comfortable pause, she stepped on future action and said she would say a prayer, and exercise her faith rather than worry, when she felt anxious.

Session II

The second session focused on listening. Alyssa asked Ben if he would be willing to use the listening skills presented in the course to listen to her talk about the way he listens to her. He agreed, and in the practice foursome, Ben used the Listening Cycle floor mat to practice the listening skills. Alyssa told Ben how annoying it had been to her, at several points during the week, when he began giving advice, rather than just trying to understand what she had been saying. Ben struggled not to say "I understand," but rather acknowledged (with a word or two that actually demonstrated understanding) what Alyssa was saying about his listening. It was also unnatural for him to invite (encourage and allow) Alyssa to continue talking, but he did. She explained how she thought that when they were first married, they did not have many differences, but now as bigger, tougher issues were emerging as a normal part of life, the need to help each other be understood was calling for more skill. Ben did not respond, but rather made an accurate summary. The other man in the foursome, moving around nervously, said, "Ben, I didn't think you were going to be able to summarize. Good job!"

When it was Alyssa's turn to listen, she also practiced the skills to give Ben a good hearing. Ben's issue was shifting into commercial real estate. At the last COUPLE COMMUNICATION session and throughout the past week, Ben had begun to let go of some negative energy as he thought about his future action zone. What kept bubbling up in his awareness was the possibility of starting his own independent business. He was excited to tell Alyssa and flowed from one idea to another, such as talking to his uncle who had done well as an attorney but had also had his hand in some other deals; borrowing some money to supplement their savings, if necessary, to get started; maybe even downsizing to a smaller house. As Ben spoke, Alyssa felt excited and anxious as she was bombarded with Ben's thinking. The coaches helped her actively focus on her listening skills rather than on reacting to and stifling Ben. Finally, Alyssa asked a question (and made a statement); "When would you quit your job? I'm concerned because we need the medical benefits."

Time for the exercise was up. The instructor urged the couples to use their skills mats to continue their discussion of issues at home during the week. He also reminded them to use "time outs" and "check process" (on the skills mats) as needed to stay on a skillful path. Alyssa commented to the rest of the foursome as they started to go back to their chairs, "I guess sometimes I am not a very good listener."

For homework between sessions, Ben chose to practice the acknowledging skill and Alyssa decided to focus on the skill of inviting.

Session III

Once partners have learned to use the Awareness Wheel (Session I) and Listening Cycle skills mats (Session II), they put the two mats together (in Session III) and use their full repertoire of skills to practice resolving an issue of conflict. The process is called "mapping-an-issue."

Ben and Alyssa's list of potential issues included time together, number of children, and borrowing money (possibly from Alyssa's parents) to start a new business. During their minicontract, they decided to focus on number of children and to lead off (together as a couple) in the evening practice foursome.

The mapping-an-issue process involves the following eight steps:

Step 1. Identify and define the issue.
Step 2. Contract to work through the issue (the minicontract covers Steps 1 and 2).
Step 3. Understand the issue completely.
Step 4. Identify wants.
Step 5. Generate options.
Step 6. Choose actions.
Step 7. Test the action plan.
Step 8. Evaluate the outcome (eventually).

Ben was eager to step onto the Awareness Wheel skills mat to begin on Step 3 (understand the issue).

He moved right to the feeling zone and said he was feeling upset because he thought (as he stepped onto the thought zone) that he had been somewhat betrayed by the suddenness of the second pregnancy, having never discussed (action zone) another pregnancy with Alyssa. Moving back to feelings, he said he felt scared about having to support two children before he was ready to do so. He also added that he was even more afraid every time he heard Alyssa (sensory data zone) mention having three children. After Alyssa accurately summarized Ben's awareness-experience, she moved to the talking mat as Ben shifted to the listening mat.

Alyssa began on the action zone by saying that when she had mentioned having three children, she was just fantasizing during the times she was enjoying staying home with their first child. She had not been aware that her occasional statements were so frightening to Ben. Shifting to thoughts, she said she did not really believe she could go through a third pregnancy physically and emotionally, even if this second pregnancy went well. And for all her worry about this pregnancy, she was happy (feeling zone) to be pregnant again (feeling zone) but heard (sensory data zone) that Ben was scared. She ended with recalling their premarried conversations about becoming a two-child family.

They checked their process and agreed to move on to Step 4. Ben began by standing on the want zone and saying, "For me, I only want two kids and I do not want to be stuck in a law practice for six more years. I want out. I also want to enjoy our kids. For you [Alyssa], I want to help share raising our children, and not just have that be your thing. For us, I would like to have more time alone together."

Alyssa took her turn on the want zone saying, "For me, I want to be at home until both of our children are in school. I want to be able to nurture our two children. For you [Ben], I want to support you in finding more engaging and rewarding work. And in all of this, I, too, would like to protect our time together and have more of it."

In Step 5 they generated (brainstormed) possible solutions based on the information they had shared. Standing on the thought zone, Ben said, "I could begin looking into commercial real estate, maybe even talk to senior partners about doing some of this work in the firm. Your dad has done well with some real estate investments. Maybe we could talk with him on our visit this summer."

Alyssa thought she could do some reading and informal study to support Ben in exploring commercial real estate. She also thought she could stop talking about having a third child and just focus on how much she enjoyed being home with their child and getting things ready for the one they were expecting. She thought it was also important to make time to be together.

For Step 6, each partner was willing to commit to a future action. Ben affirmed his intention to support Alyssa through her pregnancy and their second child's early months. He also determined to start exploring the field of commercial real estate. Alyssa committed herself to no longer scaring Ben with talk of having three children and said she would be willing to cut back on some of her time at church activities to be sure she and Ben had more time alone together.

As they visualized themselves carrying out their action plans in Step 7, Ben expressed some caution about not letting her dad take over their interest in real estate if they spoke to Alyssa's parents about it this summer.

Notice that, while partners are discussing real issues in each session, the major focus of COUPLE COMMUNICATION is on *process*: using the skills mats to coach skill use. Even in these examples, we are more interested in the process of how a couple talks and listens to each other than with the particular *content* or *outcome* of the issue. Our experience confirms that if partners learn how to process issues effectively, they can tackle any content and create their own best-fit, collaborative solutions.

Session IV

This last session introduces couples to "styles of communication," a map for recognizing and altering, if necessary, their own ways of thinking and listening. In this session they practiced style III (search talk and explorative listening) and style IV (straight talk and attentive listening) while considering the possibility of asking Alyssa's parents to loan them money to back up Ben's career shift. They found this potential rehearsal enlightening and useful.

☐ Empirical Evaluation and Research

Over the years, COUPLE COMMUNICATION has become a seasoned and well-researched program. Many independent investigators have continued to study COUPLE COMMUNICATION. The strengths of COUPLE COMMUNICATION, as evidenced by the research findings, have been maintained in its 1991 revision. Also, the revised program has addressed the areas where research suggested a need for improvement.

Over 40 independent, quantitative outcome studies have been performed, including 34 doctoral dissertations and six published articles, as well as a meta-analysis (Butler, Wampler, & Serovich, 1995; Wampler, 1990). (An additional 25 masters-level or unpublished studies have been conducted.)

The impact and effectiveness of CC have been tested on over 500 couples since its inception in 1971 (Butler, Wampler, & Serovich, 1995). The program has been studied in counseling and therapy centers, educational institutions, and the community at large, literally all over the United States (Butler, Wampler, & Serovich, 1995). More research is currently in process.

COUPLE COMMUNICATION's credibility as a foundation for short-term, solution-oriented treatment intervention is well established. The collection of research on the program indicates that couples make significant changes in four to six sessions. Findings relevant to clinical practice are discussed below.

Distressed Couples and Problem Solving

In research exploring the effectiveness of COUPLE COMMUNICATION with distressed couples, findings show that it:

- affects highly distressed couples positively and is capable of helping these couples turn their relationships around. The impact of the program on distressed couples has been compared with that on non-distressed couples (Aldridge & Aldridge, 1983; Sarnoff, 1988).
- increases the problem-solving communication between partners (Glander, 1985; Trost, 1985).
- allows the couple to work out problems in a constructive way so that both partners feel satisfied with the solutions reached (Larson & Holman, 1994; Smith, 1989).

Communication Skill and Relationship Satisfaction

Researchers have examined the effectiveness of COUPLE COMMUNICATION for constructive communication skill use and marital satisfaction in relationships. The findings about the program show:

- consistent, positive, and very large effects on communication behavior within relationships, when compared to relationships of couples who do not participate in COUPLE COMMUNICATION training (Busick, 1982; Russell, Bagarozzi, Atilanao, & Morris, 1984);
- consistent, moderate positive effects on couple perceptions of the quality of their communication and the overall quality of their relationship (Miller, 1971; Nunnally, 1972; Sarnoff, 1988; Trost, 1985);
- an extended impact. As with other intervention programs, the impact of COUPLE COMMUNICATION lessens as time goes on; however, the program still has a positive impact on relationship satisfaction and on communication behavior several months after it is completed (Busick, 1982; Sarnoff, 1988).

Self-Esteem and Self-Disclosure

Believing that a person's own self-esteem has a significant impact on the success and viability of a relationship, several researchers have explored how self-esteem and statements of self-disclosure are improved using the COUPLE COMMUNICATION program. Findings show that:

- self-esteem and self-concept improve as a result of learning the skills offered in COUPLE COMMUNICATION (Busick, 1982; Coleman, 1979; Dillon, 1976);

- a significant increase in the number and the content of self-disclosure statements between partners results from involvement in COUPLE COMMUNICATION. Improvements in statements of self-disclosure often demonstrate a healthier self-esteem (Fleming, 1977; Valenti, 1989).

Various Age and Socioeconomic Groups

Research documents that COUPLE COMMUNICATION is successful with a wide range of couples, including:

- couples of different ages (Schaffer, 1981);
- couples from varying socioeconomic groups (Burnham, 1984).

In general:

- the program is effective for distressed couples as well as for well-functioning couples;
- couples seem to enjoy the experience, as few drop out of the program;
- no negative effects of the program were found.

☐ Summary

The following characteristics of COUPLE COMMUNICATION make it practical and accountable. The program is:

- *treatment-plan friendly:* offers simple and straightforward objectives and interventions;
- *structured:* provides better learning;
- *time bounded:* supports brief therapy;
- *widely applicable:* can be taught effectively as enrichment or relationship education;
- *built on experiential methods:* uses accelerated learning tools;
- *focused on life-long competencies:* empowers participants to create their own solutions to issues, and to resolve conflicts.

Future Research on COUPLE COMMUNICATION

Several studies on COUPLE COMMUNICATION are in process and more research is welcome. Future research could well focus on these areas:

1. The effects of skill mats on communication-skills learning. All of the studies reported in this paper were conducted before the invention and incorporation of the skills mats into the COUPLE COMMUNICA-

TION program. The responses to using skills mats as a teaching tool have been very positive. However, no comparative study has been done to date on the impact of these new tools.

2. The effects of different training designs and intervention formats. While the positive outcomes of COUPLE COMMUNICATION have been well documented, more study needs to be done comparing, for example, weekend workshops with once-a-week training and other mixed group and conjoint variations.

3. The relative outcomes of couple therapies that do and do not build the COUPLE COMMUNICATION program into the treatment plan.

4. The managed care delivery context. COUPLE COMMUNICATION meets all the criteria for time- and cost-effective managed-care preventive psychoeducation. The coauthors of COUPLE COMMUNICATION are eager to collaborate with a managed care organization (and, in fact, have a research design ready) to study the short- and long-term effects of COUPLE COMMUNICATION in this relatively new health care delivery context.

☐ Contact References

For a brochure about COUPLE COMMUNICATION instructor training, materials, and certification, call 1-800-328-5099.

☐ References

Aldridge, R. G., & Aldridge, C. H. (1983). Couple communication: An analysis of two divergent student groups. *Corrective and Social Psychiatry and Journal of Behavior Technology, Methods, and Therapy, 29*, 36–38.

Bertalanffy, L. V. (1950). An outline of General System Theory. *British Journal of the Philosophy of Science, 1*, 134–65.

Blanchard, K., & Johnson, S. (1993). *The One Minute Manager.* New York: Berkley.

Boszormenyi-Nagy, I., & Spark, G. (1973). *Invisible loyalties.* New York: Harper & Row.

Burnham, R. A. (1984). Effects of the Couple Communication Program on the marital and family communication of high and low socioeconomic status couples (Doctoral dissertation, University of Notre Dame, 1984). *Dissertation Abstracts International, 45*, 1006B–1007B. (University Microfilms No. 84-14128)

Busick, C. A. (1982). The effects of communication training on marital communication, marital satisfaction and self-concept (Doctoral dissertation, Texas A & M University, 1982). *Dissertation Abstracts International, 43*, 725A. (University Microfilms No. 82-19094)

Butler, M. H., Wampler, K. S., & Serovich, J. S. (1995). *An update of meta-analysis of the Couple Communication research.* Unpublished manuscript.

Coleman, E. J. (1979). Effects of communication skill training on the outcome of a sex counseling program (Doctoral dissertation, University of Minnesota, 1978). *Dissertation Abstracts International, 39*, 7234A. (University Microfilms No. 79-11, 990)

Dillon, J. D. (1976). Marital communication and its relation to self-esteem (Doctoral dissertation, United States International University, 1975). *Dissertation Abstracts International, 36,* 5862B. (University Microfilms No. 76-10, 585)

Fleming, M. J. (1977). An evaluation of a structured program designed to teach communication skills and concepts to couples: A field study (Doctoral dissertation, Florida State University, 1976). *Dissertation Abstracts International, 37,* 7633A-7634A. (University Microfilms No. 77-13, 315)

Glander, M. H. (1985). A case study approach to the "Couple Communication Program" (Doctoral dissertation, North Carolina State University at Raleigh, 1984). *Dissertation Abstracts International, 46,* 613A. (University Microfilms No. 85-06994)

Larson, J. H., & Holman, T. B. (1994). Premarital predictors of marital quality and stability. *Family Relations, 43,* 228–237.

Markman, H. J. (1987). *The prediction and prevention of marital distress: Summary of results.* Annual report. Washington, DC: National Institute of Mental Health.

Miller, S. L. (1971). The effects of communication training in small groups upon self-disclosure and openness in engaged couples' systems of interaction: A field experiment (Doctoral dissertation, University of Minnesota, 1971). *Dissertation Abstracts International, 32,* 2819A-2820A. (University Microfilms No. 71-28, 263)

Miller, S. L., Miller, P. A., Nunnally, E. W., & Wackman, D. B. (1992). *Couple communication instructor manual.* Denver-Littleton, CO: Interpersonal Communication Programs.

Miller, S. L, Nunnally, E. W., Wachman, D. B., & Miller, P. A. (1991). *Talking and listening together.* Denver-Littleton, CO: Interpersonal Communication Programs.

Miller, J. G. (1978). *Living systems.* New York: McGraw-Hill.

Notarius, C., & Markman, H., (1993). *We can work it out: Making sense of marital conflict.* New York: Putnam.

Nunnally, E. W. (1972). Effects of communication training upon interaction awareness and empathic accuracy of engaged couples: A field experiment (Doctoral dissertation, University of Minnesota, 1971). *Dissertation Abstracts International, 32,* 4736A. (University Microfilms No. 72-05, 561)

Russell, C. S., Bagarozzi, D. A., Atilanao, R. B., & Morris, J. E. (1984). A comparison of two approaches to marital enrichment and conjugal skills training: Minnesota Couples Communication Program and Structured Behavioral Exchange Contracting. *American Journal of Family Therapy, 12,* 13–25.

Sarnoff, S. M. (1988). *The effectiveness of a communication skills training program with maritally distressed couples.* Unpublished doctoral dissertation, California Coast University.

Schaffer, M. (1981). An evaluation of the Minnesota Couple Communication program upon communication of married couples (Doctoral dissertation, University of Southern Mississippi, 1980). *Dissertation Abstracts International, 41,* 4643B. (University Microfilms No. 81-09,897)

Smith, P. (1989). *Couple communication skills training: Its impact on the individual, couple relational life, and perceived satisfaction.* Unpublished doctoral dissertation, California Graduate School of Family Psychology.

Trost, J. A. (1985). The influence of Couple Communication Program on the marital satisfaction of distressed couples (Doctoral dissertation, The Professional School for Psychological Studies, San Diego, CA 1985). *Dissertation Abstracts International, 49,* 1715A. (University Microfilms No. 88-16, 361)

Valenti, F. T. (1989). *Effects of the Couple Communication Program I on the marital adjustment, self-disclosure, and communication style of therapy and non-therapy participants.* Unpublished doctoral dissertation, University of North Carolina.

Wampler, K. S. (1990). An update of research on the Couple Communication Program. *Family Science Review, 3,* 21–40.

7
CHAPTER

Jon Carlson, Psy.D., Ed.D.
Don Dinkmeyer, Sr., Ph.D.

TIME for a Better Marriage

☐ Introduction

The movement to enrich marriages and to provide education rather than therapy for couples is usually credited as beginning a little over two decades ago. The historical roots of marriage enrichment are generally traced to Barcelona, Spain, where a group of married couples met in January 1962 for a weekend marriage enrichment retreat with Father Gabriel Calvo. It is from this meeting that the worldwide network of marriage encounter resulted.

Historians, however, appear to be unaware that Dreikurs published the book *The Challenge of Marriage* in 1946. This book was based on the thoughts he had developed 10 or more years earlier. Dreikurs predicted correctly that "normal" people would need help in dealing with the "normal" problems and frustrations of living together. He saw the shifting switch from autocratic to democratic living and hoped to help partners learn to live as equals.

Since that time, many programs have been developed to help couples learn how to build loving, satisfying, and lasting relationships. Most married couples want to stay married. They want the advantages of a happy marriage: a longer and healthier life, love, acceptance, emotional support, greater economic achievement, and children. Couples need skills for living in today's companionate relationships. Traditional marriage was based on roles fixed by gender. Men worked and provided home and food, while women bore children and nurtured the family. Marital success was judged by how well these roles were fulfilled.

In companionate marriages, marriage roles and relationships are discussed and negotiated. Both partners have the skills necessary to:

1. identify and align their goals with their partner's;
2. encourage their partners, including through "encouragement meetings" and "encouraging days";
3. develop honest, congruent communication;
4. develop an understanding of how their beliefs, feelings, and goals influence their communication;
5. listen empathically, express feelings accurately, and practice these skills in marriage meetings;
6. learn to make helpful choices in their marriage;
7. develop a process for resolving conflict; and
8. develop self-help skills for building and maintaining an equal marriage.

Marriage begins on a high note with expressions of love and respect between bride and groom. However, when partners in a couple do not have the necessary skills to sustain good relationships, the marriage can deteriorate.

In reviewing the literature, we could not find any comprehensive resources that dealt with the roles and skills that partners needed to learn. The response to previous publications that attempted to teach these skills, including *Systematic Training for Effective Parenting* (STEP; Dinkmeyer & McKay, 1976), *Systematic Training for Effective Parenting of Teens* (STEP/Teen; Dinkmeyer & McKay, 1983), *Developing Understanding of Self and Others* (DUSO; Dinkmeyer & Dinkmeyer, Jr., 1982), and *Systematic Training for Effective Teaching* (STET; Dinkmeyer, McKay, & Dinkmeyer, Jr., 1980) was overwhelming. People did want to learn effective living skills and they were willing to go to group meetings to learn these skills.

As psychologists trained in the work of Alfred Adler, we were very interested in prevention and in teaching people skills before problems occurred. We also realized that all of our previous work grew out of the primary relationship, that between husband and wife, but nowhere in our work did we directly deal with this relationship. In response to the need for a skill-based marriage program, Training in Marriage Enrichment (TIME) was developed.

TIME is an educational program designed to help married couples learn the skills they need to build a loving, supportive relationship. In TIME groups, couples develop skills that enable them to enrich their marriages and to deal with particular challenges that they experience. Couples define the marriage they want and develop and retain the skills to maintain that relationship. Participation in a TIME group does not imply that a couple has an ineffective marriage or marriage problems. Rather, a couple's participation is an indication that they want to grow and to strengthen their relationship.

☐ Theoretical Underpinnings

TIME reflects a primarily Adlerian (Adler, 1931; Dreikurs, 1950) or sociopsychological approach to human relationships. Many concepts are similar to those that appeared in *Systematic Training for Effective Parenting* (Dinkmeyer & McKay, 1976) and *Systematic Training for Effective Parenting of Teens* (Dinkmeyer & McKay, 1983).

The basic assumptions underlying Adlerian theory are that people are decision-making and socially oriented beings, and that all human behavior is purposeful (Dinkmeyer, Dinkmeyer, & Sperry, 1987). We behave according to the expectations of the social group in which we seek to belong. We are all trying to belong to and be a part of the social group in a manner that makes us unique. People belong by being the smartest, prettiest, angriest, etc.

We seek to understand marital relationships in terms of their purposes. Partners' goals for their marriage determine their behavior in it. We do not seek a causal explanation for behavior. There is no blaming of the past, parents, or other external factors. Instead, we look for the purpose of the symptom that keeps the marriage from being enriched. We believe marriages can be enriched because each partner has the capacity to choose—to act, not to react. People are relatively self-determining.

We behave according to how things seem to us—the subjective perceptions we create. Thus, our behavior is always a function of perception. However, perceptions can be modified through educational and enriching experiences.

An enriched marriage can be contrasted with a marriage in which the partners experience enthusiasm, energy, commitment, and mutual involvement infrequently. In an enriched marriage, each spouse has a feeling of personal worth and self-esteem. Each is willing to cooperate in the give and take of the relationship, to be willing at times to give without expecting to immediately receive. The system, then, is open, congruent, and cooperative.

Basic Principles of TIME

1. Developing and maintaining a good marriage relationship requires a time commitment. For a marriage to succeed, couples must make their relationship an important priority now and in the future.

2. Specific skills essential to a healthy marriage can be learned. When partners understand how a marriage works and the necessary skills for building a successful marriage, they can develop skills that create a positive, rewarding relationship.
3. Change often takes time, but all change begins with the individual. The first step in enriching a marriage involves a commitment to change. Partners begin by understanding how each of them has shaped their marriage and what each can do to make desired changes. Change takes time. Couples are encouraged to be patient with their rates of progress.
4. Feelings of love and caring that have diminished or disappeared often return with behavior changes. Romantic feelings, intimacy, and love can diminish over time in a marriage relationship. When feelings change, many couples needlessly believe that the relationship is over. The change in feelings may mean that partners are not being reinforced in the marriage and that the relationship deserves a higher priority. By viewing their relationship as intimate and satisfying, a couple can establish new behavior and feelings.
5. Small changes are very important in bringing about big changes. A happier relationship results from many small changes over a period of time. Even though both partners are committed to change, there may be times when unwanted patterns reappear. This does not mean that their new skills are not working. Couples are encouraged to continue focusing on the positive relationship they want.

Marriage Skills

The TIME program is organized systematically. Each of the 10 sessions is designed to present the principles of, and provide opportunties to practice, the necessary skills for enriching the marriage. The goal is to help couples apply and integrate the ideas and skills into their marriage relationship. This goal is achieved through reading, meaningful discussions, and application of the ideas and activity assignments and exercises. The couple is expected to work on specific skills (through "daily dialogue" and "encouragement meetings") and to assess goals and progress through the "My Plan" format. A cassette, *Time to Relax and Imagine* (Dinkmeyer & Carlson, 1984c), is a personal audiocassette designed to improve the marital relationship. In TIME sessions, couples learn and apply skills that will help them accept responsibility for their behavior; identify and align goals; encourage each other; identify factors that influence a marriage relationship and understand their responsibility in creating the desired relationship; communicate honestly and congruently; make choices (e.g., of thoughts, words, and actions) that support marriage goals; learn a process for resolving conflict; apply the conflict resolution to common marital challenges such as children, money, in-laws, friends, sex, religion, recreation, and alcohol and drug abuse. The couples themselves must commit to the process of maintaining an equal marriage.

☐ Specific Methods and Strategies for Intervention

Encouragement is basic to the TIME enrichment process. Encouragement provides the unconditional acceptance and valuing that all married partners need, regardless of whether their marriages are currently satisfying or unsatisfying.

While encouragement is a philosophy and attitude, it must be implemented by specific actions and skills. Some specific ways for TIME leaders to help couples put encouragement into practice are as follows.

1. Begin sessions by asking, "What's new and positive in your marriage?" This helps couples to refocus on the progress they are making.
2. Share with members your positive feelings and observations. "I like the way you listen"; "That sounds encouraging."
3. Encourage any movement towards incorporating encouragement meetings and "encouraging days" into couples' lives. Encouragement meetings provide a regular, systematic way to allow each partner to share the positive things they are seeing in each other and the relationship. Encouraging days are vehicles for learning what pleases your partner and ways to provide it on a daily basis.
4. Have an encouragement meeting in a session, asking members to share what they like about the way the marriage enrichment experience is going for them.
5. Encourage members to share any positive experiences. They can begin with phrases such as "I enjoyed," "I liked," or "I appreciated."
6. Have members write down five personal strengths that enable them to be encouraging partners.

☐ Format of Application

Participants prepare for each session by reading in advance the appropriate chapter of the couple resource book, *TIME for a Better Marriage* (Dinkmeyer & Carlson, 1984b).

The sessions proceed in the following sequence.

1. *Building Communication.* Several activities are used that focus on building communication. The activities are usually done as couples but may

involve some group interaction. These activities are designed to create an atmosphere of readiness for ensuing activities.

2. *Discussion of Activity for the Week.* Each week couples are expected to do one or more activities that reinforce the skill introduced in the previous session. At this point in the session, couples share their experience working with the activities of the week, followed by group discussion to provide support and encouragement. It is essential that couples participate regularly and enthusiastically in the activity assignments. These activities help to improve the marital relationship.

3. *Discussion of Reading.* Participants express the ideas, feelings, and attitudes that emerge as a result of the reading assignment. The discussion focuses on what they learned about themselves and the relationship.

4. *Presentation of the Recording.* The audiotapes for each session focus on the skill presented in the session. Participants practice the skill by responding to the audio-recorded interactions.

5. *Application.* The skill or concept introduced in the session is experienced and practiced through an activity.

6. *The "My Plan" form,* found at the end of each chapter, is filled out. This is a form on which partners write their concerns and commitments and assess their progress each week.

7. *Summary.* The summary is an essential part of each session. Each member contributes and identifies what he or she has learned during the session.

8. *Activities and Reading for the Week.* This is the assignment of the week's activity and reading for the next session.

Session 1: Accepting Responsibility

Session 1 focuses on the need for partners to individually accept responsibility for their behavior and for the success of their marriage. Couples learn about the positive goals of marriage—cooperation, contributing, accepting responsibilities, and encouraging—and they learn to recognize relationship-destroying goals, such as excusing shortcomings, power, control, and vengeance. They learn the importance of spending planned time together and preserving time for relaxation and time alone through a process called daily dialogue. In this process, the couple establishes a daily time for sharing. Each partner has five minutes of uninterrupted time to share hopes and fears, excitement and anxiety, joy and sorrow, pride and embarrassment, and apprehension and anger while their partner listens.

Session 2: Encouragement

Session 2 introduces the skills of encouragement, which include unconditional acceptance, recognizing effort, focusing on strengths, listening, empathy, being enthusiastic, and creating positive meanings or perceptual alternatives. It helps couples establish encouragement meetings and encouraging days, important activities that bring encouragement to their marriage on a regular basis. The importance of self-encouragement is also discussed.

Session 3: Priorities and Values

In Session 3, couples develop a better understanding of factors that influence their relationships, including their priorities, lifestyle, values, and destructive "games." They learn to identify their priorities and values. Discussions of lifestyle priorities include being in control, maintaining superiority, pleasing, and comfort seeking. The games that couples play are sophisticated, patterned maneuvers that are destructive to a marriage relationship. They tend to focus on individual power rather than on the growth of the relationship. Couples are taught to develop game-free relationships characterized by flexibility and empathy.

Session 4: Congruent Communication

Session 4 introduces the concept of congruent communication, which involves expressing whatever we are feeling and experiencing at the moment. Partners identify their communication styles. Four negative styles are: the placator, the blamer, the super responsible communicator, and the irrelevant communicator (Satir, 1972). Couples develop skills by using "I messages" that indicate that they are sharing a subjective view. Partners learn to express feelings and thoughts openly without being insensitive to their partner's needs.

Session 5: Listening and Responding to Whole Messages

In Session 5, couples develop an understanding of how beliefs, feelings, and goals influence communication. Partners practice communicating their thoughts and feelings on subjects of concern in their relationship. The following guidelines are recommended for improving communication:

1. Be aware of the feelings being shared.
2. Be aware of the intentions being shared.
3. Be aware of the beliefs being shared.
4. Strive for level, equal communication.
5. Be empathic. Hear, identify, and verbalize the other person's feelings.
6. Be responsible for your feelings.
7. Free each other to be. Encourage uniqueness.

Session 6: Communication Skills

Session 6 provides couples with the opportunity to practice effective listening skills, to hear the full message in the partner's words, and to indicate that they have heard and understood feelings as well as thoughts. This involves understanding nonverbal behavior and developing an awareness of our ideas, intentions, and feelings in order to communicate honestly, fully, and accurately. Also, guidelines for the marriage meeting are introduced and couples learn the procedure for marriage meetings.

Session 7: Choice-Making Skills

Session 7 focuses on the process of making choices that are helpful to a relationship and provides practice in identifying available choices and applying choice-making skills. When couples delay making choices that can improve marriage, they are in effect choosing to keep the marriage as it is. The importance of being realistic and honest with oneself and one's partner when making choices is emphasized. Couples are encouraged to make choices they can or will act upon. Choices are helpful when they encourage the development of a better relationship and harmful when they restrict the marriage.

Session 8: Conflict Resolution Process

Session 8 introduces the four-step conflict resolution process: show mutual respect, pinpoint the real issue, identify areas of agreement, and mutually participate in decisions. To resolve conflict, be specific and concentrate on the present and future rather than the past. Couples establish a procedure for using the four-step process. They also develop skills for dealing with anger.

Session 9: Applying the Conflict Resolution Process

Session 9 continues the development of conflict resolution skills. Couples apply the four-step process to an issue of concern in their relationship. The following areas of concern are highlighted: sex, finances, recreation, children, in-laws, religion, friends, and alcohol and drugs.

Session 10: Equal Marriage

Session 10 enables couples to clarify what they have learned in the TIME program and to identify and discuss marriage goals for the next 6 months. The following self-help procedures for maintaining an equal marriage are offered:

1. Encourage each other often.
2. Communicate frequently.
3. Deal with conflict.
4. Develop the courage to be imperfect.
5. Support each other fully.
6. Spend regular time together having fun.
7. Be aware of choices you can make in your relationship.
8. Develop shared dreams, goals, and interests.
9. Be self-accepting.
10. Have realistic expectations.

TIME can be used in a wide variety of settings, including:

1. A 10-session weekly marriage enrichment program. Each session focuses on skills and activities presented in one chapter of *TIME for a Better Marriage* (Dinkmeyer & Carlson, 1984b). The leader follows the *Leaders Manual* (Dinkmeyer & Carlson, 1984a) session outlines and serves as a facilitator for the entire program. The 10-session format is a complete study program. Groups will consist of couples for whom the TIME program is the first marriage enrichment experience, as well as couples who have participated in other programs and wish to continue their study.
2. An intensive workshop or retreat. With modifications of reading and activity assignments, TIME can be used in an intensive weekend workshop or retreat for couples. It is recommended that a weekend experience be limited to 12 couples. All couples should read *TIME for a Better Marriage* (Dinkmeyer & Carlson, 1984b) prior to the weekend. The TIME *Leaders Manual* (Dinkmeyer & Carlson, 1984a) has information on planning an intensive weekend.

3. A beginning experience for an ongoing marriage support group.
4. Church study, adult education program, or university course in family life, counselor training, or home economics.
5. As part of support material for marriage and family therapists. Marriage therapists can effectively use *TIME for a Better Marriage* (Dinkmeyer & Carlson, 1984) as a resource in marriage counseling and therapy. The book provides background reading on the skills of marriage. For bibliotherapy, the therapist may assign specific readings that relate to marriage skills that need strengthening or to problem areas the therapist has identified. The therapist may ask the couple to do specific activities as homework. For example, the therapist may ask the couple to hold a marriage meeting or encouragement meeting and assign the appropriate reading and skill card.
6. Individual sessions related to an individual TIME skill.
7. A follow-up experience for couples who have been in marriage encounter or marriage enrichment groups. By forming a marital C group (Dinkmeyer, Carlson, & Dinkmeyer, 1994), couples who have completed the TIME program and other enrichment experiences can receive continued group support in dealing with specific challenges in their marriages. In a caring, confidential atmosphere, couples look at specific challenges in their relationships. Couples help each other clarify beliefs and feelings and develop a commitment to change that will continue to enrich their respective relationships. *TIME for a Better Marriage* (Dinkmeyer & Carlson, 1984) serves as the basic resource.

To develop interest in TIME, use the materials provided in the publicity packet. A publicity campaign outline and schedule are included. We have not found screening helpful and believe that all couples can benefit from the TIME experience.

Be creative in how you attract couples to the TIME class. We have found it helpful to hold TIME group meetings in churches, adult education centers, and mental health centers. Also, holding an orientation meeting in one of these settings, announced in advance by the media and posters, can be an excellent way to attract potential members.

Working with leaders in churches and synagogues helps TIME leaders find their largest source of participants. The TIME program has been well received by members of the religious community. TIME can be used within the regular schedule of church education classes, or as a special study program at any time during the church year. TIME leaders can contact a member of the ministerial staff. In this initial contact, leaders may be referred to others in the church who have responsibility for overseeing the educational program.

Individuals who have participated previously in STEP or STEP/Teen groups may be interested in participating in a TIME group. If you are leading or have led STEP or STEP/Teen groups, tell the group members about TIME and let them know when you are holding an orientation meeting.

Couples who previously have been involved in group marriage enrichment experiences already recognize the value of such experiences and often are eager to find another opportunity to continue their learning. Contact leaders of groups such as Marriage Encounter or the Association of Couples for Marriage Enrichment (A.C.M.E.) and let them know how TIME relates to the objectives of their organizations. Tell them when you are holding an orientation meeting and invite their members.

Professionals such as marriage therapists, medical doctors (for example, those in family practice or obstetrics and gynecology), psychologists, counselors, ministers, rabbis, priests, and social workers are good referral sources. These professionals recognize the value of group educational enrichment activities but frequently do not have time available to conduct such groups for their clients. Let them know when you are holding orientation meetings.

☐ Qualities and Role of the Leader or Facilitator

A qualified TIME leader is an individual who cares about helping married couples create more satisfying relationships, who has the ability to lead discussion groups, and who is willing to study the theory, principles, and techniques presented in *TIME for a Better Marriage* (Dinkmeyer & Carlson, 1984b) and the *Leaders Manual* (Dinkmeyer & Carlson, 1984a).

TIME group leaders often are persons trained in the helping professions: psychology, psychiatry, social work, counseling, the ministry, education, nursing, or medicine. Also, persons who have led other group-discussion programs like STEP and STEP/Teen can lead TIME groups.

A TIME leader does not have to be an authority on marital relationships. The concepts and procedures in the program provide the basis for discussion. The leader organizes the group experience, conducts sessions by following the *Leaders Manual* (Dinkmeyer & Carlson, 1984a), and facilitates group discussion. The following personal skills or traits are helpful for TIME leaders:

- the ability to build an open, trusting group climate that promotes mutual respect and self-disclosure;
- the ability to establish guidelines for sharing, with the focus on listening and noncritical acceptance of differences;
- the ability to serve as a model as group members learn to share, listen, and noncritically accept differences;

- a sense of humor that helps self and others keep large or small challenges in perspective;
- the ability to identify alternative positive ways to view challenges or conflicts;
- the ability to provide structure that allows the group to meet its goals.

The leadership role focuses on promoting involvement and dialogue. The leader serves as a facilitator whose goal is to stimulate questions and encourage involvement in the exercises. The leader need not be an expert on marriage enrichment. Actually, too much expertise, which may encourage the leader to launch into lectures, is a deterrent to the couple and the group process.

The leader's role is to create an atmosphere and a process that promote growth between participating spouses. The leader makes materials available, presents the program for each session, leads discussion and exercises, guides the group to stay within the structure of the program, helps members apply the ideas, and encourages members to do the exercise assignments.

It is recommended that leaders be married couples. Effective leaders become models for the group in relating, communicating, and resolving issues. They believe that encouragement is a major force for bringing about positive change. They regularly use encouragement skills in the group process and for specific couples.

Organizing a TIME Session

Physical Setting

Select a location that assures privacy. Couples must feel free to discuss their concerns about their most personal relationship, their marriage. By selecting a quiet, comfortable setting that is free of distractions you demonstrate that you recognize the importance of privacy.

Arrange seating so that members can easily see and hear each other and hear the audio cassettes. For group activities, chairs should be arranged in a circle if possible. The circular setting gives equal importance to all group members and stimulates open discussion. If the room does not accommodate circular seating, arrange the chairs in either a semicircle or a rectangle. Sitting around a table is not recommended. A table can create a psychological barrier to open communication. There should be ample space for activities in which couples meet for private discussion.

Time

Participants' and leaders' schedules determine the times of meetings. It is anticipated that most meetings will be held in the evenings or, in some cases, on weekends (an intensive weekend experience, for example). When groups are held in churches, synagogues, or adult education facilities, the meeting time may conform to the organization's schedule.

Length and Frequency of Sessions

The typical session will take 2 hours. Some groups will want to extend the sessions to 2½ hours.

TIME groups usually meet once a week. One week between sessions allows participants time to absorb and apply the ideas.

Leader Preparation Time

Plan time to become acquainted with the entire program. Understanding the sequence of activities of the total program will greatly enhance your effectiveness as a leader.

Before each session, review the assigned reading and activities in *TIME for a Better Marriage* (Dinkmeyer & Carlson, 1984b) as well as the sequence of activities in the session. The leader's outline card for the session will be a handy reference. Also, listen to the audiotape to be used in the session, or review the tapescript printed in the *Leaders Manual* (Dinkmeyer & Carlson, 1984a).

Arrive early enough to make sure the seating arrangement is satisfactory and to allow yourself time to organize materials.

Materials

Be certain that each member of the group has a copy of *TIME for a Better Marriage* (Dinkmeyer & Carlson, 1984b). The personal copy allows each person to do the write-in activities, to record thoughts and goals, and to conveniently use the planning and evaluation forms. Also, each couple should have a copy of the personal audiocassette, *TIME to Relax and Imagine* (Dinkmeyer & Carlson, 1984c).

A cassette tape player in good working condition will be needed for each meeting. The TIME kit contains all other necessary materials.

Guidelines for Discussion

Guidelines for group discussion help the leader evaluate the effectiveness of the discussion process. The skilled leader keeps in mind the following questions:

1. Is the group right now working within the goals, structure, and time frame of the program?
2. How can I universalize and link the concerns and observations being shared in the group?

3. Is the group becoming more cohesive? Do the members listen attentively to each other?
4. Is communication open and congruent? Are members coming to know each other better? Do they provide helpful feedback to each other?
5. Do members understand the purposeful nature of behavior? Do they understand their goals and the goals of their partners? Do they understand how to move toward constructive, positive goals?
6. Are group members learning how to use encouragement? Are they focusing on what is positive in their relationship and identifying positive alternatives?
7. Are the couples acquiring skills as well as understanding concepts?
8. Do members spend too much time on single issues? Do they intellectualize?
9. Are the members talking with each other during open discussion, or are they directing their comments to the leader?
10. Do the end-of-session summaries reveal new insights and progress?

☐ Application of the Preventive Model to a Couple at Risk

Ben and Alyssa joined 11 other couples at the local nondenominational Christian church. The couples responded to local advertisements and were interested in having a better marriage. The focus of the TIME program was especially of interest to Ben and Alyssa, as it was a group of normal couples with normal problems. Ben and Alyssa are a very high-functioning couple, and the opportunity to learn skills rather than to have to explore pathology and problems seemed to be a good match for their place in life. They believed that if they had the tools, they could solve their own problems. In addition, being in a group with other couples who were having similar struggles was very comforting to Ben and Alyssa. As the couples went around the room, giving their names, occupations, and number of years married, Ben and Alyssa no longer felt as though they were the only couple dealing with problems.

Despite the fact that Ben and Alyssa's problems seemed serious, due in part to differences such as families of origin (separated vs. enmeshed), he being an only child and she being the oldest of three, growing up in the inner city vs. suburbs, religious backgrounds and attitudes, etc., the couple seemed to have a lot in common, such as education, value placed on children, and three years spent together with common goals. These commonalities led them to believe that they could work out their problems. Although this couple had not been married for too long, it was long enough to realize that their problems were not going to go away. This seems to be an important juncture in the life of couples, when they have to decide whether to stay together and work on their problems or to separate. The fact that Ben and Alyssa chose a TIME group (rather than an attorney) was indicative of their mutual goal of making their marriage work.

The couple found the first session of the TIME program particularly helpful. They began to stop blaming each other and to look instead at their own roles in why the marriage wasn't working. The goals of marital behavior helped each to gain some insight into some of the common problems that they were experiencing. It became clearer to both Ben and Alyssa that they wanted their marriage to work. Each day of the following week, the couple practiced the skill of daily dialogue. This skill involves setting aside 10 minutes a day for discussion with one another. Each partner was allowed 5 minutes of uninterrupted time to share their thoughts and feelings. Daily dialogue helped each of them learn to accept what their partner was saying and to share their feelings with greater ease. Both Ben and Alyssa shared their hopes and joys and excitement and worries about the future. In addition, feelings of anger, frustration, and fatigue were topics that frequently came up. Perhaps the biggest benefit came from the fact that both felt encouraged that the other was making time for their marriage.

The second session helped Ben and Alyssa learn the skill of encouragement. Although the couple realized that they weren't dealing with the real problems in their marriage, they knew that they needed to develop the skills in order to better handle the myriad of problems that faced them in this early stage of their marital relationship. In the audiotape exercise, they both began to see that they did have choices in how they responded to each other and that there are positive as well as negative ways to express the same message.

In the week following the second session, the couple continued daily dialogue and also began having encouragement meetings. Encouragement meetings are brief times in which each person finishes the following two statements:

1. The most positive thing that happened to me today was. . .
2. Something I appreciated about you today is. . .

This activity opened up some new understandings for the couple. Ben had not fully understood just how much Alyssa appreciated his working so hard for the family, and Alyssa had never understood that it was important for Ben that she be home to raise Benny. Additionally, she realized that he really did appreciate the extra efforts that she would make for him, such as changing into something sexier before he got home. Ben also was surprised to learn how much Alyssa really appreciated his involvement when Benny was younger, such as taking the 5 a.m. shift and doing dinner dishes. Many of these efforts, although acknowledged, were now acknowledged in a more meaningful fashion. Often, "thank you's" are given in a reactive fashion and go unnoticed.

By the time the third session came around, Ben and Alyssa were feeling more encouraged, and their relationship seemed to be on a different track. In the third session, the couple learned about setting priorities in marriage. They were able to develop some insight into the kind of relationship that they were having and how experiences from their families of origin were actually affecting who they had become. In the week following this meeting, the couple continued to hold daily dialogue and encouragement meetings and completed the encouraging days activity. Encouraging days is a popular marriage intervention that asks couples to list ten small pleasant behaviors your partner can do to please you. The behaviors should be specific, positive, and unrelated to past conflicts between them. The couple is asked to choose behaviors that are possible for their partner to do on a daily basis, such as "call me and tell me you love me" or "take a 10 minute walk with me." Partners then exchange lists with each other, and each partner strives to do two encouraging behaviors each day. After completing this activity, Ben and Alyssa gained new insight into one another. Ben had not realized how much it meant to Alyssa that he call just to say "hi" during the work day. Alyssa was surprised to know how much Ben appreciated her greeting him at the door with a hug and a kiss. The couple found this exercise particularly meaningful, as it helped them to gain more insight into one another and what is important to each. It seemed as though each of them was doing to the other what they wanted done to themselves, rather than what the other wanted. For example, Alyssa was calling Ben at the office, which he found annoying. Ben was seeking her out when he came home, when she felt as though he were treating her as a sex object.

At the fourth session, Ben and Alyssa learned the importance of effective communication. Congruent communication was taught, along with learning to take risks. Although the couple understood the importance of this concept at a theoretical level, they had not been aware enough of their deeper feelings to discuss them with their partner. Throughout the week the couple tried to practice congruent communication, sharing feelings openly and letting their partners know that they had been heard accurately.

At the fifth session the couple focused on further communication skills. Specifically, they learned the importance of identifying roadblocks and problems in their communication pattern. The sixth session was the final session on communication. Ben and Alyssa were gaining greater understanding of the importance of effective listening and clear, congruent communication. The couple realized that these were important if they were ever going to learn to negotiate the differences in their marriage.

During this week, the couple continued to hold daily dialogues and encouragement meetings, and they also held a marriage meeting. The marriage meeting is held at a regularly scheduled time when the couple will not be interrupted. A minimum of 40 minutes is set aside. Ben and Alyssa prepared an agenda for the meeting, with each coming up with items they wished to discuss. Issues such as alcohol, religion, and sharing financial responsibilities were listed. The couple followed the other suggested guidelines from the TIME program, and, although no problems were resolved, the couple was able to revisit the common problems in their marriage in a much more rewarding fashion. Both reported that although no changes were made, they felt understood and more helpful.

In the seventh session, the couple learned to identify the choices that they could make and realized that many of the frustrations and problems in their marriage resulted from a failure to recognize the choices that were available to them. During the ensuing week the couple worked at realizing ways that they could choose to show more love and concern for each other. The choices involved changing their thoughts, words, feelings, and actions.

During the first seven sessions, the couple had begun to learn the important skills of effective marriage and had developed new levels of respect for one another. The development of the skills necessary for the couple to negotiate problems and to learn how to accept their differences had begun. In the eighth session, the couple learned what they had entered the program to learn: a method to resolve the conflict in their marriage. Even though Ben and Alyssa realized that conflict was an inherent part of life, they had been unable to manage it. Ben and Alyssa learned to view conflicts as challenges and, now that they had the skills necessary to resolve the conflicts, they realized that conflict would not destroy their relationship. It might, in fact, help them to strengthen their togetherness.

The four steps to resolving conflict that the couple learned were:

1. Show mutual respect. This is accomplished by using the communication skills to clearly understand how their partner sees the conflict.
2. Pinpoint the real issue:
     "You feel a threat to your status or prestige."
     "You feel your superiority is being challenged."
     "Your need to control your right to decide is being challenged."
     "You feel that your judgment is not being considered and you are being treated unfairly."
     "You feel hurt and need to retaliate or get even."
3. Seek areas of agreement: concentrate on what you are willing to do; make no demands that your partner change; agree to cooperate rather than bicker.

4. Mutually participate in the solution. This is accomplished by each partner having some input into how to solve the conflict.

In this week and during session 9, Ben and Alyssa worked very diligently at applying this model to the problems that brought them into the TIME program. The couple learned that throughout their marriage it was going to be necessary to change some agreements. Different stages and different steps in the development of their family life called for different levels of involvement and closeness with one another. They learned the skills of negotiation and the fact that not having your way all the time was just part of the deal of being married.

The major problem the couple worked on over the 2-week period was their religious differences. Using this process the couple listened very carefully to one another's position. Alyssa explained that it was very important to her to be a good Christian mother and wife. She believed that this was what she could offer and that it was the right thing to do for her family. Ben discussed the importance of his Jewish heritage, but indicated that he believed that religion was something that was more a personal thing that didn't need to be conducted within a formal church setting. As the couple discussed this process further, it became clear that formal religion was very important to Alyssa, and that when Ben did not go to church with her, she felt that her views were not being respected and that she was being treated unfairly. Ben began to understand her position more clearly and did not feel as though his status was being threatened anymore. As the couple talked about how they wanted to raise Benny and their yet-to-be-born child, it became clear that they wanted the children to have some type of formal religious training from which to make their own decisions. With this in mind, Ben was willing to support Alyssa in raising the children in her Christian faith, provided that he did not have to participate. Alyssa agreed with this solution, provided that Ben would go to at least one service per month and to any services in which the children were involved.

As the couple came to the tenth and final session, they began to realize that they felt more connected as a couple and that things were running much more smoothly in their life. They realized, however, that there still were many issues that needed work. In the final meeting, the couple identified ways to continue the gains that they had made during the TIME sessions. The couple agreed that they wanted to continue daily dialogue and encouragment meetings and the weekly marriage meeting. At this final meeting, the TIME group members were very interested in having the group meet again. A follow-up meeting was scheduled for 6 weeks later in order to continue friendships that had developed and to provide an opportunity to share the progress that the couples made in using the TIME skills in their relationships.

The TIME program proved to be an ideal intervention for the high-functioning Ben and Alyssa. Although the couple wanted to resolve their problems more quickly, they did not have the skills. By participating in a marriage enrichment group, the couple learned that they were not alone and that it would be possible to change the way that they lived together.

☐ Empirical Evaluation and Research

Mattson, Christensen, and England (1990) examined the effectiveness of the TIME program using nonrandom pre- and posttreatment and controlled group designs. The treatment group attended eight 2-hour sessions using a slightly modified form of TIME. Results indicated that TIME couples, when compared with the no-treatment group, showed significant differences in areas of marital self-evaluation, dyadic adjustment, and relationship change.

A comprehensive study of the TIME program was conducted by Hawley and Olson (1995). Their study took 71 couples and divided them among three treatment groups and a control group. The TIME program group scored significantly higher on conflict resolution, adaptability, and communication. It is interesting to note that 98% of the participants reported that they would recommend any of the programs to other newlywed couples. It is likely that the high effectiveness of the TIME program in areas of conflict resolution and communication would have accounted for Ben and Alyssa's positive reactions to the TIME group. Although this research is on newlywed couples, it is likely to be indicative of the positive reactions that others report when using a 10-session TIME program.

☐ Summary

The TIME program is a general marriage enrichment program reflecting an Adlerian theoretical perspective. The TIME program consists of 10 sessions that primarily emphasize encouragement, communication, and conflict resolution skills. It is highly skill oriented, using a text and audiotape and couple exercises to introduce various skills related to its primary topics. The TIME group utilizes facilitator presentations, group discussion, and couple exercises as primary intervention methods. The limited research conducted on this program has been very positive and encourages wider application of its use.

☐ Contact References

For more information on the TIME program or its materials, contact the American Guidance Service at 1-800-328-2560, or contact one of the authors: Jon Carlson, jcarlson@genevaonline.com, or Don Dinkmeyer, Ddjr@wku.edu.

☐ References

Adler, A. (1931). *What life should mean to you.* New York: Capricorn Books.

Dinkmeyer, D., & Carlson, J. (1984a). *Leaders Manual: TIME program.* Circle Pines, MN: American Guidance Service.

Dinkmeyer, D. & Carlson, J. (1984b). *TIME for a better marriage.* Circle Pines, MN: American Guidance Service.

Dinkmeyer, D., & Carlson, J. (1984c). *TIME to relax and imagine* [Cassette]. Circle Pines, MN: American Guidance Service.

Dinkmeyer, D., Jr., Carlson, J., & Dinkmeyer, D., Sr. (1994). *Consultation: School mental health professionals as consultants.* Muncie, IN: Accelerated Development.

Dinkmeyer, D., & Dinkmeyer, D., Jr. (1982). *Developing understanding of self and others (DUSO).* Circle Pines, MN: American Guidance Service.

Dinkmeyer, D. C., Dinkmeyer, D., Jr., & Sperry, L. (1987). *Adlerian counseling and psychotherapy* (2nd ed.). Columbus, OH: Charles Merrill.

Dinkmeyer, D., & McKay, G. D. (1983). *Systematic training for effective parenting of teens (STEP/Teen).* Circle Pines, MN: American Guidance Service.

Dinkmeyer, D., & McKay, G. (1976). *Systematic training for effective parenting (STEP).* Circle Pines, MN: American Guidance Service.

Dinkmeyer, D., McKay, G., & Dinkmeyer, D., Jr. (1980). *Systematic training for effective teaching (STET).* Circle Pines, MN: American Guidance Service.

Dreikurs, R. (1950). *Fundamentals of Adlerian psychology.* Chicago, IL: Greenberg.

Dreikurs, R. (1946). *The challenge of marriage.* New York: Hawthorn Books.

Hawley, D. R., & Olson, D. H. (1995). Enriching newlyweds: An evaluation of three enrichment programs. *The American Journal of Family Therapy, 23*(2), 129–147.

Mattson, D., Christensen, O., & England, J. (1990). The effectiveness of a specific marital enrichment program: TIME. *Individual Psychology, 46,* 88–92.

Satir, V. (1972). *Peoplemaking.* Palo Alto, CA: Science and Behavior Books.

8

CHAPTER

Harville Hendrix, Ph.D.
Helen Hunt, M.A.

Imago Relationship Therapy: Creating a Conscious Marriage or Relationship

☐ Introduction

Imago Relationship Therapy is a theory and therapy of committed partnership with a focus on marriage. Its major thesis is that the purpose of the unconscious, in marital choices based on romantic attraction, is to finish childhood. Partner selection, therefore, is the result of an unconscious match between a mental image of one's parents or caretakers created in childhood (called the *imago*) and certain character traits of the attractive partner. The imago match is the determining factor in selection because it is driven by the *unconscious* purpose of recovering wholeness by restoring the connection, both personal and transpersonal, that was ruptured in childhood by need frustration. While the match between the composite of positive and negative caretaker traits and similar traits in the partner constitutes the basis of attraction, the intensity of the attraction is a result of the match in negative traits—those connected to need frustration. Romantic love, therefore, at one level, is the result of anticipated need satisfaction. At a deeper level it is a transient experience of original wholeness and connection to the whole. Since unmet needs from childhood are brought into adult intimate partnerships for resolution, and since the selected partner shares the same limitations as one's par-

169

ents, inevitably those frustrations are reactivated and reexperienced. Romantic feelings diminish as partners attempt to coerce the other into becoming the ideal parent. The power struggle that inevitably ensues often leads to chronic conflict, a parallel marriage, or a divorce.

Imago Relationship Therapy offers couples another option: to cooperate with the intention of the unconscious by creating a "conscious marriage/committed relationship" in which they intentionally meet each other's unmet childhood needs. To achieve this goal, Imago therapists use as their primary therapeutic intervention a three-stage structured process called the "couples dialogue" or "intentional dialogue." The use of this process restores contact and connection, thus achieving mutual emotional healing, restarting the developmental engine, and eventuating in the recovery of personal wholeness. Reconnection to the personal, where the rupture occurred, reestablishes awareness of one's intrinsic connection to the social, natural, and cosmic order. When used consistently, dialogue becomes *the* way of being in relationship and eventually evolves into a spiritual practice, transforming the conscious marriage into a spiritual path.

☐ Theoretical Underpinnings

Imago Relationship Therapy was birthed in the personal and intellectual partnership of Harville Hendrix, Ph.D. and Helen Hunt, M.A. Hendrix is a pastoral counselor with extensive clinical experience in couples therapy, and Hunt is a social activist who has a degree in psychology and is working on a doctorate in theology. Both having experienced divorce, they shared a deep interest in understanding their failed marriages. Finding little information in the literature on marriage that was relevant to their personal experiences, they used their relationship before and after their marriage in 1984 as a laboratory in which to study the dynamics of intimate partnership. In addition, Hendrix augmented their personal observations by studying the couples in his practice and the relational insights of the various schools of depth psychology, personality theory, behaviorism, systems theory, the western spiritual traditions, and contemporary physics. The resulting synthesis led to an extension of ideas and processes that Hendrix and Hunt systematized and named Imago Relationship Therapy (imago is the Latin word for "image"). In l984 they cofounded the Institute for Imago Relationship Therapy (IIRT), which offers workshops for couples and training for therapists in many areas of the world. The results of their collaboration were published in 1988 in a book titled *Getting the Love You Want: A Guide for Couples,* authored by Hendrix.

Although Imago Relationship Therapy originated as a clinical theory of marriage and marital therapy, reflection upon the larger implications of the unconscious dynamics of marital interaction led the authors to develop a set of metatheoretical assumptions about the nature of the universe (cosmology) and thus of human nature (anthropology). These assumptions posit the self's cosmic origins, its evolutionary inheritance, its psychological development, and its social adaptation, with special reference to their influence on the unconscious purpose and dynamics of intimate partnership.

Our Cosmic Origins

The first cosmological assumption is that human beings come from the same source and are made of the same stuff of which the universe is made (Zohar, 1990). We are "animated stardust" (Davis, 1992). Since we are an incarnation of the essence of the cosmos, by studying ourselves we can learn something about the nature of the cosmos. In turn, the clarification of our cosmic dimension informs and gives specific direction to our lives and thus to clinical theory. With regard to the nature of the cosmos, two clinical observations give us some clues from which we can retrospectively infer something about its nature. First, couples in therapy are unconsciously trying to restore connection in order to achieve healing, recover their wholeness, and complete their developmental evolution. Second, when couples become conscious (self-reflective) and intentionally cooperate with their unconscious strivings, they achieve the above goals.

These observations suggest that since we are an instance of the universe, the universe is in the process of self-expansion, self-completion, self-repair, and self-awareness. Further, since consciousness is the basic fact of human experience, it follows, given that we are the point where the universe has become conscious of itself, that the "stuff" (inanimate stardust) of the universe is consciousness Itself.[1]

From this we can posit that all "things" (animate and inanimate) are mutations of consciousness into form, first into energy and then into

---

[1]See Zohar (1990, pp. 76ff). Zohar makes clear, and we agree, that quantum physics nowhere posits the position that Consciousness is the substance of the universe. Although attempting to account for consciousness, her theory maintains a split between matter and consciousness, giving to matter qualities and relationships that infer consciousness. It is clear that physics is a theory of matter, not of consciousness, and physics encounters consciousness in its exploration of matter; it does not possess the methodology for its discovery. For the moment, the assumption that Consciousness is the substance of the universe must rely upon logical inference from the fact of consciousness or mystical intuition, as Davis (1992) suggests in *The Mind of God*, pp. 226ff.

matter. Thus every "thing" is a nodule of consciousness interconnected in a field of consciousness. We are connected with everything because we share the same substance. From this it follows that the obsessive drive in humans, most dramatically evident in couples, for the restoration and maintenance of connection reflects our participation in the processes of the cosmos. Thus we are connected not only because we are of the same substance but also because we participate in the same processes.

These assumptions suggest that the structure of being is relational—a paradigmatic shift from the prevailing ontology, which posits the individual (from person to atom) as primary, self-contained, and self-sufficient, and its separateness as ontological.[2] In an ontology of relationship, which is suggested by this cosmology, all individual things (from persons to atoms) have their characteristics and boundaries, but they constitute a unified field and are connected by essence and purpose. Thus we humans are embedded in the universe, are radically interdependent with each other and all of nature, and are open systems which continuously influence and are influenced by each other, whether in proximity or at a distance.[3]

Imago Relationship Therapy, reflecting this ontology, focuses on what Buber (1958) calls the "between" as the primary reality for couples. While there is no deemphasis on the reality and importance of the individual nor denial of the intrapsychic, there is a shift of attention to the quality of the "between." It is the character of the connection, namely, whether it is safe or dangerous, that sustains or ruptures the organization of the individual psyche and that, in turn, maintains or disturbs connection. The prevailing ontology of separation is thus amended by an ontology of relationship.

The Evolutionary and Psychosocial Journeys

A neonate comes equipped with a tripartite brain consisting of the brain stem, the limbic system, and the cortex (MacLean, 1973). These primi-

---

[2]An ontology of separation is implicit in the Newtonian, mechanistic view of the world. In the Newtonian world, all things are separate and essentially closed. How they are related and interact constitutes the principles of scientific investigation. In an ontology of relationship, all things are intrinsically connected; relationship is fundamental. The scientific question has to do with how they influence each other and with how they appear to be separate.

[3]Bell's theorem of nonlocality states the paradox that the influence of one particle on another is not determined by its locality. In fact, influence can be measured simultaneously across infinite distances, effects of which exceed the speed of light. See Davis (1983), *God and the New Physics*, pp. 105ff.

tive layers, aptly labeled the "old brain," are "atemporal" and "nonspatial." Having little awareness of time and space, the old brain tends to fuse the past and future into the present, and the self and other into a symbiotic union. Its primary function is to insure the survival of the organism and the species. When the conditions are safe, the organism experiences "relaxed joyfulness," its original condition. If the context becomes unsafe, it automatically responds with a defensive posture and, depending upon the perceived danger, *constricts* energy by freezing, hiding, or submitting, or *explodes* energy by fleeing or fighting.

To deal more effectively with these directives, the cortex developed, allowing humans to make distinctions between the past, future, and present, to distinguish actual from potential danger, and to differentiate between self and other. In addition to the development of language and logic in the cortex, the development of the forebrain enabled humans to reflect upon the functions of the cortex and the old brain, to observe and interact with their interpersonal and intrapsychic world, and to design and intend outcomes.

A neonate arrives with this tripartite brain connected to all parts of itself and possessing a rudimentary level of organization called a "nascent" self (Stern, 1985), which exists in a nonsymbiotic but essential connection with its caretaker(s). The core of this primitive self is conscious pulsating energy, which manifests through the brain as the function of thinking. When this energy takes the form of the muscles, it is expressed in the function of movement. Through the five senses, it is experienced as the function of sensation. In the emotional center, the pulsating energy is expressed through the feeling function.

Psychologically, the infant self is guided by an innate developmental program and appears to be intuitively aware that its personal evolution is dependent on its context. This "innate sociality" is evident in the infant's curiosity about others, in its obsession to be connected, and in its exhibition of protoempathic responses at birth. It also expresses itself in the infant's awareness of its essential connectedness to a larger whole.

Given an environment of physical and emotional safety, these stages and functions will manifest as connectional impulses in a specific order and at a proximally specific time. From birth to 18 months, for example, the impulse of the infant is to remain connected to the caretaker, basically through the function of the senses. If that impulse is grounded by parental support, between the ages of 18 and 36 months, the infant will proceed to the next stage, that of connecting to and exploring its environment through the function of movement. This begins the child's differentiation, but not separation, from its caretakers. Between 36 and 48 months, using the function of feeling, the child will experiment with a variety of character and affective identifications that consolidate into a cohesive self-identity. For the next 3 years or so, the child will develop the function of thinking and become obsessed with connecting to, understanding, and manipulating the environment until it achieves a sense of competence.

For the next 5 years, the child's interest turns outward to the nonfamilial world of its peers. In this new social context, the child goes through a repetition of the same developmental impulses, and the four functions are further expressed. Concerned about its relationship to others, the child connects with this new social organization and learns to care for nonfamily members by attaching to a "chum" (Sullivan, 1953), usually of the same sex. This stage is preparation for the transition to adolescence, ages 12 through 18, when the teen connects to and expresses itself in an intimate relationship, generally with the opposite sex. If the journey from infancy through adolescence has been appropriately supported, the young adult will commit to an intimate partnership and will care for the personal and collective welfare and survival of the species.

The Fate of the Self

However, human beings have not yet evolved to the point where they know how to maintain connection with the child and preserve its wholeness. Wounding is the result of the failure of semiconscious parents to support the connectional and developmental impulses and functions of the child's self. Frustration of developmental needs leads to developmentally specific wounds, such as rejection and abandonment at the attachment stage or feeling smothered or neglected at the stage of exploration. As a result, children may come to fear their own impulses and deny them to consciousness, resulting in a "denied self." To avoid further need frustration, they may adapt by either exploding or constricting their energy. Unless the situation is relieved, these patterns of energy management become dominant character structure defenses. In addition to wounding during the developmental process, children are vulnerable to the inhibition or repression of the functions of self during the socialization process. As a result of negative messages by the parents or social mores, children may feel they have no right to be, to think, to feel, to move, and/or to enjoy their senses, eventuating in the removal of the functions, in whole or in part, from consciousness. These split-off self functions constitute the "lost self."

Thus, instead of wholeness and relaxed joyfulness, the child experiences intrapsychic conflict, interpersonal alienation, and a deep yearning for the missing pieces of the self. To deal with this yearning, the child develops a presentational self, projects its denied traits onto others, and connects with others whose complementary functions were impaired. This spurious sense of wholeness, however, is not satisfactory and results in a continual search for the missing self. The pain caused by the connectional rupture results in a self-absorbed subjectivity in which the self constructs the grand illusion that it is the "center" of all cognitions and others are at the periphery. We call this cognitive-emotional state "symbiosis." In this centric consciousness, others become an extension of the self and its split-off parts. In experiential terms, symbiosis is the belief by some that "we are one and I am the one," and by their counterparts that "we are one and you are the one." Since the symbiotic self becomes the definer of the "world," that which does not conform to the self's definition is dangerous and becomes the source of anxiety, enhancing the sense of separation. But this condition is psychological, not ontological. The fact of structural connectedness is lost only to consciousness.

The Imago and the Selection Process

The fate of the self greatly influences the type of person chosen as an intimate partner in adulthood and the quality of the relationship with that person. While the imago match is the primary basis of selection, two other factors also influence this choice. The first is the similarity of developmental wounding and the complementarity of defenses. For example, both partners may have been wounded around attachment issues, but one responded by maximizing (attempts to get needs met by exaggeration and dependency) and the other by minimizing (attempts to avoid need frustration by denying needs and avoiding contact). The second is the complementarity of the functions of the self. For example, a partner who has repressed his or her thinking function will be attracted to a person whose thinking function is intact. The partner whose thinking function is intact may have repressed his or her feeling function and will therefore be attracted to a partner who has access to his or her feelings.

While all these factors fuel romantic love, they also constitute emotional and characterological incompatibility, precipitating a power struggle in the relationship. In this second and natural stage, partners will use coercive tactics like criticism, devaluation, and intimidation to force the partner to remain symbiotic, that is, to fit their image and become the ideal parent who restores connection. Failing to achieve these goals, each partner proceeds through the stages of shock, denial, anger and depression, bargaining, and finally acceptance of defeat. Through Imago Relationship Therapy, couples learn that their incompatibility is, in fact, the potential for emotional and characterological growth. Thus, it appears that nature brings incompatible people together as a means of healing and growth. When the consciousness of couples becomes self-reflective and intentional, relationships flourish as they participate in the cosmic agenda of self-repair and self-completion.

☐ Intervention Model

The main method for helping couples move towards a conscious relationship is to provide the couple with a cognitive and experiential understanding of the purposes of romantic love and the power struggle, to create a safe environment, to establish a process for breaking the symbiotic fusion, and to assist in recovering the core, energetic self and its functions. The primary educational and therapeutic tool is the couples dialogue and its modifications.

Psychoeducation

One feature of Imago Therapy is psychological education. Through learning about the journeys of the self, the unconscious purpose of the mate selection process, and the natural stages of marriage, couples can begin shifting away from the "Cinderella/Prince Charming" expectations of romantic love. By learning specific information about the intentions of their unconscious and by demonstrations of connectional processes, couples can become aware of and thus facilitate nature's agenda for bonding together two people who can intentionally become surrogate parents to each other. In order to cooperate with the goals of the unconscious, couples are taught that commitment to the relationship, to each other, and to the connectional process of dialogue must be unconditional and absolute, thereby keeping the necessary energy focused on maintaining safety and connection. In addition, couples are taught about the concept of intentionality, the process of focusing on outcomes, which enables them to design and engage in nondefensive behaviors that will reach specific goals and foster characterological growth. Together, couples can actively participate in creating a safe and passionate relationship.

☐ Specific Methods and Strategies for Therapeutic Intervention

Dialogue and the Restoration of Empathy

The three-step couples dialogue is the primary and singular intervention facilitated by the therapist throughout the psychoeducational process and therapy procedures. The first step, mirroring, is essentially active listening, a reflective process that assures both partners that the content of a discussion is accurately heard. Mirroring typically begins with a sentence stem, "If I heard you correctly. . . ." Acting as a flat mirror, the message receiver reflects an exact paraphrase of the partner's message. Mirroring achieving a triple purpose: (a) It placates the reactive old brain by providing a cognitive structure that allows the receiver to focus on content, rather than on his or her own reactions; (b) it allows the receiver to accurately hear the sender, rather than responding with distortions such as projections, archaic perceptions, and emotional reactions, and thus beginning the process of differentiation; and (c) it allows the sender to experience being heard, which simultaneously increases sender differentiation. The mirroring process helps partners create a safe environment in which they can nondefensively learn about each other's needs.

However, mirroring alone can sometimes lead to further polarization within the dyad if one or both partners assert only one true reality—their own. The second step, validation, begins to bridge that chasm. Based on Buber's (1958) work and readings on the impossibility of pure perception (perceptions are relative based on interpretation within the perceiver's intrapsychic world), we developed validation as a way of not necessarily agreeing with the other, but acknowledging that the reality of the other "makes sense," given the framework and the context within which he or she resides. Like mirroring, validation often begins with the sentence stem, "You make sense because. . . ." Validation demands suspending judgment about the other's world and accepting the validity of the other's perceptions of the world as equal to one's own. Validation allows both sender and receiver to simultaneously experience greater self-delineation, with the receiver discovering that the partner is "not me," thus breaking the symbiotic fusion. The validation process is distinct from traditional forms of differentiation through self-assertion, in which differentiation is established by impinging one's reality on that of one's partner.

To add an affective and empathic component to the process, the authors drew upon the work of Rogers (1961), Kohut (1978), and Hoffman (1990). Imago Therapy distinguishes between two levels of empathy. At the first level, cognitive empathy, the receiver *imagines* the affective world of the sender: "And given all that, I can imagine you might feel. . . ." At the second level, participatory empathy, the receiving partner experiences the sending partner's feelings while still being able to hold onto his or her own world. (This is in contrast to sympathetic identification: "I am experiencing your feelings because I also had a similar experience. . . .") This second level of empathy means: "I understand what you are understanding, because I am experiencing what you are experiencing, yet I am remaining myself." Such is the goal of every dialogical encounter, but it is a difficult goal to achieve, requiring a transcendence of the self. Ultimately, participatory empathy—the authentic, empathic acceptance of the other as delineated from the self—constitutes the space "between" the partners, allowing *content* to become secondary to *contact*. In this space of connection, the self as other is born, and the illusion of separation is dissolved.

Through empathic attunement, couples make a deep emotional connection which is itself healing. After they have engaged in this process for a while, many couples cannot remember the precipitating incident that ignited their conflict. When they can recall it, they recognize it as being about an actual or threatened connectional rupture, and the dialogue, which restores connection, obviates the need to explore the initiating incident.

Mirroring is a way of making contact, validation a way of creating equality, and empathy a way of arousing the affective capacity. Through these three procedures, both sender and receiver experience a heightened sense of self *and* connection. Ultimately, the other becomes a nonthreat to the old brain, piquing motivation to stretch into altering characterological defenses in order to meet the needs of the other.

Although the couples dialogue is initially rigid, clearly delineating the three steps helps the couple to eventually master the structure. Beginning at the mechanical level, the couples dialogue evolves to an artistic level at which the starkness of the three steps blends into a singular flow, so that nonsymbiotic interactions become a continuous way of relating.

The couples dialogue is the fundamental structure for intervention in Imago Relationship Therapy. The outcome facilitates healing, restores personal wholeness, and reconnects one to the whole, thus bringing the cycle of human yearning to an end. Couples then live life from their core energy, rather than from their needs, experiencing the original condition of relaxed joyfulness and spontaneously expressing their aliveness as care for the world. Their marriage, through the practice of dialogue, thus becomes a spiritual path.

As the therapeutic process progresses, five variations of dialogue are applied for specific purposes. These include:

1. *Reimaging the Partner.* The procedure for reimaging the partner as wounded rather than as dangerous occurs in the parent–child dialogue and in the holding exercise. In the parent–child dialogue, the receiver assumes the role of the "as if" parent, and the sender assumes the role of himself or herself as a child. In the holding exercise, the sender lies across the lap of the receiver and talks to the partner "as partner" about his or her childhood wounds. The holding partner, while containing and guiding the process, asks, "What can I do now that would heal that with your parents?" and responds by mirroring. These

two processes help partners understand each other's childhood vulnerabilities, deepen the partners' contact while increasing differentiation, and enhance empathy and compassion.

2. *Behavior Change Request.* This variation of dialogue is designed to help partners communicate their needs without using criticism, devaluation, or intimidation. It assists partners in identifying the childhood needs hidden in their frustrations and teaches them to state needs in the form of a request for behavior change. The receiving partner responds by agreeing to a concrete, specific, time-limited behavior (to ensure success), granting the request as an unconditional gift without imposing an obligation for reciprocity. This process facilitates mutual growth: Since what one partner needs is usually the most difficult thing for the other to give, the giver, by stretching into the requested behavior, activates the denied and/or lost parts of himself or herself that were repressed in childhood. In this way, partners call each other into mutual wholeness.

3. *The Container.* Anger is common in relationships and is a natural response to frustration, but it is often expressed in destructive ways. The variation of dialogue called "the container" enables couples to deal with their anger and remain connected while converting their energy into passion. Consisting of seven steps, the container is the most complicated Imago process. Beginning with a request for an appointment, the container has the sending partner state his or her frustration and then intensely escalate the angry feelings attached to it. The receiving partner asks, "Is there more?" to invite the continuing expression of angry feelings and emotionally holds those feelings until all are expressed. Since underneath most anger is hurt and sadness, tears tend to replace the discharge of anger. When this happens, the receiving partner physically holds the sender and encourages the full expression of tears until they stop. At that point, the receiver gives a summary mirror and then asks the sender to make a behavior change request. After the behavior change request, the container ends with a behavior that provokes laughter, a transition which chemically replaces adrenalin with endorphins and leaves the couple in passionate connection.

4. *Reromanticizing.* Pleasure in Imago Therapy means dipping into the river of full aliveness, our essential nature, which contributes to a sense of well-being and connection. Reromanticizing has partners intentionally creating and mutually exchanging pleasure in their relationship. The "other" that emerges becomes not only nonthreatening but a source of imminent pleasure, thus enhancing emotional safety, intensifying passion, and deepening connection.

5. *Re-visioning.* Most couples who become therapy clients do not have a

distinct "vision" of their relationship, nor do they have specific relationship goals. In the re-visioning process, couples envision the qualities and behaviors of their dream relationship. They are encouraged to define specific goals with clear strategies, which are imprinted through behavioral rehearsal and daily meditation. This creates a relationship that is healing and recovers wholeness.

In addition to the five dialogical procedures discussed above, couples are taught eight therapeutic principles, the tenets of Imago Relationship Therapy's clinical perspective:

1. *Containment.* The main therapeutic task is to establish, maintain, and increase the couples' contact with one another by keeping all exchanges in the session dialogical. By using in-between session assignments that arise from the context of the session, the dialogical environment is transferred to the home. Assignments may also include reading *Getting the Love You Want* (Hendrix, 1988) or listening to an audiotape of the previous therapeutic session.

2. *Safety.* An Imago therapist maintains an environment of safety in order for growth and healing to occur. Since confrontation produces anxiety and shores up defensive patterns, the therapeutic encounter is nonconfrontational and serves as a model of safety for the couple.

3. *Suspension of Judgment.* Because "truth" is relative and colored by personal biases, and since the focus of therapy is on the "between," the Imago therapist never takes sides or engages in traditional diagnostic judgments. In the Imago framework, insight is secondary to contact; thus, the goal of therapy is the restoration of connection.

4. *Listening.* An Imago therapist listens to discern the underlying wound, developmental arrests, and presence of the lost self in the partner's complaint. Often, the therapist provides a stimulus for the sender's message through the use of sentence stems, which elicits recollection of the wound. Such stems might include, "And that reminds me of. . . "; "Stay with that. . . "; "And when you do that. . . ".

5. *Seeing Couples Together.* All therapeutic procedures are facilitated between partners or in the presence of the partner. When couples choose to take the Getting the Love You Want Couples Workshop, they must remain in the workshop until it ends. This conjoint structure is essential to prevent the deleterious effect of uneven growth and the danger of triangulation, both of which interfere with the quality of connection between partners.

6. *A Process of Small Changes.* Imago is a process of small, slow, and consistent changes. Since each change can stir a defense, the pace of change and its integration is a determinant of permanence. When small changes are made slowly over a period of time, a transformation of the rela-

tionship occurs even if the impasse, the issue which arises out of the deepest wound and activates the strongest defense, has not been addressed. Ultimately, the impasse issue dissolves as a result of the restored connection that is created by the dialogue process.

7. *Commitment.* Since commitment is a condition for change, partners are asked to commit to the relationship, to each other, to the dialogue process, and to the procedures of change. Usually the therapist asks for a 12-session time commitment, stressing the importance of the couple investing sufficient energy in their relationship. Some couples may be able to commit to only one session at a time, but as safety increases and contact deepens, commitment tends to grow. Thus, at the end of the 12 sessions, depending upon the goals of the couple, the time commitment becomes open-ended.

8. *Therapy Is Not About Solving Problems.* Since problems are seen as functions of developmental immaturity, the resolution of childhood issues restarts the developmental process. "Problems" thus dissolve in the dialogical process through empathic attunement, a quality of relationship that facilitates psychological growth and differentiation.

☐ Format of Application

There are currently three formats of Imago Relationship Therapy: (a) couples counseling with a certified Imago therapist; (b) attendance at a 20-hour Getting the Love You Want Couples Workshop; and (c) the seven-hour *Getting the Love You Want Home Video* (Hendrix & Hunt, 1993), which is a videotaped abbreviation of the Getting the Love You Want Couples Workshop. This section will briefly describe the format of the workshop. The couples counseling format will be demonstrated later in its application to the case study.

The Getting the Love You Want Couples Workshop is designed for couples to work in privacy, at their own pace, and can be adapted by all couples to fit the stage of their relationship. The 20-hour workshop is generally given over a 2-day weekend and offers lectures (making preattendance readings unnecessary), written exercises, guided imageries, live demonstrations, and working one-on-one with one's partner. Certified Imago Therapists are available for clinical support.

In the first section of the workshop, "The Unconscious Marriage/Relationship," the leader lectures on an historical and evolutionary framework for understanding one's relationship and the purpose of romantic love. Charts and written exercises are provided for identifying developmental wounds and the lost functions of the self, enabling participants to become conscious of their own and their partner's unmet needs.

By lecturing on the purpose of the power struggle, couples learn that their chronic frustrations are the result of symbiotic fusion and the interaction of their character defenses of minimizing and maximizing. The workshop leader explains the incompatibility producing the power struggle as the catalyst for change, thus reframing the power struggle as "growth trying to happen." The aims are to challenge the belief of most partners that they married the wrong person and to offer them the option of a conscious relationship.

A volunteer couple is solicited to teach and demonstrate mirroring, the first step of the couples dialogue. Guided by the workshop leader, one partner takes on the role of sender, with the other being the receiver. By discussing a real-life frustration in front of the group, the demonstrating couple teaches the mirroring technique and demonstrates its superiority over couples' typical ways of discussing conflictual issues.

The second section of the workshop, "The Conscious Marriage/Committed Relationship," is designed to show couples how to intentionally focus their energy to create a conscious relationship. To facilitate this focus, partners participate in the "no-exit decision," which encourages them to make a commitment to each other, to the relationship, and to the dialogue process. "Exits" are defined as any behavior or activity a person engages in that diminishes intimacy between partners. Exits can be terminal (divorce, suicide, murder), catastrophic (affairs, addictions), intentional, or functional. An intentional exit is a feeling expressed as a behavior ("acting out" instead of "talking out" feelings), with the clear motivation to avoid involvement with the partner. A functional exit is a behavior that one enjoys but which pulls energy away from the relationship. Working, playing golf, watching television, "surfing the Web" on the Internet, shopping, or going out with friends are behaviors that can be used as either functional or intentional exits. The no-exit decision process identifies one's exits, facilitates dialogue about why one engages in the exits, and has partners commit to: (a) immediately closing terminal or catastrophic exits (with certain exits like addictions, outside intervention may be necessary), and (b) working towards modifying the intentional and functional exits to increase involvement and intimacy in the relationship.

After couples have made the no-exit decision, the workshop leader lectures on the destructive power of criticism. Since criticism is a coercive attempt to get one's partner to remain symbiotic and meet one's needs while attempting to escape the symbiotic pull of the partner, couples are introduced, by demonstration and practice, to the behavior change request process. Because of the complexity of the container, the workshop leader demonstrates the process but recommends that, if intense anger needs to be discharged, couples initially work with an Imago therapist to ensure the completion of all seven steps.

The reromanticizing processes introduced towards the end of the workshop include the "caring behaviors dialogue," "surprises," and "positive flooding." The caring behaviors dialogue is designed to educate the partners about behaviors that make them feel cared about and loved. It acknowledges not only current behaviors but also behaviors from the courtship phase, and in addition allows the opportunity for expressing secret desires. Each partner is encouraged to intentionally begin and/or continue engaging in these caring behaviors. The surprise process is designed to keep the relationship actively alive with spontaneity by encouraging partners to randomly furnish gifts that match the desires of the recipient. The purpose of the positive flooding process is to mutually express and amplify the positive resources of each partner, including physical characteristics, character traits, behaviors, and global qualities.

The workshop ends by having couples design a dream relationship, a process which helps them construct a mutual vision of their future relationship and internalize it as their goal. This process will be discussed further in the case study.

In the participant's manual, there is a week by week schedule of exercises to help the couples continue the Imago work at home. Participants are encouraged to see a certified Imago therapist, if necessary, to begin a support group with other couples engaged in Imago work, and to purchase the *Getting the Love You Want Home Video* (Hendrix & Hunt, 1993) for review.

☐ Qualities and Role of the Leader or Therapist

The Role of the Therapist

In Imago Therapy, the traditional role of the therapist as an expert in a hierarchical system is replaced by an egalitarian model of "therapist as facilitator." The healing process occurs in the couple's relationship, rather than in the client–therapist partnership. Interpretation, analysis, confrontation, and other invasive transactions, along with the anxiety they evoke, are absent in this approach. Instead, the Imago therapist empowers partners to sustain their own healing by helping them to: (a) acquire information that deepens their awareness of each other and promotes empathy; and (b) understand and internalize the process of healing and its procedures, so that they can continue to work on their own.

Qualities of the Certified Imago Therapist and Workshop Leader

Professionals who have been trained in Imago Relationship Therapy come from a variety of the therapeutic disciplines: social work, pastoral counseling, psychology, marriage and family therapy, and psychiatry. All are licensed or certified to practice psychotherapy and have an advanced degree in one of the healing professions. Because of the role shift from the traditional view of therapist to that of facilitator, the Imago therapist must be rigorously trained and highly skilled.

Admission requirements for entering into the basic clinical training in Imago Relationship Therapy include: (a) possession of an advanced degree in the mental health field and membership in a recognized professional association (e.g., NASW, AAMFT, APA, American Association of Pastoral Counselors [AAPC], etc.); (b) a current clinical practice with couples; (c) a license to practice psychotherapy if required by their state; and (d) 300 hours of postgraduate supervision.

To obtain certification, the applicant must participate in a Getting the Love You Want Couples Workshop prior to the first day of training (experientially introducing the therapist to the processes), attend 96 hours of training, receive a positive evaluation from the clinical instructor(s), and serve as a support therapist in a Getting the Love You Want Couples Workshop. This latter requirement enables the Instructor to receive an evaluation from the workshop presenter on the trainee's integration of Imago Therapy and his or her ability to use it with couples in the workshop context. Three months, and again 6 months, after completion of the formal course, trainees must write a 1-page report on what they have learned and submit it to their clinical instructor.

Having successfully completed all of these requirements, the trainee may then apply to IIRT for clinical membership. Upon acceptance he or she may use the title of certified Imago therapist. Although continuing education credits are not required to maintain certification, Imago therapists are encouraged to remain current with these, and those who do are awarded standing as advanced clinicians.

To enter into the workshop presenter's program which, upon certification, allows the therapist to lead Getting the Love You Want Couples Workshops, the applicant must be a certified Imago therapist, have experience speaking to public audiences, and have practiced Imago Relationship Therapy with couples for 1 year since certification as an Imago therapist. The course requirements include 96 hours of formal training, required readings, and leading two couples workshops. Postcourse requirements include writing and submitting a workshop manual and leading two additional couples workshops, with the second workshop being evaluated by an on-site certified clinical instructor.

Certified Imago therapists who wish to become clinical instructors and master trainers build upon these achievements and meet other requirements pertinent to the function of each level. All requirements and admissions processes are outlined in the *Professional Training Catalogue* (Institute for Imago Relationship Therapy [IIRT], 1998).

By requiring stringent prerequisites, IIRT and its faculty members work with therapists who have gone through a formation process and who are mature, exhibit professional competence, and have clinical experience. In addition, because of the diversity among therapeutic disciplines and clinical orientations, graduates of the program participate in cross-theoretical dialogues in annual meetings, through journal writings, and by taking advanced courses, thus maximizing and enhancing academic and clinical awareness.

☐ Application of the Preventive Model to a Couple at Risk

This section describes how the first several sessions of Imago Therapy might proceed, applying specific strategies that might be used with Ben and Alyssa, the couple at risk.

General Overview of the Therapy Session

Throughout the course of therapy, the therapeutic process includes the application, relevant to the specific needs of the couple, of the therapeutic tenets of Imago Relationship Therapy discussed earlier. Because working within the time constraints of a 45- to 50-minute session often cuts short affective processing, Imago therapists typically work in 1½-hour sessions. With the couple's permission, the therapist will audiotape the session and then give the audiotape to the couple to review between sessions. The therapist provides other between-session assignments to help the couple practice what they have learned, maintain their connection, and achieve an environment of safety at home.

Session 1

Often, premarital couples who are on second or later marriages go to an Imago therapist to ensure that they don't make the same mistakes they made in their earlier marriages. Remarried or early-married couples with relatively minor levels of conflict might seek therapy because they heard, by word of mouth, that Imago Therapy is skills-based, offering tools that help make good marriages better. Couples whose conflicts are intense (hot marriages) or who have given up (parallel marriages) often go to therapy to find a mediator or referee, with the option of divorce in mind.

In the first session, the Imago therapist would ask Ben and Alyssa to take turns "sending" and "mirroring" while discussing why each of them thinks the other chose to enter therapy and what the partner wants to achieve. He or she might then ask the other to respond to the question, "How have I prevented the marriage we both want from happening?" The purpose of this structured process is to prevent them from engaging in a recitation of their frustrations with each other, so that a safe therapeutic environment can be created.

Next, the therapist would attempt to elicit the "core scene" by asking Ben to tell Alyssa what he thinks is her deepest frustration with him and having Alyssa mirror him: "Alyssa, from my perspective, your deepest frustration with me is. . . . " When Alyssa finishes mirroring, the therapist would prompt her to validate Ben's perceptions, suggesting the sentence stem, "You make sense, because. . . . " Alyssa would then have the opportunity to express empathy, with the therapist prompting her with the phrase "And I can imagine that makes you feel. . . . " (Note: The movement to validation and empathy requires a clinical judgment that the couple can do it. If, by experimentation or intuition, the therapist decides they are not ready, he or she asks them to limit their response to mirroring, and introduces the other processes later on in therapy.) The therapist would then ask Ben to respond by confirmation.

Then Alyssa would switch to the sender role and communicate her views of Ben's deepest frustration with her, with the therapist facilitating in the same way. In the process, the therapist might provide a sentence stem like "And that reminds me of. . . . " This is done to evoke conscious connections between current frustrations and childhood experiences.

As they discuss their marriage and their childhoods, the Imago therapist would listen for clues to their developmental wounds and observe their defenses. In the case of Ben and Alyssa, the therapist would note that they appear to have been wounded in the transition stage from exploration to identity. Ben appears to have been smothered by his single mother and to have defended himself by minimizing his responses. Not having a father in the home, he seems to have overidentified with his maternal uncle, who encouraged him to be a lawyer and internalized his reserve, thus reinforcing his tendencies toward minimization and being controlling. Alyssa appears to have been wounded by her mother's neglect and her father's controlling manner; she seems to have identified with her mother's affableness and her father's sternness as well as, later on, his religion. Although she appears compliant, she maximizes her affective responses through exaggeration. Because this particular couple was not suffering from early wounding (attachment and early exploration stages), and because of their education and sophistication, the therapist might decide that they could now engage in the full dialogue process.

The therapist might close the session with some psychoeducational information about the importance of commitment to the relationship and to the therapy process. He or she would suggest a 12-session commitment, to be revised later if necessary. Before they left, the therapist would assign them to practice the dialogue process in their daily interactions and to limit discussions of their relationship to small issues.

By the end of the first session, the Imago therapist has already: (a) taught the couples dialogue; (b) begun fostering differentiation by putting one in the shoes of the other; (c) increased the awareness of the frustrations of each partner; (d) decreased criticism and defensiveness by having the partners identify the *other partner's* frustrations, rather than allowing partners to talk about how frustrating the other person is; (e) allowed the couple to experience the projections and distortions they may have had regarding the other's frustrations; (f) gotten an initial commitment to the therapy process; and (g) with the between-session assignment, had the couple begin to integrate dialogue into their lives. Simultaneously, the Imago therapist took an informal case history of the couple, noting important issues related to family of origin, their nurturing deficits from childhood, and their character defenses. The therapist also has some information about their career choices and their sexual relationship.

Session 2

At the beginning of this session, the Imago therapist would continue to emphasize the dialogue process by asking Ben and Alyssa to alternate sending and mirroring about their experiences of the first session and their between-session assignments. Then the therapist might talk about the human tendency to use defenses whenever one is emotionally threatened, underscoring the importance of establishing emotional safety whenever emotionally laden issues are discussed. He or she might explore with the couple the ways they have been dealing with conflictual issues, for example, whether one "flees" from conflict while the other "fights." This would confirm his or her impression of which partner is the minimizer and which is the maximizer in the relationship.

The therapist might then turn to deepening Ben and Alyssa's understanding of the quantity and depth of their frustrations by using an exercise called the "frustration list," with "frustration" being the generic term for behaviors that produce negative emotions. Through this process, the therapist helps them discover the pattern in their frustrations, that is, how their frustrations lay the foundation for and build up to their "core scene." The process has the partners write down, in session, a list of the things each of them does that they perceive frustrates the other partner. The partners then rate each item on their list on a 1 to 10 scale, to indicate how much their frustrating behavior appears to disrupt their relationship. When the lists are finished, the therapist would then ask the partners to share each item on their list with one another: "Ben, please share with Alyssa what you do that you believe makes her feel frustrated with you." Ben would then read an item from his list: "You get frustrated with me for not being religious." The Imago therapist would facilitate Alyssa's mirroring of Ben's message. The therapist would then ask Alyssa to share with Ben an item on her list. "You get frustrated," Alyssa might state, "that I don't spend as much time with you as I did before Benny was born." Ben would then respond by mirroring Alyssa's statement. After each frustration on both partners' lists had been shared and mirrored, the therapist would elaborate on the three phases of the dialogue process (mirroring, validation, and empathy) and coach them in discussing a "moderate-level" frustration on one of their frustration lists.

In Imago Therapy, frustrations are considered the "royal road to the unconscious," which provides a glimpse into unresolved issues from childhood. Thus, frustrations are often used as the benchmark for gauging childhood wounds and developmental lags. To demonstrate, suppose Alyssa lets Ben know that she gets frustrated when he doesn't listen to her talk about the nightmares she's been having. From this, the therapist might surmise that "not being heard" may be a painful issue for Alyssa, one possibly left over from the identity stage of development (around 3 to 5 years of age, according to Imago theory). If Ben, for his part, expresses the frustration that he is being overly controlled by Alyssa ("Women have choices; men don't," as he stated), the therapist might observe that Ben, too, could have issues stemming from the identity stage as well as residue from wounding at the stage of exploration.

After the dialogue, the therapist asks each partner to share how he or she experienced the exchange. The therapist goes on to explain that, although the process might feel mechanical or unnatural, it is vital to developing a healthy relationship and will feel more natural as they master the process.

At session's end, the therapist would give one or more between-session assignments. A typical assignment would be to spend 10 minutes a day discussing low- or moderate-level frustrations from each partner's frustration list, alternating the roles of sender and receiver. The therapist might also give them an article on Imago Relationship Therapy to read aloud together.

Session 3

At the beginning of the third session, the Imago therapist would ask Ben and Alyssa to share the positive intentional behaviors they engaged in since the last session and to acknowledge what they saw their partner do for them. This exchange encourages a focus on the positive aspects of the relationship. Next, the therapist would check on how successfully the couple completed the between-session assignment.

The third session might include another psychoeducational component on the theoretical notion of the imago and its role in the partner selection process. The therapist would present the concept that marriage, according to Imago theory, is viewed as nature's way of bringing together two people for the purpose of healing and characterological growth.

The therapist would next have them discuss a small frustration, this time stating their own frustration rather than their perception of their partner's frustration. This discussion would lead into the behavior change request process. Alyssa, for example, might be frustrated that Ben does not take the time to listen to her talk about her anxieties over the upcoming birth of their second child. After the partners discuss this for a while, the therapist would direct Alyssa to generate three specific, measurable, and time-limited requests for behavior changes from Ben, changes that would ease the frustration Alyssa just expressed. In light of her frustration, one of her requests might be, "During the next 2 weeks, if I have a nightmare, I would like you to hold me and to mirror, validate, and empathize with the details of my nightmare, either immediately after I wake up or before you leave for work the next morning." After Alyssa has stated two other requests, which Ben mirrored, the therapist suggests that Ben select the easiest of the three, to ensure that he succeeds in fulfilling Alyssa's request. Once Ben commits to granting Alyssa one of her requests "as a gift," the therapist has Alyssa initiate some "high-energy fun" with Ben, intentionally engaging him in an enjoyable physical behavior, such as a 30-second hug, which promotes a sense of pleasurable connection.

Toward the end of this session, the therapist leads Ben and Alyssa through a guided visualization of their "dream relationship," as it would look 3 to 5 years in the future. Afterwards, the therapist gives each partner a worksheet entitled "Your Relationship Vision." The between-sessions assignment for the week is for each to write down positive statements that describe their ideal relationship, using the pronoun "we," with each statement written in the present tense, as though that segment of the vision were already fulfilled. Next, they are to spend time sharing their vision list, mirroring back each sentence and noting the items on which they mutually agree. These agreed-upon items are then listed on the "Our Relationship Vision" form, which they complete and bring in to their next therapy session.

With couples who are deeply engaged in the power struggle, unlike Ben and Alyssa, the relationship vision process would not be effective this early in therapy; however, the vision list should be completed as soon as possible after therapy commences, as a means of guiding the direction of therapy.

Session 4

In the fourth session, the therapist would begin by reminding the couple that this was the last session to which they initially committed. The therapist asks how they have experienced the process and effects of therapy, particularly the dialogue process. He or she would also discuss with them their desire to continue or terminate the therapy with this session.

The therapist next asks Ben and Alyssa to share their mutual relationship vision list, then teaches them how to transform their general vision statements into behavioral goals by using a "Model Goal Sheet." For example, the vision statement, "We have fun regularly," can be rewritten as an objective that would help to attain that goal: "We will have high-energy fun once a week." The therapist then assists them in developing strategies to achieve their goals. For instance, one tactic that would create fun is "See a funny movie once a week and play a silly game each Sunday." The partners would also list the likely sensory effects of engaging in such strategies, such as: "We will feel lighthearted and relaxed." The goal sheet allows the couple to record their progress toward their goals as well as revise their plan if necessary. The therapist would suggest that Ben and Alyssa place their relationship vision form somewhere in their home where they can read it together regularly, review it, and change it if they so desire.

To close the session or the therapeutic process, depending on the decision Ben and Alyssa made, the Imago therapist reviews different types of exits and the no-exit decision. Because Ben and Alyssa both state that they do not engage in any catastrophic or terminal exits, they discuss the intentional and functional exits they use. For example, Alyssa might say, "I think I use spending time with Benny as a functional exit." By this, Alyssa means that spending time with their child is necessary and enjoyable, but that there are times when her overinvolvement with Benny results in an underinvolvement with Ben, a depletion of time and energy for their relationship. Ben and Alyssa then discuss the effects of Alyssa's exit on Ben. This dialogue might be followed by a behavior change request of Alyssa by Ben, which might be, "On the next two Saturdays, I'd like you to leave Benny with a babysitter for 3 hours so that we can have an intimate picnic in the park."

At the end of this session, the therapist would describe the benefits of introducing passion, via the reromanticizing process, into their relationship. Finally, if the couple contracted to continue therapy, the therapist would give an overview of what future sessions would cover.

General Comments

Ben and Alyssa came into therapy with an already-firm commitment to their relationship, which was not yet highly conflicted (they wanted to "make a good relationship better"). They also already showed signs of empathy and intentional behaviors. Thus, they found it relatively easy to engage in the couples dialogue and were readily receptive to the idea of gifting one another through the behavior change request process. In addition, both Ben and Alyssa expressed that they had been feeling unheard and misunderstood. The dialogue process, therefore, would likely have had an immediate and positive effect on their relationship.

If, however, the couple found themselves having difficulty in listening to one another, following through on commitments to change behaviors, or remaining dialogical with one another, the Imago therapist would engage them in some regressive work. This would enable the couple to understand the deeper emotional roots of their relationship problems. For instance, if Alyssa found it difficult to empathize with Ben's unhappiness over his job, Ben could be led to recall times during his childhood and adolescence when he felt pressured by his uncle's role modeling and by his mom's high expectations of him, as well as his overall sense of being controlled by others. Once such connections to childhood wounding are experienced and expressed, typically an affective shift toward empathic attunement occurs between partners. In this case, because of Alyssa's enhanced empathic understanding of Ben, she might feel more motivated to grant Ben behavior change requests that would ease his frustrations, frustrations that were rooted in his childhood experiences and reenacted in his marriage.

☐ Empirical Evaluation and Research

Empirical research on Imago Relationship Therapy is still in its infancy. Anecdotal feedback includes thank you letters and referrals from people who have worked with a certified Imago therapist, attended a Getting the Love You Want Couples Workshop, read the books on Imago Therapy, or viewed the home video (Hendrix & Hunt, 1993). Other data include the increase of clinicians who have taken Imago professional training (IIRT has certified over 1,400 therapists worldwide) and who report, after their certification, a greater success rate in working with couples.

Recently, there have been some preliminary empirical findings on Imago Therapy. One study, conducted by Luquet and Hannah (1996), analyzed nine married couples before and after a six-session short-term Imago Relationship Therapy format (Luquet, 1996). Each participant completed the Marital Satisfaction Inventory (MSI; Snyder, 1981) prior to the first session and again one week after the sixth and last session. All three MSI scales selected for analysis—Global Distress, Affective Communication, and Problem-Solving Communication—improved significantly from pre- to posttreatment. These findings were limited, given the absence of a control group and the small number of subjects.

Another study was conducted by Hogan, Hunt, Emerson, Hayes, and Ketterer (1996) on participant satisfaction with the Getting the Love You Want Couples Workshop. Two hundred sixty-eight participants of couples workshops, all led by Hendrix in Chicago, Los Angeles, and New York City, completed pre- and posttest measures. Of the 268 participants, 104 (39%) filled out and returned a third follow-up questionnaire, which was mailed to their home 3 months after the workshop.

Ninety-six percent rated the workshop experience "enjoyable." Ninety-nine percent rated their experience to be either "excellent" (58%), "very good" (34.5%), or "good" (6.5%), with only 1% rating their experience as "fair" or "poor." Ninety-six percent of the participants rated the workshop to be either "extremely relevant" (67%) or "very relevant" (29%). No participants rated the weekend as "not relevant at all." Again, given the absence of a control group and of random assignment, along with the tendency for participants to rate such experiences positively due to their monetary investment, these findings must be considered equivocal.

Hannah, Luquet, and McCormick (1997) found, on a sample of approximately a dozen couples, positive changes on a number of relationship and personal distress measures subsequent to a six- to eight-session format of Brief Imago Therapy (Luquet, 1996). Like those of the earlier studies, these findings must be considered preliminary.

Although such efficacy studies represent a promising beginning, Berger, in his article "What Can Clinicians Learn from Research?" (1997), addressed Imago's lack of sound longitudinal research studies. Berger challenged Imago clinicians and theorists to conduct more extensive efficacy studies using long-term follow-up, control groups, randomization of couples, and objective measures. He also recommended process studies that explore couples' reactions to variations in the therapist's role (e.g., passive facilitator vs. active leader) and theoretical studies that would examine hypotheses emerging from Imago theory (e.g., whether or not couples display complementary adaptations to emotional woundedness and/or complementary functions of the self). Discussions are currently underway among the board members of IIRT, the Association of Imago

Relationship Therapy (AIRT), and its clinical members to generate the financial resources to launch more comprehensive studies.

☐ Summary

Imago Relationship Therapy is effective with all couples, regardless of the difficulties in their relationships. Screening is generally unnecessary; the most relevant diagnostic parameters are the approximate developmental age of each partner, their emotional wounds, and their characterological defenses. These assessments enable the therapist to pace the dialogical processes according to the developmental maturity of the partners and the rigidity of their defenses. With couples who were wounded early in childhood, it is necessary for the Imago therapist to pace the dialogical procedures most slowly, because these couples are more defended than couples who were wounded later on developmentally. Thus, they are more symbiotic and have greater difficulty mirroring and, especially, validating the reality and feelings of the other. However, when the pace is slowed and the couple's interaction is contained by the Imago therapist, safety increases and anxiety simultaneously decreases. Ultimately, all couples can grow to become dialogical.

When physical abuse or addictions exist, it is often useful to seek auxiliary resources, such as shelters or treatment center programs *parallel* with Imago Therapy. Couples need to work together on these catastrophic issues, integrating the work into their relationship. Unfortunately, many of these auxiliary programs center on healing the individual rather than the couple. Perhaps Imago work could be joined with ancillary treatments either by creating a training program within the Imago clinical framework or by forming a partnership with ancillary programs, which would embrace Imago's "relationship as central" motto within their own addiction and/or abuse framework.

Additionally, Imago theory and practice could be enhanced through a studied comparison and contrast with other conjoint couples therapies. One area in need of theoretical development is the role of the body in characterological defenses, that is, how the body holds memories that are difficult to verbally access; thus, developing cognitive or emotive exercises, learning how to use the body as a diagnostic tool, and developing body work to relax defenses, access memories, and release feelings would enrich the therapy. Imago Therapy would be enhanced also by its consideration of hereditary, constitutional, and temperament factors.

Imago Therapy's main strengths are the support of its clinical procedures by its metatheoretical assumptions, the dialogue process for facilitating safety and connection, the opportunity for couples to participate in couples groups and/or workshops that offer support and modeling, and the focus on the relationship as nature's evolutionary healing structure. Ultimately, this focus on marriage or a committed relationship as a path towards wholeness reduces stress in the family environment, raises conscious awareness for the prevention of developmental wounds in future generations, and restores an awareness of connection to the larger whole, becoming essentially a process of spiritual evolution.

☐ Contact References

For more information on Imago Relationship Therapy, contact the Institute for Imago Relationship Therapy, 335 N. Knowles Ave., Winter Park, FL 32789; rickimago@aol.com; http://www.imagotherapy.com.

☐ References

Berger, R. (1997). What can clinicians learn from research? *The Journal of Imago Relationship Therapy, 2*(1), 71–80.

Buber, M. (1958). *I and Thou.* New York: Scribner & Sons.

Davis, P. (1983). *God and the new physics.* New York: Simon & Schuster.

Davis, P. (1992). *The mind of God: The scientific basis for a rational world.* New York: Simon & Schuster.

Hannah, M. T., Luquet, W., & McCormick, J. (1997). COMPASS as a measure of the efficacy of couples therapy. *The American Journal of Family Therapy, 25*(1), 76–90.

Hendrix, H. (1988). *Getting the love you want: A guide for couples.* New York: Henry Holt.

Hendrix, R. A., & Hunt, J. A. (1993). *Getting the Love You Want Home Video* [Video]. Winter Park, FL: Institute for Imago Relationship Therapy.

Hoffman, M. L. (1987). The contribution of empathy to justice and moral judgment. In N. Eisenberg & J. Strayer (Eds.), *Empathy and Its development* (pp. 47–80). New York: Cambridge University Press.

Hoffman, M. L. (1990). Empathy and justice motivation. *Motivation and Emotion, 4,* 151–172.

Hogan, T., Hunt, R., Emerson, D., Hayes, R., & Ketterer, K. (1996). An evaluation of satisfaction with the "Getting the love you want" weekend workshop. *The Journal of Imago Relationship Therapy, 1*(1), 67–75.

Institute for Imago Relationship Therapy. (1998). *Professional training catalogue.* Winter Park, FL: Author.

Kohut, H. (1978). *The search for the self: Selected writings of Heinz Kohut: 1950–1978,* Vols. I & II, P. H. Ornstein (Ed.). New York: International Universities Press.

Luquet, W. (1996). *Short-term couples therapy: The Imago model in action.* New York: Brunner/Mazel.

Luquet, W., & Hannah, M. T. (1996). The efficacy of short-term Imago therapy: Preliminary findings. *The Journal of Imago Relationship Therapy, 1*(1), 67–75.

MacLean, P. (1973). *A triune concept of the brain and behavior.* Toronto, ON, Canada: University of Toronto Press.

Rogers, C. (1961). *On becoming a person.* Boston: Houghton Mifflin.

Snyder, D. K. (1981). *Marital Satisfaction Inventory manual.* Los Angeles: Western Psychological Services.

Stern, D. (1985). *The interpersonal world of the infant.* New York: Basic Books.

Sullivan, H. S. (1953). *The interpersonal theory of psychiatry.* New York: Norton.

Zohar, D. (1990). *The quantum self: Human nature and consciousness defined by the new physics.* New York: Quill/William Morrow.

David H. Olson, Ph.D.
Amy K. Olson, B.A.

PREPARE/ENRICH Program: Version 2000

☐ Introduction

Historical Background

The choice to marry is one of the most important decisions in life, yet many people do not invest time and energy into preparing for their marital relationship. Couples typically spend more time preparing for their marriage ceremony than building skills to help them have a happy and lasting marriage.

Current statistics verify a divorce rate of over 50% (Olson & DeFrain, 1997). A significant proportion of married couples experience serious marital conflict early in their relationship, as indicated by the high divorce rate early in marriage. In fact, the average length of a marriage is only 6 years. Clearly, couples are not prepared to deal with the challenges of marriage.

Theory and Issues Related to Couples

Table 9.1 gives an outline of some of the more common issues that couples face in marriage, along with the corresponding areas addressed by the PREPARE/ENRICH Inventories.

196

TABLE 9.1.   Common conflict issues in couples and PREPARE/ENRICH areas

Common Conflict Issues	PREPARE/ENRICH Areas
	Personality Issues
Expressing self	Assertiveness
Self-esteem	Self-confidence
Denial/avoidance	Avoidance
Control issues	Partner dominance
	Intrapersonal Issues
Idealization/social desirability	Idealistic distortion
Personality/habits	Personality issues
Incompatible values/beliefs	Spiritual beliefs
Interests/activities	Leisure activities
Expectations	Marriage expectations
Satisfaction	Marriage satisfaction
	Interpersonal Issues
Communication	Communication
Arguments/anger	Conflict resolution
Children	Children and parenting
Commitment	Couple closeness
Marital roles	Role relationship
Sex/affection	Sexual relationship
	External Issues
Relatives/friends	Family and friends
Money/work	Financial management
Family issues	Family closeness & family flexibility

Factors Influencing Development of PREPARE/ENRICH

PREPARE was originally developed after learning about the difficulty of working with premarital couples. In the late 1970s, David Olson was approached by three premarital programs in the Twin Cities that were running large lecture programs for groups of 50 couples. An evaluation demonstrated that these programs were generally ineffective and that they too often turned couples off to the idea of couple enrichment programs. The question was what could be done to help couples get better prepared for marriage.

The initial idea was to create a couple questionnaire that would get the couple talking with each other about their relationship. By including in the questionnaire relevant issues for couples, it was hoped that they would begin discussing and even resolving some of these issues before marriage. After the initial questionnaire was developed, a research project was designed to determine the impact of a premarital "inventory" and counseling for couples (Olson, Fournier, Druckman, & Robinson, 1979). The study included five groups: couples who had had no premarital preparation; those who had participated in some type of program; those who had participated in PREPARE with no feedback; those who had participated in PREPARE with 2 hours of feedback; and those who had participated in PREPARE with four 2-hour feedback sessions. The study clearly demonstrated that the PREPARE groups made more important changes than the first two groups. Also, the group with PREPARE and four feedback sessions made the most positive change. These findings led to the further development of the PREPARE Inventory—a questionnaire used to assess couples—and more clearly defined feedback sessions.

Overview of Version 2000

PREPARE was developed in 1978 as a result of extensive research and has been revised three times (1982, 1986, 1996). In 1996, major revisions were made in the PREPARE, PREPARE-MC, and ENRICH Inventories, and they were expanded into the PREPARE/ENRICH Program with six couple exercises. The goal of the program was to build on the strengths of these well-designed inventories, and to add a more comprehensive skill-based program for couples. Table 9.2 summarizes the improvements that the program's "Version 2000" make.

For Version 2000, the 20 categories in each of the inventories were expanded and revised, so there are now 165 items in each inventory. About 40% of the items are new, 30% were revised extensively, and the remaining 30% had minor revisions. Major revisions were made to the items in order to reduce double negatives, expand the areas covered, and increase the clarity and quality of the items. Unclear and unreliable items were dropped, increasing the reliability of all the scales. The reliability of the scales now averages .80 and the range is from .73 to .90 for all the inventories.

Thirty background questions are now contained in all the inventories,

---

TABLE 9.2.   Improvements in Version 2000 of the PREPARE/ENRICH Inventories

- Major item revision with 40% new items and 30% revised
- 30 background questions with 15 questions on abuse
- Four newly created personality scales
- New typology of couples with 4 premarital types and 5 marital types
- Expanded focus on family of origin & couple system using Couple & Family Map (Circumplex Model)
- Six couple exercises

with 15 items added that focus on various types of abuse. The abuse questions deal with alcohol and drug abuse, and other types of abuse, including emotional, physical, and sexual. The abuse questions pertain to abuse from parents, partner, and others.

In order to enhance the understanding of couple dynamics, four personality scales were added to the inventories and they focus on: self-confidence, partner dominance, assertiveness, and avoidance. All the scales are integrated into the feedback process and couples complete exercises in the workbook that are designed to improve their assertiveness skills.

The categories Family-of-Origin (two scales) and Type of Marriage (two scales) were added to all inventories. Each person describes their relationship regarding couple closeness and couple flexibility, and their family of origin regarding family closeness and family flexibility. These descriptions are plotted onto the Couple & Family Map (based on the Circumplex Model of Marital and Family Systems; Olson & DeFrain, 1997). This provides a more comprehensive picture of the family of origin and its relationship to the couple system.

A 25-page *Building a Strong Marriage Workbook* was expanded from the earlier booklet to include six couple exercises on communication (two), conflict resolution skills, linking family of origin to the couple's relationship, financial management, and goal setting.

☐ Theoretical Underpinnings

The theoretical assumption is that the quality of the marital relationship can be predicted from the premarital relationship. Therefore, we can identify the relationship factors that, if improved, will make a difference to the quality of a marriage (Fowers and Olson, 1986). Version 2000 of the PREPARE/ENRICH Program is a comprehensive premarital program that has a theoretical and empirical foundation and clinical relevance to couples.

This program applies four important characteristics of an effective preventive approach. First, factors that relate to marital success need to be identified. Second, couples need to be assessed on those critical variables. Third, feedback and exercises need to be given to couples, which will help them deal with problem areas. Fourth, couples need skill-building exercises that focus on communication and conflict resolution skills.

An instrument and program that attempts to improve a couple's relationship should be able to obtain information on the most critical factors in premarital relationship formation and development that are predictive of later marital satisfaction and stability. In a recent study, Stahmann and Hiebert (1997) attempted to identify factors that relate to marital success. A diverse group of 238 clergy who conducted premarital counseling were asked to estimate the percentage of premarital couples experiencing problems or complaints in 29 possible areas. For first marriages, the five problem areas ranked as occurring most frequently were: communication (63%), unrealistic expectations of marriage or spouse (62%), money management and finances (60%), decision making and problem solving (55%), and power struggles (51%). For remarriages, the five problem areas ranked as occurring most frequently were: communication (57%), children (57%), problems related to previous marriage (49%), power struggles (48%), and money management and finances (47%).

J. H. Larson and Holman (1994) reviewed 50 years of published longitudinal and cross-sectional research on premarital factors that predict future marital quality and stability. Marital stability was defined as the status of a marriage (i.e., separated or divorced), and marital quality was defined as a subjective evaluation of a couple's relationship. Based on an ecological or ecosystemic perspective, Larson and Holman concluded that premarital predictors could be organized into three major categories. First, background or contextual factors include family-of-origin effects, sociocultural factors like education and age at marriage, and current contexts like support for the relationship from family and friends. Second, individual traits and characteristics include emotional health, self-esteem, and interpersonal skills. Third, couple interaction processes focus on interpersonal similarity. Based on their research, Larson and Holman concluded that individual traits and behaviors and couple interactional processes are the two most important categories of factors in predicting marital quality and stability.

J. Larson et al. (1995) reviewed five premarital assessment questionnaires (PAQs) available to educators and premarital counselors. The authors evaluated the five PAQs based on theoretical and psychometric criteria pertaining to their usefulness in educational and counseling settings. Building on J. H. Larson and Holman's (1994) previous and extensive review of literature, they evaluated each PAQ for the inclusion of premarital items that were found to predict future marital success. PREPARE assesses most (85%) of the premarital factors defined in their research as good predictors of marital satisfaction and stability. Based on J. H. Larson and Holman's evaluation of PAQs, they found PREPARE to be "most psychometrically sound" and rated it as "the best instrument for premarital counseling" (J. Larson et al., 1995, p. 251).

In summary, these reviews clearly demonstrate the importance of having a couple assessment tool and couple program that focus on at least the following five areas: communication, conflict resolution, family of origin, finances, and goals. The PREPARE/ENRICH Program builds on these important areas and provides both a couple assessment and couple exercises on these topics.

☐ Intervention Model

Linkage of Intervention Model and Theory

The theory and research on couples identified the most salient issues to focus on with couples. The PREPARE/ENRICH Program built directly on these findings and includes two steps: (a) couple assessment with relevant inventory, and (b) several feedback sessions using six couples exercises. Each of these steps will be briefly described.

In step 1, couples take one of the four couple inventories: PREPARE, PREPARE-MC, ENRICH, or MATE. PREPARE is designed for couples planning to marry who do not have children. PREPARE-MC is designed for couples planning to marry who have children (either together or from previous relationships). ENRICH is designed for married couples seeking enrichment and counseling and for couples who have cohabited for two or more years. MATE is designed for older couples (50 or older) planning to marry or facing other life transitions such as retirement or relocation.

All four inventories contain 165 items designed to identify and measure the couple's relationship in 20 areas. There are 12 content areas, 4 personality scales, and 4 scales focusing on the family-of-origin issues. The specific categories are: Idealistic Distortion, Marriage Expectations (PREPARE and PREPARE-MC only) and Marital Satisfaction (ENRICH only), Personality Assessment, Communication, Conflict Resolution, Financial Management, Leisure Activities, Sexual Relationship, Children and Parenting, Family and Friends, Role Relationship, and Spiritual Beliefs.

The PREPARE/ENRICH Inventories contain two family-of-origin scales (assessing Family Cohesion and Family Flexibility) and two scales assessing the couple system (Couple Cohesion and Couple Flexibility). These scales help to show the relationship between the family of origin and the couple relationship, since a person's family provides a frame of reference for evaluating a couple relationship. These four scores (two from each person) are plotted onto the Couple & Family Map.

There are also four personality scales (Assertiveness, Self-Confidence, Avoidance, and Partner Dominance) that are assessed in the PREPARE/ENRICH Inventories. Assertiveness measures a person's ability to express feelings to a partner and to be able to ask for what he or she would like. Self-Confidence focuses on how good a person feels about himself or herself and his or her ability to control things in life. Avoidance measures a person's tendency to minimize issues and reluctance to deal with issues directly. Partner Dominance focuses on how much a person feels a partner tries to control him or her and dominate his or her life.

Six Goals and Six Couple Exercises

There are six goals in the PREPARE/ENRICH Program and there is one couple exercise for each goal. The six goals are: to assist the couple in identifying and building upon their relationship strengths and to identify areas of the relationship that may be problematic or in need of enrichment; to teach the couple to communicate more effectively about important issues; to resolve problematic issues using the 10-step Conflict Resolution Model; to explore family-of-origin issues using the Couple & Family Map; to develop a plan for achieving personal, couple, and family goals. The PREPARE/ENRICH Program contains six couple exercises to help the couple achieve these goals. The exercises are designed to encourage communication and planning together about how to deal with important topics. For each goal there is a corresponding couple feedback exercise. The six couple feedback exercises are summarized in Table 9.3.

☐ Strategies for Intervention

There are six couple exercises, and the materials for completing these exercises are included in the 25-page *Building A Strong Marriage Workbook* that is given to each couple when they come back for the feedback session. The six exercises are now described in more detail in the following sections.

Sharing Strength and Growth Areas: Couple Exercise I

Each partner in a couple independently chooses three areas from the 12 PREPARE/ENRICH scales that they feel are relationship strengths, and three areas they feel are relationship growth areas. Then each partner is encouraged to share what he or she believes the strengths are in their relationship. One partner proposes a strength area and discusses the

---

TABLE 9.3.   Six couple goals and six couple exercises in PREPARE/ENRICH program

- Exploring relationship strengths and growth areas
- Strengthening couple communication skills, including assertiveness and active listening
- Resolving couple conflict using the 10-step Conflict Resolution Model
- Exploring family-of-origin issues using Couple & Family Map
- Developing a workable budget and financial plan
- Developing personal, couple, and family goals

strength; then the other partner indicates one strength he or she has selected. This process is repeated until all three strength areas have been
discussed by both partners. As partners share their perceptions, the counselor interjects the results found in the inventory regarding the strengths
and illustrates them with some specific items.

The same discussion process is used to share and discuss growth areas.
After the partners have shared their chosen strength and growth areas
with each other, they are encouraged to discuss questions such as, "Did
your partner's responses surprise you?" When the partner's perceptions
concur with inventory results, the counselor should interject one or two
specific items from the area to generate discussion about how the area
under consideration is problematic or beneficial for the couple. If the inventory results do not concur with the partners' perceptions, the counselor may have the couple discuss the concern more fully with one another.

Sharing strength and growth areas helps the couple to understand each
other better, by increasing each other's awareness of how each views the
relationship. This exercise also encourages communication and clearly
defines relationship strengths that can be built upon in the future.

Creating a Wish List: Couple Exercise II

Assertiveness and active listening are two specific communication skills
emphasized in Couple Communication Exercise II. Teaching assertiveness
and active listening skills helps to increase the positive cycle of increasing
assertiveness and self-confidence and reduces the negative cycle of avoidance and partner dominance for both the individuals and the couple (based
on four personality scales).

Partners make "Wish Lists" of three things they would like their partners to do more often and they take turns sharing these wishes. Sharing
their wishes with each other encourages each partner to be assertive with
the other. As the partners share their wishes with each other, the counselor provides them with feedback related to their assertiveness and active
listening skills. The counselor would also give feedback from the four
personality scales (Assertiveness, Avoidance, Self-Confidence, Partner
Dominance) and the Communication scale. The counselor would conclude by giving the couple positive feedback about their assertiveness
and active listening skills and how to continue to build these skills.

A typical example is Susan and Michael, who shared their wishes with
each other. Susan asked Michael: "Would you tell me more often how
you are feeling and what you are thinking?" Michael responded: "I will
try, but I will need to be reminded." Michael had a special request for
Susan: "I wish you would be willing to come to a baseball game with

me." Susan responded: "I will go to a game if you let me know a couple of weeks in advance so I can plan for it." In both of these cases, the partners showed not only that they understood the request, but that were willing to comply with the request. Agreeing is not a necessary step in active listening since the goal is only to demonstrate that one understands what the other person has requested.

Ten Steps for Resolving Couple Conflict: Couple Exercise III

For this exercise, the counselor would walk the couple through the 10 steps exercise during a feedback session using an issue from one of their chosen growth areas to introduce the process. Then the couple would select an issue to work on as a homework assignment to be reviewed at the next session. Table 9.4 identifies the 10 steps for resolving couple conflict which were developed based on current research and theory regarding relevant steps that have been used in a variety of conflict resolution models.

Feedback Using the Couple & Family Map: Couple Exercise IV

When we marry, we marry not only another person but also that person's family. Because of the importance of family of origin in shaping a person's view of the world and expectations for a relationship, we focus on family of origin in each inventory. Each person describes their couple relationship and their family of origin in terms of closeness and flexibility on the inventory. These four descriptions are plotted on the Couple & Family Map. The goal is to help the couple see the importance of their family relationship in their couple system. Also, it helps the couple be more

---

TABLE 9.4.   Ten steps for resolving couple conflict

1. Set a time and place for discussion.
2. Define the problem or issue of disagreement.
3. How do each of you contribute to the problem?
4. List past attempts to resolve the issue that were not successful.
5. Brainstorm: List all possible solutions.
6. Discuss and evaluate these possible solutions.
7. Agree on one solution to try.
8. Agree on how each individual will work toward this solution.
9. Set up another meeting.
10. Reward each other as you each contribute toward the situation.

proactive in thinking about what they want and do not want to bring from their family into their couple relationship.

During the feedback process, the counselor would define couple and family closeness and couple and family flexibility for the couple, and give a general overview of the Couple & Family Map. The counselor would then show the partners how their family of origin and couple relationship categorizations were plotted on the Map, and allow them to react to his or her perception. Discussions of similarities or differences are explored, as the couple explores questions such as, "How similar are the couple's descriptions of their families of origin?" and "What would the couple like to change about their couple relationship?" This information is summarized with the couple and they are asked to share what they learned.

A sample of the Couple & Family Map is presented in Figure 9.1 which illustrates how one couple (male and female) described their couple relationship and how they described their families of origin. Carla and Justin not only see their couple relationship differently in terms of closeness and flexibility, but they also come from very different families. Carla describes the couple relationship as "somewhat flexible" and "very connected," whereas Justin describes it as "flexible" and "connected." Their description of the couple relationship is in part influenced by the differ-

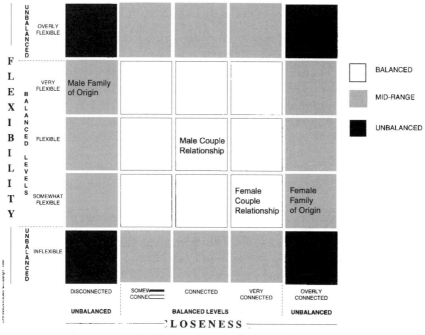

FIGURE 9.1. Couple & Family Map

ent families in which they grew up. Carla had a "very connected" and "somewhat flexible" family, while Justin had a "disconnected" and "very flexible" family. Justin said: "I was surprised to see how different my family is from Carla's family" and Carla responded that: "Justin's family is not very close and not much fun to be with." This couple is starting the process of exploring their families of origin with each other, and this exercise is designed to facilitate this discussion.

Financial Plans and Budget: Couple Exercise V

Financial management is a problematic issue for most premarital and married couples. In fact, 37% of all married couples indicate that the number-1 problem in their marriage is money (Olson & DeFrain, 1997). Couples are asked to complete the Budget Worksheet and each partner makes a list of short- and long-term financial goals. These materials are in the *Building a Strong Marriage Workbook* and are often assigned as a homework assignment. The counselor may help facilitate a realistic and workable budget and help the couple set both short-term and long-term financial goals. The counselor also reviews with the couple the financial management area from a computer report obtained from the inventory, focusing on strength and growth areas.

Personal, Couple, and Family Goals: Couple Exercise VI

Developing and sharing goals as a couple promotes closeness and bonding, as well as communication. Couples in which partners are aware of what each person wants often pull together to help each other achieve goals. Couples are given the individual homework assignment of describing two or three personal, couple, and family goals. They develop an action plan for one or more areas of life using the "CHANGE" model; the goals should be attainable within 1 to 5 years (see Table 9.5). During a feedback session, the counselor will have each partner take turns sharing

TABLE 9.5.   CHANGE model

C	Commit yourself to a specific goal
H	Habits: Break old ones; start new ones
A	Action: Take one step at a time
N	Never give up—lapses might occur
G	Goal-oriented: Focus on the positive
E	Evaluate and reward yourself

goals, while they focus on the similarities and differences between them. Throughout the sharing process, the counselor also gives feedback on the assertiveness and active listening skills of each person.

☐ Format of Application

Recruitment of Couples

Premarital couples most often hear about the PREPARE Program from a clergy member when they are interested in getting married. Married couples typically hear about the ENRICH Program when they are seeking marriage counseling or when they are attending a marriage enrichment program. Because of the increasing interest in and awareness of the PRE-PARE/ENRICH Program stimulated by the media, couples often contact the PREPARE/ENRICH office directly to locate a counselor or clergy members with whom they can complete the program.

Couple Assessment

Once a couple is connected with a counselor, the counselor describes the complete program, which includes taking the relevant inventory and completing the six couple exercises. The counselor introduces the inventory to the couple and reminds them that it is not a test, but a tool to evaluate their relationship in terms of their strengths and potential areas of growth. A couple number is assigned to protect the couple's identity when the inventory is scored. Only the counselor can match the identity of a couple with the resulting computer report. The counselor then sets a date to administer the inventory and a date for the initial feedback session.

When the couple is taking the inventory, it is important that they be in separate rooms so they do not discuss the items with each other. Separating them facilitates more privacy and honesty in answering the questionnaire. After the inventories are completed, the counselor collects the question booklets and answer sheets and sends the answer sheets in for scoring. Couples are encouraged to discuss the inventory before returning for the future feedback sessions.

Materials Provided to the Counselor

The counselor receives a 15-page computer report assessing the couple's strengths and growth areas from 12 different categories. This computerized summary provides a comprehensive profile description of the particular relationship along the various dimensions of a couple relationship. The counselor also receives a 25-page *Building a Strong Marriage Workbook,* which is given to the couple during the initial feedback session. The counselor will meet with the couple for several (3–6) sessions to encourage them to complete the six couple exercises.

☐ Qualities and Role of the Leader or Facilitator

The program is used by professional counselors, clergy of all denominations, and lay couples. Professional counselors can choose the option of purchasing a *Self-Training Counselor Manual* and videotape by completing an application form. Persons not trained as professional counselors, such as clergy and lay couples, are required to attend a 1-day workshop in order to be trained on how to administer and use the PREPARE/ENRICH Program.

The counselor is trained to facilitate the couple's discussion of the relevant issues with each other in a direct and open manner. The counselor is also encouraged to teach and reinforce the communication and conflict resolution skills. This is a semistructured program that provides the basic materials and design but permits the counselor some flexibility in how it is delivered based on individual counseling skills and amount of time the counselor can work with the couple.

☐ Application of the Preventive Model to a Couple at Risk

While all couples going through the program would participate in all six of the couple exercises, we have chosen three of the exercises to illustrate how this program could be helpful to Ben and Alyssa. We will describe Exercise II, on communication; Exercise IV, on family of origin, and Exercise VI on personal, couple, and family goals.

In Exercise II, the couple creates a wish list, which is designed to teach them how to be more assertive with each other and to use active listening. Ben reads from his wish list: "I would like to have more attention and love from you rather than what is left over after caring for Benny." Rather than using active listening, Alyssa reacts by saying: "I wish I wasn't so exhausted so I could have more energy to give attention to you." The counselor then encourages her to first use active listening to show that she understands before she agrees or disagrees with Ben. Both Ben and

Alyssa need to improve their assertiveness and active listening skills and find quality time to talk with each other like they did in the past.

Exercise IV focuses on family-of-origin issues, which are becoming more prominent for Ben and Alyssa now that they have children. The counselor gives a brief overview of the Couple & Family Map and shows Ben and Alyssa how each perceives their relationship and their families of origin. Alyssa's family was "rigid" and "very connected," while Ben's family was "flexible" and "connected." Alyssa is behaving more like her parents now than she did when she was first dating Ben. She has become more religious, less interested in her career, and more like her mother. Ben is becoming more frustrated because he would like their family to be more flexible and he is feeling less connected to Alyssa. The counselor will try to help the couple explore how they see their couple relationship now and how they would like their relationship to be in terms of flexibility and closeness in the future.

Exercise VI focuses on each person identifying their personal, couple, and family goals with each other. One of Ben's personal goals is to start his own business; a couple goal is to get more connected with Alyssa; and a family goal is spend more time with her and their son Benny. Alyssa's personal goal is to become more active in church groups; a couple goal is for Ben to be more understanding of her and her concerns; and a family goal is to be a good mother and wife. The counselor then encourages them to develop an action plan using the CHANGE model; they choose to work on their couple relationship. They develop a plan to get a sitter and spend one evening each week with each other outside the home. The overall goal is to help them improve their couple relationship so that they can be better for each other and for their children.

☐ Empirical Evaluation and Research

Reliability and Validity of Inventories

An important strength of the PREPARE/ENRICH Inventories is their strong psychometric properties. High levels of reliability and validity have been found for each instrument, making them valuable tools for research as well as clinical use. Each of the 20 scales in PREPARE, PREPARE-MC, and ENRICH have been assessed for alpha reliability and test–retest reliability. High reliability coefficients were found for both internal consistency and test–retest on all instruments. The internal consistency ranged from .74 to .89 for PREPARE (n = 7,846; average = .79), from .73 to .84 for PREPARE-MC (n = 2,530; average = .78), and from .74 to .89 for ENRICH (n = 1,962; average =.85).

Four separate studies have tested the predictive validity of PREPARE and ENRICH. PREPARE has been able to predict with about 80%–85% accuracy which couples will be satisfied with their marriages and which couples are likely to experience difficulties. These findings are based on two 3-year longitudinal studies of premarital couples who had participated in a PREPARE program 3 months prior to marriage (Fowers & Olson, 1986; A. S. Larsen & Olson, 1989). ENRICH is able to discriminate between happily married and unhappily married couples with about 90% accuracy (Fowers & Olson, 1989). This is based on a major study of 5,039 couples who took ENRICH as part of either a marital therapy or a marital enrichment program.

The potential of the PREPARE Program for preventive work was demonstrated in a follow-up study by Fowers and Olson (1986). Based on a couple's marital status 2 to 3 years after the wedding, and their current responses to a marital satisfaction questionnaire, four groups were defined: (a) married satisfied, (b) married dissatisfied, (c) divorced or separated, and (d) canceled. An analysis of variance indicated significant differences between the four groups in 8 of 11 subscales. As hypothesized, it was found that couples with higher marital satisfaction scores had scored significantly higher on the PREPARE Inventory prior to marriage than had dissatisfied couples, divorced couples, and couples who canceled their weddings. Couples who had canceled their wedding plans had scores that were very similar to those couples who were divorced or separated and significantly different from those of happily married couples.

Typology of Couples Based on PREPARE/ENRICH

Four types of premarital couples and five types of married couples were derived by using the *positive couple agreement* (PCA) scores from the PREPARE and ENRICH Inventories using cluster analysis. Using data from 5,030 premarital couples who took PREPARE, Fowers & Olson (1992) identified the four types of premarital couples: *vitalized, harmonious, traditional,* and *conflicted.*

Five types of married couples were created using a sample of 6,267 married couples (Olson & Fowers, 1993) who took ENRICH. It was validating to find that the four premarital types identified from the PREPARE inventory also emerged from the ENRICH inventory, with one additional type, the devitalized type. Thus four of the five marital types are identical to the four premarital types: vitalized, harmonious, traditional and conflicted. The one additional marital type is called devitalized (see Figure 9.2).

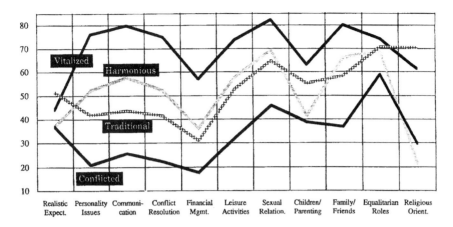

FIGURE 9.2. Four types of premarital couples based on PREPARE

An important replication study of the types from ENRICH was completed with a sample of 450 African-American married couples by Allen (1997). Cluster analysis replicated the same five types of couples as from a sample of Caucasian couples. This replication supported the existence of five couple types, and the percentage of African-American couples in the various types were very similar to that of the Caucasian couples.

Vitalized Couples

The vitalized couples were the happiest couple type because they had the highest PCA scores on many areas. They had many strengths (high PCA scores) and few growth areas (low PCA scores).

Harmonious Couples

The harmonious couples had many strengths, but not as many as the vitalized couples. They like many areas of their relationship, but often have low scores in the children and parenting area.

Traditional Couples

These couples are called traditional because they had more strengths in traditional areas including children and parenting, family and friends, traditional roles, and spiritual beliefs. However, they had lower scores on more internal dynamics, where they indicated problems with personality issues, communication, and conflict resolution.

Conflicted Couples

These couples had numerous growth areas and few relationship strengths. They were called conflicted since they seemed to disagree about many areas, and they had low scores on communication, conflict resolution, and many other areas. As premarital couples, they are at high risk for eventual divorce; as married couples, they commonly seek marital therapy (Fowers, Montel, & Olson, 1996).

Devitalized Couples

These couples (from ENRICH only) had growth areas in almost all aspects of their relationship. They are typically very unhappy and have few strengths as a couple, although they might have had strengths earlier in their relationship. These couples also commonly seek marital therapy.

Validation of Four Premarital Types From PREPARE

In order to validate the four premarital types, 328 premarital couples were followed for 3 years after marriage to assess their marital success (Fowers et al., 1996). These 328 couples were classified into the four premarital types and outcome measures focused on whether they were happily married, unhappily married, separated or divorced, or had canceled their wedding plans.

The most significant validation of the value of the typology was the finding related to the marital outcomes of the premarital couples (see Table 9.6). As hypothesized, the vitalized couples produced the highest percentage of happily married couples (60%) and the lowest percentage of separated and divorced couples (17%). Conversely, the conflicted couples produced the most separated or divorced couples (49%) and the least number of happily married couples (17%). The traditional couples produced the lowest percentage of separated or divorced couples (6%), but the highest percentage of unhappily married couples (50%). The high percentage of unhappy couples is to be expected because their traditional orientation would encourage them to stay together even if the marriage was problematic.

There were 89 couples who canceled their wedding plans as a result of taking PREPARE and receiving feedback. As predicted, the highest percentage of those who canceled their weddings were from conflicted couples (35 couples; 40%), followed by traditional couples (23 couples; 26%), then harmonious couples (20 couples; 22%), and, least often, vitalized couples (11 couples; 12%).

TABLE 9.6. Premarital types based on PREPARE and marital outcomes

Premarital Type	Happily Married		Unhappily Married		Separated Divorced		Total Percent	
	N	%	N	%	N	%	N	%
Vitalized	38	60%	15	23%	11	17%		100%
Harmonious	30	46%	19	29%	16	24%		100%
Traditional	17	34%	25	50%	8	16%		100%
Conflicted	10	17%	18	30%	32	49%		100%
Totals	95		77		67			239

Interconnection of Four Personality Scales

There is a *positive cycle* linking assertiveness and self-confidence and a *negative cycle* linking avoidance and partner dominance (see Figure 9.3). In the positive cycle, as a person uses more assertiveness, their level of self-confidence tends to increase. As a person's self-confidence increases, their willingness and ability to be more assertive increases. In the negative cycle, when one person perceives their partner as dominating, a common reaction is for that person to avoid dealing with issues. As one person uses more avoidance, the other person will tend to become more dominant.

An empirical analysis of these personality scales demonstrates how they are interconnected with each other and with some of the other content scales like communication and conflict resolution (see Table 9.7). People who have high scores on assertiveness tend to be low in avoidance, to be low in partner dominance, to like the personality of their partner (Personality Issues scale), to feel good about their communication (Communication scale), and to like how they resolve couple conflict (Conflict Resolution scale). Clinically, it would be common for people who have high scores on the negative cycle to have a greater tendency to be abusive (background questions) and controlling of their partner (partner dominance).

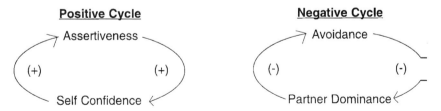

FIGURE 9.3.   Positive and negative cycles

TABLE 9.7. Assertiveness and personality assessment

People high in assertiveness tend to:
Be low in avoidance ($r = -.72$)
Be low in partner dominance ($r = -.50$)
Like the personality of their partner ($r = -.49$)
Feel good about communication with their partner ($r = .49$)
Feel good about conflict resolution with partner ($r = .68$)

The personality assessment is designed to increase the counselor's understanding of each partner and how their personality characteristics are related to the underlying couple dynamics. These four areas are interrelated with each other and together provide a rather comprehensive picture of each person. Research on couples has found that successful couples tend to be those in which both people are high in self-confidence, low in partner dominance, high is assertiveness, and low in avoidance (Olson, 1996).

☐ Summary

The PREPARE/ENRICH Program is designed to facilitate communication within couples about meaningful issues in their relationships. The program has six goals and one couple exercise for each goal. The program is designed to increase couples' awareness of their relationship strengths and growth areas and to provide them with skills so that they can improve their relationship. The program includes first taking a relevant couple inventory (PREPARE, PREPARE-MC, ENRICH, or MATE) and then getting feedback about its results from a trained counselor.

There are a variety of strengths in the PREPARE/ENRICH Program, and one is that it begins with a comprehensive couple inventory. The couple takes one of the four inventories (PREPARE, PREPARE-MC, ENRICH, and MATE), which have been designed to maximize their relevance to couples in different stages in their relationships. The inventories have been scientifically developed and have high reliability, high validity, and large national norms ($n = 250,000$ couples) with couples from various ethnic groups. The inventories are based on systems theory, and the Circumplex Model of Couple and Family Systems (Olson & De Frain, 1997) is used in the assessment and program. Numerous studies have been published that demonstrate the rigor of the inventories and their relevance to couples from a variety of ethnic groups. The program has been adopted by professional counselors and clergy from many diverse religious groups.

The program does, however, have some limitations. The inventories are lengthy, with 165 items and 30 background questions, and are at about the sixth grade level, so that persons with lower reading levels would have some difficulty with them. It is a requirement that both people in a couple relationship complete the questionnaire and, therefore, it is not designed for one person. The program is also not designed for individuals with very severe emotional problems or for couples having intense marital conflict.

Future directions for the program include continued research on its effectiveness and on the value of various aspects of it. A new feature is a group version of the program called GROWING TOGETHER. In this group program for couples, the couple receives a *Couple Report* and a *Building a Strong Marriage Workbook,* and they view the *PREPARE/ENRICH Video* that illustrates the six couple exercises. The couple completes the exercises with their partner and they then share their experiences with the other couples in the group.

☐ Contact References

For more information, contact Life Innovations, P.O. Box 190, Minneapolis, MN 55440; 800-331-1661; http://www.lifeinnovation.com

☐ References

Allen, W. (1997). *Replication of five types of married couples based on ENRICH.* Unpublished doctoral dissertation, University of Minnesota, St. Paul.

Duvall, E. M. (1971). *Family development* (4th ed.). Philadelphia: Lippincott.

Fournier, D. G., & Olson, D. H. (1986). Programs for premarital and newlywed couples. In R. F. Levant (Ed.), *Psychoeducational approaches to family therapy and counseling* (pp. 194–231). New York: Springer-Verlag.

Fournier, D. G., Springer, J., & Olson, D. H. (1979). *Conflict and commitment in seven stages of premarital and marital relations.* Unpublished manuscript, Dept. of Family Social Science, University of Minnesota, St. Paul.

Fowers, B. J., Montel, K. H., & Olson, D. H. (1996). Predictive validity of types of premarital couples based on PREPARE. *Journal of Marital and Family Therapy, 22, 1,* 103–119.

Fowers, B. J., & Olson, D. H. (1986). Predicting marital success with PREPARE: A predictive validity study. *Journal of Marital and Family Therapy, 12,* 403–413.

Fowers, B. J ., & Olson, D. H. (1989). ENRICH marital inventory: A discriminant validity and cross-validation assessment. *Journal of Marital and Family Therapy, 15,* 65–79.

Fowers, B. J., & Olson, D. H. (1992). Four types of premarital couples: An empirical typology based on PREPARE. *Journal of Family Psychology, 6*(1), 10–21.

Kitson, G. C., & Sussman, M. B. (1997, April). *Marital complaints, demographic characteristics, and symptoms of mental distress among the divorcing.* Paper presented at the meeting of the Midwest Sociological Society, Chicago.

Larsen, A. S., & Olson, D. H. (1989). Predicting marital satisfaction using PREPARE: A replication study. *Journal of Marital and Family Therapy, 15,* 311–322.

Larson, J. H., & Holman, T. B. (1994). Premarital predictors of marital quality and stability. *Family Relations, 43,* 228–237.

Larson, J., Holman, T., Klein, D., Busby, D., Stahmann, R., & Peterson, D. (1995). A review of comprehensive questionnaires used in premarital education and counseling. *Family Relations, 44,* 245–252.

Olson, D. H. (1996). *PREPARE/ENRICH Counselors Manual: Version 2000.* Minneapolis, MN: Life Innovations.

Olson, D. H., & DeFrain, J. (1997). *Marriage and the family: Diversity and strengths* (2nd ed.). Mountain View, CA: Mayfield.

Olson, D. H., Fournier, D., Druckman, J., & Robinson, J. (1979) *Effectiveness of premarital counseling with PREPARE.* Unpublished manuscript, University of Minnesota, St. Paul.

Olson, D. H., & Fowers, B. J. (1993). Five types of marriage: An empirical typology based on ENRICH. *The Family Journal: Counseling and Therapy for Couples and Families, 1*(3), 196–207.

Rappaport, R. (1963). Normal crises, family structure and mental health. *Family Process, 2,* 68–80.

Stahmann, R. F., & Hiebert, W. J. (1997). *Premarital counseling: Professionals handbook* (2nd ed.). Lexington, MA: Lexington Books

10
CHAPTER

Lori Heyman Gordon, Ph.D.
Carlos Durana, Ph.D., M.Ac.

The PAIRS Program

For one human being to love another: that is perhaps the most difficult of all tasks, the ultimate, the last test and proof, the work for which all other work is but preparation . . . so we must not forget, when we love, that we are beginners, bunglers of life, apprentices in love and must learn love . . .

—Rainer Maria Rilke

☐ Introduction

Intimacy, a critical process in the development of close relationships (Hinde, 1978), is now a major concern in our culture. Significant technological, cultural, socioeconomic, and religious changes in our society have contributed to a shift in the primary function of marriage, from one of providing security and stability for the raising of children to one of developing love and intimacy between partners (Diskin, 1986; Mace & Mace, 1975). Modern marriage requires greater interpersonal competence and equality than was needed twenty to forty years ago, when marriage demanded role competence (Mace & Mace, 1986).

The PAIRS (Practical Application of Intimate Relationship Skills) program was developed as a 4- to 5-month, 120-hour, comprehensive psychoeducational course designed to enhance self-knowledge and to develop the ability to sustain a pleasurable intimate relationship. The

217

approach integrates a wide range of theories and methods from psychology and psychotherapy and presents them in an educational format. The program is unique in the field, acting as a bridge between therapy and marital enrichment.

PAIRS teaches skills as well as engaging the participants in an in-depth exploration of self and relationship dynamics. Although certain skills are necessary for success in marriage, including commitment, effective communication (openness, honesty, empathy), and the ability to make creative use of conflict (Mace & Mace, 1986), these may not be sufficient. Essential as well is a knowledge of the self, that is, an understanding of how past experiences can be transferred into the present marriage in disruptive ways (Paolino & McGrady, 1978).

The broad conceptual framework of the PAIRS program utilizes concepts and techniques from the experiential, object relations, communication, behavioral, and family systems approaches of various therapists and theoreticians, most notably, Virginia Satir (communication, family systems and rules, self-worth, and psychosyntheses), Murray Bowen (differentiation and family of origin), Ivan Boszormenyi-Nagy and Geraldine Sparks (invisible loyalties and the revolving ledger), Bernard Guerney (empathic listening), George Bach (conflict resolution and the fair fight for change), Erik Berne and Claude Steiner (ego states and life scripts), Paul McLean (triune brain), Daniel Casriel (bonding, the logic of emotion, emotional expressiveness, and levels of emotional maturity), Ira Progoff (stepping stones), Roger Gould (stages of growth in the adult life cycle), Nathaniel Branden (sentence stems, journaling), Jean Houston and Helen Bonny (guided imagery), Bernie Zilbergeld (sensuality and sexuality), Richard Stuart (social learning and behavior modification), and Clifford Sager (contracting for change). The PAIRS integrative model seeks to change destructive relationship interactions by affecting the psychodynamic underpinnings of the individual through cognitive, affective, and behavioral interactions within an experiential relationship or group context.

On a personal note, I (Lori Gordon), born as the younger of two sisters, was a romantic who fervently believed in happy endings. My father, a dentist as well as a chess player, taught me the strategic challenges of chess when I was 6. My mother, a homemaker, nursed me through lengthy acute ear infections in the years before penicillin was available by singing me to sleep with lullabies. Both of my parents were easily affectionate. Their joy in each other and in their children was obvious. My parents never openly argued. I grew up believing in my parents' devotion and in family ties, with the expectation that my life would follow that same path. But the tragic loss of both of my parents, when I was between the ages 14 and 16, demolished these expectations. My father died suddenly of a coronary; my mother died a year later of cancer. My sister precipitously married at the age of 21 and became my guardian. Although I still trusted in love, I distrusted fate.

I learned to confide my deepest feelings with my first romantic partner, a young poet and writer who enlisted at age 18 in the Marine Corps. At the end of my sophomore year at Cornell University, I met and married a law student whom I had known for only three months. I expected the same kind of trusting, confiding relationship with him that I had with my first love and that I had seen in my parents' marriage. To my surprise, disappointment, and dismay, this was not to be.

During the 17 years of this marriage, I had four children and ultimately returned to graduate school, seeking an understanding of my unhappiness with my relationship. It took years of exploration to discover that what I had expected from my marriage was totally disparate from what my husband, the only child of divorced parents, had learned: not to trust and not to confide. For us, therefore, intimacy and mutuality were not possible.

Following my graduate training and commencing work at a community health center, I made a clear decision to either improve my marriage or end it. Unwilling to seek counseling earlier in our relationship, my husband now agreed to consult a therapist. To my dismay, I was appalled to discover that there were no therapists seeing couples or helping marriages. My marriage ended in a bitter divorce that was deeply wounding for my children. It became my life's passion to find a way to help others as well as myself to avoid the tragic waste of what was, at the start, a loving, nurturing relationship.

PAIRS was initially developed when I was invited to create the first course for future marriage and family counselors at the Graduate School of Counseling Education at American University. I began with graduate students in the helping professions. My training at that time consisted of an undergraduate degree from Cornell University, with a double major in Child Development and Family Relationships and Psychology, and a master's degree in Clinical Social Work from Catholic University. In addition, I had created the Family Relations Institute in the Washington area for postgraduate training by pathfinders in the developing field of marriage and family therapy. I was the senior therapist at a community mental health center and a family therapist at two innovative adolescent family treatment centers. I had developed an active private practice in individual, couple, family, and group therapy.

PAIRS integrates a compilation of wisdom from my life's journey, my clinical practice, and my experience with masters in the experiential, educational, and therapeutic helping professions. In developing the PAIRS program, I drew upon my academic, professional, and personal experiences with marriage, divorce, and life as a single parent raising four children. I based PAIRS on my own exploration of intimacy, which had been fueled by my desire to understand the passages and pitfalls of romantic love and commitment. Receiving an invitation to develop a semester-long university course gave me the opportunity to integrate my most significant learnings into a course that would help future counselors be effective.

Upon discovering the transformative power of this course in the lives of my graduate students, I chose to add a modified version of the course to my clinical practice at the Family Relations Institute. During those early years, I refined and experimented with the material to create the most effective vehicle for producing and sustaining positive change for the participants in my classes.

After a happy remarriage to a community leader and member of the clergy, I was encouraged by Virginia Satir to present my work to other therapists.

☐ Theoretical Underpinnings

By far the primary influence on PAIRS was Satir (1967, 1972), a founder of experiential family therapy. Satir's authenticity and respect for the personhood of each human being, her encouragement of open and honest communication, and her heartfelt and humanistic approach to clients are foundational elements that PAIRS models and utilizes as a context for therapeutic change. The PAIRS program's use of congruent communication styles, its emphasis on developing self-esteem, its use of psychodrama, and its emphasis on the role that family rules play in influencing development are all aspects integrated from Satir's work.

The second major influence on PAIRS was psychiatrist Daniel Casriel's psychodynamically based cathartic group therapy (New Identity Process), designed to reeducate a person's attitudes, emotions, and behaviors. According to Casriel (1972), a person makes decisions, based on early conditioning, to pursue pleasure and avoid pain while meeting biological needs. Casriel viewed bonding (the ability to be physically close and emotionally open) as a biologically based need which, when not met, becomes a central determinant in the development of psychological dysfunction and influences the later development of intimacy in relationships. PAIRS draws from Casriel's use of holding techniques and intensive emotional expression in eliciting repressed attitudes and emotions and providing corrective emotional experiences.

PAIRS was influenced also by the work of George Bach (Bach & Wyden, 1968) on the "fair fight for change," a process that clarifies in simple steps what is destructive and what is constructive in conflict resolution. This approach to resolving differences, along with Sager's "contracting model" (Sager, 1976), became the basis for the contracting component of PAIRS, the concluding section that teaches that love is a feeling, marriage is a contract, and a relationship is work. The contract of the relationship is formed by the series of expectations that both partners identify and negotiate in order to sustain the pleasure of the relationship.

The PAIRS integrative approach provides deep understanding of the dynamics of couple relationships. PAIRS highlights the importance of the couple as a crucible from which pleasure, healing, personal growth, and the development of higher capacities can emerge. With its emphasis on bonding as a biologically based need, PAIRS facilitates a deeper union and love, a love that goes beyond sex toward a sense of spiritual union that differentiates the need for sex from the need for love. Through its focus on emotional evocation and expression, PAIRS clarifies the importance of accessing and exploring emotional experience in order to lower defenses, access core beliefs, enhance intimacy, and facilitate conflict resolution (Durana, 1994, 1996b, 1996c). By integrating intrapsychic and interpersonal approaches, PAIRS shifts the focus from the therapist as the agent of change to the couple. Finally, PAIRS enhances the experience and expression of emotions and affirms bonding among men as well as between women as a powerful mechanism for personal and couple transformation (Durana, 1996b, 1996c).

PAIRS uses a multidimensional framework for understanding the nature of personal relationships. The interventions proposed by this approach stem from several underlying assumptions. Below are a few of the most significant ones.

First, a human being is viewed as an integrated whole with cognitive, affective, and behavioral aspects. Change can begin at any point in this cognitive, affective, and behavioral triangle. Each section of the PAIRS course attempts to affect each of these three. For example, in the first section, participants learn about their style of communication (Satir, 1972), how hidden assumptions (Gordon, 1996a) about love and intimacy undermine relationships, how caring behaviors and concrete requests for change (Bach & Wyden, 1968; Sager, 1976; Stuart, 1980) can enhance the well-being of the individuals and the couple, and how to experience and express powerful emotions such as anger in a structured manner and in a safe environment (Bach & Wyden, 1968; Casriel, 1972).

Second, a basic tenet of humanistic psychology, as expressed by Satir (1972), is that the potential of any individual can be released within a context of caring when the value, beauty, and uniqueness of the person are acknowledged and encouraged. The establishment of basic positive attitudes about the self, as outlined by Casriel (1972), is seen as an indispensable foundation for successful relationships. At the center of these attitudes are the beliefs in a right to exist as a separate person with needs and the right to not have to be perfect in order to feel good and lovable. Drawing forth the resources and competencies of the individual releases his or her organismic capacity for growth. Concepts such as self-esteem, empathic understanding, and genuineness of expression are integrated in PAIRS by lectures and exercises that help to develop these capacities. Treasuring oneself enables the treasuring of one's partner.

Third, the notion of *bonding* (Casriel, 1972), a biological need for connection that gives rise to symptoms when not met, lies at the core of what it means to be intimate (Gordon, 1993; Durana, 1996c). This is a key assumption in the PAIRS program. The need an infant has to cling to another human being is as primary as the need for food (Bowlby, 1958, 1977). Snuggling and sucking create biochemical reactions in the brain that affect functioning and development (Restak, 1979). Infants appear to develop a sense of self from experiencing care giving and sensing the inner feelings of the care givers (Mahler & McDevitt, 1982). The ability of an individual to enjoy giving and receiving physical nurturing, as Montague (1978) has suggested, is a measure of his or her development. Attachment behaviors such as bonding appear to act as social releases of instinctual responses in relationships (Fairbairn, 1952).

In PAIRS, participants are enabled to experience bonding (physical closeness and emotional openness) and other forms of affection between partners. Bonding increases self-exploration, provides symbolic parenting, and dissolves resistance between partners. It helps to differentiate the need for sex from the need for love, helps convey acceptance and trust, facilitates communication and attachment behaviors, and makes way for love and commitment (Durana, 1994, 1996b, 1996c, 1998).

Another important assumption in PAIRS is the psychoanalytic notion that a fundamental human motive is to develop satisfactory object relationships (Fairbairn, 1952). Childhood developmental patterns create nonadaptive adult relationship patterns in which partners become repositories of childhood's unmet needs, fears, and expectations for meeting those needs. Part of the work of a relationship is to own these projections and work through the loss and the grief for those early unmet needs. This work is carried out in PAIRS by means of techniques and exercises adapted by Gordon from Casriel's (1972) cathartic self-exploration techniques and from Satir's (1967, 1972) psychodrama techniques, such as the "Parts of Self" and "Parts of Couple" exercises.

An intimate relationship can serve as a crucible where two people can grow and develop, learn to satisfy their biologically based need for bonding and how to soothe each other's disappointments and wounds, clarify the projection process, provide symbolic parenting for satisfying early unmet needs, and develop compassion, forgiveness, truthfulness, and courage as they attempt to meet their own and each other's needs. All of the exercises, experiences, and lectures in PAIRS stem from this premise.

One of the goals of PAIRS is to encourage couples' personal experience of an "I-Thou" mutuality (Buber, 1970). Experiential family therapists such as Satir (1967, 1972) believe that existential encounters in which people become present to each other often result in a transformation in how they relate to one another. The healing potential of relationships is released in the I-Thou encounter. Growth can then take place through the dialogical process. This process is taught in PAIRS through talking and listening skills (Guerney, 1977; Satir, 1972), as well as through the techniques of bonding, emotional openness, and emotional expression (Casriel, 1972). Partners can then become empathic witnesses to each other's wounds and early unmet needs.

Basic to PAIRS is the postulate that affective expression in itself is therapeutic and growth producing (Casriel, 1972; Satir, 1967). Our emotional brain (MacLean, 1973) cannot be ignored. Because emotions have their own logic of pleasure and pain, the development of emotional literacy is a goal of PAIRS. Teaching participants how to more fully experience and appropriately express a wide range of emotions can lead to a variety of outcomes: reduced stress, corrective emotional experiences, increased awareness of need, enhanced self-disclosure and communication, uncovered unconscious feelings, transformed maladaptive interpersonal and intrapsychic patterns, and enhanced attachment bonds (Durana, 1996c, 1998; Gordon, 1993; Greenberg & Johnson, 1986; Nichols & Zax, 1977; Satir, 1972). PAIRS's use of evocative techniques encourages new affective experiences that provide participants with opportunities to choose new ways of feeling, thinking, and interacting.

Two other assumptions merit mention: the value of groups for facilitating therapeutic change (documented by Yalom, 1985) and the equality of each partner as a necessary part of the marital relationship. PAIRS makes wide use of group interactive techniques such as "peer coaching," where couples assist each other in resolving conflicts and providing support. These peer techniques add an important element to the impact of the PAIRS program (Durana, 1996a).

PAIRS encourages and supports the shift from the dominant/submissive model to one of the equality of each partner through empowering each gender with the knowledge and tools necessary to sustain the new equality. For example, the process of male bonding that takes place during the "bonding weekend" in PAIRS allows males whose nurturant capacities and needs have been curtailed and repressed (Chodorow, 1978, p. 7) to express the pain and fear that are repressed in so many men due to socialization. Their experience of symbolic fathering with each other can lead to the enhancement of intimate relationships (Durana, 1996b). On the other hand, women who have been taught by their culture to not express anger have the opportunity to access feelings of assertiveness, anger, and power.

☐ Intervention Model

The specific goals of intervention are clearly described in the PAIRS "Content of Course" description. They are written in a manner that is easily understood and relatively free of technical jargon.

General:

1. To know and nurture both yourself and your partner, so that you can recognize, acknowledge, and even enjoy your differences rather than seeing them as a threat or an attack.
2. To learn how to enjoy your partner and to sustain your relationship as a continuing source of mutual pleasure.

Communication:

3. To recognize when your style of communication is more of a problem than the problem you are communicating about.
4. To avoid the mind-reading that so often leads to misunderstandings with your partner, checking out your assumptions before you act on them and not expecting your partner to know without being told.
5. To learn how to make sure that each partner is being heard by the other, using the processes of empathic listening and shared meaning.
6. To communicate all of your feelings (including anger) without destroying love, by learning to accept and express those feelings comfortably, directly, and nondestructively.
7. To recognize and deal with covert, indirect expressions of anger, or a fight-phobic partner or aggressively hostile partner.
8. To learn how to clear the air of strong fear, pain, or anger before attempting to resolve conflicts or solve problems.
9. To fight in such a way that you actually resolve the issue at hand, including problems related to sex, money, children, time, in-laws, ex-spouses, your home, housework, fidelity, and jealousy.

For the Self:

10. To trace the emotional history of your family and to discover which family models influence the way you relate to intimates now.
11. To trace your own emotional history including the "revolving ledgers" or "emotional allergies" that influence your relationships today.

12. To uncover the hidden expectations and defensive communication styles you learned from parental messages and family models which may be sabotaging your relationships in the present.
13. To identify your own needs and get them met, freeing you to feel real empathy for your partner instead of secretly resenting your role as caretaker or provider.
14. To become intimately acquainted with the richness and complexity of your own unique personality.
15. To recognize the different roles that you and your partner play, the masks you don, the behaviors you assume in different moods and circumstances, and find out how they work, or don't work, together.

Sensual and Sexual Pleasuring:

16. To learn the differences between affection, comfort, bonding, sensuality, and sexuality so that sex is not your only avenue to closeness.
17. To satisfy your biological need for that combination of physical closeness and emotional openness we call bonding.
18. To be able to communicate openly and honestly about your sexual and sensual needs and to get them met.

Clarifying Expectations:

19. To negotiate using a style where each feels heard, respected and considered, instead of attempting to control or use power, which make the loser want to withdraw emotionally or get even.
20. To negotiate a relationship you both can live with joyfully.

Gordon developed the PAIRS "dialogue guide" clinically as a specific tool to facilitate confiding about a range of thoughts, feelings, and assumptions via Satir's leveling style. The list of Gordonian "love knots" was compiled over time to identify those typical assumptions that cause marital distress and to offer ways to resolve them in a nonblaming mode. Both were specifically designed for PAIRS and have proven highly effective in enhancing and facilitating committed relationships.

Interventions are accomplished through carefully sequenced class lectures, graphics and overheads, exercises, peer coaching, group discussion, journaling, guided reflections, reading of handbook content and selected texts, homework, and guided couple dialogue. Each class has a specific content and goal.

The 120-hour course provides the necessary time for each concept to be introduced and described and for the exercises to be experienced, allowing for an integration of the content and the building of a foundation for intimacy. Experimentation in the early years of developing the PAIRS program clarified the importance of beginning the course with the logic of emotion or love and then developing skills in communication and conflict resolution prior to delving deeper into self-understanding. Many course participants are new to the understanding that emotion has its own logic and that there are specific skills associated with confiding. These skills include talking, listening, clarifying, mind-reading, identifying assumptions, and conflict resolution.

Following the establishment of safety within the group, specific skills in confiding in one's partner are taught, including Satir's "daily temperature reading," the PAIRS dialogue guide, and peer coaching, along with the concepts of self-worth, emotional levels of development, and caring behaviors. The course content then progresses into deepening levels of self-understanding through a series of exercises that include surfacing hidden expectations (love knots), study and development of individual genograms, early decisions, family sculpting, life scripts, emotional allergies, revolving ledgers, negative emotional allergy infinity loop, personality typology, psychodrama, and, ultimately, the powerful experience of bonding with emotional openness, intensity, and physical closeness with a partner. The course continues with a sequence on sensuality and sexuality, including pleasuring touch, and concludes with a segment on contracting for change. Contracting for change includes specific topics such as jealousy, money, sex, and parenting, as well as decision making.

It is important to note that, despite the depth and intensity of this program, humor is sprinkled liberally throughout the course to illuminate typical relationship pitfalls and assumptions.

☐ Format of Application

The PAIRS intensive program, consisting of 120 hours of training, is spread over 4 to 5 months. PAIRS is designed to enhance self-knowledge and the participant's ability to sustain a pleasurable intimate relationship. The format includes weekly or biweekly 3-hour classes and four or five weekend workshops lasting 19 to 21 hours. Groups are composed of 15 to 35 participants.

Participants come to PAIRS primarily with the hope of learning relationship skills in a structured group educational setting. Participants come mostly on the recommendation of partners, friends, PAIRS graduates, and therapists, as well as due to dissatisfaction with the results of therapy. Advertising accounts for only a small percentage of participants. For the most part, participants' self-selection into the program is the most common form of screening. Some PAIRS leaders conduct interviews to assess whether the two partners are candidates for therapy as opposed to PAIRS.

A profile of the issues and problems of participants (Durana, 1996a) suggests that most desire improvement in communication skills (recognizing and expressing needs, feelings, and listening), understanding and accepting the other partner, resolving differences, experiencing more positive feelings in the relationship, and understanding and increasing the level of intimacy. Other outcomes less strongly desired include understanding oneself and relationship issues, having more satisfying sexual relations, and clarifying money issues.

Thus far, PAIRS participants have consisted of mostly white, middle- and upper middle-class couples. A study by Durana (1996a) of 137 participants from five different classes throughout the United States found that the average participant was 42 years old and had been married for 13.4 years. Participants ranged from those in a well-functioning relationship to highly distressed couples; in fact, these couples appeared to be significantly more distressed and lower in intimacy, as compared with the general population. About one half of Durana's sample had received therapy prior to coming to PAIRS. Highly volatile, alcohol or drug abusing, antisocial, and borderline couples were not part of the sample.

Divided into five sections, the program (Gordon, 1996b) is designed to help couples reexamine their relationship with the goal of reeducating attitudes, emotions, and behavior. The first section involves developing empathic listening skills and learning to speak on one's own behalf, identifying caring behaviors, discovering dysfunctional communication styles, and uncovering hidden expectations and beliefs about love and relationships, as well as identifying negotiating styles and developing conflict resolution skills.

The second section involves exploration of the self. Participants learn about early messages and decisions made about love and relationships. The three-generation family map (genogram) is used in conjunction with learning about family-of-origin rules, myths, and loyalties and about how these affect current relationships. In addition, leaders teach how differing parts of self, roles, and personality styles affect intimacy. This section of the course begins with the process of self-differentiation, which is carried to a deeper level in the following segment.

The third section, Bonding and Emotional Reeducation (B.E.R.), involves learning and experiencing bonding, emotional intensity, and emotional expressiveness. Acceptance of one's need for bonding is viewed as crucial to sustaining an intimate relationship. Participants are taught to differentiate the need for bonding from the need for sex, to free repressed emotions from the recent past and from childhood, to provide symbolic parenting, and to facilitate attachment behaviors that lead to an increase in empathy for one's partner. This section also includes restructuring negative attitudes with positive beliefs and revising early decisions that sabotage relationships.

The fourth section focuses on enhancing physical intimacy in its variety of manifestations, ranging from affection, tenderness, and bonding to sensuality and sexuality. Included are lectures and discussions on early decisions about sexuality, sexual myths, jealousy, sexual preference, and sexuality, as well as films, massage, and other techniques.

The fifth part involves clarifying expectations and goals. At this stage, the participants' use of the skills and insights acquired through the PAIRS programs leads to the creation of a mutually pleasurable marital contract.

Throughout the course, PAIRS makes use of group processes and peer coaching. Peer coaching provides participants with the experience of giving and receiving from others. It facilitates learning by guiding and providing feedback to those being coached. One of the aims of PAIRS is to enhance the ability to confide in one's partner; this ability is encouraged by a leader/facilitator model that seeks to move the client-to-therapist transference to one's partner, who then becomes a confidant. Homework assignments include readings from the participant's manual and from eight popular books, keeping journals, and practicing exercises learned in class.

☐ Qualities and Role of the Leader or Facilitator

In 1984, PAIRS was launched through a 4½-day professional training program given by Virginia Satir. After participating at a national AAMFT conference, Lori Gordon was approached by a number of clinicians about creating an intensive professional training program.

Upon discovering the life and death voltages of emotions that were often elicited during the PAIRS course, Gordon chose to place the teaching of the course into the hands of mental health professionals. She believed professionals would be best able to make referrals to individual, couple, family, or group therapy for those participants who needed more help than a course could provide. Gordon's clinical practice included a range of helping modalities, and there was often a flow from her practice to the class, and vice versa. Many individuals who would not have considered therapy came to the class, and others, having been in a variety of therapies, found that the class provided knowledge they hadn't received in therapy.

PAIRS views the most important qualities for an effective class leader, beyond a graduate mental health degree and state licensing, to be authenticity, personal life experience, humor, values regarding intimacy, a capacity for self-disclosure, and the ability to participate in and model an intimate relationship. The role of the PAIRS leader is that of a guide, a coach, and a participant in life's journey. He or she is egalitarian, has a capacity for humor, is open to learning and to change, has respect for each individual, and is committed to the structure and values of PAIRS.

☐ Application of the Preventive Model to a Couple at Risk

Ben and Alyssa are a typical couple arriving at PAIRS. They want to be happier, and they need a new "contract." They need to face many realities: becoming parents, growing up, their family-of-origin differences, the loss of their earlier, more carefree years. Ben, having always been the "special" one, had several difficulties: sharing his partner, his wife, with his children; being the sole breadwinner; feeling trapped in his law career; being a father who had never had time with his own father. Alyssa was dealing with her own role changes and the worries associated with becoming a mother.

Ben and Alyssa will gain the following from their participation in PAIRS.

1. They will experience hope and humor in a community of involved couples and individuals guided by a knowledgeable, empathic, skilled leader. They will find a class environment where they can be open about their fears, their hopes, their disappointments, and their assumptions, as well as about themselves, their life, and their relationship.

2. They will identify their communication styles. For example, Alyssa has been a placater; Ben has been superreasonable—styles which have been augmented by her maternal role model and his law school training.

3. They will learn how to level with each other using the dialogue guide and the love knots exercises. These will help them realize that Ben has been either dismissing Alyssa's feelings or trying to fix them. They will learn to identify and resolve specific knots pertinent to their relationship. Self-worth will be enhanced as they learn to level, to listen with empathy, and to share their deepest feelings.

4. They will be guided to nurture their relationship; to deal with complaints, wishes, hopes, and dreams; and to develop a new contract using the daily temperature reading.

5. In the fair fight for change, through peer coaching, they will learn to be honest about their disappointment and anger. They will learn the difference between dysfunctional communication styles, or dirty fighting, and constructive fighting on behalf of their relationship.

6. In the Self section, through the "Family Systems Factory," "Couple and Family Sculpting," and "Genogram," exercises they will begin to understand the different expectations each brings to their relationship as a result of their diverse backgrounds and unique personalities. They will face the impact that their son and the child soon to arrive will have on their relationship.

7. In the B.E.R. workshop, Ben will confront his feelings about his father, his son, and becoming a parent. He will experience closeness and empathy with other men, and he will come to understand more about women's feelings. Alyssa will be afforded the opportunity to confront her dislike of her mother's subservience and her feelings about herself when she acts in similar ways. Both will come to realize the emotional impacts of their early life decisions. They will discover their individual life scripts and become familiar with experiencing and expressing varying levels of emotional intensity. The concepts of emotional allergy,[1] the revolving ledger,[2] and the negative emotional allergy infinity loop,[3] as they affect their relationship and each of them individually, will become part of their ongoing dialogue. For example, Ben may well be allergic to Alyssa's time and attention to her Christian church and to their child, since in his developing years Ben was the sole recipient of his mother's and grandmother's attention. He consciously or unconsciously would like this desirable situation to continue and wants to withdraw from Alyssa or even to punish her when this doesn't happen. In effect, he is expecting her to continue to pay the positive bill that was paid in the past in his earlier family.

8. Through the journal meditation, "Period/People/Events/Emotional Impact/Decisions," they will realize how their unique life events and decisions affect them in the present. These reflections will enrich their couple dialogue.

9. The "Caring Behaviors" and "Turn-Ons/Turn-Offs" exercises will bring new awareness of how to nurture their relationship.

10. In "Emotional Levels of Development," they will realize the necessity of being grown-up enough or adult enough to develop the new contract of the parental stage, which includes sacrifice, cooperation, and role changes.

---

[1]Emotional allergy: An intense emotional reactivity to a situation or behavior that carries an affective load, either because it is similar to an historical event that was wounding or painful or because it is wounding in that it denies a positive hope from the past into the present.

[2]Revolving ledger: The transference onto a present partner of an emotional bill or invoice for events that occurred in the past with some other person. This, in effect, implies a desire to have the painful past events atoned for by the present partner or the desire to actually punish or get even with the present partner for what someone in the past did or did not do.

[3]Emotional allergy infinity loop occurs when a behavior triggered in one partner by an emotional allergy to a behavior of the other partner, in turn triggers a reactive behavior or emotional allergy in that other partner, thus creating a negative infinity loop that will continue in a destructive pattern unless consciously raised to awareness and interrupted.

11. In "Death and Loss," they will be powerfully rebonded to each other with empathy, mutual appreciation, and compassion.
12. In "Parts of Self" and "Parts of Couple," along with the Myers Briggs Personality Inventory, they will realize their complexity, diversity, and uniqueness and will learn a new language for individuation and strategic problem solving.
13. The Sensuality, Sexuality, and Pleasuring Workshop will reopen doors to passion and provide access to a fuller range of pleasures through bonding and touch, as well as through sensuality and sex, which will be particularly valuable at this time of pregnancy, child bearing, and parenthood.
14. The Jealousy section will allow further discussion of:
    a. Ben's parents, particularly his father's infidelity;
    b. Ben's suppressed jealousy of the time Alyssa devotes to church and children.
15. The Contracting section will provide the integrating vehicle for working and reworking their wishes, hopes, and dreams into a new contract, both in having coaches and in acting as peer coaches for others. It will enlist their creativity, intelligence, and good will for problem solving aimed toward creating a new foundation, for example, borrowing money for Ben to start a new career.

On reaching the close of the PAIRS course, the couple will have arrived at a joyful, bonded relationship with new skills, language, and concepts for understanding and nurturing themselves and for parenting their present and future children. Open lines of communication will have been established, enabling them to confide pain, fear, anger, and disappointment as well as appreciation, pleasure, and love. They will have become part of a caring network of PAIRS couples who can continue to support each other, often functioning as extended family. Ben will have other male figures to relate to, and Alyssa will have other women. Many PAIRS participants continue meeting periodically, both in separate gender groups and as couples.

☐ Empirical Evaluation and Research

The first research study of PAIRS (Gordon, 1984) was a pre- and post-assessment of 11 couples measuring state–trait anxiety and personality and relationship dimensions. The results suggested that the majority of participants entering PAIRS exhibited state anxiety in the top quartile of the U.S. adult population, feelings of anger in the upper third, and state and trait curiosity in the lower quartile.

Postparticipation measures showed significant changes in state and trait anxiety, with greater changes in trait anxiety, suggesting the possibility of a change in personality dynamics. In addition, there were improvements in self-esteem and in appreciation of the partner. While the size of the sample was small and the design lacked control for extraneous variables, this study hinted at important changes within individuals and couples.

An exploratory study conducted by Turner (1993) examined the effectiveness of PAIRS using a pretest/posttest, one-group design. The study measured the change in relationship cohesion, consensus, satisfaction, affection, and adjustment using the Dyadic Adjustment Scale (DAS) subscale and total scores. Eighty-seven participants in six PAIRS classes from four major cities throughout the United States volunteered to take part in the study; the numbers of participants completing questionnaires ranged from 10 to 19 per class. The sample consisted of higher educated, middle-class, and mostly married male and female participants. Using paired t-tests, the analysis indicated gains at posttest on all subscales as well as on total DAS score.

To assess the use of bonding and emotional expressiveness in the Bonding segment of the PAIRS class, Durana (1994) conducted a pilot study. From a group of 31 participants, nine volunteers took part in a pre- and postassessment, which included an in-depth interview. Results indicated an increase in compatibility between partners and a significant reduction in state anger (feelings of hostility). Most participants found that the workshop enhanced empathy for others, encouraged emotional openness and listening, and led to conflict resolution.

In a recent article, Durana (1996b) explored the use of emotions and bonding in the B.E.R. segment of the PAIRS training. By means of a case study and a review of relevant psychotherapy literature with respect to emotions, catharsis, and touch, Durana proposed that bonding and catharsis within a context of cognitive and behavioral integration can facilitate change by allowing the remembrance of painful experiences, by gratifying unsatisfied needs, by providing symbolic parenting, and by facilitating attachment behaviors, thereby making way for love and commitment in marital relationships.

A research study by Durana (1996c) used quantitative and qualitative research methods to evaluate the impact of bonding and catharsis in the B.E.R. segment of PAIRS. Fifty-four participants were assessed at four different points in time throughout the PAIRS program (pre-PAIRS, pre-B.E.R., post-B.E.R., post-PAIRS) using measures of marital adjustment, self-esteem, depression, anxiety, control, and support.

The results suggested that B.E.R. can lead to significant improvements in marital adjustment, cohesion, self-esteem, and emotional well-being. Findings from a structured questionnaire developed by Durana suggest that B.E.R. is valuable in expressing feelings, enhancing intimacy, identifying negative interactions rooted in family-of-origin history, and helping differentiate between the need for bonding and the need for sex. The results also showed significant differences for PAIRS participants in marital adjustment, consensus, affection, satisfaction, and self-esteem.

A study by Goss (1995) examined changes subsequent to PAIRS on problem solving, communication, individuation, and distress. Using a pretest/posttest one-group design, the analysis showed increases on all of the variables except spousal individuation.

To evaluate the long-term effectiveness of PAIRS, Durana (1996a) studied married participants from five different PAIRS classes throughout the United States. The volunteers ($N = 137$) were evaluated pre-PAIRS, post-PAIRS, and 6 to 8 months after the PAIRS course ended. Measures included marital adjustment, marital satisfaction, conflict and unhappiness, and client satisfaction. Open-ended questions developed by Durana solicited clients' experiences with the program, incorporated their evaluation of its impact, and explored gender differences.

Most subjects experienced enduring improvements regarding marital adjustment, marital satisfaction, and conflict and unhappiness, among other areas. Participants also reported positive changes in relationships with children, friends, and family of origin.

Another study (Durana, 1998) explored the enhancement and maintenance of intimacy, a critical element in the development of healthy relationships. Pre-PAIRS, post-PAIRS, and 6 to 8 months after PAIRS, 137 married volunteer program participants from five different classes throughout the United States were evaluated. These participants tended to be more distressed and less intimate than the general population. Most participants (76%) experienced significant gains in intimacy that were sustained at follow-up. Gender differences in intimacy had been reduced at follow-up, as well.

DeMaria (1998) conducted a national survey and explored the characteristics of 129 married couples enrolled in the PAIRS course. The study included a semistructured survey and intensive interviews. The study explored marital satisfaction and how couple types and level of satisfaction relate to sexual satisfaction, divorce potential, conflict tactics, romantic love, and attachment style. The study also explored motivations to enroll in the PAIRS program using a qualitative analysis.

According to the results, the participants were highly distressed, conflicted, and devitalized. They were also securely attached and reported high levels of romantic love despite low levels of sexual satisfaction, some consideration of divorce, occasional episodes of physical violence, and previous experience in marital therapy. The findings also suggested that these couples were highly motivated to participate in the PAIRS program.

A recent study by Turner (1998) assessed the impact of PAIRS on individual outcomes, adult interaction styles, use of projective and perceptive identification, and marital discord. The study included 75 participants and 45 controls. *T*-test comparisons of group change scores suggested that the PAIRS intervention had a positive impact on interaction style, social support, and marital discord. Qualitative observations showed an improvement in adult interaction style for couples demonstrating perceptive identification but not for those demonstrating projective identification.

☐ Summary

At the conclusion of the PAIRS program, a male attorney who, with his wife, shared many similarities with Ben and Alyssa, wrote, "I never wanted a child, as I never wanted to subject a child to the kind of upbringing that I had. . . . Now I think it would be the luckiest child in the world, to have parents who not only want to love and do love, but *know how to love.*" (He and his spouse now have two children.)

The PAIRS integrative model, with its broad theoretical base, offers a wide range of techniques and accommodates a broad range of participants. The language of the lectures and exercises is simple, avoiding technical jargon. The length of the program and its highly interactive nature, which includes peer coaching, allows participants to develop friendships and supportive relationships that can last for many years.

An often-cited concern by participants (Durana, 1996a) is the large amount of material presented. This dilemma may speak to the needs for greater conceptual integration of all of the different components of PAIRS and for underscoring the common themes underlying the different exercises and lectures. Some of this does take place, for example, in the "relationship roadmap," a conceptual structure that offers a unifying view of the goals and processes of self-actualization and of the establishment of a nurturing intimate relationship. PAIRS could also be enhanced by including a section on gender differences in communication.

The PAIRS program may be contraindicated for couples with extended pathology, such as borderline, antisocial, highly volatile, or drug and alcohol abusing couples. The program is lengthy, and the cost (an average of $1200 per person) is prohibitive for many. Some couples may not be seeking the in-depth exploration that takes place in the PAIRS program, but instead are merely seeking to learn communication and conflict resolution skills. Several brief programs (If You Really Loved Me, a one-day workshop, PAIRS FIRST, an eight-session course, and Passage to Intimacy, a weekend workshop) have recently been developed to accommodate such couples. They are being well received. An intensive couples week has been developed, and along with PAIRS FIRST, provides a wide range of choice.

The program needs to be taught to a wider range of socioeconomic and minority groups to determine its applicability to other populations. Thus far, the program has been taught in several countries, with adaptations made to accommodate various populations.

Expansions of PAIRS to the high school and adolescent population through programs like PAIRS for PEERS are in the pilot stage. Other adaptations have been developed to address relationships dealing with medical illness, military couples, newlyweds, singles, long-term marriages, separated and divorcing couples, and the formerly married.

Lori Gordon offers this final commentary: "The PAIRS program presents a culmination of my life's wisdom. I have had the unique privilege of passing it on to many able hands. Profoundly tormenting and challenging experiences provided powerful life lessons; that this knowledge is now a source of transformation and positive life change for people I haven't ever met is a source of gratification more satisfying than mere words can fully express. The ageless prose of Henry Wadsworth Longfellow in *A Psalm of Life*, "footprints that perhaps another, sailing o'er life's solemn main . . . a forlorn and shipwrecked brother, seeing will take heart again. . . ," expresses the depth of my hope.

☐ Contact References

For further information about classes, leaders in your area, resources such as books, audiotapes, and videotapes, as well as teaching and training opportunities, call 1-888-742-7748 or visit http://www.pairs.com

☐ References

Bach, G. R., & Wyden, P. (1968). *The intimate enemy.* New York: Avon Books.

Bowlby, J. (1958). The nature of the child's tie to his mother. *International Journal of Psychoanalysis, 39,* 350–373.

Bowlby, J. (1977). The making and breaking of affectional bonds. *British Journal of Psychiatry, 130,* 291–310.

Buber, M. (1970). *I and thou.* New York: Scribner's.

Casriel, D. (1972). *A scream away from happiness.* New York: Grosset & Dunlop.

Chodorow, V. (1978). *The reproduction of mothering.* CA: University of California Press.

DeMaria, R. (1998). *A national survey of married couples who participate in marriage enrichment: Satisfaction, couple type, divorce potential, conflict styles, attachment patterns, and romantic and sexual satisfaction of married couples who participated in PAIRS (Practical Application of Intimate Relationship Skills), a marriage enrichment program.* Unpublished doctoral dissertation, Bryn Mawr College, Bryn Mawr, PA.

Diskin, S. (1986). Marriage enrichment: Rationale and resources. *Journal of Psychotherapy and the Family, 2,* 111–125.

Durana, C. (1994). The use of bonding and emotional expressiveness in the PAIRS training: A psychoeducational approach for couples. *Journal of Family Psychotherapy, 5*(2), 65–81.

Durana, C. (1996a). A longitudinal evaluation of the effectiveness of the PAIRS psychoeducational program for couples. *Family Therapy, 23,* 11–36.

Durana, C. (1996b). Bonding and emotional re-education of couples in the PAIRS training: Part I. *The American Journal of Family Therapy, 24*(3), 269–280.

Durana, C. (1996c). Bonding and emotional re-education of couples in the PAIRS training: Part II. *The American Journal of Family Therapy, 24*(4), 315–328.

Durana, C. (1998). Enhancing marital intimacy through psychoeducation: The PAIRS program. *The Family Journal, 5*(3), 204–215.

Fairbairn, W. R. D. (1952). *An object-relations theory of the personality.* New York: Basic Books.

Gordon, L. (1984). *PAIRS.* Unpublished manuscript.

Gordon, L. (1993). *Passage to intimacy.* New York: Fireside/Simon & Schuster.

Gordon, L. (1996a). *If you really loved me.* Palo Alto, CA: Science and Behavior Books.

Gordon, L. (1996b). *Training manual and curriculum guide.* (Available from PAIRS International, 1152 North University Drive, Suite 203, Pembroke Pines, FL 30024)

Goss, M. (1995). *The effects of the PAIRS training on communication response, individuation and global distress among married couples.* Unpublished doctoral dissertation, Howard University, Washington, DC.

Greenberg, L. S., & Johnson, S. M. (1988). *Emotionally focused therapy for couples.* New York: Guilford.

Guerney, B. (1977). *Relationship enhancement.* San Francisco, CA: Jossey-Bass.

Hinde, R. A. (1978). Interpersonal relationships: In quest of a science. *Psychological Medicine, 3,* 373–386.

Mace, D., & Mace, V. (1975). Marriage enrichment—wave of the future? *The Family Coordinator, 2,* 131–141.

Mace D., & Mace, V. (1986). The history and present status of the marriage and family enrichment movement. *Journal of Psychotherapy and the Family, 21,* 7–17.

MacLean, P. (1973). *A triune concept of the brain and behavior.* Toronto, ON, Canada: University of Toronto Press.

Mahler, M., & McDevitt, J. (1982). Thoughts on the emergence of the sense of self, with particular emphasis on the body self. *Journal of American Psychoanalytic Association, 30,* 827–848.

Montague, A. (1978). *Touching.* New York: Perennial Library.

Nichols, M. P., & Zax, M. (1977). *Catharsis in psychotherapy.* New York: Gardner.

Paolino, T. J., & McGrady, B. S. (1978). *Marriage and marital therapy.* New York: Brunner/Mazel.

Restak, R. M. (1979). *The brain.* New York: Warner Books.

Sager, C. (1976). *Marriage contracts and couple therapy.* New York: Brunner/Mazel.

Satir, V. (1967). *Conjoint family therapy.* Palo Alto, CA: Science and Behavior Books.

Satir, V. (1972). *Peoplemaking.* Palo Alto, CA: Science and Behavior Books.

Spanier, G. B. (1976). Measuring dyadic adjustment: New scales for assessing the quality of marriage and similiar dyads. *Journal of Marriage and the Family, 38,* 15–28.

Stuart, R. B. (1980). *Helping couples change.* New York: Guilford.

Turner, L. (1993, May). *An exploratory study of PAIRS: An integrative group approach to relationship change.* Paper presented at the Eighth Annual Symposium on Group Work, Ann Arbor, MI.

Turner, L. (1998). *The impact of a psychoeducational group intervention on marital discord, adult interation style, projective identification, and projective identification.* Unpublished doctoral dissertation, Catholic University, Washington, DC.

Yalom, I. D. (1985). *The theory and practice of group psychotherapy.* New York: Basic Books.

Les Parrott III, Ph.D.
Leslie Parrott, Ed.D.

Preparing Couples for Marriage: The SYMBIS Model

☐ Introduction

As codirectors of the Center for Relationship Development (CRD) at Seattle Pacific University, we primarily emphasize marriage preparation and early marriage mentoring in our work. A psychoeducational approach that incorporates essential skills and highlights up-to-date information about contemporary marriage is crucial to correcting faulty information and equipping couples with an accurate understanding of themselves and what they bring to the relationship, so that they can have a successful marriage. The marriage mentoring component compliments the psychoeducational approach by shifting the reliance from classrooms, books, videos, and counseling to a relational connection between a giver and receiver of knowledge and experience. A marriage mentor is defined as a happy, more experienced couple who empowers a newly married couple through sharing resources and relational experiences, particularly throughout the first year of marriage.

CRD was established in 1992 with the overarching goal of nurturing healthy relationships through preventive interventions. In conjunction with Seattle Pacific University's Department of Psychology, CRD sponsors curricular offerings that are academically rigorous and based on solid theoretical and applied research. Currently these offerings consist of two psychology courses in relationship development, the first of which focus on practical principles for building healthy relationships in general (family, friendships, dating, etc.). The second course is more advanced and presents practical tools for marriage and family relationships over the life cycle. Students must complete the first course and have advanced status to enroll in the second course. More then 200 upper division students have completed this course. The relevance of these relationship courses to our marriage preparation model is readily apparent. A recent issue of *American Demographics* reported that two thirds of today's college students say that "having close relationships with other people is always on their minds" and ranks highest as a "personal value" (Walker & Moses, 1996, p. 36). By tapping into this felt need, a rapport is established for those individuals that eventually become engaged to be married and, as a result of the course content, understand the need for quality preparation for marriage.

Therefore, in addition to the relationship development courses, CRD sponsors an ongoing marriage preparation model entitled "Saving Your Marriage Before It Starts" (SYMBIS). Over the past 3 years, 250 couples have participated in SYMBIS, which has experienced annual increases in enrollment. A unique feature of this program includes the Marriage Mentor Club, which links newlyweds with a seasoned married couple throughout the first year of marriage.

We believe deeply in the impact of preventive interventions on the permanence, intimacy, and satisfaction of marriage (see McManus, 1993, for a summary of intervention models). Research has underscored a tendency for minor problems in marriage to escalate into major rifts if they are not addressed promptly. Lasswell (1985), for example, reports that half of all serious marital problems develop in the first 2 years of marriage. Our experiences in marriage and family therapy are consistent with this prognosis and have shaped our emphasis on treating marriages in their early phase.

☐ Theoretical Underpinnings

The overarching modality of the SYMBIS program is shaped by the family-systems approach, particularly by family-systems theory as presented by Bowen (1978) in his seminal work, *Family Therapy in Clinical Practice.* SYMBIS has also been influenced by the contributions of Friedman (1985), a former student of Bowen, who has been a pioneer in applying systems theory to religious congregations and families within the church and synagogue. Other significant influences on our approach to marital preparation and therapy are Carter and McGoldrick (1989), systems therapists who emphasize the importance of the family life cycle in marital therapy.

The SYMBIS model attempts to weave into its fabric the Bowenian concepts of self-differentiation and viewing the couple in the context of their transgenerational family system, especially in the first few counseling sessions. For example, the Bowenian theory suggests that extended family dynamics transfer relationship and communication patterns (myths, secrets, and legacies) into the marital system. We believe that a crucial element of marriage preparation is the identification of the family legacy each marriage partner unconsciously brings into the marriage, specifically in uncovering unspoken rules and unconscious roles that shape each partner's expectations for marriage. Bringing both of these aspects out into the open is an important step in marriage preparation and can be accomplished through constructing a family genogram as well as through a variety of exercises.

Helping couples who progress through the SYMBIS model to become aware of their own unspoken rules gives them the freedom to accept, reject, challenge, or change those rules from their family of origin for the sake of their own relationship. Identifying unconscious roles is equally important. Without knowing it, a bride and groom are drawn into acting out roles (e.g., the navigator, the money manager, the decorator, etc.) that they form from a blend of their personal dispositions and family system dynamics. Once partners become aware of the assumed and prescribed roles each tends to take, they can then discuss how to write a new script together.

In addition, as the couple moves through the developmental passages of the life cycle (marriage, birth, raising children, launching young adults, retirement, and death), these transitions dynamically impact the extended family system. Symptoms or problems may occur in healthy marriages when there is extraordinary developmental stress (untimely death, chronic illness, birth of a handicapped child). However, even minor developmental stressors can cause problems for a family that is coping with dysfunctional extended-family relationship dynamics (Carter & McGoldrick, 1989).

The role of the family of origin is central to marriage counseling from our perspective. In other words, the couple cannot be considered in isolation from the extended families of origin of both partners. Friedman (1985) eloquently states, "The position we occupy in our families of origin is the only thing we can never share or give to another while we are still alive. It is the source of our uniqueness, and hence, the basic parameter for our emotional potential as well as our difficulties. . . . [T]he more we understand that position, therefore, and the more we can learn to occupy it with grace and savvy, rather than fleeing from it or unwittingly allowing it to program our destiny, the more perfectly we can function in any other area of our life" (p. 34).

From our family-systems perspective, there are three significant measures of marital health: (a) the marriage relationship (how much conflict and distance is present); (b) the physical and emotional health of each marriage partner, including evidence of an overfunctioning/underfunctioning reciprocity; (c) the emotional and physical health of each of the children, including relationships with each of the parents and with the siblings that might indicate the presence of entrenched relational triangles. Marriages are considered to be healthy to the extent that the entire family system is symptom free. It would be impossible to measure the health of the marriage without an understanding of the entire extended family. From a family-systems perspective, difficulties in marriage have less to do with the differences between marriage partners than with what is causing the differences to be highlighted at the present time (Friedman, 1985).

Also stemming from the Bowenian perspective is the idea of fostering true marital intimacy through strengthening self-differentiation. Self-differentiation, according to Bowen, is the ability to have well-thought-out life values, principles, and convictions and to hold onto them in the face of anxiety and pressure for conformity and togetherness. It is the capacity to maintain relationships based on emotional separateness, equality, and openness. The self-differentiated person is able to say, "This is who I am, what I believe, what I stand for, and what I will do or will not do, in a given situation." Bowen states, "A more differentiated person can participate freely in the emotional sphere without the fear of becoming too fused with others. He or she also is free to shift to calm, logical reasoning for decisions that govern life. A well differentiated person is not changed by coercion or pressure, or to gain approval, or enhance one's stand with others" (quoted in Gilbert, 1992, pp. 193–194). This concept should not be confused with autonomy or narcissism. Differentiation includes the capacity to maintain a nonanxious presence in the midst of anxious systems while taking full personal responsibility for one's emotional well-being (Friedman, 1985). This is critical to marriage preparation because true intimacy is often misunderstood (Oliker, 1989; Larson, 1988; Crosby, 1976). As misguided couples attempt to achieve emotional closeness (i.e., intimacy), they become ensnared by their own need for the relationship to magically complete and improve their own identity and esteem. Relational fusion (masquerading as intimacy) leads to a high level of relational stress and these dependent couples, with low levels of self-differentiation, cultivate an enmeshed relationship, characterized by a general reliance on their spouse for continual support, assurance, and wholeness. When either of the fused partners becomes dissatisfied, their stress is defined solely within the relationship and blame is inevitably placed on the other person.

The opposite of an enmeshed marriage is a relationship of rugged self-reliance, often called the disengaged relationship. Spouses who are attempting to earn their sense of wholeness by relying on no one, not even their marriage partner, also exhibit symptoms of a low level of self-differentiation and the result is gradual frustration and dissatisfaction with marriage. The goal of SYMBIS is to help the couple achieve an interdependent relationship through strengthening self-differentiation. Issues that involve high levels of anxiety and emotional reactivity for the couple are reframed as opportunities for further self-differentiation within the extended-family context and within the marital dyad.

Gilbert (1992) suggests the following characteristics in relationships characterized by self-differentiation: (a) emotional calm (a nonanxious presence); (b) intellectual objectivity (the ability to observe self in a relationship pattern and make changes without expectations for the other); (c) maintaining one-to-one relationships with one's spouse and the individuals in one's extended family; (d) viewing others as anxious or fearful (rather than malicious or manipulative) in conflict; (e) the ability not to react in kind to the anger or anxiety of others; (f) the ability to make choices or define positions that do not jeopardize love, approval, acceptance, and nurturing; (g) focusing more on personal responsibility than on the behavior of others in the relationship; and (h) calm and thoughtful decision making. Our goal in marriage preparation and marital therapy is to enable the couple to move toward self-differentiation and a more authentic, healthy intimate connection.

☐ Intervention Model

The SYMBIS model is designed to support a couple in building a successful marriage through 8 to 10 sessions, each with a distinct goal: (a) demythifying common marital myths and developing healthy expectations for marriage; (b) developing a realistic concept of love and its malleability; (c) cultivating an attitude and outlook toward life that will sustain marriage in spite of unforeseen difficulties; (d) teaching effective communication skills; (e) accurately understanding and accepting gender differences; (f) teaching effective skills for resolving marital conflict; and (g) exploring the value of a spiritual foundation and the ways couples can build it. In addition to exercises and discussion on each of these seven topics (see Table 11.1), the SYMBIS model also includes administration and interpretation of the PREPARE assessment (Olson, Fournier, & Druckman, 1987).

Critical to the SYMBIS model is the facilitation of a year-long relationship with a marriage mentor couple. Once a couple marries, many issues arise in the relationship that were never imagined during the engagement period. In addition, issues that were explored during premarital

TABLE 11.1:   SYMBIS session goals and methods

Session	Goal	Sample of Methods
1	Establish rapport and begin initial assessment	Administer PREPARE assessment Develop a preliminary family genogram
2	Expose common marital myths and develop healthy expectations of married life	Exercises: "Your Personal Ten Commandments" and "Making Your Roles Conscious"
3	Establish a realistic understanding of love and its fluidity	Exercises: "Defining Love" and "Your Changing Love Style"
4	Cultivate a life-attitude that will sustain marriage (free from blame, self-pity, and resentment)	Exercises: "Avoiding the Blame Game," "Adjusting to Things Beyond Your Control"
5	Cultivate the personal qualities and teach the specific skills of healthy communication	Self-test: "How Well Do You Communicate?" Role-play: clarifying content and reflecting feeling
6	Explore and bridge common gender differences while reviewing communication skills	Exercise: "Your Top Ten Needs" Role-play: communication skills within gender context
7	Teach, model, and practice effective conflict resolutions skills	Exercise: "Mind-Reading" Role-play: "Sharing Withholds" and other skills
8	Explore faith journeys and provide tools for melding spiritual paths	Exercises: "Your Spiritual Journey" and "Improving Your Serve"
9	Inform couple of their strengths and areas for growth	PREPARE interpretation
10	Facilitate relationship with marriage mentor couple	Follow-up sessions

counseling suddenly become more salient. Research regarding commitment in marriage indicates that the first year of marriage is the time couples are most likely to become disillusioned with marriage (Surrah & Hughes, 1997). Mentoring allows for a connection with a seasoned, healthy couple who serve as a sounding board and much more as they invest in the newly married couple to sustain them during this often tumultuous period of adjustment. The two couples typically meet a minimum of three times: at 3 months after the wedding, at 7 months, and near the 1-year wedding anniversary. The value of marriage mentoring, in great part, is that it short-circuits unnecessary anxiety by normalizing the experiences of early marriage. It also supports the preventive structure established in the premarital counseling sessions by providing real-life models and opportunities to reinforce insights and skills (e.g., communication and conflict resolution skills) that can keep detrimental patterns from becoming entrenched ways of relating. Marriage mentor couples are recruited, screened, and trained in mentoring strategies that support the premarriage work and, as an aside, they typically report a "boomerang effect" of receiving as much good out of the process as the newlyweds (see Parrott & Parrott, 1995a; Parrott & Parrott, in press).

Since we know of no aspect of marital interaction about which recent research has shown more astounding results than conflict resolution, we work to integrate the findings on this area into our approach. Research at the University of Denver, for example has predicted with 80% accuracy who will be divorced 6 or 7 years after marrying based on conflict within the relationship (Clements, Stanley, & Markman, 1998). Research at the University of Washington has established a 94% accuracy rate on the prediction of marriage success, again, based solely on conflict in marriage (Gottman, 1994). This preponderance of research has underscored the importance of incorporating conflict resolution skills into our psychoeducational approach. Our goal is to contextualize these findings within the family system and to help couples understand both what unhappy couples do wrong and what healthy couples do right. In a didactic fashion, we explore the disastrous ways of arguing that will sabotage a couple's attempts to resolve conflict and, through role-playing exercise, we work to help couples gain skills to identify and avoid the presence of these saboteurs.

Our intervention model also utilizes Yale psychologist Robert Sternberg's triangular theory of love. We work to strengthen marital commitment by helping couples understand that love has three essential ingredients: passion, intimacy, and commitment (Sternberg, 1986). This is presented in the context of God's covenantal love as the model that shapes and sustains our faithfulness to each other. The bottom line is that we try to help couples understand the fluidity of love and equip them with tools that will cultivate the type of commitment that will sustain their love over the life cycle.

☐ Specific Methods and Strategies for Intervention

The SYMBIS model of marriage preparation incorporates a comprehensive marriage preparation curriculum into its 10-session counseling model. The book *Saving Your Marriage Before It Starts* (Parrott & Parrott, 1995b), addresses seven key relationship areas by posing "Seven Questions to Ask Before (or After) You Marry" (stemming from the theoretical foundations elaborated above). These questions are: (a) Have you faced the myths of marriage with honesty? (b) Can you identify your love style?

(c) Have you developed the habit of happiness? (d) Can you say what you mean and understand what you hear? (e) Have you bridged the gender gap? (f) Do you know how to fight a good fight? (g) Are you and your partner soul mates? Companion SYMBIS workbooks (male and female) are used in conjunction with the book to engage the couple in strategic exercises during the counseling process (Parrott & Parrott, 1995c). There are 22 optional exercises built into the SYMBIS model.

The goal of SYMBIS session 1 is to establish rapport and begin initial assessment with the couple through the administration of the PREPARE Inventory (to assess the relationship) and to construct a family genogram for each individual (to assess transgenerational family dynamics). The family genogram incorporates information about family structure, functioning information, and critical life-cycle events. Patterns of emotional distance, emotional cut-off, conflict, and relational triangles will be explored through family myths, rules, roles, relationships, legacies, etc. Particular attention is paid to the level of self-differentiation each partner learned from their parents. The PREPARE inventory also measures the perceived and ideal levels of cohesion and adaptability of each partner's family.

The purpose of session 2 is to expose common marital myths and develop healthy expectations for married life. The exercises "Your Personal Ten Commandments" and "Making Your Roles Conscious" were designed specifically for the task of helping a couple openly discuss their transgenerational family legacy of unspoken rules and unconscious roles and enable them to create a healthy shared vision for marriage that is unique and fulfilling to the two of them.

In session 3, the counselor works with the couple to establish a realistic understanding of love and its fluidity. The exercises "Defining Love" and "Your Changing Love Style" have been designed to facilitate this process. The process of providing accurate and complete information about what love is and how love is experienced over the life-cycle is crucial to this model. The exercise "Your Changing Love Style" is based on the triangular model of love developed by Sternberg (1986), which identifies the elements of passion, intimacy, and commitment. Each partner divides the relationship into three phases, charting a love triangle that best suits each phase of the relationship (allowing for the fluidity of passion, intimacy, and commitment over time). The couple then discusses the unique style of love that characterizes their relationship currently and in times past. The exercise "Defining Love" allows couples to accept responsibility for cultivating passion, intimacy, and commitment in their relationship through identifying in their own terms how each partner defines love from a list of 12 attributes most frequently identified with love: acceptance, caring, commitment, concern for the other's well-being, friendship, honesty, interest in the other, loyalty, respect, supportiveness, trust, and wanting to be with the other. From this list of attributes, each partner chooses their top three and writes a definition of love that incorporates them. The partners compare their priorities and definitions with one another to see what differences, if any, emerge when it comes to defining love.

The goal of session 4 is to enable the couple to cultivate a life-attitude that will sustain marriage (free from blame, self-pity, and resentment). The exercises "Avoiding the Blame Game" and "Adjusting to Things Beyond Your Control" focus on developing a healthy, differentiated demeanor in the relationship.

Session 5 focuses on communication. The goal is to cultivate a solid foundation for shared empathy and to equip couples with specific communication skills for their relationship. The self-test "How Well Do You Communicate?" and a role-play that establishes the ability to clarify content and reflect feelings in the relationship are utilized.

The central task of session 6 is the exploration of common gender differences, particularly in the area of personal needs and communication patterns. The exercise "Your Top Ten Needs" and a role-play focused on communication skills within the context of gender facilitate this process. Another important exercise designed to bridge the gender gap is the "Couple's Inventory." This exercise helps the couple take stock of the role they each play, consciously and unconsciously, in their relationship. This area is a special focus, particularly because of the importance of unconscious roles that each partner is affected by as a result of his or her own family of origin. The exercise is a list of 15 sentence stems that each partner completes as honestly as possible. Selected sentences include, "I feel central to our relationship when. . . ," "I feel peripheral to our relationship when. . . ," "I feel most feminine/masculine in our relationship when. . . ," "Our finances are controlled by. . . ," "Our social life is planned by. . . ," "The role I play as your wife/husband is. . . ," and so on. The couple then is asked to compare the statements with each other and discuss how their gender influenced the way they responded.

Session 7 tackles the area of effective conflict resolution. The exercises "Mind Reading" and "Sharing Withholds" engage the couple in effective conflict resolution. The "Sharing Withholds" exercise is designed to help the couple keep a clean emotional slate and avoid needless conflicts. This is a key technique for ongoing, effective conflict resolution. We call it "sharing withholds" because it gives partners the chance to share thoughts and feelings that they have withheld from each other. It takes the couple about 10 to 15 minutes to do this. They begin by writing two things the other has done in the last 48 hours that they sincerely appreciated but did not acknowledge. For example, "I appreciate the help you gave me in writing my proposal last night." Next, each individual writes one thing the other has done in the last 48 hours that irritated them but that they did not complain about. For example, "I didn't like it when you borrowed my umbrella without telling me." Once both partners have written their statements, they takes turns sharing them. One person shares all three statements, one after the other. Then the other person shares his or her three statements. And here is an important part of this exercise: The person on the receiving end can say only "thank you" after each statement. That's all. Just "thank you." This rule allows couples to share something that bugs them without fearing a blow-up or a defensive reaction. It also allows couples to receive critiques in the context of affirmation. Once the couple understands the process, this exercise can be done every day to keep repressed feelings from causing damaging and explosive conflicts.

The eighth SYMBIS session focuses on an exploration of the faith journeys for the purpose of providing tools to integrate spiritual paths, values, and experiences into the relationship. The exercises "Your Spiritual Journey" and "Improving Your Serve" have been designed to engage the couple in this task.

Session 9 in the SYMBIS model provides concrete information about the couple's strengths and opportunities for growth through the interpretation of the PREPARE results. The 10th session incorporates any specific issues the couple is facing, as well as the facilitation of a marriage mentor match for this couple. Follow-up sessions are scheduled (preferably within the first 3 months of marriage).

☐ Format of Application

The SYMBIS model targets engaged, about-to-be-engaged, and newly married couples. Couples are recruited to participate in the program through CRD at Seattle Pacific University, by regional marketing, pastoral referrals, regional and national media attention, and word-of-mouth referral. Couples range in age from their 20s to 50s, with the majority of participants in their late 20 and early 30s. While most of the participating couples are anticipating engagement, preparing for a first marriage, or in the early phases of a first marriage, some couples are entering a second marriage. SYMBIS programs have been established at a variety of colleges, universities, and churches nationally to serve local college students and congregations. No screening or assessment is required for participation in the SYMBIS program.

☐ Qualities and Role of the Leader, Facilitator, or Therapist

The SYMBIS model is flexible. It is designed to be used in a wide variety of therapeutic, educational, and congregational settings. In its most rigorous and thorough format (individual counseling sessions for engaged couples), SYMBIS requires an M.A.-level therapist or pastoral counselor with a basic understanding of family-systems dynamics. Training and certification to administer and interpret the PREPARE/ENRICH assessment tools is also required (and is equally available to lay counselors); see chapter 9 of this volume for more information on PREPARE/ENRICH.

As a psychoeducational group experience, the SYMBIS model can be implemented by a facilitator through the use of an eight-session video curriculum for couples that includes a leaders guide, a complete curriculum for the course, and the follow-up design for a marriage mentor program. This complete marriage preparation program has been implemented on college and university campuses and in Protestant and Catholic churches successfully. Couples without a formal facilitator may even use the curriculum on their own by reading the book, viewing the video sessions, and completing the exercises.

☐ Application of the Preventive Model to a Couple at Risk

Because the SYMBIS model is primarily focused on preparing couples for marriage, the traditional SYMBIS program cannot be applied to this case. However, the underlying therapeutic assumptions that inform our work can be honored and applied in this situation, as can many of the intervention techniques utilized in the SYMBIS model.

As cotherapists, we would approach Ben and Alyssa's situation from two angles: (a) focusing on family-systems issues, and (b) giving attention to special issues in the relationship. Because Ben and Alyssa are highly motivated to work on their relationship issues, our therapeutic work with this couple would probably require between 3 and 6 months of weekly sessions.

Assuming the initial intake interviews have occurred (information is provided by the case), the first 4 to 6 weeks of therapy for Ben and Alyssa would involve placing their relationship in the broader context of their extended families through (a) identifying unspoken family rules; (b) assessing unconscious relationship roles; and (c) reestablishing intentional connections with the family of origin.

This therapeutic approach seems to have great merit for couples who have become myopic and see their partners as the source of all pain in their lives. The presenting issue with the couple is "making a good marriage better." However, Ben and Alyssa are clearly caught in a struggle to maintain intimacy while negotiating a major life-cycle transition together (the creation of a family) and simultaneously coming to terms with unfinished business from their own original families.

Unspoken Rules

Ben and Alyssa are walking through a marital minefield of unspoken rules they absorbed from their families of origin. One unspoken rule that is apparently in operation is, "the wife should agree (reflexively) with the husband" (see Ben and Alyssa's immediate assumption that they would relocate for his career). This directly fulfills family-of-origin rules from both sides. Helping the couples we counsel to become more aware of their unspoken rules can keep little problems from becoming big ones. We often have each of the partners complete an exercise entitled "Your Personal Ten Commandments." This exercise is designed to identify the expectations that emerge (almost involuntarily) from their family backgrounds, sibling positions, and personal dispositions. Making secret (unconscious) expectations known allows for conscious examination and incorporation or elimination. To generate material, we often provide a list of incomplete sentence stems for each partner to complete:

Women are . . .
Men are . . .
Marriage is . . .
Sex is . . .
Children are . . .
Success is . . .
Failure is . . .
Being a woman and having a career is . . .
Being a man and having a career is . . .
Spirituality is . . .
Being self-giving is . . .

The answers the clients provide would then be reworded as commands, thus formulating unspoken rules.

Breaking an unspoken rule can be perceived as a sign of betrayal to the partner. Never talking about unspoken rules is like walking through a marital minefield. Heightening awareness can help the couple avoid needless explosions. It will help them to recognize their freedom to accept, reject, challenge, and change their rules for relating.

Unconscious Roles

With the life-cycle transition into a new phase of family life, Ben and Alyssa have each uniquely experienced their new roles as parents. Just as a dramatic performance follows a script, so married couples almost involuntarily discover themselves falling into unconscious roles. Consciously or unconsciously, Ben and Alyssa are acting out the roles that they had observed in their families of origin. Once Ben and Alyssa are aware of the roles they each tend to take, they can then discuss how to write a new script together that is fulfilling for both of them. We would engage them in the exercise "Making Your Roles Conscious." First, we would have them each of them indicate how their parents handled a list of tasks, dividing them up according to "mother," "father," or "both parents." Tasks include a wide variety of relationship responsibilities, such as providing income, staying home with children, handling finances, initiating discussion about the relationship, disciplining the children, initiating sex, making major decisions, etc. Then, Ben and Alyssa would each be asked to divide this same list of tasks up between "you," "your spouse," or "both of you." Next, each would determine how they would like to divide up the tasks, according to their understanding of their own and their spouse's interests, time, and abilities. Finally, we would have Ben and Alyssa compare theirs lists and discuss the results. This exercise can uncover the unspoken assumptions behind their current roles and enable them to readjust their role assignments to bring fulfillment to both of them.

Understanding Cultural Differences in the Family System

A note about cultural difference: Although Ben and Alyssa come from culturally and religiously different families (Alyssa from a stable, Protestant, suburban family and Ben from a single-parent, Jewish, urban family), and we believe that culture plays an important role in family process, we also view culture as "the medium through which family process works its art" (Friedman, 1985, p. 122). Bearing this in mind, we would continue to be sensitive to cultural themes, but we would seek to do so in a way that doesn't allow culture to camouflage family process. In the case of Ben and Alyssa, the most obvious link to the family process are issues of faith. With the birth of their first child, Alyssa experienced a new commitment to her Christian faith, resulting in noticeable changes. Our goal would be to work with Ben and Alyssa to understand why this difference in faith and life-style choices (i.e., church attendance, alcohol consumption) has been emphasized between them at this point in time. This work would be done in the context of their transgenerational family genograms.

Reworking Family-of-Origin Relationships

From our perspective, the same emotional process that Ben and Alyssa are experiencing in their relationship was operating in their families of origin. Only limited improvement of their relationship will occur without work in the families of origin by each of them. We would encourage each of them to spend individual time with, or make contact with, every family member. Their objective is not to confront or accuse, but rather to become aware of the tone and type of intimacy they experience in each one.

One of the most helpful tools for reworking family-of-origin relationships is the constructing of a family genogram. Developed from research on family systems by Bowen, genograms are widely used to help people unravel family mysteries (Carter & McGoldrick, 1989). The genogram is constructed in the counseling session. This relational family tree reveals recurring life patterns across three generations, and it can speed up the process of awareness and facilitate the intentional reworking of family connections. Basically, the genogram enables the couple to map their family structure and relationships and to chart their family interaction patterns. This information, collected as the result of personal knowledge and strategic conversations with individual family members, often becomes an agent of change for the couple. The backbone of the genogram is a graphic depiction of the family structure across three or four generations. Each male is represented by a square and each female is represented by a circle. A marriage is represented by a solid line connecting the two persons, and so on. Then the counselor puts the genogram to work by addressing relationship dynamics, life-cycle issues for the extended family, and family themes, rules, and roles that become evident as the information unfolds.

It is to be predicted that after a measure of rewarding work within the family of origin, an intense conflict will erupt (possibly over faith, roles, or their shared vision as a couple). At this point, it is important to begin to address specific current issues between the couple.

Addressing the Life Cycle Transition

As a couple, Ben and Alyssa are facing the major transition into parenthood, with all of the resultant increased stress it introduces into their marital system. This often causes a quantum leap in anxiety, intensifying the entrenched style of relating the couple has developed.

For a woman, bearing a child is often considered a confirmation of her femininity and a rite of passage into legitimate adulthood. This may be particularly true in Alyssa's case, since the role of the woman (in Alyssa's mind) may be closely associated with her mother, who did not work outside of the home. Ben, on the other hand, did not have a "stay-at-home" mom, nor did he have a father. This new phase of the life cycle is stretching him into unknown territory.

Addressing the New Pregnancy

We would address the "surprise" pregnancy and the resultant impact it has had on their intimacy, passion, and commitment. For a pregnancy to occur without a shared vision and decision-making process for this couple seems to symbolize a significant pattern in their current relationship. This situation calls us to address issues of power, trust, and self-differentiation.

Dealing With Conflict

With an escalating level of marital conflict, Ben and Alyssa are more in need of effective tools to navigate relationship conflict then they have ever been. Because their marital style has not incorporated conflict significantly in the past, we would work with them to equip them for healthy conflict. Two possible tools for Ben and Alyssa might be the "XYZ Formula" and the "Conflict Card." The "XYZ Formula" (In situation X, when you do Y, and I feel Z) can enable them to state their feelings in a nonattaching, noncontemptuous manner (Stanley, Markman, St. Peter's, & Leber, 1995). The use of this formula helps couples to avoid the vicious cycle of criticism and contempt that Gottman has identified as fatal to marriage.

On the "Conflict Card" is a scale from 1 to 10 ranking the intensity of a person's feelings, ranging from 1: "I'm not enthusiastic, but it's no big deal to me," to 10: "Over my dead body." Using an objective measurement of the intensity of feelings allows for a partner who tends to be less expressive to communicate on even grounds with a more expressive partner.

Gender Differences

Research and experience consistently point to a fundamental and powerful distinction between the sexes. As we work with couples, we find that, typically, men try to meet needs that they value and women do the same. We believe that couples can celebrate male–female differences in marriage by accurately understanding and meeting the unique needs that are part of their spouse's gender. While there will always be exceptions to the rule, a wife's most basic needs in marriage are to be: (a) cherished, (b) known, and (c) respected. Men, on the other hand, tend to desire (a) admiration, (b) autonomy, and (c) shared activity. It is clear that both Ben and Alyssa are feeling the weight of unmet needs. Ben, who has lost his autonomy (and now is bearing the responsibility of being the provider) and Alyssa, who isn't experiencing Ben as a good listener (is not feeling known and cherished). We would help them begin to work together to meet these most basic individual needs.

Relationship Assessment

The importance of objective and accurate relationship information leads us to place a high value on relationship assessment tools such as the EN-RICH (Evaluation and Nurturing Relationship Issues, Communication and Happiness) Inventory (Olson et al., 1987). This tool effectively incorporates important family-of-origin influences and provides a high level of accurate relationship information. We would probably use this early in our work with Ben and Alyssa as a foundation for our work with them as a couple.

☐ Empirical Evaluation and Research

While the ultimate indication of success in the SYMBIS model resides in the quality of the relationship that participants achieve in the future, evaluations of SYMBIS programs over the course of 4 years have indicated significant improvements ($p < .001$) in realistic beliefs and attitudes about marriage (Hammersla, Parrott, & Parrott, 1995).

Longitudinal research on the program is in progress which measures the relationship of the couple on many dimensions before the SYMBIS program, immediately following the SYMBIS program, 1 month later, and 1 year later. Many unsolicited anecdotal reports, from both facilitators and participants, indicate a positive evaluation of the SYMBIS model. Because couples who participate in SYMBIS do not begin their marriage mentor connection until after their weddings, we are able to stay in contact with them over the course of their engagement and immediately before and after their weddings. The process of selecting the marriage mentor couple and making the initial match has served as a channel of continuity with couples. This has provided a rich supply of positive feedback (both from couples who successfully marry and from those who end their relationship prior to marriage based on learning that has occurred throughout the process). Participants in the marriage mentor program evaluate their experiences for effectiveness and enjoyment three times yearly. In addition, seasoned couples participating in the mentoring process report a happy by-product of the program: a boomerang effect. That is, they report that mentoring a new couple strengthens their more mature marriage by default.

☐ Summary

As a relatively new preventive program, SYMBIS has many areas that could be reshaped and improved. Not least of these is the need for much more empirical research. With a more stable base of basic research, the SYMBIS model will be able to articulate its effective efforts with greater confidence. Some may also argue that the approach needs a more explicit skill-building emphasis. This is yet to be determined.

Perhaps the program's major strengths are its relevance and its accessibility. The model reaches a felt need of the current generation of couples by identifying their most salient issues. The program is also one that is quite plausible for most individuals to access. Since it can be conducted in a variety of settings with varying degrees of rigor, SYMBIS can reach a great number of couples.

When we consider what is important in preparing couples for life-long marriage, there are many skills and strategies stemming from a variety of modalities that can be incorporated into the SYMBIS model. As a psychoeducational approach continually influenced by new research findings, SYMBIS is continually being reshaped. All the while, the soil of Bowenian family systems provides a stable context for correcting faulty information and equipping couples with an accurate understanding of themselves and what they bring to the relationship.

☐ Contact References

Readers who would like more information about the SYMBIS program can reach the authors at Center for Relationship Development, Seattle Pacific University, Seattle, WA 98119; (206) 281-2178; http://www.realrelationships.com

☐ References

Bowen, M. (1978). *Family therapy in clinical practice*. New York: Jason Aronson.

Carter, B., & McGoldrick, M., (1989). *The changing family life cycle: A framework for family therapy* (2nd ed.). Needham Heights, MA: Allyn & Bacon.

Clements, M. L., Stanley, S. M., & Markman, H. J. (1998). *Prediction of marital distress and divorce: A discriminant analysis.* Manuscript submitted for publication.

Crosby, J. F. (1976). *Illusion and disillusion: The self in love and marriage* (2nd ed.). Belmont, CA: Wadsworth

Friedman, E. H. (1985). *Generation to generation: Family process in church and synagogue.* New York: Guilford.

Gilbert, M. (1992). *Extraordinary relationships: A new way of thinking about human interactions.* Minneapolis, MN: Chronimed.

Gottman, J. M. (1994). *Why marriages succeed or fail.* New York: Simon & Schuster.

Hammersla, J., Parrott, L., & Parrott, L. (1995). *Beliefs and attitudes about marriage.* Report on research submitted to Murdock Charitable Trust, January 25, 1995.

Kerr, M. (1981). Family systems theory and therapy. In A. Gurman & D. Kniskern (Eds.), *Handbook of family therapy* (pp. 226–264). New York: Brunner/Mazel.

Larson, J. H. (1988). The marriage quiz: College students' beliefs in selected myths about marriage. *Family Relations, 37,* 43–51.

Lasswell, M. (1985). Illusions regarding marital happiness. *Medical Aspects of Human Sexuality, 19,* 144–158.

McManus, J. J. (1993). *Marriage savers.* Grand Rapids, MI: Zondervan.

Oliker, S. (1989). *Best friends and marriage.* Los Angeles: University of California Press.

Olson, D. H., Fournier, D. G., & Druckman, J. K. (1987). *Counselor's manual for PREPARE/ENRICH* (rev. ed.). Minneapolis, MN: PREPARE/ENRICH.

Parrott, L., & Parrott, L. (1995a). *The marriage mentor manual.* Grand Rapids, MI: Zondervan.

Parrott, L., & Parrott, L. (1995b). *Saving your marriage before it starts: Seven questions to ask before (and after) you get married.* Grand Rapids, MI: Zondervan.

Parrott, L., & Parrott, L. (1995c). *Saving your marriage before it starts: Workbook for men/women.* Grand Rapids, MI: Zondervan.

Parrott, L., & Parrott, L. (in press). *Mentoring engaged and newly married couples.* Grand Rapids, MI: Zondervan.

Stanley, S. M., Markman, H. J., St. Peters, M., & Leber, P. (1995). Strengthening marriage and preventing divorce: New directions in prevention research. *Family Relations, 44,* 392–401.

Sternberg, R. (1986). A triangular theory of love. *Psychological Review, 93,* 119–135.

Surrah, C. A., & Hughes, D. K. (1997). Commitment processes in accounts of the development of premarital relationships. *Journal of Marriage and the Family, 59,* 5–21.

Walker, C., & Moses, E. (1996). The age of self navigation. *American Demographics, 18,* 36–47.

12
CHAPTER

Richard A. Hunt, Ph.D.
Joan A. Hunt, M.A.

The Caring Couples Network

☐ Introduction

The Caring Couples Network (CCN) involves married couples, pastors, and professional consultants as teams with an integrated network of ministries to couples and families. These ministries include mentoring to prewedded and newly married couples, couples with children, and couples facing major problems.

Several historical and theoretical factors influenced the development of the CCN team approach. The concept of couples as influencing other couples is part of most theoretical understandings of marriage, family dynamics, and therapy (e.g., Paolino & McCrady, 1978; Stuart, 1980; Jacobson & Gurman, 1986; Popenoe, Elshtain, & Blankenhorn; 1996). The concept of the CCN team as mobilizing married couples for action grew out of seeing the gap between the needs of couples and the availability to them of couples who model healthy marriage and family living.

The CCN team is a multitheoretical, multidisciplinary, multimodel approach to delivering specific nurture, support, mentoring, and interventions to couples at their points of felt need. The CCN team is both a mobile delivery system of couples reaching and supporting other couples in many practical ways and an administrative unit in a local church or other setting to facilitate these nurturing ministries.

The *nurture* function involves CCN team members and others in providing caring friendship ministries, such as mentoring and support for couples, presentations on marriage and family issues, and outreach to couples and to other agencies concerning needs of couples and families. The CCN team decides how to prioritize and coordinate the ministries they choose to provide.

The marriage bond is at the heart of families (Everett, 1990). Churches need to find more ways to enable marriages to succeed in being the healthy bond that enables families to function successfully as well as minister to disrupted and hurting families. When marriages are seriously dysfunctional or fail, then ministries to single parents, stepfamilies, and families with violence, substance abuse, and other concerns become needed and can be offered through the CCN team.

Too often, unfortunately, communities hear only from those couples who divorce or otherwise have destructive relationships, creating a culture of divorce (Popenoe et al., 1996). There are millions of married couples who are succeeding in their marriages, providing good parenting, and creating new models of healthy marriage for the future. CCN seeks to mobilize these healthy couples to share their successes and reach out to nurture other couples at every stage of life.

The Need for the Caring Couples Network

The emphasis of both the Council on Families in America (1995) and of McManus (1995) is upon reaching and supporting couples early, as they consider marriage, and before initial conflicts develop into chronic negative patterns that produce marital dysfunction and divorce. However, effective ministries of the church are still needed to help couples and families even in deepest distress.

The need for better marriage ministries calls churches to organized action beyond just the publication of books and magazines on marriage and family living. In response, the United Methodist Church has established CCN to implement many of these marriage support suggestions.

Many local churches already have some marriage ministries, such as couples classes and programs, premarital and early marriage mentoring, marriage enrichment, and marriage counseling. Through its CCN team, a church or group of churches can coordinate these ministries and reach more couples with greater potential benefit for couples, families, congregations, communities, and the general society.

The Origin of CCN

For many years the United Methodist denomination has provided several resources for couples. The official marriage manual of the United Methodist Church is *Growing Love in Christian Marriage,* which consists of a couples book (R. A. Hunt & J. A. Hunt, 1981), used by over 300,000 couples, and a pastors book (Smith & Smith, 1981). A marriage enrichment program, Celebrating Marriage, has been available since 1982.

In 1995 the General Board of Discipleship of the United Methodist Church established CCN to implement a system for integrating, supporting, and expanding marriage ministries through local churches. A system of CCN resources and procedures was planned, and a design team of couples met in Nashville in July 1995.

In November 1996, the *Caring Couples Network Handbook* (R. A. Hunt & J. A. Hunt, 1996) and CCN video, *Caring Couples Network: A Team in Action* (R. A. Hunt, Hunt, Gentzler, & Hughes, 1997) describing the CCN team's ministries were published. A book of real-life stories about couples who have been helped by other couples is in preparation. The Growing Love in Christian Marriage and Celebrating Marriage enrichment programs have been revised and updated to become part of CCN.

It is intended that CCN teams be organized within one local church, yet a CCN team may also be in other settings, such as several churches in a community or county. The goal is to have a CCN team in every church and community as soon as possible.

Although originated in the United Methodist Church, CCN teams can be established in other churches and denominations and among ecumenical groups of churches. Materials are written with minimum reference to United Methodist terminology and structures and from an ecumenical perspective. One of the goals of the program is to find ways to make CCN available through other denominations and churches.

Specialized CCN teams can also minister among clergy where the married couples are all clergy and/or other professional persons who work in church settings.

Key CCN Concepts

CCN is a team of married couples working with their pastor (and pastoral staff in larger churches) and with professional consultants (therapists, physicians, attorneys, family finance experts, and other experts) to minister with and to engaged and newly married couples, couples with children, and couples with serious difficulties, such as substance abuse, violence, losses, and other negatives that damage marriage and family life.

CCN sees marriage as a spiritual journey of the spouses, undertaken for the spiritual formation and growth of themselves, their children, other relatives and friends, and those in their churches and communities (Everett, 1990; R. A. Hunt & J. A. Hunt, 1996). The family is God's 7-day-a-week "home church" for the nurture and support of the household, and the wife and husband are the "coministers" who guide and shape those in the household.

CCN incorporates and builds upon basic principles of couple mentoring, friendship, marriage enrichment, and outreach. The goal of CCN is to *network* couples, pastors, and consultants with many resources in active outreach to serve the needs of couples and families.

Within the United Methodist Church, CCN brings together three existing resources: *Growing Love in Christian Marriage* (R. A. Hunt & J. A. Hunt, 1981; Smith & Smith, 1981), the denominational guide for engaged and married couples; Celebrating Marriage, the United Methodist marriage enrichment program; and the United Methodist expressions of the Marriage Encounter and Engaged Encounter programs. To these resources, CCN adds the *CCN Handbook* (R. A. Hunt & J. A. Hunt, 1996), the CCN video, *Couples Who Care* (Ives, 1997), and other resources for mentoring, nurturing, and supporting couples. Each local CCN team is welcome to use additional resources and approaches according to the needs, training, and goals of their ministries with couples and families.

☐ Theoretical Underpinnings

The CCN approach emphasizes the important dimension of supportive friendships among couples in many informal ways, as well as enrichment and therapy (R. A. Hunt, Hof, & DeMeria, 1998). CCN is more about implementing existing theory than about creating new theory. CCN seeks to reach couples who otherwise would not be reached with the good information, models of marriage, and supportive nurture that help to make needed changes early.

CCN emphasizes marriage as a permanent covenant between husband and wife as coequals before God, as the basic optimal context for raising children, and as a relationship of mutual sharing, nurture, and comfort between spouses (Everett, 1990). Marriage is the relationship between two consenting adults around which other family relationships are formed. The quality of the covenant of marriage is the key to the quality of parent–child and other family relationships in both the household and the extended families.

CCN is based in a specific type of "committed romantic relationship" in the marriage of one man and one woman who "espouse" each other before God through a wedding and/or other public acknowledgment of their relationship (in contrast to unwedded, living-together couples). The phrase *committed romantic relationships* uses three key words that have special meanings in the CCN approach to couples.

To be either committed or romantic implies a relationship. The CCN approach sees marriage as a special relationship between one man and one woman before God. Among CCN couples, the emphasis is heavily on marriage and married couples as the preferred and most challenging human relationship. Individual couples and CCN teams may have differing opinions about unmarried couples and about homosexual couples. The official CCN approach is that a wedded, lifelong marriage between one woman and one man is the optimal way to organize sexual relationships, promote individual growth, and form the most solid basis for organizing family life. While other types of relationships may provide some benefits that appear similar to a one-woman–one-man marriage, they are not equal to marriage in all respects. Therefore a one-man–one-woman marriage is unique among ways to organize human relationships. Other relationships may substitute when those involved are unable or unwilling to make a one-man–one-woman marriage work, but those are not equivalent to marriage.

The word *committed* points to the question of whether the partners intend their relationship to continue into the future and under all circumstances. *Committed* includes the sense of being pledged, promised, involved, obligated, dedicated, intentional, resolute, and unalterable. Commitment gives the overall stability and confidence of the relationship through the ebb and flow of emotional feelings and daily living. Commitment allows the roots of the relationship to deepen, providing support and stability for each partner.

The committed element is most clearly shown in a public wedding. In the wedding, each partner "espouses" the other in this vow of developing permanent love. In the wedding each partner vows before God and announces to the world (as represented by those present) the intent to love and care for the other under all circumstances. Whether simple or elaborate, one purpose of the wedding is to remind both the partners and those around them of the promise to be present and available to each other across all life circumstances. This is quite a challenge, yet it is through meeting the challenges of marriage that the partners forge the marriage bond that stabilizes their relationship and frees them for growth, both individually and as a couple. Families, friends, and others are called to respect this commitment and to not try to distort or break it. In those times when either spouse would prefer to escape rather than work on the relationship, the wedding vow reminds both of the possibilities of greater love. Thus the relationship is not a temporary agreement to be abandoned at the unilateral discretion of either partner.

The word *romantic* points to the intense, intimate, affectionate, erotic, fervent, attached, tender, mystical, and "beyond words" nature of the deepest relationship between a woman and a man. While some would see romance as some type of unrealistic fantasy, the interplay between the high times of intense positive "personal chemistry" between spouses and the long-term sober commitment to stay establishes marriage as a very special, unique, secure relationship that allows for safety, intimacy, and growth.

Marriage is a complex system of units that can be viewed simultaneously from many perspectives. Among these perspectives are these units: legal, social, economic, religious, educational, leisure, and sexual (R. A. Hunt & Rydman, 1979, p. 16).

The committed romantic relationship called marriage is a lifelong journey with many stages and changes. Borrowing from experiences of travel, the metaphor of "lifelong journey" also points to the many ways each partner changes and grows as each sees his or her past childhood and family relationships in new ways. The growing confidence in each other gives a basis for growth, for support, and for coping with new challenges, variations, reversals, and unexpected changes.

Philosophically, marriage is a way to answer the question of how to structure one's priorities in life in order to maximize the good and minimize the bad. Marriage structure and process embody the partners' value systems, life experiences, and choices (Hendrix, 1988; Markman, Stanley, & Blumberg, 1994). Although marriage structures and emphases have changed over the centuries, all are expressions of the answers to basic life questions about human nature, the relationship of men and women, the purpose and place of children, parent–child relationships, family interaction, and how society and the married family household should interact.

It is necessary to separate the concept of being *religious* into inner spirituality and outward expressions through organized religious groups. The spiritual dimension is the heart of marriage and permeates everything a couple does (R. A. Hunt, 1987; Everett, 1990).

Inner spirituality (personal religion) includes the very personal communion between marriage partners that finds expression through their common experiences, including sex, parenting, coping with adversities, worship, adventures, and more. Spirituality also includes the partners' world views and the answers they give and live to fundamental life questions, such as what our place in the universe is, who God is, and how to love. Spirituality calls couples to deeper levels of caring, warmth, and meaning from which to challenge and improve outward expressions of religiosity (R. A. Hunt, 1987).

Outward or social religion involves questions about how a couple relates to others, including other couples, families, work, and society. These involve standards and norms (expectations about what should happen), interventions in situations to achieve justice and fairness, and merciful actions to minister to those in need. Social and organizational religion, along with other agencies, call couples to become involved with the world as a balance to their focus on themselves.

Psychologically, marriage involves all of each partner's personality and character, including physiological, perceptional, motivational, emotional, intellectual, volitional, and behavioral systems, as each person interacts with a partner, with other family members, and with other parts of society (Fincham & Bradbury, 1990). All of one's past contributes to who the person is at the moment, yet at any given moment a person can make choices about directions to take in the future. Thus each theoretical approach, including psychodynamic, social learning-cognitive, structural-strategic, family systems, imago, and others, contributes helpful perspectives on marriage. To function well in marriage requires both sufficient levels of personal competence and interpersonal skills in communication, problem solving, and goal setting.

Socially, marriage is a system composed of two persons, in the context of other systems, such as family and community (R. A. Hunt & Rydman, 1979). Each system affects the marriage just as the marriage affects the other systems. These results are constantly in process, yet are based on past experience. "Caring couples" are a part of these systems.

The preventive interventions of CCN stem from the central assumption that every couple needs a variety of models of successful marriage. Couples get these models both by observing other couples and by hearing how those couples are conducting their marriage journey. Just as travelers tell others about road conditions and what to see, so couples can share insights about their own journey with other couples who either have not yet reached that situation or are in the middle of a similar situation. Although a novice storyteller may improve with guidance from those who are more experienced, the essential elements of the story are still valuable to others who are making similar journeys. The major essential for the CCN couple is to nurture and mentor, yet give freedom and flexibility to the other couple.

☐ Intervention Model

The model of intervention follows from the theory described above by way of several principles that the CCN intervention model assumes.

1. There are many married couples who have healthy relationships.
2. There are many other couples who need and want to know these models.
3. Marriages can be improved by having these two types of couples interact.

4. Religious groups are a major channel for mobilizing these services with couples.
5. The most efficient way to improve families and, through parenting, to nurture the next generation of children, is by improving marriages.
6. Training will enhance the effectiveness of a healthy couple's influence on other couples.

The specific goals of intervention are: (a) to give positive hope, support, and nurture to all couples; (b) to enable couples in need to get the help they need; (c) to present a variety of models of healthy marriage to couples, families, and others in ways that address their current needs.

There are two major tasks associated with the CCN goals, nurture or supportive and administrative:

1. The primary goal of the CCN team is to enable couple-to-couple support through mentoring, enrichment, education, and other channels.
2. In order to achieve the many expressions of support and nurture, the administrative goals of CCN are to organize, train, and support CCN teams.

There are several skills for preventing couple or marriage distress and enhancing committed romantic relationships (e.g., Miller, Wackman, Nunnally, & Miller, 1988; Hendrix, 1988; Markman et al., 1994). CCN teams may use a variety of formulations of skills, yet these couple skills can be summarized following the "love-power" approach to couples (J. A. Hunt & R. A. Hunt, 1994).

Preliminary to identifying skills is understanding the two major dimensions of caring and sharing. Love (caring) and power (sharing) are the basic dimensions of marriage. Everything else in marriage follows from this perspective. Learning to love in all kinds of challenges and circumstances is the ultimate goal (or end) across the marital journey. The means to this end is the power (ability, resources, capability) to express love in ways that the recipient recognizes. This is often a very complex process, since both words and actions can have so many different meanings.

These two basic dimensions of love and power are found by other names in most theoretical approaches to marriage. For example, in Olson's (1996) circumplex model, his term *cohesion* refers to an optimal balance of caring (love) patterns of closeness and distance, and *adaptability* refers to an optimal balance of power as expressed in structure and freedom.

Love is a process of continuing to share and care for another person in ways that the other person recognizes as loving and caring. The intent to love is the first step, with some type of loving action being the expression of that intent. However, love is completed when the recipient recognizes the care and concern the giver is trying to express.

Love: Choosing your future. Since love is the ultimate end or goal of marriage, the choices a couple makes about their future express their understanding and desires in love. Future is both short term (e.g., what to do today, this week; scheduling) and long term (e.g., career, children, world concerns). In choosing directions, a couple is prioritizing the ways to love and choosing among these. Included in love (as care, respect, concern) is love of God, self, partner, family, friends, environment, and world—all laced with many issues of goals and priorities.

Power: Evaluating your resources. Resources are the means (power) to an end (love) that each partner has. Resources are broadly defined as including abilities, character, personality, habit patterns, finances, background, and heritage. The central question for the couple is how to combine these resources to maximize the love they want, both today and into the future. Power struggles erupt between partners because each has a different goal or vision of their shared future.

Communication: Connecting these dimensions. Communication includes the often emphasized skills of listening, expressing, problem solving, and conflict resolution. In addition, communication points to the positive ways that partners connect their love, resources, and evaluations to produce joy, satisfaction, pleasure, and a sense of accomplishment in their marriage and their lives, and with the persons with whom they have contact (children, relatives, work associates, neighbors, friends, society).

Communication includes both verbal and nonverbal dimensions. Communication also refers to the "how" and the "what": how the sender conveys his or her meanings to the receiver as well as what the message is. In this sense, "good communication" refers to accuracy, in which the impact on the receiver matches the intent of the sender.

Good: Increasing your positives. Positive results occur when a couple uses their resources to implement love in ways they intend. For most couples, "positives" include descriptions such as being able to do what they want, having joyful times together, enjoying affection (both sexual and other types), being honest and dependable, having sufficient finances, enjoying satisfying living and working conditions, and many other specifics. However, when it comes to details, every couple has their own specific criteria for determining what is "positive" and what is "negative" in their marriage.

Bad: Decreasing your negatives. Negative results occur when a couple uses their resources in ways that hurt themselves and/or others.

For most couples, "negatives" probably include being verbally, physically or emotionally hurt; addictions (alcohol, other drugs, food, gambling, sex, etc.); being ignored, devalued, or left out of decisions (as in extramarital affairs, family issues, etc). In addition, the absence of positives may itself be a negative.

The positives and negatives categories are expressions of the common underlying "good/bad" scale that every couple uses to evaluate what is happening in their marriage and other relationships. Many nuances are included in making judgments of good vs. bad. Among these are: "Which specific action, pattern, or situation is being evaluated?" and "Good or bad for whom?" Judgments about positives and negatives (good/bad) always involve the match between what one wanted or expected and what is (or has) actually happened, as seen from the perspective of the person making the judgment. In marriage, having two persons involved complicates decision making and challenges the spouses to clarify their perspectives and to find consensus as a basis for making decisions about their future and resources.

Each couple constantly evaluates the results (positive and negative) of how they connect their resources to their goals.

☐ Specific Strategies for Intervention

The CCN approach takes a "metaframework" approach (Breunlin, Schwartz, & Kune-Karrer, 1992) that invites use of any activities and techniques from any source, a few of which are listed in the references. CCN has created some resources and procedures, yet so many good resources are already available that can be used by CCN teams. CCN encourages the use of any resources and techniques that enable couple growth, nurture, friendship, and mentoring.

The primary activity or procedure is the interpersonal relationship between couples in which they share their stories and insights (Wimberly, 1997). Although one couple may be the "caring couple" and the other couple may be a "partner couple" (the couple receiving care), both couples benefit from the friendship exchange. A caring couple can see the good in and learn from even the most dysfunctional couple, while that couple benefits from the mentoring and nurture of the caring couple.

A caring couple seeks to express friendship and mentoring in specific ways that the recipient couple can understand and accept. The *CCN Handbook* (R. A. Hunt & J. A. Hunt, 1996) offers suggestions concerning many situations. Some of these are described below in the application of CCN to the couple (Ben and Alyssa) being considered in this volume.

The basic rationale for interventions is that partner couples need the personal contact and support that can only be provided by other couples who are perceived to be "real" and who are seen to be coping successfully with situations similar to their own. In this personal, nonthreatening, and supportive relationship the receiving (or partner) couple has the opportunity to ask questions of the caring couple, and the caring couple can address specific issues that they may see at work in the partner couple's relationship. Out of their own experience, their knowledge of marriage resources, and their training in psychoeducational skills, the caring couple becomes a "living book" in a language that the partner couple can understand and apply to themselves.

☐ Format of Application

Couples are recruited to the CCN program at two levels: caring couples and couples who receive their care (recipient couples or partner couples).

The CCN team is composed of these three types of persons: married couples, the pastor and/or other church staff members (if any), and professional consultant(s). Together, these team members covenant with God, each other, and their church to minister to couples in need as a direct expression of the congregation's outreach to all couples and families.

Caring couples are volunteer married couples who:

- commit themselves to grow in their own marriages;
- want to reach other couples with friendship and support;
- express their own faith through their personal relationships with others;
- support spiritual qualities in marriage and family living;
- seek to improve society's support for healthy marriages and families.

Within each caring couple, the spouses decide how they want to function effectively together in reaching other couples. It is expected that both spouses will participate in the CCN team although one partner may take primary initiative or leadership on specific ministries.

Pastor (and staff, if any): The CCN team must have support and involvement from the local church pastor (and staff, if any) for several reasons. The pastor(s) are most likely to know of the needs of couples and to see how the caring couples can provide nurture and support in specific situations. Since one goal of the CCN team is to assist in the pastoral care of couples, the pastor(s) are usually the key persons in facilitating contacts between mentor couples and the couples and families who need their ministries. The CCN team benefits from the enabling support and perspectives of the pastor.

The pastor and consultants also benefit from the CCN team in many ways, because caring couples, out of their experiences in their own marriages and families, are in a unique position to provide ministries to couples that greatly expand and supplement the pastor's work with couples.

Professional consultant(s) have expertise in marriage-related areas, such as couples therapy, marriage enrichment, family finance, social services, women's shelters, law enforcement, health maintenance, family medicine, personnel management, and divorce and family mediation. It is assumed that professionals who identify themselves as marriage counselors or therapists will be licensed or certified in an appropriate discipline such as psychology, marriage and family counseling, social work, pastoral counseling, psychiatry, or professional counseling.

Professional consultants cooperate with the pastor and couples, provide information about couple and family dynamics as needed, and assist the pastor and couples to connect with community resources.

According to the needs of the church and the CCN team, professional consultants may participate in training team members, provide backup consultation to caring couples, assist in referrals, and be available to couples for marital and family assessment and therapy, provided all parties do not see this as a dual-role relationship (as a therapist and consultant or trainer).

Screening and assessment of caring couples follows the general guidelines given in the *CCN Handbook* (R. A. Hunt & J. A. Hunt, 1996), some of which are listed in the foregoing discussion of caring couples.

The CCN approach can be used with any population of couples. This seemingly grandiose catch-all assertion is possible because the CCN team has three major means of contact with couples in need.

For couples who are functioning well and are open to receiving mentoring about marriage and family matters, either the pastor can introduce the caring couple to the partner couple or the caring couple can introduce themselves. In turn, the caring couple can use both couple-to-couple and group formats for mentoring and other enrichment and educational approaches.

For couples who recognize that they are in difficulty and are seeking ways to proceed, the pastor may provide counseling assistance and also may refer the couple to other professional treatment. The caring couple can be part of the treatment plan by being available to the dysfunctional couples as a support and as a real-life example of a more healthy marriage.

For dysfunctional couples who seem to be less open to receiving care, the CCN team consultation process among caring couples, professional consultants, and pastoral staff can create the best intervention plan for that couple. Where the skills and resources of the CCN team are not sufficient, the team can then obtain more input in order to decide which direction to take.

There are usually many needed ministries among couples and families in the typical parish, yet in the beginning, the CCN team will need to identify a few specific goals and situations in which they will minister. Among the many possibilities are these:

1. assisting in the preparation for marriage with adolescents and single adults;
2. information and support for couples considering marriage;
3. mentoring engaged and newly married couples;
4. addressing parenting issues for previously married spouses forming step-families;
5. supporting new parents around pregnancy, birth, and the initial parenting of their children;
6. supporting couples with fertility or pregnancy concerns;
7. finding ways to address parenting issues with children, adolescents, and young adults;
8. assisting couples in conflict or who are considering divorce to find broader perspectives on the issues involved and to get professional help as needed;
9. reaching out to couples with addictions such as alcoholism, food or substance abuse, and gambling;
10. finding ways to enable couples with domestic violence, emotional or sexual abuse, or other hurtful patterns to get appropriate help;
11. being available to support couples in crises such as the death of a family member, a major accident, or illness;
12. finding ways to assist couples in the loss of a job, work or career changes, or moves to a new location;
13. providing support to couples concerned about children leaving home and about "empty nest" transitions;
14. facilitating support for couples with aging parents or other intergenerational issues;
15. providing support and nurture for older adults' marriage issues in relation to retirement, financial planning, health, and other issues;
16. finding ways to assist couples in coping with major financial difficulties;
17. supporting couples with chronic illness or physical challenges;
18. facilitating couple and family ministries in times of community disasters and crises of any type;
19. addressing additional marriage and family situations to which the CCN team can provide nurture, information, support, and ministry.

☐ Qualities and Role of the Leader or Facilitator

In the CCN team, all members serve as leaders or mentors in some way according to the needs being addressed. It is expected that pastors, church staff, and professional consultants will have the education, training, and background required for their certification, licensing, or ordination, according to their professional identity. It is expected that caring couples will exemplify successful marriages and will continue to obtain training and enrichment that increases their skills and effectiveness with other partner couples.

The effectiveness of the CCN team depends heavily upon the characteristics of the persons on the team. Each local CCN team may adapt and refine the following criteria to fit their own situation. Since the CCN team is based in a church setting, these characteristics are stated in terms of a Christian religious setting. They can be adapted to other religious traditions. All CCN team members (pastors, couples, consultants) need to:

1. demonstrate clear commitment to marriage and family as systems in which each person mutually nurtures the other family members. This nurture and support is informed by their values and faith perspectives.
2. be able to incorporate Christian spiritual dimensions of marriage in all aspects of their work with couples and families.
3. have experienced in their own marriage the major elements of high-quality Christian marriage and family living and be able to identify and respect these in any couple and family.
4. have understanding and empathy with others.
5. be recommended by the pastor or equivalent person who knows them well enough to be confident of their ability to serve on the CCN team.

Qualities of Caring Couples Who Participate in the CCN Team

1. They must model the qualities of Christian marriage in their own lives and relationships.
2. They should be married long enough to give evidence of a stable, healthy, and growing relationship with each other, with their children, and with others.
3. The should be interesting, caring, and winsome to other couples.
4. In their own marriage and family relationships, they should have experienced nurture and support from other couples and individuals.
5. Both spouses should be active in the local church and willing to volunteer time and resources for friendship, mentoring, and other ministries with others.
6. They should be able and willing to talk about their Christian faith and understanding of marriage and to share their own experiences in ways that are helpful to others.
7. Some CCN couples may have special training or information in mar-

riage-related areas, such as finance, health, sexuality, parenting, coping with major dysfunctions, or other areas, which they can share with others.

8. Some couples may have useful insights and skills from their own life experiences of overcoming serious marital and/or personal crises, such as alcoholism, abuse, divorce and remarriage, infidelity, illness, financial loss, or career disasters.

Qualities of Pastors and Church Staff Members Who Sponsor a CCN Team

1. They need a vision of the many ways that the CCN team expands ministry with other couples and families and a willingness to connect caring couples with others who need their friendship and support.
2. They must be willing to work with caring couples and consultants, and feel comfortable doing so.
3. They must be able to take the lead or join in the initiative to form and encourage a CCN team.
4. They should genuinely and comfortably support CCN's goals and models.
5. If married, they should embody the caring couple qualities in their own marriages. If not married, adapt the caring couple qualities to their single lifestyle.
6. If married, they should be clear about how their spouses will be involved in the CCN team.
7. They should be able to use existing discipleship and spiritual nurture programs and organizations in the training and support of caring couples.
8. They should know how to network with other professionals and agencies regarding the objectives of the CCN team.

Qualities of Professional Consultants to the CCN Team

1. Consultants provide professional competency in treatment and services to specific areas of marriage and family living that the CCN team may need.
2. Each consultant's vision, values, and standards for marriage and family need to be compatible with the CCN team's visions, values and standards.
3. Consultants need to be open and comfortable working with volunteer couples, pastors, and churches.

4. They need to be willing to volunteer consultation time with CCN team.
5. They should be sensitive to the spiritual and religious dimensions in marriage in relation to other dimensions, such as physical and mental health, finances, and emotional relationships.
6. They should know how to network and facilitate cooperation with other professionals and agencies regarding the objectives of the CCN team.
7. Consultants who provide therapy need to be well trained in marriage and family assessment, therapy, and enrichment methods and procedures.

☐ Application of the Preventive Model to a Couple at Risk

In the case of Ben and Alyssa there are at least five possible contact points for the CCN team to make contacts. The exact CCN intervention will vary according to which contact point is assumed. For the first contact opportunity, we will assume that Alyssa and Ben have taken the initiative to participate in a marriage enrichment retreat.

Contact Point 1: A CCN Celebrating Marriage Retreat

Ben and Alyssa have signed up for a 1-day version of the CCN Celebrating Marriage enrichment retreat. Alyssa found out about the program through publicity from her church, which is sponsoring the event, and Ben reluctantly agreed to attend with her. The sponsoring church has provided child care for children of couples participating in the retreat. Ben and Alyssa are the fourth of nine couples to arrive just before the 9:00 a.m. starting time. The retreat is being held in a separate retreat house on the church property.

The leader couple for the day has arranged for snacks, lunch, and a seated dinner, with the retreat to end around 7:00 p.m. The morning begins with fun music and a short worship. The program for the day has four major blocks of work time (about 90 minutes each), with brief presentations and demonstrations by the leader couple and time for the couples to meet in small support groups of three couples each.

The exact topics and procedures are designed by the leader couple, using suggestions from the Celebrating Marriage manual and the *CCN Handbook* (R. A. Hunt & J. A. Hunt, 1996), so the exact topics may vary for each retreat. For the retreat that Alyssa and Ben attend, the leader couple invites the couples to form three support groups of three couples each.

In the first time period, the leader couple uses a group exercise in which the men and women are in separate groups. Using newsprint, each group compiles two lists: "Ways my spouse shows love to me" and "Ways I show love to my spouse." After lists are compiled, the couples return to the large group and compare the lists.

In the second time period, with the entire group, the leader couple uses an imaging exercise to enable couples to remember some good times in their lives, and then the leader couple share their own appreciations to illustrate the next small group activity. In the support groups each couple in turn shares some appreciations, after which the other couples give feedback and share viewpoints.

In the third period, the leader couple describes how to use good communication skills to make a request for change in some area of the marriage and how to then plan to make the change. In smaller support groups, couples do this and receive feedback and support from the others present.

In the fourth period (before dinner), attention is given to ways to increase mutual affection and nurture through words, actions, sexuality, and other ways. After modeling by the leader couple, again in support groups, each couple practices giving and receiving expressions of affection with feedback from the other couples.

After the romantic seated dinner, the leader couple invites couples to describe gains they have made during the day and to make plans to continue their support groups in informal ways as nurture boosters for continuing the gains they have made in the retreat. The leader couple also describes how trained caring couples are available to any couple at points of need.

Ben and Alyssa participated well in these activities. Alyssa wanted to continue as one of the three couples in their support group, but Ben was not sure about it. In his friendly off-hand way, however, Ben commented that he would welcome someone to take care of little Benny "to give them time to get their own marriage back, especially now that we are expecting our second child."

The leader couple then suggested that there were some caring couples who had themselves experienced the premature delivery of a child and who had worked on career change issues much like Ben and Alyssa were working on, and who would be willing to provide child care once a month or so. Alyssa welcomed this possible supportive couple, and Ben agreed. After the retreat, the leader couple contacted two of the caring couples to ask them to contact Alyssa and Ben, who had agreed to the contact.

Over the following months, a caring couple, Bill and Sue, do provide some child care for little Benny so Ben and Alyssa can have some evenings out. In addition, the couples and their children have two family picnic times together. Bill also connects Ben to an attorney friend (another caring couple) who, 2 years earlier, had started his own specialty practice in family law. Sue, a nurse now working in an elementary school, helps Alyssa to get more information about her pregnancy concerns.

Some 6 months later, the leader couple invites Alyssa and Ben to an evening "booster session" follow-up for the couples who participated in the Celebrating Marriage retreat. In the evening booster session the couples share their progress, identify current needs, and make connections with other caring couples. In addition, one of the CCN team consultants has a seminar on family-of-origin issues, which many couples attend. After these meetings, Ben decides to join Alyssa in a couples class.

There are at least four other, earlier contact points that CCN might use to reach Ben and Alyssa. Each of these moves to a progressively earlier point of possible intervention. Although these opportunities are there primarily because of the church background of Alyssa, other opportunities might have become available through work or school contacts with Ben as well.

Contact Point 2: When Alyssa Began Attending Church

As part of participating in church activities, Alyssa most likely has met other women her age with similar time-pressured life experiences, both current and recent. As part of her introduction to the church, the pastor and/or other leaders would discover Alyssa's concern for her husband and child. During this orientation period these leaders would describe the CCN and ask her if she would like to be introduced to a caring couple who had resolved successfully some of the faith issues that Alyssa and Ben have, while dealing with getting started in a career, a difficult delivery, and the neonatal development of a child. Perhaps two or three caring couples would be available to represent these issues.

Assuming that Alyssa agrees to contacts with these caring couples, then they would plan ways to meet Ben, to have some joint friendship activities (including children), and, at times, to provide child care for Benny so that Ben and Alyssa can have some renewal time alone. Through these friendship contacts, Ben and Alyssa may also find names of others in the church and/or community who could help them with questions of child development, career changes, the second pregnancy, and other concerns.

Contact Point 3: At the Early Birth of Their Child

If some of the CCN team members at Alyssa's church had taken as their special ministry the contacting of mothers of new babies in the community, then a caring couple would have met Alyssa and Ben shortly after the emergency C-section and become acquainted with them and their needs. These friendships with Alyssa and Ben would open more opportunities for nurture.

Contact Point 4: Around the Wedding Time of Alyssa and Ben

One goal of the CCN team is to have a caring couple available to every couple from the time the couple contacts the pastor or church about their potential engagement and wedding through 2 years after the wedding. Assuming that Alyssa's church has a CCN team, this would have been a supportive, mentoring contact between Alyssa and Ben and their caring couple. Both couple-to-couple and group activities are part of this nurturing process. The caring couple would find ways to encourage Ben and Alyssa to address some of their issues, such as completing education, beginning their careers, and finding a common faith involvement in either a church or synagogue.

Since Ben and Alyssa either were away from home at college or moved from the community after their wedding, their caring couple would find ways to maintain contact with them by telephone, email, or other means, as well as try to find an equivalent caring couple to contact in their new community.

Contact Point 5: With Alyssa's Parents

Since it seems that Alyssa's parents, Jack and Caroline, are (and were) active in their church, the CCN team there would also have some type of outreach to midlife couples whose young adult children are leaving home for college, getting married, and having children. It is likely that Jack's views are somewhat more dominant and rigid than other midlife couples in the congregation. It is also likely that Jack and Caroline have other couple friends with whom they may mutually discuss how midlife couples feel about their children growing up and perhaps being less active in church, interfaith marriage, and other matters that affect Ben and Alyssa.

The caring couple focus may also involve ways to assist these midlife couples to balance their lingering control of their children at this launching stage of family life with the freedom of becoming more like equal adult friends rather than domineering parents. The CCN team may also sponsor marriage enrichment events for midlife couples as well as seminars and workshops on parenting and other midlife issues. The somewhat different dynamics of being "parents of the bride" vs. "parents of the groom" can also be identified.

At each of these five possible contact points, caring couples may suggest to Ben and Alyssa the value of some short-term marriage therapy as an additional way to address some of the deeper family-of-origin and faith issues that they have. It is clear that Ben and Alyssa have many strengths and have already made constructive changes in their marriage and parenting practices. The friendship and support of caring couples would certainly help Alyssa and Ben to know that the difficulties and reactions they have faced are typical of all couples.

Being part of an ongoing couples class or group in a church or synagogue gives each couple mutual friendship, information, and support. Although formal theological beliefs are important, the deeper vitality of faith emerges out of the human relationships individuals and couples have in families and among friends in church. Both Ben and Alyssa are blessed with strong, vigorous parental support. While the parents may differ on specific theological premises, it seems that they certainly agree on the importance of determination, commitment, mutual support, and clear positive values. One of the purposes of the CCN is to enable every couple to connect their resources to their visions and goals in order to increase their positives and decrease their negatives.

☐ Empirical Evaluation and Research

Informal, anecdotal reports of couples helping other couples are plentiful. The video, *The Caring Couple Network: A Team in Action* (R. A. Hunt et al., 1997), presents some examples of couples sharing their marriage experiences. *Couples Who Care* (Ives, 1997) provides more real-life reports from couples who have been helped by other couples. Most therapists and pastors can recall situations in which couples have reported how they were helped, or discouraged, by observing other couples and by comments that others have given them.

The importance of couples helping other couples has been clearly demonstrated in a wide variety of couple support and intervention models (McManus, 1995). The importance of couples modeling successful ways to express positives and cope with negatives is emphasized by many marriage enrichment programs (such as Association for Couples in Marriage Enrichment, 1992).

Research in the Planning or Implementation Stages

The CCN approach assumes that we know enough to take action now, and in doing what we do know, we can learn more about mentoring couples, networking, and creating a culture of healthy marriage and family relationships. Thus, ongoing empirical research on the many aspects of the CCN approach is needed and planned.

Many churches are starting CCN teams. Leaders in CCN will be in close contact with some of these churches to obtain feedback and to work together to improve resources and procedures. In addition, as finances and opportunities become available, empirical studies of specific components of CCN will be conducted. Persons in graduate programs are especially invited to consult with CCN about research projects.

☐ Summary

Both the major strength and the potential limitation of the CCN approach is the quality of the couples, pastors, and consultants on a given team. Caring couples must themselves have a satisfying marriage, high motivation, and good training for specific types of mentor and other nurturing relationships with other couples.

Among CCN's strengths are the availability of caring couples according to the needs of others couples for realistic friendships at no financial cost. The couple-to-couple approach, involving both men and women in all situations, both models good marriages and helps to prevent inappropriate sexual relationships. The ready availability of professional consultants enables caring couples to obtain consultation as needed, make referrals, and avoid situations that may be beyond their competence and resources.

Among CCN's limitations can be less-than-helpful matches between caring couples and those with whom they work. Inadequate or incompetent professional consultants and/or pastors and staff may place caring couples at greater risk than necessary, and caring couples may move too quickly with a partner couple or may not sufficiently heed consultation.

There are two primary requirements for using caring couples. First is that potential receiving couples must be open to being mentored, supported, or helped. Any lack of openness would be, of course, a pervasive problem for any intervention approach and would challenge the CCN teams to find innovative ways to reach couples in need.

The second requirement is to insure the safety of caring couples in their contacts with other couples. One purpose of the consultants is to assist the CCN team members to be aware of situations when a specific type of CCN approach is likely to be ineffective or harmful.

At a theoretical level, the CCN approach can be enhanced by relating theoretical work concerning sources of influence on marriage quality, such as family of origin, attachment, modeling, and family interaction theories, to a theoretical understanding of the social influence from other couples. Theoretical work on the biopsychosocial understanding of marriage (e.g., Gottman, 1994) usually focuses on individual couples—a "micro" approach to interaction between couples.

A theoretical understanding of the relationship between marriage and other areas of society is also important for building a theory of why couple-to-couple nurture works. The crucial importance of society in creating support for marriage and parenting represents a "macro" approach to interaction between couples (e.g., Glendon & Blankenhorn, 1995).

Biopsychosocial theory and theological understandings of marriage (e.g., Everett, 1990) need to be related. Recent work on the role of promises (Popenoe et al., 1996) and on commitment and core belief systems (Markman et al., 1994) point in this direction. Several approaches to marriage integrate theological and psychosocial perspectives (e.g., Hendrix, 1988; Balswick & Balswick, 1991).

Clinically, the CCN approach can be enhanced as CCN teams receive feedback on their work from consultants and pastors. As more CCN teams are established, they will help to test training procedures, brief assessment methods, guidelines for friendship contacts, ways to use marriage enrichment resources, and the effectiveness of various couple, group, and institutional programs. As funding becomes available, CCN teams are ready to participate in research programs to strengthen the CCN approach in every way possible.

The major purpose of CCN is to connect couples to existing resources at the points of the couples' need and openness to help. One assumption is that couples use other couples as models (both good and bad) of marriage. This modeling process is intrinsic to family life, primarily through children observing how their parents treat each other as husband and wife. The range of models expands as persons, from childhood through adulthood, observe man–woman couple interactions and hear family stories among their relatives, neighbors, friends, and the mass media.

CCN seeks to increase the number of positive models of marriage and make them realistically available to other couples at their points of need. Thus CCN is open to using all avenues, including books, video, marriage enrichment, therapy, and other resources, to reach couples everywhere. This provides mobile, readily available relationships among couples for support, mentoring, nurture, and action. As part of the CCN team, pastors and professional consultants train caring couples, give information and perspectives on marriage and family issues, and are available for referral when couples need professional help.

CCN involves volunteer healthy couples in helping to deliver a wide variety of approaches and ministries for many types of couple and family situations. Couples and families need so much nurture and support that no concerned group can afford to waste time fighting other groups that also have positive concerns for marriage and families. Rather than fight each other, CCN wants to make the circle larger by finding cooperative ways to bring marriage and family ministries to all.

☐ Contact References

The authors may be contacted at Fuller Seminary: 818-584-5553. Information about CCN may be obtained from the Family Ministries Unit of the United Methodist General Board of Discipleship, Nashville, TN, 615-340-7074. CCN materials may be purchased through Cokesbury Book Stores. For more information on adapting and using CCN in non-Methodist and ecumenical settings, contact the authors or the United Methodist General Board of Discipleship.

☐ References

Association for Couples in Marriage Enrichment. (1992). *Basic training workshop: Participants guide and resource manual.* Winston-Salem, NC: Author.

Balswick, J. O., & Balswick, J. K. (1991). *The family: A Christian perspective on the contemporary home.* Grand Rapids, MI: Baker Book House.

Breunlin, D. C., Schwartz, R. C., & Kune-Karrer, B. M. (1992). *Metaframeworks: Transcending the models of family therapy.* San Francisco: Jossey-Bass.

Council on Families in America. (1995). *Marriage in America: A report to the nation.* Summary available from Institute for American Values, 212-246-3942. (Also published as chapter 13 in Popenoe et. al., 1996.)

Everett, W. J. (1990). *Blessed be the bond: Christian perspectives on marriage and family.* Lanham, MD: University Press of America.

Fincham, D., & Bradbury, T. N. (Eds.). (1990). *The psychology of marriage.* New York: Guilford.

Glendon, M. A., & Blankenhorn, D. (Eds.). (1995). *Seedbeds of virtue.* Lanham, MD: Madison.

Gottman, J. M. (1994). *What predicts divorce?* Hillsdale, NJ: Lawrence Erlbaum Associates.

Hendrix, H. (1988). *Getting the love you want.* New York: Harper & Row.

Hunt, J. A., & Hunt, R. A. (1994). *Awaken your power to love.* Nashville, TN: Nelson Press.

Hunt, R. A. (1987). Marriage as dramatizing theology. *Journal of Pastoral Care, 41*(2), 119–131.

Hunt, R. A., Hof, L., & DeMaria, R. (1998). *Marriage Enrichment: Preparation, mentoring, and outreach.* Philadelphia: Brunner/Mazel.

Hunt, R. A., & Hunt, J. A. (1981). *Growing love in Christian marriage* (Couples book). Nashville, TN: Abingdon.

Hunt, R. A., & Hunt, J. A. (1996). *Caring couples network handbook.* Nashville, TN: Discipleship Resources.

Hunt, R. A., Hunt, J. A., Gentzler, R., & Hughes, D. (1997). *The Caring Couple Network: A team in action* [Video]. Nashville, TN: Discipleship Resources.

Hunt, R. A., & Rydman, E. J. (1979). *Creative marriage* (2nd ed.). Boston: Allyn & Bacon.

Ives, J. (1997). *Couples who care* [Video]. Nashville, TN: Discipleship Resources.

Jacobson, N. S., & Gurman, A. S. (Eds.). (1986). *Clinical handbook of marital therapy.* New York: Guilford.

Markman, H., Stanley, S., & Blumberg, S. L. (1994). *Fighting for your marriage.* San Francisco: Jossey-Bass.

McManus, M. J. (1995). *Marriage savers* (Rev. ed.). Grand Rapids, MI: Zondervan.

Miller, S., Wackman, D., Nunnally, E., & Miller, P. (1988). *Connecting with self and others.* Littleton, CO: Interpersonal Communication Programs.

Olson, D. H. (1996). *PREPARE/ENRICH Counselors Manual: Version 2000.* Minneapolis, MN: Life Innovations.

Paolino, T. J., & McCrady, B. S. (1978). *Marriage and marital therapy.* New York: Brunner/Mazel.

Popenoe, D., Elshtain, J. B., & Blankenhorn, D. (1996). *Promises to keep: Decline and renewal of marriage in America.* Lanham, MD: Rowman & Littlefield.

Smith, A., & Smith, L. (1981). *Growing love in Christian marriage* (Pastors book). Nashville, TN: Abingdon.

Stuart, R. B. (1980). *Helping couples change: A Social Learning approach to marital therapy.* New York: Guilford.

Wimberly, E. P. (1997). *Recalling our own stories: Spiritual renewal for religious caregivers.* San Francisco: Jossey-Bass.

Scott M. Stanley, Ph.D.
Susan L. Blumberg, Ph.D.
Howard J. Markman, Ph.D.

Helping Couples Fight for Their Marriages: The PREP Approach

☐ Introduction

Helping couples fight for their marriages is more important than ever before. Professionals from many fields, including psychology, religion, education, law, and social work have turned increasing attention to programs designed to reduce marital distress and divorce. In the past few decades, much research has been devoted to better understanding both the development and prevention of marital distress. The Prevention and Relationship Enhancement Program (PREP) has its foundation in this research.

The specific roots of this work go back to the mid 1970s, when many researchers were studying marital distress. At Indiana University, Howard Markman and Clifford Notarius teamed up with John Gottman to investigate the specific causes of marital distress. Along with other researchers around the United States (e.g., Birchler, Weiss, & Vincent, 1975), the group at Indiana was particularly interested in how distressed couples communicated, compared to better functioning, happier couples. This team stud-

Preparation of this chapter was supported in part by National Institute of Mental Health, Prevention Research Grant 5-RO1-MH35525-12, Long Term Effects of Premarital Intervention.

ied actual couple interaction through the use of trained observers. In brief, such research highlighted the fact that distressed couples were particularly deficient in their ability to communicate well.

While at Indiana University, Markman began a key longitudinal study to test the hypothesis that the communication variables that had discriminated between distressed and nondistressed couples in earlier research would predict the development of marital distress and divorce (Markman, 1981). Markman found that the quality of communication before marriage, and before distress had developed, was one of the best predictors of future marital distress. It was from this beginning that Markman founded a preventive program for couples based on empirical research. Over the years, Markman has been joined in the research, development, and refinement of this work by others, notably Frank Floyd, Scott Stanley, and Susan Blumberg (e.g., Markman, Floyd, Stanley, & Jamison, 1984). Studies have continued on the effectiveness of PREP over the past 20 years (Stanley, Markman, St. Peters, & Leber, 1995). The most up-to-date version of the program is embodied in a variety of materials for couples (e.g., Markman, Stanley, & Blumberg, 1994; Stanley, Markman, & Blumberg, 1994).

From its inception, PREP has been based, where possible, on empirical research. In particular, PREP emphasizes a skills-oriented approach based on etiological factors underlying marital failure. Studies to assess the short- and long-term effectiveness of the intervention strategies have also been employed. In the past decade, work on PREP has expanded in concept, techniques, the kinds of couples targeted (married as well as engaged couples), content (e.g., Christian PREP; Stanley & Trathen, 1994; Stanley, Trathen, & McCain, 1996), and format. A business was begun for the purpose of facilitating the dissemination of training and materials for those wanting to help couples in this approach. The program and materials are regularly updated to reflect new research findings and new opportunities for helping couples build strong and happy relationships.

☐ Theoretical Underpinnings

PREP is based on the cognitive-behavioral tradition of change, with significant influence coming from the field of behavioral marital therapy. Therefore, the focus is on ways of thinking (attitudes and expectations) and behaving (communication and conflict management) that are associated with marital success and failure. The skills-oriented approach rests on the assumption that couples can learn new behaviors that can help them prevent the deterioration in relationship quality commonly seen in marriage. In addition to the cognitive-behavioral roots, PREP is largely based on a broad range of marital research.

By taking into account a broad range of empirical findings on marriage, one can develop a rich model of marital success and failure. The current version of PREP is based on the seminal research on communication begun in the 1970s (e.g., Gottman, Notarius, Gonso, & Markman, 1976; Guerney, 1977; Markman, 1981; Miller, 1971; Wampler & Sprenkle, 1980), with the addition of concepts and techniques from more recent research bearing on such dimensions as conflict management, gender differences, commitment, religion, cognitions, fun, and friendship (Stanley et al., 1995).

While there is not a singular pathway to marital distress or divorce, Figure 13.1 portrays a comprehensive model that reflects a common path to marital failure based on findings from many different studies on marriage and relationships (Stanley, 1995).

In this model, two people initially become attracted to one another out

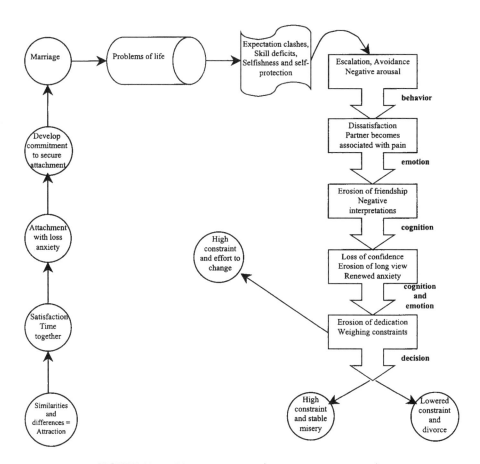

FIGURE 13.1.   How a marriage dies: One common path.

of the mix of similarities and differences (and proximity). As they spend time together that is satisfying, the two partners feel a growing sense of attachment. Along with this bond comes a sense of anxiety over the potential loss of the loved one. In this context, commitment develops, in large measure to remove this anxiety by the promise of a future together (Stanley, Lobitz, & Dickson, in press). For many couples, this commitment culminates in marriage.

Prior to the wedding day, most first-time married couples have had few tests of their ability to handle conflict. They simply have not encountered many significant issues or disagreements during courtship. That is partly why satisfaction tends to be very high at this stage (Stanley & Markman, 1992). Yet, there is clear evidence that how couples communicate and handle conflict foretells an important story about their future—more important than their premarital level of satisfaction (Markman, 1981; Markman & Hahlweg, 1993). Over time, this committed couple must increasingly deal with the problems of life *together*. This explains why many couples can start out so committed and so happy only to find their attachment being eroded by the constant irritation of upsetting and unresolved conflicts.

What they argue about and how they argue is a function of both their expectations and their abilities to communicate and negotiate effectively, most of which is based on previous experiences in life with their families of origin, past relationships, and the cultural context. Certain patterns of mismanaged conflict that are destructive for relationships will be repeatedly expressed in many couples (Gottman, 1993; Gottman & Krokoff, 1989; Markman et al., 1994; Notarius & Markman, 1993). Out of this mix, a very important change occurs over time in the relationship: *the presence of the partner becomes increasingly associated with pain and frustration, not pleasure or support.* For most couples, this violates a basic assumption about what being together is all about: having a most intimate and supportive friend for life.

Negative interpretations about the partner may become commonplace as a "me versus you" environment takes hold. These negative interpretations lead each to consistently interpret the actions of the other as more negative than is warranted (Baucom & Epstein, 1990). Confidence erodes and the sense of attachment that led to commitment in the first place becomes more fragile. In fact, we have observed that many couples will begin regularly threatening the future of the relationship as commitment becomes a pawn to be sacrificed in the heat of tormenting conflicts (Stanley et al., in press).

Ultimately, the marriage becomes a shell of its former state, with the view that each partner holds of the other radically changing, as in the classic reversal of figure and ground (Gottman, 1993). In this case, the initial view becomes harder and harder to reinstate. At this point, the keys to the stability of the marriage lie less in commitment as *dedication* and more in commitment as *constraint* (Stanley & Markman, 1992). In other words, decisions to stay or leave now have more to do with the costs of leaving than the desire to stay. As constraints keeping marriages together weaken in our society, couples who get to this point are increasingly likely to divorce, whereas in the past many stayed together in stable, miserable marriages. Of course, some couples rebound from this place of high constraint and low dedication to redevelop dedication, love, and positivity in their marriages (the third circle in Figure 13.1).

This model of marital failure suggests a number of targets for intervention. These include certain patterns of communication, conflict management, dysfunctional beliefs, and understandings and motivations regarding commitment. The good news is that couples are not predestined to this path of destruction. There are things they can learn and act on to stay off the path of failure and on the path of friendship, support, and intimacy. But many of these skills and attitudes are anything but natural for most couples.

☐ Intervention Model

While it is not always possible to help couples before distress develops, prevention is strongly preferred to interventions that come after much damage has already occurred. A framework now gaining popularity in prevention efforts draws attention to the key goals of reducing *risk factors* and raising *protective factors* (e.g., Coie et al., 1993).

Consistent with the theoretical model of marital distress just covered and this framework for prevention, PREP has four major goals. The two key goals under the rubric of reducing risk factors are to teach couples better communication and conflict management strategies and to aid couples in clarifying and evaluating expectations. The two key goals under the rubric of raising protective factors are to boost understanding of and choices reflecting commitment and to enhance the positive bonding that comes from fun, friendship, and sensuality. These aims (described in more detail below) are accomplished through cognitive-behavioral strategies, which seek to directly modify cognitions and behaviors associated with marital success and failure.

As discussed earlier, many couples experience the erosion of their relationship as they encounter the problems of life together, and they do not have the skills for coping with those problems. But even without encountering problems per se, many couples have styles of interaction that are inherently irritating to the partners. That is why PREP focuses so much on communication, conflict management, expectations, and commitment. Whatever the background, problems, and differences two people face, it is how they handle these issues that will be the key in determining whether they grow more deeply together or further apart as they go through life. PREP focuses on key factors that are both strongly related to the ongoing health of relationships and also changeable through education and skills training.

Communication and Conflict Management

There is an intense focus in PREP on helping couples to identify and re-duce specific patterns of negative interaction that are believed to be par-ticularly corrosive to the marital bond over time (for further review of such negative patterns, see Gottman, 1994; Levenson & Gottman, 1985; Markman & Hahlweg, 1993; Markman et al., 1994; Matthews, Wickrama, & Conger, 1996). At the heart of it, PREP focuses on helping couples learn how to control their conflicts rather than having their conflicts con-trol them. This focus is preeminent because of our belief in the salience of poorly handled conflict in the erosion of the marital bond (see Notarius & Markman, 1993; Gottman, 1994). Hence, many strategies of PREP are aimed at teaching couples *positive* strategies for effectively handling the more *negative* side of the relationship. When partners are capable of this in the context of a secure commitment, they are able not only to handle conflict well, but to thrive in the development of a deeper intimacy forged from mutual respect.

In PREP, structure is emphasized for helping couples manage the more difficult, volatile, and negative emotions that intimacy and conflict can generate. Structure is defined as agreed-upon ground rules for handling differences and conflict. Since few people have learned how to handle such matters well, very clear rules give couples a road map for getting through discussions that they are otherwise not likely to handle well. For example, couples are taught the speaker–listener technique, which is a very simple, structured method for good communication that couples can engage in when needed (see details later in this chapter). The structure of simple rules brings a degree of safety to a conversation that allows for greater openness and less negative affect.

This leads to a crucial theoretical point. We do not teach the speaker–listener technique (and other structured techniques) because we think such skills are necessarily required for a great relationship. In fact, the speaker–listener technique employs active listening skills such as para-phrasing that are clearly not normative for couples. Rather, practicing the skills embodied in the technique helps couples to learn how to counter-act the negative patterns of interaction that can bring a marriage to its knees. Further, when stressed by conflict, couples can employ the artificial structure to help them communicate more effectively and reduce the tendency toward "danger signs," such as escalation, invalidation, negative interpretations, and withdrawal (Markman et al., 1994). In fact, following the rules of the technique virtually guarantees that certain negative patterns will not be expressed, but it does not necessarily bring more joy and closeness. Those outcomes are linked more to increasing protective activities such as fun and friendship—experiences that are very vulnerable to the negative patterns. In summary on this point, we are much more interested in reducing the negative patterns of interaction than in the speaker–listener technique per se. The technique is employed as one means of helping couples achieve this crucial end.

The intervention model also is directed at specific cognitive patterns that intensify resentment and conflict. When partners hold negative presuppositions about one another, they misinterpret events, communication, and motives, generating more intense negative affect and defensiveness. In several different places, the material cautions partners about the destructive impact that negative interpretations, mind-reading, and score-keeping can have on perceptions of the other. Partners are specifically advised of the importance of recognizing cognitive biases and distortions that, ultimately, only the individual holding them can change. Partners are encouraged to actively look for evidence that is contrary to the often unfair, negative views one adopts of the other.

Expectations

Couples are at increased risk when either or both partners hold expectations that are either unreasonable or unexpressed (Eidelson & Epstein, 1981). Unmet expectations lead to disappointment and frustration, increasing the likelihood of negative interchanges that can erode and damage the relationship per the mechanisms outlined above.

In PREP, couples are encouraged to work through their expectations through a combination of self-exploration and communication exercises. This part of the intervention model is the most insight-oriented module of the entire PREP program. Partners are encouraged to uncover expectations (good or bad) that have developed from their past experiences in families of origin, previous relationships, the media, religious beliefs and institutions, etc. Thus, key cognitive changes targeted in PREP involve bringing expectations to light and negotiating a mutual vision. By doing so, partners not only are drawn together now, but can also reduce future conflicts fueled by erroneous expectations.

As a special example of the importance of expectations, PREP encourages partners to explore their *core belief systems,* which for most people would preeminently comprise religious and spiritual beliefs (Markman et al., 1994). This domain can be either an area of risk for couples (such as when two people from differing religious backgrounds marry and attempt to ignore the implications) or a source of increased protection for the relationship. Couples are encouraged to openly explore not only what they believe, but how they express those beliefs in their life together, today and in the future.

Dealing With Commitment

Attitudes and choices associated with commitment are emphasized in the PREP intervention model. Whereas using greater structure when discussing difficult issues fosters safety in interaction, enhanced and clear commitment fosters safety in terms of trust and a secure future. This part of the intervention strategy of PREP is geared toward motivational change, encouraging partners to make the kinds of choices that foster a relationship of mutual dedication and teamwork. As with the work on expectations, the changes aimed for here are primarily cognitive (e.g., Stanley et al., in press). Developing strategies for fostering the long-term view, clarifying priorities, and protecting the relationship from alternatives are emphasized.

Fun, Friendship, and Sensuality

The bond between two people in marriage thrives when there is a consistent, shared base of fun, friendship, and sensuality. The experiences of talking together as friends, having fun together, and feeling sensual attraction are a large part of how couples develop an attachment in the first place. Unfortunately, many couples do not preserve these positive experiences over time. Key interventions in PREP are geared toward helping couples recognize the importance of preserving time for these experiences and the need to protect such time from the ravages of poorly handled conflict. For most couples, such positive bonding experiences do not simply fade away over time. They are either (a) actively eroded by the intrusion of issues and disagreements into time for positive connection, or (b) not made a priority over other demands of life that consume time and energy. For many couples, time for relaxation becomes increasingly invested in passive, relationship de-enhancing activities like watching television. In PREP, couples are taught simple behavioral strategies for preserving and enhancing the experiences that can fuel the continued growth and bond in the marriage.

☐ Specific Methods and Strategies for Intervention

PREP embodies many cognitive-behavioral strategies (see Markman et al., 1994, for details). Five are described here.

Highlighting Danger Signs

While many patterns of interaction damage a relationship over time, PREP highlights four patterns to make couples aware of the kinds of behaviors that are likely to be corrosive to their relationship over time. These are escalation, invalidation, negative interpretations, and withdrawal. Certainly, others could be discussed (or these four could be labeled differently), but the important point for couples to grasp early on in PREP is that they need to have ways to prevent or reduce such patterns if they are going to keep their relationship on the best path.

The Speaker–Listener Technique. The speaker–listener technique is a structured approach to good communication and conflict management. In this technique, the couple uses an object to designate who has the "floor," thus clearly marking who is the "speaker" and who is the "listener," a distinction most couples find hard to make in their normal conversation. Simple, clear rules are associated with each role (see Figure 13.2). For example, the speaker is to speak only about his or her own thoughts,

THE FLOOR

Speaker-Listener Technique

Rules for the Speaker:
1. Speak for yourself. Don't mind read!
2. Keep statements brief. Don't go on and on.
3. Stop to let the Listener paraphrase.

Rules for the Listener:
1. Paraphrase what you hear.
2. Focus on the Speaker's message. Don't rebut.

Rules for Both:
1. The Speaker has the floor.
2. Speaker keeps the floor while Listener paraphrases.
3. Share the floor.

To Order Fighting *for* Your Marriage books, audio, or video tapes:
Call 1-303-759-9931   © PREP Educational Products, Inc. 1991

FIGURE 13.2.

feelings, and needs. The listener is to paraphrase what he or she heard, in order to provide feedback to the speaker and focus attention. In addition, the listener must edit out his or her own thoughts and feelings during the paraphrase, reducing the tendency to form or express rebuttals while listening. Speakers must focus on expressing their thoughts or emotions about a given situation, resisting mind-reading, blaming, or unproductive venting of anger.

These rules have been taught in many communication models, but here they are directly connected to the danger signs that they counteract. For example, by having one person speak at a time and keeping the amount of content small, the tendency to escalate, or to build up negative emotion, is lessened. As the listener paraphrases, the speaker knows whether he or she was heard correctly, providing an automatic check on the clarity of the communication. What is different here from many other approaches to communication is that this technique is taught as a structure to use when needed, with clear acknowledgment of its artificiality. Indeed, couples are told that the artificial rules are the very reason the technique works—because the more natural responses of many couples at times of frustration or vulnerability are often counterproductive.

Couples describe feeling able to tolerate negative emotion more effectively within the speaker–listener format. It is not expected or recommended that couples would use this much structure for most conversations in life. The key is for couples to learn to adopt the structure when necessary. Couples who practice the technique also appear to benefit from longer term changes in communication quality, whether or not they regularly find the actual structure of the technique useful. That is because spending time engaging these rules builds better communication skills that can generalize beyond the use of the structure.

Time Out. This technique is likely to be familiar to many readers and can be very powerful when used correctly. The key as presented in PREP is for couples to have an agreed-upon way to stop escalation or other kinds of communication sequences that are damaging or unproductive. Time out is emphasized as a way not only to stop a negative process, but also to shift into either a better communication mode at that time (e.g., using the speaker–listener technique) or to come back to the issue later, at an agreed-upon time. This technique is particularly helpful for getting couples out of pursuer/withdrawer interchanges, in which one partner retreats from the other who is pursuing. Time out allows for a mutually agreed upon way to stop a frustrating interchange, a way that includes accountability for follow-up on the matter of concern.

Ground Rules. Strategies such as the speaker–listener technique and time out are combined with numerous others in a presentation of ground rules for protecting a relationship from poorly handled conflict. The heart of this strategy is helping partners develop agreed-upon ways of handling issues that will protect their relationship. The paramount goal is for the couple to protect their relationship from the danger signs that are identified in PREP—danger signs that are based on empirical research of marital success and failure. Among other things, couples will leave PREP having worked openly on the suggested ground rules and equipped with a plan to use the principles in their relationship.

Commitment. Based on the latest findings in commitment research, a number of specific strategies are suggested in PREP. For example, research shows that people who are more committed to their partners think less often and less seriously about what it would be like to be with another person (Stanley & Markman, 1992). Furthermore, when committed, people are more likely to actively devalue attractive alternatives in order to protect commitment to the partner (Johnson & Rusbult, 1989). Such research results are directly translated into simple cognitive and educational strategies for people to use in committed relationships. Lecture and reading materials stress that people have choices about what they think about, and that there are predictable consequences to thinking a lot about real, available, attractive alternatives. Instead, people are encouraged to put that energy into making their own relationship better rather than engaging in a cognitive process (alternative monitoring) that is guaranteed to breed deeper resentment and, ultimately, dissolution of the relationship. As such, the strategy employed here is purely cognitive and motivational, with exercises designed to help the participants think through their own levels of dedication to one another.

Another commitment-related intervention stresses the value of a long-term view of marriage (e.g., perseverance and continued investment even when discouraged). This is contrasted with the destructive effects of holding a short-term view (i.e., being more reactive to current events, being oriented to taking rather than giving) that fosters score-keeping and resentment. Regular talks about the future (e.g., goals, dreams, vision) are promoted as one way to foster this long-term view, since research shows that committed, happy couples tend to do just this.

A third intervention regarding commitment helps couples focus on how the choices they make in life reflect priorities, with the relationship often taking a back seat to the frenzy and noise of life. Essentially, PREP emphasizes that commitment to the relationship involves active choices for partners—choices that will greatly affect their chances of having a satisfying, secure relationship over time. An optional written exercise encourages each participant to identify his or her own priorities, the perception of his or her partner's priorities, and guesses of the partner's perception of his or her own priorities. Then, in sharing together the results of these personal reflections, partners confront whether or not they are each living in ways that reflect their priorities.

Resources for PREP. When presenting PREP workshops, leaders have a variety of materials available for getting the points across to couples. The key resource for couples (and leaders) would be the book *Fighting for Your Marriage* (Markman et al., 1994). The lecture materials closely parallel the book chapters, and all the workshop exercises are explained in detail. Trained leaders also have other materials to choose from that can be used in teaching the concepts to couples, such as manuals, notes for helping couples follow along with the lectures, videotapes, and audiotapes. The book chapters are often assigned as homework in longer versions of the program, so that couples can reinforce their learning at home and have guidance as they do their practice sessions.

☐ Format of Application

Applicable Couples and Settings

The PREP approach is applicable to couples at widely different stages in life, such as engagement, early marriage, and long-term, mature marriages. In fact, much of the theoretical and skill content could be applied to almost any significant relationship in a person's life. The material is directly applicable to happy couples, where prevention is the key, as well as to distressed couples who need to make specific changes to begin to turn their marriages around. PREP is also flexible in that its strategies can be employed in counseling, programmatic group settings, or in self-study by couples. The most common group settings are those with an educational, service orientation. These have included churches, synagogues, mental health centers, HMOs, work settings, health care settings, and chaplaincy or family support centers in the armed forces.

Screening and Assessment

Since the approach is readily used and adapted to couples in various developmental stages and degrees of happiness and distress, screening of couples is not usually needed or desirable. The primary screening issue might be to select out couples who are coming to an educational, skills-oriented program in place of therapy. Beyond this, attendance at the program can facilitate therapy that a couple is already participating in with a trained therapist. Further, a couple who needs more help may be encouraged by the approach of the workshop to seek further help in therapy. Even partners with personality or character disorders can benefit greatly from the structured techniques of this approach, although any kind of intervention with such populations is hard work.

Perhaps the most controversial screening dilemma for those doing PREP involves the issue of domestic violence. Clearly, PREP is not a domestic violence treatment program. However, many of its strategies are quite appropriate for some couples with low levels of physical aggression that emanate from a dynamic involving mutual difficulty in managing conflict well. The issues concerning domestic violence and couples interventions are generally too complex for this discussion. What is clear to us is that some leaders prefer to attempt to screen out couples who may be engaged in physical aggression and some prefer not to do so. The issue boils down to complex concerns about settings, confidentiality, population served, etc. Those who choose not to screen for such couples often adopt this view out of a belief that this could be a step toward such couples getting more help.

Program Details

For the rest of this discussion, the focus will be on PREP as a program that can be delivered to couples in a group format. The full version of PREP takes 12 hours to present to a group of couples. This can be formatted into a six-session, 2-hour-per-session version, a weekend version, a full day with two follow-up weeknight evenings, or other formats as needed. Data from the PREP research in Germany suggests that couples can benefit as much from weekend formats as from sessions spaced out over a number of weeks.

In all of the formats, couples attend a series of lectures and are given small segments of material along with clear explanations and demonstrations. Following most lectures, couples are immediately given an opportunity to practice and apply the skill or exercise covered in the lecture. Each new segment of material builds on previously taught skills, so that couples can experience early success and apply it to the next step.

☐ Qualities and Role of the Leader or Facilitator

Ideally, the PREP leader should have training and knowledge in a field that emphasizes understanding and helping couples. This includes psychology, clergy, social work, or education. Many lay leaders in religious settings also make excellent presenters of PREP, even though they may have less of a specialized background in marital issues.

The leader has dual responsibilities: (a) to present the lecture material to the couple, facilitating discussion and answering questions; and (b) to supervise and support the coaching staff who work directly with the couples. If coaching by paraprofessionals is not used, the leaders would also try to be available to answer questions and coach couples having trouble with the exercises.

Delivering the lectures is the central role of the PREP leader. Potential leaders attend an intensive training seminar which reviews not only the material to be presented but also the theoretical concepts and research basis underlying the development of the techniques. Leaders receive a detailed manual with outlines of all lecture material, and they have the option of using prepared videotaped presentations to supplement their oral presentations.

The educational nature of the program emphasizes presentations by the leader, with couples deciding how much to participate. The leader must be flexible in regards to responding to questions versus directing couples to deal with private issues on their own, with their coach, or with the leader. As couples have indicated in their evaluations over the years, comfort with public speaking is a must. Personal examples, whether taken from the lecture material or from the leader's own experience, are another powerful tool that couples respond to strongly.

Paraprofessional Coaching

Presenters have the choice of training coaches to work along with them in teaching couples the skills, or they may choose to present the material without such aid. The program probably is most effective when paraprofessional coaches are used. However, this is not possible in many settings, and when coaches are not used, leaders can be quite effective in moving the couples along in their practice (often spending a bit more time with couples who are having more difficulty). When coaches are used, the leader is responsible for their training and supervision. This might not include "supervision" in the formal sense of complete oversight of the interaction, but instead may involve an informal discussion of the direction and progress the couple is making and guidance in dealing with problems.

We highly recommend that coaches be nonprofessionals, for several reasons. First, it is less intimidating to the couples, and it emphasizes the educational versus therapeutic nature of the program. Second, in our experience, therapists who act as coaches are more likely to blur the lines and engage in more interpretation and other therapeutic techniques than is appropriate in an educational program. Third, paraprofessional staff are often easy to find and train. We have used undergraduate and graduate students, homemakers, business persons, nurses, and many others interested in working with couples.

☐ Application of the Preventive Model to a Couple at Risk

Ben and Alyssa chose to attend a "Fighting *for* Your Marriage" weekend for couples, the most commonly offered format. Like many couples, they thought awhile before signing up. Ben was the one who took the initiative: A colleague at work had taken the seminar and brought some brochures to the office. This colleague spoke positively about having experienced an unpressured approach while getting away for a weekend without the kids. Ben read the brochure and felt it offered an opportunity for him and Alyssa to talk about some things before the new baby arrived. He especially liked the fact that the program was not counseling, therapy, or an encounter group. Alyssa, feeling more and more like her mother as she tried to avoid conflict, read the brochure and agreed, feeling surprised that Ben would go to a workshop to help their marriage. An educational program that taught communication and conflict management skills didn't sound too threatening, and now that Benny was sleeping through the night, an older friend from her church might be willing to watch him overnight. Besides, there would be even less time for the two of them to go away once the new baby arrived. At the same time, Alyssa was a little upset that Ben hadn't even thought about how hard it might be to leave Benny for the night. For his part, Ben was surprised and relieved that Alyssa agreed without much argument.

They arrived at the hotel meeting room along with about 20 other couples. They looked with interest at the materials: a copy of the book *Fighting for Your Marriage* (Markman et al., 1994), a notebook with copies of handouts and worksheets, and a magnet that looked like a piece of linoleum, labeled "The Floor." The room was set up in rows, with a television and a VCR in the front.

The introductory lecture gave the background and research about this approach. The leader discussed the difficulty many couples have in negotiating conflict and summarized the research showing that this problem predicted marital distress and divorce. More importantly, the leader discussed the danger signs (escalation, invalidation, negative interpretations, and pursuer–withdrawer patterns) that mark many relationships headed for trouble. Ben recognized that he had been feeling invalidated by Alyssa when he'd tried to talk to her about the pressure he felt over being the sole provider. Recently, she had said, "I know it's hard right now, but this is what we *both* wanted." Well, it wasn't what he had wanted, and it became clearer to him that the two of them had some really different expectations. He was also thinking about his growing resentment over the new baby—something they might have discussed if they had not been so busy and so much in the habit of avoiding discussions about key things happening in their lives.

Alyssa, too, was thinking about the message of the morning. She was becoming more aware of how afraid she was to talk freely with Ben about their marriage, plans, and life together. "How did we get so distant from one another?" she thought.

Ben also wondered if he was making negative interpretations by assuming that some of Alyssa's recent behaviors indicated a disregard of him and his needs. "Maybe she's just as tired and worn out as I am," he thought now. Alyssa thought about feeling invalidated by Ben's lack of understanding about her feelings, particularly about the new baby. He seemed to dismiss her fears instead of listening to them. Maybe she was interpreting his reactions incorrectly, though she was very hurt whenever he told her not to worry. They never argued much, but that last argument had been a bit louder than usual. Both were strongly responding to the core message of the morning: that it was not emotionally safe for them to talk together about their needs, fears, and desires. Alyssa wondered if her mother had felt unsafe around her father; maybe that was why her mother always gave in to whatever her father wanted.

The presentation of the speaker–listener technique interested both Ben and Alyssa, especially the live role-play and the videotaped examples of real couples. They went back to their room for their first practice session. Ben discovered that he was pretty good at giving feedback as the listener. Alyssa had a harder time putting aside her own thoughts to listen to Ben, and it became apparent to both how little direct communication they'd had in their relationship for some time. They talked about the danger signs and were surprised to discover that they both felt invalidated. Both partners thought they were the only one feeling that way.

The end of the first day brought a discussion of how to preserve and deepen fun and friendship in their marriage. They thought that this material explained precisely why they had been losing their sense of connection. They had been doing exactly what the lecturer said most couples do over time: They did not make time for the positive side of their relationship, and all they ever really talked about anymore was problems. Ben thought to himself, "It's really true that we don't talk the way friends talk anymore." Alyssa whispered to Ben, "No wonder we don't feel very close. We never do anything that we used to do that helped us *be* close."

This was a turning point in the workshop for them. This simple lecture had awakened in Ben and Alyssa the realization that, although they really did like each other, simple neglect and the pressures of life had caused them to drift apart. Both were recognizing the central message of this workshop: Most couples need to do a better job of handling their problematic issues, but also need to do a better job of making room in their lives for the really great things about being a couple.

Ben and Alyssa dug right into that evening's assignment. They were to first practice the speaker–listener technique, then take a night off from issues, pressures, and conflicts. The lecturer had pushed hard on the point that, after the brief practice, the couples were to put the work of their marriages away for the evening and have fun. Alyssa commented, "What a great idea. We can just agree to be together for an evening and make our issues and conflicts *off limits*." Their practice of the communication technique was not perfect, but they made a genuine effort to use it to talk about their feelings of disappointment in their marriage.

After calling home to check on the baby, they took seriously the admonition to go have fun and not deal with the cares of life for an evening. They did just that. They had dinner, talked like friends (about things like wanting to go to Europe for a vacation), and played. They even went dancing in the lounge of the hotel. "I think it's been years since we did anything like that," Alyssa noted. "Too long," Ben agreed. Afterward, they retreated to their room for some relaxing massage. It seemed like ages since they spent that kind of time together.

The next morning, Ben and Alyssa were both struck by the lecture on expectations. Ben initially thought, "Big deal. Of course expectations are important." But as the information unfolded, Ben realized how often he assumed that he and Alyssa had the same goals and desires, even though he rarely talked to Alyssa about what he expected. In truth, he was feeling a great deal of disappointment about the way some things in their life together had turned out.

Meanwhile, Alyssa was reflecting on growing up her family. "Can it really be that we are acting out my parents' patterns?" At the same time, she felt Ben had unrealistic expectations about the way life with children should be, especially after the problems they had faced with Benny. Alyssa realized that she had never talked with Ben about the emotional changes she'd experienced since Benny came along, or about how Benny's birth had changed her expectations about the way she would live her life. She sensed that Ben had expected that children would not really change their lives much, although he had not said this out loud. "We really need to talk about this stuff, and about where it is we are headed," she thought to herself.

The lecturer turned their attention briefly to the particular expectations that come from religious and spiritual beliefs. Both Ben and Alyssa tensed considerably when they heard this topic. Of all the subjects they dreaded talking about, this one was at the top of the list. The lecture stated the obvious: "Many couples, when they get married, think that this stuff is really not that important to them, only to find out later that they have major differences over their religious beliefs and practices, and these problems end up dividing them. " "That's us," Alyssa thought. The leader pointed out that there was an entire chapter in the book dealing with these matters and that the work of identifying and talking through these issues would take a good deal of time. Ben leaned over to Alyssa and said, "We've really been avoiding this. We need to work on it." Alyssa nodded, reaching for his hand to hold.

The presentation on "issues and events" clarified what happened during their conflicts, in particular, how they would get quite upset about things that seemed so minor. They became subdued at the realization that the differences between them might be deeper than they had thought. "No wonder it feels more like a minefield than a marriage," Ben thought. "We've got all this stuff under the surface that we have not been dealing with openly." He felt some relief when the leader emphasized that what couples really need is a sense of hope in their ability to handle their major issues over time, rather than a promise that they will get rid of all their issues and conflicts once and for all.

The presentation on "problem solving" made Ben feel more in control. Both partners liked the problem-solving model, and they had plenty of issues about which to problem solve. The model was, in fact, similar to those he had studied in law school; he had used such problem-solving methods in his practice, but he had never realized that they could be useful in marriage. Once again, the presenters noted the value of structure as a kind of road map for getting through the more difficult issues in their relationship terrain. As before, the presenter suggested that couples practice the technique on a less conflictual issue at the beginning, in order to get the hang of the strategy.

Practice time for problem solving was next. They decided to apply the model to the problems they had with finding a reliable babysitter. This problem was very specific, and both could see how important it was in reaching their goal of getting their relationship back on track. They defined their solution as finding a babysitter they could count on weekly. Alyssa came up with a number of reservations concerning the kind of person she would feel comfortable with, and Ben validated her concerns by paraphrasing. That was enough to help Alyssa stay with the process, instead of vetoing all Ben's suggestions, as she had done in the past. They came up with several practical ideas to try the following week, with each of them agreeing on what steps they would take and what day and time they would review their progress, so that adjustments could be made if necessary. They had not had such a clear sense of working together on something in ages, and it felt good.

The last afternoon of the weekend workshop, "ground rules" were presented. These summarized the major strategies used in PREP for protecting a relationship from poorly managed conflict. Ben and Alyssa learned how they could incorporate the skills into their daily routine, though they weren't sure that they really needed to have a weekly couple meeting. The presenter pointed out the benefits of such a meeting but also acknowledged the difficulty many couples had in doing this regularly. On the other hand, Alyssa and Ben couldn't argue with the presenter's point that couples eventually pay a high price for not taking time to be proactive about their relationship issues. The two agreed to try all the ground rules, including having couple meetings on Thursday evenings. As Alyssa pointed out to Ben, "Look, what could it hurt? Look how good it has been for us to take this weekend to think about where we are heading!"

The final lectures on forgiveness and commitment moved them deeply. They realized that they had many constraints keeping them together, including the children and financial concerns, as well as their parents' potential disapproval of divorce. They also recognized their strong reservoir of dedication toward one another. But they also realized that their marriage had slid down on their priority lists, and both had been doing some score-keeping. They could finally see how unfair that was and how great an effect their interpretations of things must have had on their feelings toward one another. On the positive side, they had always seen themselves as a team, but they needed to get back to nurturing that spirit in their relationship. They left the weekend thinking deeply about what they needed to change. There was no miracle, but neither had expected one. They did feel closer than they had in years, and they now had a clear sense of what would work to get their marriage back on track.

Alyssa and Ben are fairly representative of many couples who come to PREP seminars. Such couples range from very happy couples who simply want to stay that way (like the premarital couples who have been the focus of much PREP research) to couples on the brink (or in the midst) of divorce. Alyssa and Ben are like the average couple who comes not terribly distressed, yet not doing very well, either. They are in the midst of the erosion that destroys all too many marriages.

Ben and Alyssa had experienced a breakdown in communication, as the range of their problems and their differences eventually outstripped their ability to effectively manage conflict and solve problems. This is a typical couple whose expectations and hidden issues surface over the course of a relationship, as they face greater and greater challenges from crises and changes in circumstances. Like many couples, they had come to believe that talking together was most likely going to lead to a fight, and so they avoided their most effective tool for improving their relationship. Such a dynamic reinforces a growing avoidance and distancing that can destroy any relationship, if it goes on long enough.

☐ Empirical Evaluation and Research

There are three streams of research that support the approach embodied in PREP. PREP is not the only program that finds its rationale in this empirical background; it is, however, directly supported by this body of empiricism. These three streams are prediction research, outcome research, and survey research (Stanley, 1997).

Prediction Research

While research demonstrates that many factors put couples at increased risk for distress and divorce (e.g., Kurdek, 1993; Karney & Bradbury, 1995), the quality of couple interaction seems particularly predictive (Clements, Stanley, & Markman, 1997; Gottman, 1993; Kurdek, 1993; Markman & Hahlweg, 1993; Matthews et al., 1996). This quality can be identified early in a relationship, before the couple recognizes any significant problems. These subtle communication patterns have increasing influence as the stresses and demands of life build up.

PREP is centered on this line of research perhaps more than any other—on interventions designed to counter the patterns, beliefs, and attitudes that research has shown put couples at great risk. Furthermore, PREP emphasizes factors that both are associated with increased risk and are relatively amenable to change (Stanley et al., 1995). Many other risk factors play a role in distress and divorce, but if they are not changeable, they make poor targets for intervention. Hence, couple interaction, expectations, beliefs, and attitudes are the primary targets of PREP because they are strongly related to future marital quality and stability and are changeable through skills-oriented interventions.

Outcome Research

Many outcome studies assessing the effects of various forms of PREP with various kinds of couples either are underway or have been completed. In a paper on premarital preparation, Stanley (1997) recently reviewed the latest findings from a number of outcome studies on PREP. These are summarized in the following quote:

> A number of studies specifically on PREP and its variations have shown very encouraging results. Behrens and Halford (1994) found that the communication skills of those coming from divorced homes could be brought up to the level of those not having this risk factor (parental divorce). Blumberg (1991) compared PREP with Engaged Encounter, finding at post-assessment that PREP couples communicated more positively and less negatively as judged by trained coders. In Germany, a version of PREP has been in use by the Catholic Church, where PREP couples (compared to a mixed control group, with about half of the couples choosing other premarital programs offered by the Church and about half receiving no premarital

program) have shown significant gains in communication and conflict management skills from pre- to post-test, and have maintained these gains at the one- and three-year follow-ups compared to their pre-test scores and to controls. Moreover, PREP couples were significantly more satisfied at the three-year follow-up and more stable as compared to controls (Thurmaier, Engl, Eckert, & Hahlweg, 1993). Perhaps most importantly, the latest data show that the PREP couples have a lower divorce rate (1.6% vs. 12.5%) than the control couples (Hahlweg, Markman, Thurmaier, Engl, & Eckert, 1998). [Authors' note: The most recent data from Germany, at the 5-year follow-up point, show a 4% divorce rate for PREP couples compared to 24% for control couples (K. Hahlweg, personal communication, February 1997).]

A recent study on another variation of PREP in the Netherlands did not show the same kinds of promising results as other PREP studies have (Van Widenfelt, Hosman, Schaap, & van der Staak, 1996). However, interpretation of results from this study is problematic for various reasons. First, PREP couples had been together an average of three years longer than controls at the beginning of the study, making group comparisons difficult. Second, since the PREP couples averaged nine years together prior to intervention, inferences to premarital "prevention" seem limited. Third, control couples were significantly more likely to drop out of this longitudinal study, which can produce a control group that is increasingly select (biased) for couples doing relatively well (Van Widenfelt et al., 1996).

Such methodological problems are very difficult to overcome in longitudinal, intervention outcome research, and studies on PREP are affected by such complicated methodological concerns in varying degrees. At the University of Denver, we are currently beginning a large scale outcome study of premarital training with the support of the National Institute of Mental Health. This new study will address some of the design concerns raised by other outcome studies on premarital training.

In the United States, the longest term evaluation of the skills-based, premarital training ever conducted has been a study comparing PREP to matched control couples (Markman, Floyd, Stanley, & Storaasli, 1988; Markman, Renick, Floyd, Stanley, & Clements, 1993; Stanley et al., 1995). PREP couples have been shown to have about half the likelihood of breaking up or divorcing, have demonstrated greater relationship satisfaction, and have shown lower problem intensity than the control couples for up to five years following training. For years following training, PREP couples have shown better communication than controls, as assessed on such dimensions as communication skills usage, positive affect, problem-solving skill, and support/validation. PREP couples have also shown less withdrawal, less denial, less dominance, less negative affect, and less overall negative communication than controls. Lastly, PREP couples reported significantly fewer instances of physical violence.

I also note that one recent comparison test of a skills-based approach (Christian PREP) compared to a comprehensive, information-based approach did not find differences in the couples' functioning at post-test

(Trathen, 1995). However, it is very hard to find significant differences shortly after premarital training, because couples come in very committed and satisfied (i.e., ceiling effects), and clear short-term differences do not typically emerge without objective coding of couple interaction (e.g., Blumberg, 1991; Hahlweg et al., 1998). In any studies of premarital preparation outcomes, the most important data will come from long term follow-up, because the outcomes of premarital training that are of greatest interest are inherently long term (e.g., stability vs. divorce). It is certainly possible that well-conceived, intense premarital training programs of various designs will ultimately prove effective.

While more research can be done and is being done, there is substantial evidence from both prediction research and outcome research of the great importance for targeting communication and conflict management skills when counseling couples premaritally. (Stanley, 1997, pp. 6–11)

Survey Research

The Center for Marriage and Family at Creighton University recently reported on a comprehensive survey of couples taking premarital counseling in the Catholic Church. A number of findings bear directly on the issues of educating couples in order for them to have happier, more stable marriages (Center for Marriage and Family, 1995). For one thing, these researchers found that couples (who were now married) rated the longer, more intense premarital programs as having been more helpful. Second, when asked what topics were the most helpful as they looked back on their premarital education, these couples ranked *communication* (73.5% rated as helpful), *commitment* (70.4% rated as helpful), and *conflict resolution* (67.2% rated as helpful) as the top three content areas. Thus, it appears that as couples move forward in their marriage, they are most likely to look back and see the relevance of these core issues. These are the core foci of PREP.

In summary, there are three streams of empirical research that independently suggest the importance of the targets and strategies found in programs like PREP. A goal in refining PREP is to keep in step with sound research to assure the usefulness and relevance of the interventions that make up the approach.

☐ Summary

While the strategies of PREP seem valid for couples at all stages in life and in various states of happiness or distress, PREP is oriented toward prevention. The goal of any prevention program is to reduce the chances of later distress or divorce by intervening before problems develop to a destructive degree. PREP shows great promise for achieving this goal, and couples, along with the institutions that serve them, have the means for doing the work of prevention.

Educational approaches to prevention have the advantage of being attractive to couples at many different stages of a relationship. There are many couples like Ben and Alyssa who have already started on a downward path, yet are at a point where an educational, preventive approach could have a powerful effect. Programs like PREP can help halt such erosion and move couples down a better path.

PREP is a program that is evolving. It is continually updated based on the latest research. New methods for disseminating the strategies will continue to be produced over time. Couples can be exposed to the model through workshops provided by those trained in the program or through freestanding products based on the approach (book, audiotapes, and videotapes).

Some couples with very complex dynamics might be better served by other models. Having seen thousands of couples respond with deepened attachment and confidence in their future, we have come to believe in the power of the simple. Simple strategies that promote emotional safety and positive connection can help many couples have the kind of intimacy they deeply long for. PREP seeks to give couples hope by teaching them the skills and attitudes they need to stay together and stay happy.

☐ Contact References

Readers interested in learning more about the PREP approach or the research underlying it can contact the authors at the Center for Marital and Family Studies, Psychology Department, University of Denver, Denver, CO 80208.

☐ References

Baucom, D., & Epstein, N. (1990). *Cognitive-behavioral marital therapy.* New York: Guilford.

Behrens, B., & Halford, K. (1994, August). *Advances in the prevention and treatment of marital distress.* Paper presented at the "Helping Families Change" Conference, University of Queensland, Brisbane, Australia.

Birchler, G. R., Weiss, R. L., & Vincent, J. P. (1975). Multimethod analysis of social reinforcement exchange between maritally distressed and nondistressed spouse and stranger dyads. *Journal of Personality and Social Psychology, 31,* 349–360.

Blumberg, S. L. (1991). Premarital intervention programs: A comparison study (Doctoral dissertation, University of Denver, 1991). *Dissertation Abstracts International, 52,* 2765.

Center for Marriage and Family. (1995). *Marriage preparation in the Catholic Church: Getting it right.* Omaha, NE: Creighton University.

Clements, M., Stanley, S. M., & Markman, H. J. (1997). *Predicting divorce.* Manuscript in preparation.

Coie, J., Watt, N., West, S. G., Hawkins, J. D., Asarnow, J. R., Markman, H. J., Ramey, S. L., Shure, M. B., & Long, B. (1993). The science of prevention: A conceptual framework and some directions for a national research program. *American Psychologist, 48,* 1013–1022.

Eidelson, R. J., & Epstein, N. (1981). Unrealistic beliefs of clinical couples: Their relationship to expectations, goals and satisfaction. *American Journal of Family Therapy, 9*(4), 13–22.

Gottman, J. M. (1993). A theory of marital dissolution and stability. *Journal of Family Psychology, 7,* 57–75.

Gottman, J. (1994). *Why marriages succeed or fail.* New York: Simon & Schuster.

Gottman, J. M., & Krokoff, L. J. (1989). Marital interaction and satisfaction: A longitudinal view. *Journal of Consulting and Clinical Psychology, 57,* 47–52.

Gottman, J., Notarius, C., Gonso J., & Markman, H. (1976). *A couple's guide to communication.* Champaign, IL: Research Press.

Guerney, B. G., Jr. (1977). *Relationship enhancement.* San Francisco: Jossey-Bass.

Hahlweg, K., Markman, H. J., Thurmaier, F., Engl, J., Eckert, V. (1998). *Prevention of marital distress: Results of a German prospective-longitudinal study.* Manuscript submitted for publication.

Johnson, D. J., & Rusbult, C. E. (1989). Resisting temptation: Devaluation of alternative partners as a means of maintaining commitment in close relationships. *Journal of Personality and Social Psychology, 57,* 967–980.

Karney, B. R., & Bradbury, T. N. (1995). The longitudinal course of marital quality and stability: A review of theory, method, and research. *Psychological Bulletin, 118,* 3–34.

Kurdek, L. A. (1993). Predicting marital dissolution: A 5-year prospective longitudinal study of newlywed couples. *Journal of Personality and Social Psychology, 64,* 221–242.

Levenson, R. W., & Gottman, J. M. (1985). Physiological and affective predictors of change in relationship satisfaction. *Journal of Personality & Social Psychology, 49*(1), 85–94.

Markman, H. J. (1981). Prediction of marital distress: A 5-year follow-up. *Journal of Consulting & Clinical Psychology, 49*(5), 760–762.

Markman, H. J., Floyd, F., Stanley, S., & Jamieson, K. (1984). A cognitive/behavioral program for the prevention of marital and family distress: Issues in program development and delivery. In K. Hahlweg & N. Jacobson (Eds.), *Marital interaction: Analysis and modification.* New York: Guilford.

Markman, H. J., Floyd, F. J., Stanley, S. M., & Storaasli, R. D. (1988). Prevention of marital distress: A longitudinal investigation. *Journal of Consulting and Clinical Psychology, 56,* 210–217.

Markman, H. J., & Hahlweg, K. (1993). The prediction and prevention of marital distress: An international perspective. *Clinical Psychology Review, 13,* 29–43.

Markman, H. J., Renick, M. J., Floyd, F., Stanley, S., & Clements, M. (1993). Preventing marital distress through communication and conflict management training: A four and five year follow-up. *Journal of Consulting and Clinical Psychology, 62,* 1–8.

Markman, H. J., Stanley, S. M., & Blumberg, S. L. (1994). *Fighting for your marriage: Positive steps for a loving and lasting relationship.* San Francisco: Jossey-Bass.

Matthews, L. S., Wickrama, K. A. S., & Conger, R. D. (1996). Predicting marital instability from spouse and observer reports of marital interaction. *Journal of Marriage and the Family, 58,* 641–655.

Miller, S. (1971). The effects of communication training in small groups upon self-disclosure and openness in engaged couples' systems of interaction: A field experiment. (Doctoral Dissertation, University of Minnesota, 1971). *Dissertation Abstracts International, 32,* 2819A–2820A.

Notarius, C., & Markman, H. J. (1993). *We can work it out: Making sense of marital conflict.* New York: Putnam.

Stanley, S. M. (1995, December). *How a marriage dies.* Paper presented at Focus on the Family Breakfast for Christian Counselors, Colorado Springs, CO.

Stanley, S. M. (1997). What's important in premarital counseling? *Marriage and Family: A Christian Journal, 1,* 51–60.

Stanley, S. M., Lobitz, W. C., & Dickson, F. (in press). Using what we know: Commitment and cognitions in marital therapy. In W. Jones & J. Adams (Eds.), *Handbook of interpersonal commitment and relationship stability.*

Stanley, S. M., & Markman, H. J. (1992). Assessing commitment in personal relationships. *Journal of Marriage and the Family, 54,* 595–608.

Stanley, S. M., Markman, H. J., & Blumberg, S. L. (1994). *Fighting for your marriage. Videotape series for couples.* Denver, CO: PREP Educational Videos, Inc.

Stanley, S. M., Markman, H. J., St. Peters, M., & Leber, D. (1995). Strengthening marriages and preventing divorce: New directions in prevention research. *Family Relations, 44,* 392–401.

Stanley, S. M., & Trathen, D. (1994). Christian PREP: An empirically based model for marital and premarital intervention. *The Journal of Psychology and Christianity, 13,* 158–165

Stanley, S. M., Trathen, D. W., & McCain, S. (1996). *Christian PREP manual for leaders: Prevention and relationship enhancement program.* Denver, CO: Christian PREP, Inc.

Thurmaier, F. R., Engl, J., Eckert, V., & Hahlweg, K. (1993). *Ehevorbereitung-ein partnerschaftliches lernprogramm EPL.* Munich, Germany: Ehrenwirth.

Trathen, D. W. (1995). A comparison of the effectiveness of two Christian premarital counseling programs (skills and information-based) utilized by evangelical Protestant churches. (Doctoral dissertation, University of Denver, 1995). *Dissertation Abstracts International, 56/06-A,* 2277.

Van Widenfelt, B., Hosman, C., Schaap, C., & van der Staak, C. (1996). The prevention of relationship distress for couples at risk: A controlled evaluation with nine-month and two-year follow-ups. *Family Relations, 45,* 156–165.

Wampler, K. S., & Sprenkle, D. H. (1980). The Minnesota Couple Communication Program: A follow-up study. *Journal of Marriage and the Family, 42,* 577–584.

John Mordechai Gottman, Ph.D.
Julie Schwartz Gottman, Ph.D.

The Marriage Survival Kit:
A Research-Based Marital Therapy

☐ Introduction

Historical Background and the Theory
Underlying Our Approach

The concept that underlies the development of the theory of our approach
is that marital intervention and prevention programs ought to be developed empirically by studying the longitudinal course of marriages and
understanding what is "dysfunctional" when a marriage is ailing. Although
there are many hypotheses about this issue, very few of them have received empirical support, and so most of them are myths that need to be
dispelled. To study this question, our laboratories have examined the correlates of marital satisfaction and misery, the longitudinal predictors of
divorce, and the predictors of marital satisfaction among stable marriages.
However, it has turned out to be the case that we also need to understand
the correlates of well-functioning marriages, and that additional information is supplied by attempting to understand what well-functioning
couples are doing to maintain intimacy in their marriages. These two
questions leave unresolved the issue of what the etiology is of the indices
and predictors of ailing marriages. We need to understand how people
get into these muddles that are predictive of marital meltdown.

   One of the major issues in the area of designing marital interventions can be called the "delay" problem. We now know that after determining that their marriages are in trouble, couples wait an average of 6 years before seeking professional help (Notarius & Buongiorno, 1992)! Hence, we need to discover what interventions can reverse this delay, which contributes to the cascade toward divorce if the destructive processes have been going on for some time. Finally, we need to know if there are any processes that can short-circuit marital meltdown, and, if so, are prevention and intervention methods the same processes?

Research Base for Answering These Five Questions. For the past 14 years, we have conducted longitudinal research on seven samples of couples totaling 670 couples using methodology that gathers behavioral, self-report, interview, and physiological data. We have tried to insure that some of these samples represent the major racial and ethnic groups in the communities from which they were drawn. Our longest follow up has been 14 years. The samples have varied across the life cycle of the family, ranging from newlyweds to couples facing retirement. Also, one sample focused on physically violent couples, comparing these to both distressed nonviolent couples and happily married nonviolent couples.

Proximal Change Studies. In addition to these longitudinal studies, in which there was no intervention, we have been conducting a series of short-term change studies whose goal was only to improve the second of two conflict resolution conversations held by the couples in our laboratory. In part, these brief changes serve as a model for relapse; we seek to obtain dramatic changes in the short term that we do not expect to last. We hope to learn what the dynamics are that determine whether specific interventions will or will not last.

Ability to Predict the Longitudinal Course of Marriages. We can now confidently predict divorce and marital satisfaction among the couples who stay married. In three separate studies, these predictions were consistently made with over 90% accuracy. We are able to predict divorce in the areas of emotional behavior, cognition and perception, or physiology. We call these three areas the "core triad of balance," because each couple establishes a balance of positivity and negativity in each area, and this balance determines the ultimate fate of the marriage. Our first finding was that in the area of emotional behavior, there was more positivity than negativity in marital interaction among couples headed for divorce, and that four negative interaction patterns were most predictive of divorce. Gottman (1994a) called these four the "Four Horsemen of the Apocalypse." They are criticism, defensiveness, contempt, and stonewalling (which is the listener's withdrawal from marital interaction). We also discovered that general, diffuse physiological arousal was predictive of divorce. Finally, the perception of the interaction and the couple's perception of the entire history of their marriage is recast in couples experiencing what we call "the distance and isolation cascade," a pattern of: (a) feeling flooded by how one's partner complains; (b) viewing one's marital problems as severe; (c) believing that there is no point in trying to work these issues out with the partner; (d) arranging one's lives in parallel so they do less and less together; and, (e) loneliness. In a recent longitudinal study with violent couples, we made similar predictions, and again the accuracy was high.

A Theory Has Emerged From All This Empiricism.   In studying the answers to the basic research questions, we have composed a theory, one that has varying degrees of empirical support. By the word "theory" we mean a mechanism for explaining our predictions. This theory attempts to explain how marriages function well or dysfunction. It includes information about prevention and intervention. The theory is called the "sound marital house."

Mathematical Modeling.   For the past 5 years, we have been working with James Murray of the Department of Applied Mathematics at the University of Washington to create a set of nonlinear difference equations that can theoretically represent our predictions (Cook et al., 1995). The idea of "balance" in marriages forms the basis of this mathematics. The equations permit us to put our theory into quantitative terms, creating a new general systems theory of couples and families. The added advantages of this mathematical modeling are: (a) it makes our theory precise; (b) it makes our theory potentially disconfirmable; (c) it allows us to *simulate* the interactive behavior, thoughts, and physiology of a couple in situations different from those in which we first observed them; and, (d) it suggests experiments for changing marriages. Furthermore, the equations provide a new theoretical language for describing marital interaction, based on the core triad of balance, which is the balance in a marriage within and between physiology, thought, and interactive behavior (Gottman, 1994b).

We will attempt to describe what we think the theory has added to the understanding of couples' relationships. The theory is an attempt to move beyond a checklist of empirical findings to a statement about the dynamics of how marriages actually work, one that will have implications for intervention and prevention. The sound marital house theory attempts to make several contributions. First, the theory links nonconflict interaction with conflict resolution. Most marital therapies assume that if the couple resolves its conflicts, the couple will be happy. Many couples also share in this myth. But actually, if they suddenly and magically resolved all their conflicts, they would be left with a void between them. These couples do not know how to work on improving the everyday and the loving aspects of their relationship, and so the only arena in which they come together is conflict. This is especially true of violent couples. Second, we have discovered that several principles in the nonconflict interaction of couples actually determine, to a significant extent, the effectiveness of repair attempts during conflict resolution. Hence, it is necessary to work on the nonconflict aspects of the relationship to improve the couple's ability to resolve conflict. Third, the theory is not a checklist of what couples need to do to make their marriages work. It attempts to explain the mechanism of how marriages work.

The research approach was guided by one paper written by Goldfried and D'Zurilla in 1969. In this paper the authors simply argued that intervention and prevention programs ought to be developed by studying how competent populations handled the very same situations that were problematic for specified target populations. We should point out a caveat, namely, that it is not necessarily logical to expect that marriages may be "fixed" by the same mechanisms that make them naturally work or dysfunction. Thus, it is a scientific hope that there is only one mechanism that is responsible for the success or failure of marriages. This would be quite parsimonious, but it may be false. It could very well be the case that ailing marriages need to be repaired by an entirely different set of principles. This question can be resolved empirically.

☐ Theoretical Underpinnings

Theoretical Understanding of Committed Romantic Relationships

We need to define a fundamental concept that we call *set points* in a marriage. These are quantities that represent the balance of negativity and positivity in emotional interaction, perception, and physiological arousal and calm. Furthermore, the marital system defends these quantities as homeostatic values that it regulates using a variety of corrective repair mechanisms. The idea is that each individual, partly due to personality, brings to the marriage a set of "uninfluenced" set points. For example, some people are more dysphoric than others, and so their own uninfluenced set points for positive versus negative emotional behavior will tend toward the irritable and depressed affects. Our theory assumes that every relationship is a system that develops its own influenced "set points" with respect to the balance of positivity and negativity in behavior, perception, and physiology. That is, the marital interactions then move the uninfluenced set points to a new set, the influenced set points. These influenced set points are an extension of the old idea of "homeostasis" in general systems theory. The idea is that people bring to every marital interaction a set of uninfluenced set points in the core triad of balance, behavior, thought, and physiology.

First, there is their average level of positivity and negativity when they are not being influenced by their partner. These "uninfluenced" set points depend on the temperaments, the histories of the individuals, and the history of the relationship. We discovered that the uninfluenced set points of couples headed for divorce were far more negative than for stable couples. This means that what each partner brings to the interaction is already more negative in couples headed for marital meltdown. Then the couple proceeds to interact, and this interaction has characteristic influence functions through which a husband affects his wife, and his wife in turn affects him, creating influenced set points in behavior, perception, and physiology. The interaction can move the individual uninfluenced set points in either a more negative or a more positive direction. In marriages headed for divorce, as one might expect, the interaction moves the partner in a more negative direction, while the opposite is true in stable, happy marriages. The marital system thus drives the uninfluenced set points in predictable ways to create the influenced set points in behavior, perception, and physiology. For relationships to work well, these set points must reflect a very large balance of positivity versus negativity in perception and behavior, or in the physiological domain, a state of calm and well-being versus a state of mobilization for fight/flight, subjective upset, vigilance, and danger.

We have discovered that the positive/negative ratio in interactive behavior during conflict resolution must be at least 5 to 1 in stable, happy marriages. In marriages headed for divorce, the positive/negative ratio is only 0.8 to 1, so that there are 1.25 as many negatives as positives. Furthermore, the basis for these ratios during the resolution of conflict lies within the everyday and romantic aspects of the marriage that have nothing to do with the resolution of conflict. By examining the same ratios during the couple's far more neutral discussions of how their day went that preceded the conflict discussion, we were able to account for between 30% and 50% of the variation in the same ratios during conflict. It is the mundane, everyday aspects of marital interaction that provide the setting conditions for the effective resolution of conflict.

☐ Intervention Model

Philosophical, Religious, Psychological, and Social Assumptions That Underlie Our View of Couplehood and Marriage

In our work we have attempted to remain objective and uninfluenced by all religious and social assumptions. Instead, we have tried to be guided purely by empiricism. We view ourselves very much like the 15th century Portuguese cartographers, who sailed the unknown waters, navigated the oceans, and drew crude maps. We are drawing similar crude maps of relationships and their developmental transitions. We are also trying to find out how expert "sailors" navigate these troubled waters. Hopefully this information will one day become commonly known by the general public, and it will help people avoid the everyday disasters that have come to be the overwhelming fate of today's marriages. The following are the basic assumptions of our approach.

Philosophy of the Intervention

Everything in our approach to intervention is designed to minimize the possibility of the couple's relapse after therapy.

The Therapy Is Primarily Dyadic.   In our therapy it is the goal to move the therapeutic context from an initial triadic context to a dyadic context in which the therapist acts as a coach. The goal of the therapy is for the couple to have the capability to make their next conversation "better," that is, less like those couples who are on a trajectory toward divorce, and more like those couples who are on a trajectory toward happy, stable marriages. Therapy can end when the couple has the ability to make their interaction (conflict and nonconflict) less divorce prone. This cannot be accomplished with the therapist remaining central to maintaining the couple's functional interaction. In the therapy, then, the couple interacts with one another a great deal, rather than talking to the therapist. The therapist then acts to give the couple one tool that they can then use with one another, and make their own.

The Role of Emotion.   Our own philosophy of the role of emotion in marital therapy is the opposite of Bowen's in two ways. In Bowen's thinking, rationality and emotion were opposed, and he viewed rationality as designed to inhibit negative affect. Papero (1995), writing about Bowen's theory of emotion, noted:

Bowen described a continuum based on the ability of the person to keep separate the emotional and intellectual systems and to maintain a choice between them, which he called the "scale of differentiation of self." People with no ability whatsoever to separate them, no matter what the conditions, were assigned the rank of zero on the continuum. They had no ability to differentiate between the emotional and intellectual systems and operated continuously under the guidance of the emotional system. From the zero point, individuals could be assigned a position on the continuum based on an assessment of their ability to separate emotional and intellectual systems and to maintain a choice between them. Bowen assigned a number 100 to the opposite end of the continuum, to designate the individual displaying full ability to separate and choose between the emotional and intellectual systems to guide behavior. (p. 13)

In the early years of psychology the Yerkes–Dodson law attempted to demonstrate how arousal and performance might be related. This view of a dialectic between emotion and intellectual functioning is now being replaced by current neurophysiological thinking (e.g., Damasio, 1994), in which emotion is coming to be viewed as essential to rational thought and rational problem solving. Our own work on metaemotion (Gottman, Katz, & Hooven, 1997) suggests that understanding one's emotions can be a guide for both insight and action.

The Therapist's Role in Soothing.   Bowen also viewed the therapist's role as similar to that of a control rod in a nuclear reactor, to intervene and soothe the couple. In this view it is the therapist's role to do the soothing in the marital system. Our view is opposite to this. The danger in Bowen's view is that it makes the therapist irreplaceable, and it may maximize the couple's relapse once therapy terminates. Particularly given what we now know about state-dependent learning, the therapist, in our view, ought to allow the couple to get very upset, even entering states of diffuse physiological arousal (DPA), and then have *them* learn how to self-soothe and soothe one another.

Low Psychological Cost.   Interventions should seem easy to do. They should not be costly psychologically or appear to be foreign to people. The reaction to interventions should overwhelmingly be, "Oh, is that all there is to this? I can do that."

How the Preventive Interventions Stem From the Assumptions

It is our view that prevention and intervention must be different processes because most couples experience very long delay times before seeking treatment. Our findings suggest to us that this delay results in a five-stage process through which "perpetual problems" become "gridlocked problems." Intervention programs must deal with this marital gridlock, but prevention programs usually do not need to give quite as much attention to this problem.

How the Model of Intervention Follows From the Theory

The model of intervention follows directly from the theory. The theory has seven hierarchical parts. Figure 14.1 organizes the theory of the sound marital house.

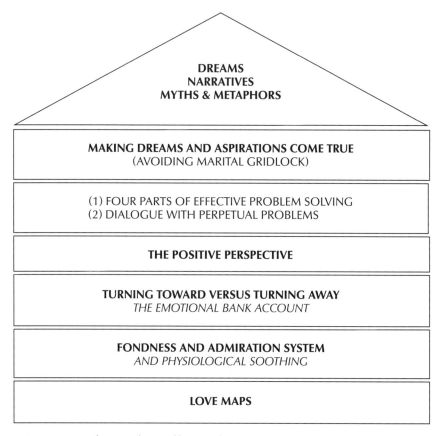

FIGURE 14.1.   The sound marital house: The Gottman theory of how marriages work. *Note.* Copyright 1998 by the Gottman Institute. Reprinted with permission.

The Gottman Theory of Marriage: The Sound Marital House

These are the seven components that marital interventions need to target. They are organized as the floors of a house.

The foundation of the house, the *love map*, involves the couple knowing one another and periodically updating this knowledge.

Assessed using our Oral History Interview, we have discovered that the amount of "cognitive room" people (especially husbands) allocate for the marriage and for their partner's world is a strong buffer against marital dissolution. By "cognitive room," we mean the amount of knowledge each person has about the relationship and the partner's world, especially their psychological world. In our longitudinal study of newlyweds, this dimension, assessed in the first few months of the marriage, was a buffer against the drop in marital satisfaction that 75% of wives experience a few months after the birth of the first child. Those couples who, in effect, had made love maps were more likely to wind up in the 25% of couples who did not experience the drop in marital satisfaction after the transition to parenthood.

The second story of the sound marital house is the *fondness and admiration system*, which is the antidote for contempt.

The fondness and admiration system is assessed by the amount of affection and respect each person spontaneously shows toward the partner. Once again, the fondness and admiration system is assessed using our Oral History Interview. Admiration and fondness are the antidotes against our most powerful predictor of divorce, contempt. Once again, in our longitudinal study of newlyweds, the fondness and admiration system, assessed in the first few months of the marriage, was a buffer against the drop in marital satisfaction that 75% of wives experience a few months after the birth of the first child. Those couples who, in the first few months of marriage, spontaneously expressed fondness and admiration about their partners were more likely to wind up in the 25% of couples who did not experience the drop in marital satisfaction after the transition to parenthood.

Taken together, the variables assessed from our Oral History Interview have been able to predict which couples will divorce and which will stay married with over 90% accuracy in three separate studies.

The third story of the Sound Marital House is *Turning Toward Versus Turning Away* in everyday moments, or what we call the *Emotional Bank Account* that exists in every marriage.

This dimension of marital interaction is assessed during nonconflict interaction. In our longest longitudinal study we had couples meet in our laboratory after having been apart for at least 8 hours. They then began by discussing the events of their day. The couple's ratio of positive to negative affect during this interaction was strongly predictive of the same ratio during the subsequent conflict interaction, in which the couple tried to resolve a major area of continuing disagreement in their marriage. About 10 years ago we built an apartment laboratory at the University of Washington, in which couples lived for 24 hours. There are no instructions, except to be as you are at home. Couples read the newspaper, watch TV, listen to music, watch videotapes, work, play games, cook dinner, eat, clean up, take naps, and so on. We are now coding the 600 hours of interaction we have of the 50 couples who lived in this laboratory. While analysis has yet to begin, it seems quite easy to code whether couples "turn toward" or "turn away" from one another during this everyday interaction. Most of this interaction is neutral in affect, but it is either connected or unconnected. An example of turning toward one's partner is responding to excitement: Wife: "What a pretty boat!" Husband: "Yeah. I think that's a schooner." So far, subjectively, it seems that the ratio of turning toward versus turning away may be related to the way the couple resolves conflict in our standard conflict-resolution interaction. However, we have yet to finish this analysis.

These three stories build the fourth story, which is Weiss's (1980) idea of positive sentiment override, or what we call the *positive perspective*.

The idea Weiss proposed was that there is a buffer that operates in marriages called positive sentiment override, or PSO. PSO is a discrepancy between insider and outsider perspectives such that messages an observer might describe as objectively negative, say irritable, are taken as neutral or even positive by the receiver of the message. Weiss proposed that this is clearly a positive buffer that overrides the more immediate proximal events in moment-to-moment marital interaction. There is an analogous negative sentiment override (NSO) in distressed marriages. Here, neutral messages are responded to as if they were attacks, and there is a surprising negative affect that results. A good example of this comes from Tannen's (1990) book. In the case of PSO, the wife says, irritably, "You're not supposed to run the microwave with no food in it." The husband says, "Oh, I didn't know that. Thanks." In the case of NSO, the wife says, neutrally, "You're not supposed to run the microwave with no food in it." The husband says, with hostility, "Don't tell me what to do, you rat! Did you read the manual? Well I did. You never read manuals. I'm always the one who has to do it." So, if a couple had PSO, repair attempts worked. If they had NSO, the repair attempts didn't work. It is our theory that PSO determines a lot of things, including the presence of positive affect in problem-solving discussions and the success of repair attempts during conflict resolution. So far we have just completed analysis of the data from our newlywed study, and these data support this hypothesis.

The next story consists of two parts. (a) For marital problems that are resolvable, we detail the *four parts of effective problem solving*. These are *softened startup, repair and deescalation, accepting influence,* and *compromise.* We have discovered that the use of positive affect in the service of deescalation is a part of this process, but it is not programmable—it just happens by itself when the positive perspective is in place. (b) For marital problems that are not resolvable, and there are many of these in most marriages, to avoid marital gridlock it is necessary that the couple establish what we call a "dialogue" with the perpetual problem.

The implication of the presence of positive affect is that, during the assessment of the marriage, we need to look not only for the absence of negativity (e.g., the Four Horsemen), but for the presence of positive affect, even during conflict resolution. Thus, many marriages that are emotionally detached will be identified in our assessment as problematic marriages. What is the basis of a continued positive affective emotional connection? The answer involves the next story, which is the marriage's effectiveness at *making dreams and aspirations come true.* This aspect of marriages is the basis of unlocking marital gridlock, in which the *symbolic values* of each person's position must be explored.

Finally we have "the attic," where the symbolic meanings of many of our ideas about emotion (our idea of "metaemotion") and the marriage live; the attic is where our *Dreams, Narrative, Myths, and Metaphors* about our marriage and family find a home. This is what you tell yourself about emotion and your marriage, and it contains your internal thoughts, metaphors, myths, and stories about the marriage. The role of the marriage in facilitating or hindering personal growth resides here, as does the meaning of what the couple feel they are (or are not) building together.

This part of the theory is related to our Dreams-Within-Conflict Interview. This interview is designed to get at the symbolic meaning of each person's position. We have discovered that within this symbolic meaning there is hidden a "life dream" that makes it very difficult for people to yield any influence on the issue. The interview uncovers these dreams and reveals their nature before creating a climate of acceptance and facilitation of one another's dreams. Gridlocked conflict eventually leads to emotional disengagement (the distance and isolation cascade). The interview is especially useful with couples who have become emotionally disengaged and affectless because of long-standing gridlocked conflict. Here the emotional power of each person's complaints is tapped by helping people get in touch with the meanings behind their own positions. This aspect of the theory also extends to dealing with very negative and painful gridlocked conflict, which we find can only be solved by exploring the symbolic meaning of each person's position. The floors of the sound marital house are interconnected because the narratives, dreams, metaphors, and myths about marriage actually cycle back to the foundation, which is knowing one another.

Specific Goals of the Intervention

The following are the eleven goals of the Gottman intervention. Clinicians are advised to terminate the treatment after these goals have been accomplished. First, during the couple's attempts to resolve conflict, the markers of divorce must be significantly and meaningfully reduced, particularly the Four Horsemen and the ratio of positivity to negativity. It is also necessary that the couple have moved from NSO to PSO. This means that there is a buffer in the marriage that leads people to interpret their partner's anger as valuable information rather than as a personal attack. It is necessary for the love map to have been created and be used on a daily basis. This means that people are continuing to know about one another's worlds and updating this knowledge periodically. The fondness and admiration system needs to have been activated or reactivated. During nonconflict, everyday interactions, partners are turning toward one another rather than away most of the time. The couple has created PSO and its maintenance through resetting the set point of turning toward versus turning away. This refers to the emotional bank account in the marriage, suggesting that the couple is more emotionally connected and engaged with one another. A lot of this connection is nonemotional, occurring in everyday, mundane, fairly neutral contexts. Each person needs to accept influence from the partner, particularly the husband from his wife. In dealing with the resolution of conflicts that can be resolved:

- The couple uses softened rather than harsh startup in dealing with conflict.
- The couple can effectively repair negative interaction chains
- The couple uses positive affect in the service of de-escalation.
- The couple knows how to physiologically soothe self and partner.
- The couple has the tools, without the therapist, to make the next conversation better than their last.

For conflicts that are basically unresolvable (about 69% of couples' conflicts are of this nature), the couple is able to turn gridlocked "perpetual" marital conflicts into what we call a dialogue with the perpetual problems. By "dialogue," we mean that they do not necessarily resolve the problem, but that the affect around which they don't resolve the problem has become more positive. They don't continually hurt each other when discussing the problem, but, instead, have developed some amusement and relationship to the problem itself. They can therefore communicate acceptance of the partner even though they are not happy about the perpetual problem area. The threshold of what we call the "marital poop detector" has been set significantly lower, and the couple has ways of repairing periods of irritability and emotional distance before too much time has passed. This is based on our evidence that people in happy, stable marriages are not adapting to high levels of negativity. Instead, they are talking things over gently before they become too negative.

Tasks Associated With These Goals

There are three parts to the marital intervention: (a) changing the setting conditions that create dysfunctional marital conflict resolution patterns; (b) changing the way couples resolve conflict, which has two parts: solving problems that *can* be solved in specific ways, and converting gridlock with perpetual problems into dialogue with perpetual problems; and (c) dealing with resistance to change. These parts of the intervention are not sequential. They are interlaced as the intervention proceeds. Within each of these parts there are tasks to be accomplished that are related to the levels of the sound marital house. These tasks are described in Table 14.1.

The intervention begins with an assessment phase, described in the left-hand column of the table. The next column describes the sound marital house. The next two columns are the tasks of the intervention. There are two columns to deal with the relapse problem in marital therapy. First, the concept is introduced and there are tasks associated with the introduction of each concept. Next, the concept is generalized to the couple's everyday life. For example, in the love map phase of the sound marital house, to introduce the concept, the couple plays the board game we invented called "Love Maps." To generalize this concept to the couple's everyday life, the couple makes a real map of their partner's world, and then makes a commitment to continually update these maps.

Resistance to change is conceptualized in terms of distortions of the sound marital house. This means, for example, that a particular individual psychopathology will be placed upon the matrix of the sound marital house to know how to proceed. A good example is that depression may be manifest in a particular case as a disorder of the fondness and admiration system. A particular client may have a lot of difficulty believing that the partner respects and admires him or her. This suggests specific interventions that need to occur, either within a conjoint context or individually. These changes will require understanding and altering the person's relational schemata, or internal working model of aspects of the sound marital house.

Buffering Children.   Another part of the therapy is training parents how to buffer children from the deleterious effects of an ailing or dissolving marriage. The resources for this part of the intervention are the book *The Heart of Parenting,* by Gottman and DeClaire (1997), and the video-

TABLE 14.1.   Tasks associated with the Gottman theory of the Sound Marital House

Assessment	Part of the Sound Marital House	Exercises Introducing Concept	Generalization to Everyday Life
Dreams-Within-Conflict Interview	Making dreams and aspirations come true: Exploring symbols, metaphors, narratives, myths. Unlocking marital gridlock	Discuss dreams, hopes	Weekly get-in-touch dates. Understanding partner's myths, dreams, and narratives in current contexts.
Observing interaction during conflict discussions	Everyday functional conflict resolution	Softened startup, accepting influence, de-escalation, effective repair attempts, soothing via positive affect (esp. humor)	Early discussions of continued low-level irritability, emotional distance (negative threshold reset)
Four Horsemen distance & isolation cascade: Flooding; DPA	Avoiding dysfunctional (Four Horsemen) and pursuer–distancer interaction patterns	Discuss flooding and parallel lives scales, understand gender differences.	Taking breaks, soothing, and making repair natural and effective
Video replay interview: Insider/outsider discrepancy	Positive perspective	Physiological soothing, in therapy: Video replay methods	Positive attributions of everyday negative affect
Everyday interaction: Events of the day discussion, positive discussion	Turning toward vs. away: The emotional bank account	Everyday Interaction Checklist Exercise	Stress reduction conversations: Requited interest, humor, excitement, affection, irritability, and complaining
Oral History Interview	Fondness and admiration system	Positive Adjectives Checklist, Thanksgivings Exercise	Appreciation and affection, thoughts about partner when apart
Oral History Interview	The love maps	Love Maps board game	Create real map of partner's everyday life

Note. Copyright 1998 by the Gottman Institute. Reprinted with permission.

tape *Emotion Coaching* (Gottman & Shulman, 1996), which trains parents in a five-step emotional coaching method.

☐ Skills for Preventing Couple or Marital Distress and Enhancing Committed Romantic Relationships

It is the point of view of this intervention that very little social skill training is necessary for most couples in the steps of the sound marital house, because all the skills are there in most couples' repertoires for dealing with friends and guests. When we interact with siblings, friends, and guests, we usually deal with their feelings respectfully; we accept their limitations and appreciate their contributions. In our view, changing marriages is primarily a matter of enabling these skills in a new context. When we invite a group of friends over for dinner, we do not say, at the end of the evening, "I am so disappointed. I was expecting real community tonight, and this evening fell far short of my hopes. I am ending these friendships." When a guest spills a glass of wine we do not say, "You are so clumsy. You have ruined my best tablecloth. I am never inviting you over again. How could you treat me this way?" We say, "No problem. Would you like another glass of wine?" and we clean up the stain. When a guest leaves an umbrella we do not say, "You are so forgetful. What am I, your slave to be constantly running after you?" We say, "Here's your umbrella."

The major issue is that these skills do not get applied in the everyday interactions of most couples, except for the couples who are the "masters" of marriage. We have studied these couples in our longitudinal studies of long-term happy marriages. What the people do in these relationships is not complex, but the secret is that they do these things often.

☐ Specific Methods and Strategies for Intervention

Activities, Exercises, Readings, and Other Techniques, Including the Frequency and Length of the Intervention

There are specific exercises in the Gottman intervention for the two steps of introducing the concept and generalizing it to the couple's everyday life. These are referred to in Table 14.1. For example, for introducing the idea of enhancing the fondness and admiration system, the Positive Adjectives Checklist is employed. Each spouse selects three positive adjectives that are characteristic of the partner and then shares the reasons for this choice with the partner and an example of when the partner displayed this positive trait.

Brief Rationales for the Interventions

The single best discriminator between happily and unhappily married couples is the reciprocation of negative affect. This means that unhappily married couples are engaged in continuing chains of negativity, without any ability to repair this interaction and make it more positive. One could argue that effective repair could be the only goal of any marital intervention. What, then, are the correlates of effective repair? We could find no aspect of the way the repair attempt was delivered or the content of the repair attempt that was predictive of its success. Michael Lorber (1996), in an honors thesis in our laboratory, discovered that even in the most distressed marriages, couples make a repair attempt about once every 3 minutes, and the rate is higher the more unhappy the couple is. He investigated the basis of effective repair attempts, which were repair attempts rated by observers as actually ending the chain of negativity. The effectiveness of repair attempts turned out to be significantly related to a concept that Weiss (1980) called "sentiment override," which we discussed earlier in the chapter. The concept depends on a discrepancy between "insider" and "outsider" perspectives of the marital interaction. A couple has NSO if even affectively neutral statements (as seen by an objective observer) are taken as negative (by the receiver). A couple has PSO if even affectively negative statements (as seen by an objective observer) are taken as neutral or positive (by the receiver). Recall the example given earlier in the chapter, in which a wife says, "You're not supposed to run the microwave oven with no food in it." Even if she says this neutrally the husband may take offense and answer: "Don't try to control me. Did you read the manual? No, you never read the manual, do you? But I always do!" That's NSO. But if the wife says: "You're not supposed to run the microwave oven with no food in it" with irritability and the husband answers: "Oh thanks. I didn't know that," that is PSO. You can see that PSO provides quite a buffer against the escalation of conflict. Lorber found that PSO was related to the effectiveness of repair attempts.

But then, we asked, what is the basis of PSO or NSO? This is akin to asking, "Why do some people start a conflict discussion with criticism (one of the Four Horsemen of the Apocalypse) rather than complaint?" The answer lies not in the way they resolve conflict but in their everyday interaction, which is represented by the first three floors of the sound marital house: love maps, fondness and admiration, and the emotional bank account. In other words, the intervention cannot focus just on conflict resolution.

Finally, in response to the long wait times for getting help and its consequences for marital gridlock, we asked the question about the determinants of marital gridlock. Gridlocked marital conflict is characterized either by emotional disengagement and deadness or by the presence of the Four Horsemen and a great deal of continual pain in discussing the issue. The answer is represented by the two top floors of the sound marital house, which are concerned with the dreams-within-conflict intervention. This intervention examines the symbolic meaning of each person's position in the gridlock and makes the marriage safe enough for these dreams, metaphors, narratives, and myths to emerge and be explored and heard before people begin solving the gridlocked marital problem.

Our approach to ending marital gridlock comes from a recent discovery that approximately 69% of all marital conflicts in our laboratory involve perpetual problems. These are problems that one inherits whenever one selects any relationship; they are basically irreconcilable differences. In our view, the role of functional conflict resolution has been greatly overrated. Our research reveals that most couples never resolve their major marital issues, and it doesn't matter very much. We find that when we study couples longitudinally, even after 4 years, they are still coping with the same marital issues. In most cases it seems as if the couple has changed clothes and hair styles, but the marriage has not really changed very much in the way issues are handled. There is remarkable stability in these marital interaction patterns over 4 years. In classifying the discussions of continuing disagreements these couples had, 31% of the discussions involved functional problem solving, 13% involved gridlocked marital conflict on perpetual problems, and 56% were conversations about perpetual problems in which the couple was trying to establish a dialogue with the problem. So, in 69% of the cases, the major issue in the marriage was a perpetual problem. What mattered was not solving the perpetual problem but rather the affect with which they discussed it!

Instead of solving problems, what seems to be important is whether or not a couple can establish a dialogue with their perpetual problems. This dialogue needs to feel good for it to be a dialogue. To feel good, the couple makes their peace with the problem to some degree. They may be able to push or pull the problem about somewhat and change their level of frustration with the problem. They may come to some acceptance of the problem.

However, if they cannot establish such a dialogue, the conflict becomes gridlocked, and gridlocked conflict eventually leads to emotional disengagement. Hence, the goal of most of our intervention around problem solving is to help the couple move from a gridlocked conflict with a perpetual problem to a dialogue with the perpetual problem. In either case the problem remains perpetual. An example is one couple where the wife described the husband as a loner, who only begrudgingly does things with the family. Both partners said their conversations about this issue were always the same. The husband says, "Alright, I'll go," and maybe adds, "Okay, sure, anything you say, honey," and then the couple reminisces about how they always go through the same scenario, joking with each other about how they are in a rut, and cannot even argue creatively. They are not happy about the perpetual problem, but they are also amused by it.

These perpetual problems are often issues without resolution that the couple has been dealing with for many years. They continue to talk about the issue, occasionally making some progress, or at least making the situation better for a short time, but then, after a while, the problem re-emerges. Somehow these couples manage to magically communicate acceptance of their partner while also communicating that they would like some improvement on this issue. Humor and affection are very important components of this magic.

☐ Format of Application

How Couples Are Recruited to the Program

The entire program consists of a 2-day workshop with a 6-month follow-up workshop, and the availability of marital therapy. We advertise in the newspaper and on radio and television, and send announcements of our workshops to local clinicians. Couples are then admitted to the 2-day workshop. After the workshop, we follow up with couples every 3 months using a relapse questionnaire. We then assess whether the couple wishes to see a therapist, and, if appropriate, we make a referral to a member of the Gottman Institute Marriage Clinic (whom we have trained). We continue to follow the couples for 2 years after termination from therapy.

How Screening and Assessment, If Any, Are Done

So far, we have done no screening, except that the cost of the workshop is $325 per couple for 2 days, which is a form of financial screening. In our research study, we will eliminate this cost. There needs to be an epidemiology of marriage, so that we can know, in depth, what kinds of marriages exist in our population, and what types of couples and what types of people come for treatment. We think that it may be advisable to assess individual psychopathology (major depression, suicidal behavior, antisocial personality, borderline diagnosis, psychosis, alcoholism, post-traumatic stress disorder (PTSD), childhood physical or sexual abuse) or what may be termed "fundamental violations of the marital contract" (for example, physical abuse or the presence of an ongoing extramarital affair) in future research. We expect different levels of success with couples that bring these additional problems to the therapy. In these cases we expect that the data will show that marital intervention may even be contraindicated.

Populations for Which the Approach Is Inappropriate

The approach is based on research for populations that are fairly normal and representative of the population. The approach will probably have less success with populations in which there are high levels of individual psychopathology, particularly major depression, suicidal behavior, anti-social personality, borderline diagnosis, psychosis, PTSD, alcoholism, physical abuse, and the presence of an ongoing extramarital affair. The intervention is probably going to have decreasing levels of success with couples who are further down the cascade toward marital dissolution, particularly our "distance and isolation cascade."

☐ Step-by-Step Description of the Program

There are three parts of the intervention, which need to be adjusted for each individual case. First, we start with the idea of *changing the setting conditions that cause dysfunctional marital conflict resolution.* The setting conditions refer to the first several floors of the sound marital house, which in turn determine sentiment override (positive or negative). In practice the therapist integrates changing the couple's conflict resolution with changing these setting conditions. Second, we move the couple toward *functional problem solving and conflict resolution.* This involves a two-pronged approach of (a) teaching functional conflict resolution for solvable problems and (b) changing marital gridlock with perpetual problems to dialogue with perpetual problems. Finally, we deal with *sources of resistance.* The specifics of each part follow.

Changing the setting conditions that cause dysfunctional marital conflict resolution. This part of the therapeutic intervention is designed to meet the need to change the way the couple thinks about the marriage (love maps), the couple's fondness and admiration system, and the way the couple moves through time together, prioritizes how they choose to be together, and addresses the balance of engagement/disengagement and turning toward/turning away. These balances affect the setting conditions that have given rise to the deadlocks in the first place. These setting conditions do not involve conflict resolution, although they have profound impact on PSO or NSO, which determines how the couple handles minor everyday conflicts. PSO and NSO also determine the couple's ability to repair interaction during conflict resolution. Hence, this part of the therapy program involves changing the way the couple moves through time, the way the two people set priorities, and how they engage and connect on an everyday basis.

The couple usually comes into therapy with the idea that if they solve some basic core issues in their marriage, everything will be okay. Furthermore, most therapists are also trained to believe this hypothesis, that is, that the resolution of conflict is the royal road to intimacy. According to our research, this assumption may be incorrect, for two reasons. First, if the couple were actually, magically and suddenly, to resolve their core conflicts, the result is that usually there would be a void. This is so because the affectional system and the admiration system have both been sorely neglected. They will be left with a lack of emotional connection. In fact, they may miss the connection that the conflicts themselves provided. Second, if they are relating, if they are making an emotional connection, say, through listening sympathetically to their partner do battle with the world, even if only for 20 minutes a day, research suggests that this alone will dramatically change the way they deal with conflict. They will be buffered with PSO instead of NSO, so the way they react to their partner's irritability will change, and this will increase the chances that repair attempts will succeed.

In practice, the therapist starts each session by listening to the couple talk about their week. Conflict and its resolution will naturally become integrated with this component of the intervention. The therapist needs to individualize this integration differently for each couple. This means that the sequence of interventions may vary across couples, and that the specific resistances the therapist will encounter will also vary.

☐ Qualities and Role of Leader, Facilitator, or Therapist

Education, Training, and Background

It is important to recognize that we are still in the phase of intervention development and testing. During this phase, the workshop leaders need to have a great deal of expertise and experience. We have done all the couples workshops ourselves, although we envision training others to do them in the future. The therapists we are training are also very experienced clinicians. Our rationale for requiring training and experience is that this is necessary to individualize the intervention for each couple. The principles of the intervention are not complex, but tailoring them for individual cases is. We think that this is particularly true of unlocking gridlocked conflict. As we learn more about what works well for whom, we will try to become more precise about the training and background needed for the leaders and therapists in our approach.

Role of Leader Vis-à-Vis Participants

We see the leaders and the therapists as having a highly professional relationship with couples. We do not see them as mentors or equals, and so friendship and self-disclosure need to follow the same general guidelines as in any professional, therapeutic relationship.

☐ Application of the Preventive Model to a Couple at Risk

The case of Ben and Alyssa, presented by the editors of this volume, is quite interesting, but it provides inadequate information about the nature of the couple's relationship for an adequate assessment. Hence, it will become necessary for us to indicate choice points in our assessment of the case and then make some assumptions about the case before we can discuss the specifics of our intervention.

In general, Ben and Alyssa are what we would call "conflict avoiders" (see Gottman, 1994a, 1994b). They have been through a series of major normative life transitions—graduating from school, getting married, moving, becoming parents (of a fragile child), Alyssa's giving up teaching, Ben's major dissatisfaction with his job and subsequent depression—without discussing what these transitions mean for each of them or for the marriage. Conflict is something that happens to them, rather than the result of them discussing and systematically examining their real differences. They would prefer to avoid examining their differences, instead relying on the assumption that the passage of time will improve things in the marriage. If the couple discussed their basic differences, they might feel far less alienated. In our therapeutic approach this begins at the most fundamental level of creating love maps, which are maps based on real knowledge of one another's psychological world. This passivity of avoiding conflict leads to a chaotic lifestyle, because things happen to them that they feel are out of their ability to control. What we don't know is the strengths of the marriage, other than that they apparently both enjoy socializing and their sex life with one another. Many conflict avoiders share a basic philosophy of life, family, goals, lifestyle, and relationships.

One thing we would want to assess is the real knowledge they each have of one another, particularly knowledge of their fundamental beliefs about God, work, family, and the meaning of life. We would also like to assess the amount of real fondness and admiration (respect) they have for one another. Does Ben share his mother's view that Alyssa is okay as long as she has a career of her own, or is this not central to his respect for her? What is their time like with the baby? Is this a source of joy for them together, or is it lonely for her as well as for him? For the purpose of our intervention, the information given about both families was not helpful. We would need to know what the family histories implied for how they thought about their marriage, something we explore in our Oral History Interview and in our Meta-Emotion Interview. In short, a lot of information is provided, but without knowing the couple's perception of this information, it would not be very useful to us. In the Oral History Interview, we obtain information about the couple's relationship history and philosophy of marriage, and their perception of their parents' marriages. In the Meta-Emotion Interview, we obtain information about how they feel about the basic emotions of anger, fear, sadness, love and pride. We try to understand the history of their feelings and philosophies about these emotions and how it affects the marriage (and parent–child relationships).

We will assume that we know the answers to these things. We will assume that these two levels of the sound marital house were strong before their first pregnancy. We will assume that there was, in each of them, a strong liberal intellectual tradition that Columbia University represents.

A great potential strength of this couple is the way they have managed to handle their in-laws without the differences becoming marital issues. Therefore, it is likely that both spouses are very tolerant of these differences between the parents, and have worked out their own approach to these issues (religion, a conservative versus a liberal life view, and women's liberation). We will also assume that Alyssa's turning toward religion after her son was saved was not at all pathological, which makes sense since we know it was not a turn toward the kind of rigidity her father represented. Instead, we will assume that Alyssa's turning toward God was actually something that could be a common bond between her and Ben, if the couple explored the basis of this change in Alyssa. So, we further assume that Ben's disinterest in Reform Judaism is a basic agnosticism, but that he is quite tolerant of Alyssa's belief in God.

Hence, everything else considered, this couple's problems are quite typical of couples who are having a rather difficult transition to parenthood. This transition is especially difficult for couples who are not talking very often and very intimately, and in which the pregnancy was a major life-changing event for the wife but not for the husband. Things have begun to slip in the marriage, but they do not seem beyond repair. They are ideal candidates for preventive intervention.

The intervention needs to progress by having Ben and Alyssa get back in touch with one another, and to change their marriage so that they make continual time for one another without little Benny around. They need to spend time on a regular basis listening to one another's stresses and worries, hopes and aspirations, and dreams. Ben needs to understand the changes that have occurred in his wife. Alyssa needs to understand why Ben is so dissatisfied with his job (we don't know from the case description). Alyssa and Ben may also need to discuss Ben's increase in alcohol consumption. Alyssa's characteristic avoidance of this change in Ben's behavior needs to be examined as well. Is she suppressing her own concerns? Regarding religion, is Ben suppressing his concerns regarding Alyssa's newfound religious convictions? Is Alyssa having feelings about Ben's lack of religiosity? What do these issues mean to them symbolically? Are there dreams and visions of, say, a "good family" that are being hidden, not discussed, with resulting emotional disengagement? These are all issues that, in their avoidance, are distancing these people from one another.

There is another issue about which information has not been sufficiently presented that Ben and Alyssa should explore. What are the circumstances surrounding the second pregnancy? Did Ben and Alyssa agree to have another child? Is this pregnancy an accident? Or is something else at work here? Clearly, Ben has negative feelings about having a second child now but does not address them. The underlying issues need to be explored by the couple. Following this work, the couple needs to deal with this new pregnancy and work out a way to be friends during this second transition. In particular, the case summary gives us the impression that while Alyssa has made a transition from wife to wife-plus-mother, Ben hasn't really become a dad yet. We would need to explore how this can be accomplished, because this transition will have major implications for their ability to become a family and to be able to grow as individuals.

Probably the most important part of our intervention would be the exploration of their individual loneliness in the context of exploring their dreams of how they want their lives to be. That seems to us to be the major lack in this couple's ability to make a successful normative transition to becoming a family with two children. The potential third child could be an important area of even further exploration.

This couple has a tendency to drift for long periods of time without really making meaningful contact with one another. We would build in this contact by changing the way they talk to one another and the way they listen to one another on an everyday basis. Right now we would have a lot to catch up on in this domain, and we would need to build in mechanisms that would prevent this drift and relapse in the future.

☐ Empirical Evaluation and Research

We are in a pilot-testing phase of the development of our intervention. We have now conducted workshops with 235 couples, and we are following these couples for 2 years. We are also now training a group of clinicians who will be our referral network for couples who relapse using this approach. Our questions are:

1. What kinds of couples sign up for these workshops?
2. What proportion of couples of each type relapse?
3. Why do they relapse? (a) What things about the intervention are working and what things are not working? (b) Are there other couple or individual characteristics that predict relapse?
4. Which of the couples who relapse will seek and which will not seek (or will refuse) marital therapy?
5. Which couples make gains and which do not make gains in therapy?
6. Which couples relapse after the marital therapy, and why?

Research in the Planning or Implementation Stages

We are doing change interventions with each of the components of the intervention in a series of eight proximal change studies. In these studies we change only one component of the couple's interactive system at a time. For example, in our first study we are changing the couple's fondness and admiration system only. In another study the couple learns to physiologically soothe themselves and each other. Couples are then followed for 2 years. These proximal change experiments and our pilot-testing is building to a research grant to do a large-scale assessment of the whole intervention. As the reader may have noted, the front end of the intervention is an "inexpensive" workshop that lasts 2 days, with a 6-month follow-up, day-long workshop. If we can show that this inexpensive intervention is effective with couples who have not progressed very far along the cascades toward divorce, then we may have made a contribution toward prevention. If we can then show that, for a certain percentage of the rest, we can reverse the deterioration created by the long delay in getting professional help, and, if we can specify what kinds of couples we fail with, then we will be on the right track toward developing a truly effective empirical theory and intervention for marriages.

What we need to demonstrate first might be called the "validity of the process equation." This simply means that we have to first show that, to the extent that couples change on the variables of the sound marital house, their marriages will remain stable and happy. We may only accomplish this with a small percentage of couples at first.

Our ultimate goal is for an overall effectiveness of between 60% and 70% of couples who are not very progressed down the cascade toward marital dissolution, which was previously spelled out by Gottman (1994a), and an effectiveness that decreases with increasing wait time on the couple's part. As conflicts become gridlocked and stay gridlocked longer, this intervention should have decreased effectiveness. The presence of either individual psychopathology or what we call fundamental violations of the marriage contract (violence, extramarital affairs) should drastically reduce the effectiveness of the approach we propose, unless it is combined with other therapies.

☐ Summary

Limitations, Strengths, and Contraindications of the Approach

This approach was developed using samples that we are fairly confident are normal and also representative of the population of marriages that exist in the communities in which we have been doing research. We do not know to what extent the unhappily married couples or divorcing couples in our samples are representative of the unhappily married couples who are seeking marital therapy or other forms of psychological help from our professionals. There may be more individual psychopathology in the distressed marriages that most clinicians see. This may be one of the limitations of our intervention.

One possibility is that our basic assumption is wrong, and that couples whose marriages did not work at one time and who need to fix their relationships are nothing like couples whose relationships work well, and therefore, these couples require an entirely different intervention. The intervention that would work for them might be based on an entirely different set of principles, perhaps derived from the study of a set of other couples who have brought their relationships back from hell. We don't think so, because from what we know of relationships, one set of principles holds for all. But, we could be wrong.

We have yet to soundly evaluate the effectiveness of this approach to intervention. As such, it must be considered highly speculative, though hopefully an interesting and provocative approach.

How the Approach Might Be Enhanced Theoretically and Clinically

What is necessary is for the approach we have presented to be evaluated in a collaborative study that spans a number of treatment facilities. In our view, the assessment and treatment of relapse is the most important problem that needs to be solved in the area of marital intervention and prevention. Replication is also critical.

Our methodology is necessarily quite slow, because, at each stage of our work, we must rely on research to guide us. We have had a great deal of speculation without an adequate research basis for the design of interventions. It is time to give this approach a chance, but it is critical to also apply the hard criteria of adequate scientific investigation to these ideas. Hence, we too stand humbly before the hard tests of Mother Nature. At present, this approach is short on experience with a wide variety of couples. In the next 5 years, these basic experiments will be undertaken.

☐ Contact References

For more information, contact the authors at the Gottman Institute, P.O. Box 15644, Seattle, WA 98115-0655, 1-800-523-9042.

☐ References

Cook, J., Tyson, R., White, J., Rushe, R., Gottman, J., & Murray, J. (1995). The mathematics of marital conflict: Qualitative dynamic mathematical modeling of marital interaction. *Journal of Family Psychology, 9*(2), 110–130.

Damasio, A. R. (1994). *Descartes' error.* New York: Grosset/Putnam.

Goldfried, M. R., & D'Zurilla, T. J. (1969). A behavioral-analytic model for assessing competence. In C. D. Spielberger (Ed.), *Current topics in clinical and community psychology, Vol. 1.* New York: Academic Press.

Gottman, J. M. (1994a). *What predicts divorce?* Hillsdale, NJ: Lawrence Erlbaum Associates.

Gottman, J. M. (1994b). *Why marriages succeed or fail.* New York: Simon & Schuster.

Gottman, J. M., Gonso, J., Notarius, C., & Markman, H. (1978). *A couple's guide to communication.* IL: Research Press.

Gottman, J. M., & DeClaire, J. (1997). *The heart of parenting: How to raise an emotionally intelligent child.* New York: Simon & Schuster.

Gottman, J. M., Katz, L. F., & Hooven, C. (1997). *Meta-emotion: How families communicate emotionally - Links to child peer relations and other developmental outcomes.* Mahwah, NJ: Lawrence Erlbaum Associates.

Gottman, J., & Shulman, D. (1996). *Emotion coaching* [Video]. Available from the Gottman Institute, P.O. Box 15644, Seattle, WA 98115-0655, 1-206-523-9042.

Lorber, M. (1996). *Sentiment override and the effectiveness of repair attempts during marital conflict.* Unpublished honors thesis, University of Washington, Seattle.

Notarius, C., & Buongiorno, J. (1992). *Wait time until professional treatment in marital therapy.* Unpublished paper, Catholic University of America, Washington, DC.

Papero, D. V. (1995). Bowen family systems and marriage in N. S. Jacobson & A. S. Gurman (Eds.), *Clinical handbook of couple therapy* (pp. 11–30). New York: Guilford.

Tanner, D. (1990). *You just don't understand: Women and men in conversation.* New York: William Morrow.

Weiss, R. L. (1980). Strategic behavioral marital therapy: Toward a model for assessment and intervention. In J. P. Vincent (Ed.), *Advances in family intervention, assessment and theory* (pp. 229–271). Greenwich, CT: JAI Press.

Ronald M. Rogge, M.A.
Thomas N. Bradbury, Ph.D.

Recent Advances in the Prediction of Marital Outcomes

☐ Introduction

The goal of preventing marital dysfunction is especially significant given the statistics on the success of traditional marital therapy: Fewer than half of the couples who seek out therapy show sustained improvement following treatment (Jacobson & Addis, 1993). Premarital interventions have a unique role to play in that they can help couples resolve potential problems before problems become entrenched within a marriage and erode the commitment to the marriage. This advantage would be most salient for the couples who are at the greatest risk for developing significant levels of marital discord and dysfunction.

In addition to targeting high-risk couples, identification of early risk factors associated with marital discord and divorce could help reveal po-

This research was supported by a Chancellors Fellowship from the UCLA Graduate Division (1995–1996) and a Graduate Research Fellowship from the National Science Foundation (1996–1997). The second author was supported in the preparation of this article by grant MH48674 from the National Institute of Mental Health.

Jennifer Abrea, Jennifer Christian-Herman, Catherine Cohan, Joanne Davila, Matthew Johnson, Benjamin Karney, Erika Lawrence, Gregory Miller, Rena Repetti, and Carol Zelden assisted with these studies; Andrew Christensen, Kathy Eldridge, Matthew Johnson, Benjamin Karney, Erika Lawrence, and Anne Peplau provided valuable comments on earlier drafts of the article. Their contributions are gratefully acknowledged.

tential causes of marital dysfunction, enabling professionals to tailor their premarital interventions to the specific needs of these high-risk couples. Thus, the prediction of marital outcomes serves two related purposes: identifying couples at greatest risk for marital discord and identifying the most salient underlying causes of that discord. In sum, analysis of the factors that predict marital discord and divorce will contribute not only to our conceptual understanding of the processes underlying marriage, but also to our practical attempts to strengthen newlywed marriages and prevent divorce.

☐ Review of Prior Prediction Studies

Prediction of Marital Stability With Behavioral Data

Recent research on prediction of marital instability has focused on the use of behavioral data to predict marital outcomes. Couples are videotaped while working to resolve a marital difficulty, and then the videotapes are coded by a team of independent raters using an objective coding system. As the data are collected objectively and in a standardized manner across subjects, it is perceived to be free of the normal biases that accompany self-report data and is thus considered to be more accurate and reliable. In a study of 90 newlywed couples, Gottman (1994) used the behavioral codes from the Specific Affect (SPAFF) coding system collected shortly after the marriage to predict marital outcomes 2 years later. Performing discriminant analyses on that behavioral data, Gottman (1994) was able to classify outcomes with 84% accuracy, predicting[1] 4 of the 5 divorces or separations and 72 of the 85 stable marriages. In this analysis, the variables of whining and emotional validation emerged as the strongest predictors of marital outcomes.

In a similar fashion, Lindahl, Clements, and Markman (in press) studied 90 premarital couples, using behavioral data and self-report data collected prior to marriage to predict marital outcomes 12 years later. With the use of the behavioral codes from the Couple Interaction Scoring System (CISS), the behavioral codes from the Interactional Dimensions Coding System (IDCS), and self-report data on problem ratings and demographics, Lindahl et al. (1998) were able to classify the outcomes of married or divorced with 80% accuracy. The variables of problem severity, emo-

---

[1]As the discriminant functions were applied to the same data set from which they were derived, this does not represent prediction in the strictest sense, but serves as an estimate of the level of prediction which could be obtained if these discriminant functions were applied to a new data set.

tional invalidation, negative communication, problem facilitation, and age differentiated between couples who stayed married and those who divorced. Thus, a combination of behavioral and self-report variables reflecting marital communication were found to predict outcomes with high accuracy. However, the results of Lindahl et al. (1998) must be taken with the caution that one third of the couples in the sample received premarital counseling as an integral part of the research project, because the primary goal of the research was to study counseling outcomes.

The results from these studies demonstrate that marital outcomes can be predicted through the close observation of couples' interactions early in marriage. That finding alone has several important implications for the field of premarital intervention. The fact that couples' behavior at the beginning of their marriage can predict later outcomes suggests that the seeds of dissatisfaction and divorce are already in place within newlyweds, embedded within their behavior toward each other. Moreover, in closely analyzing the specific behaviors that predict divorce, these studies identify specific domains of behavior that need to be targeted by premarital interventions. Consequently, these studies are an important step toward clarifying the behavioral antecedents of dissatisfaction and divorce.

Although the results obtained with observational data are encouraging, this type of data comes at a high cost. The data are expensive to collect and the process of training a team of coders in a microanalytic behavioral coding system is very demanding, often requiring 6 to 12 months of training before adequate levels of inter-rater reliability are achieved. Furthermore, once trained, significant amounts of time are required to code tapes with microanalytic coding systems, often requiring an hour or more to code 10 minutes of interaction. Thus, at every step in the process of collecting this data, there are high costs of time and effort. If the purpose of prediction is to effectively identify the couples at risk for divorce in order to target them for premarital intervention, then the use of behavioral data to accomplish that prediction would require that thousands of professionals and paraprofessionals be trained in these behavioral coding systems and collect this expensive type of data. Such an undertaking is simply not practical. Thus, although observational data are invaluable for specifying the interactional processes that might give rise to marital dysfunction, the high cost of behavioral data prohibits its widespread application to the problem of identifying high-risk marriages.

Prediction of Marital Stability With Self-Report Data

Traditional self-report data collected by means of questionnaires provide a low-cost alternative to behavioral data; the questionnaires can be quickly collected and scored with no need for special training. Several studies examine the predictive power of the premarital inventories used by various religious organizations. Fowers and Olson (1986; see also Olson & Olson, chapter 9 of this volume) identified clergy who had been routinely giving couples the PREPARE Inventory, a 125-item questionnaire that consists of 11 subscales covering different relationship domains. They asked each clergy member to select 2 to 5 couples whom they had counseled using PREPARE 2 to 3 years earlier, specifically asking them to identify even numbers of couples who were married and satisfied and couples who were divorced, separated, or married but dissatisfied. Using this methodology, Fowers and Olson compiled a retrospective sample of 164 couples who had been married 2 to 3 years and had taken the PREPARE Inventory prior to marriage. When husbands' and wives' subscale scores were independently entered into prediction analyses, Fowers and Olson were able to classify happily married and separated or divorced couples with 81% accuracy. Similarly, when predicting between the happily married and the unhappily married couples, they were able to achieve a level of accuracy of 77%. Fowers and Olson did not try to classify all three outcomes simultaneously, nor did they indicate which subscales were most predictive in their different analyses. However, their results do suggest that self-report data can yield comparable levels of predictive power to those found with behavioral data in the process of identifying high-risk couples.

In a replication of this study, Larsen and Olson (1989) used a similar retrospective method to assemble a sample of 179 couples who had been married for 2 years and who had taken the PREPARE Inventory as part of their premarital counseling. Following the analyses of Fowers and Olson (1986), Larsen and Olson (1989) only reported dichotomous predictions without attempting to classify all three marital outcomes simultaneously. Using a combination of husbands' and wives' data, Larsen and Olson were able to classify happily married and divorced or separated couples with 84% accuracy. The PREPARE subscales of Equalitarian Roles and Leisure Activities were weighted most heavily in this classification, followed by Realistic Expectations, Conflict Resolution, Family and Friends, Religious Orientation, Children and Marriage, and Sexuality. Thus, using highly similar methodologies, Larsen and Olson replicated the findings of Fowers and Olson, further demonstrating the power of self-report data to classify couples according to their eventual marital outcomes.

In a similar vein, Williams and Jurich (1995) studied the predictive abilities of the FOCCUS (Facilitating Open Couple Communication, Understanding and Study) premarital inventory. This inventory consists of 15 subscales covering different relationship domains such as communication, problem solving, values, personality match, and friendships. Williams and Jurich contacted 333 couples who had taken the FOCCUS inventory 4 to 5 years prior to the study and had provided enough tracking information that they could be located. Of these couples, 207 returned completed questionnaires and were consequently included in the retrospective sample. Because only 8 out of the 207 couples were separated or divorced 5 years after their wedding, the unstable group was combined with the married but dissatisfied couples to form a poor-quality group. When Williams and Jurich used the FOCCUS subscale scores to predict high-quality verses low-quality outcomes in discriminant analyses, they were able to classify with as much as 75% accuracy. Their results suggested that 14 of the 15 subscales significantly contributed to the prediction, with the Problem Solving, Personality Match, Sexuality, and Personal Issues subscales contributing most heavily to that prediction. Thus, self-report variables once again demonstrated levels of predictive ability comparable to those found with behavioral data.

Despite the fact that Fowers and Olson (1986), Larsen and Olson (1989), and Williams and Jurich (1995) found reasonable levels of accuracy in their classifications, the methods employed by these studies prevent them from being directly comparable to the prospective, behavioral studies reviewed earlier. To begin, in all three of these studies, couples completed the premarital inventories in the context of premarital counseling and thus their marital outcomes may have been affected. As a consequence, they cannot be compared directly to couples who do not receive a premarital intervention. Furthermore, the manner by which the samples were collected effectively excluded all couples except those who were religious enough to seek premarital counseling through their church, a procedure which may yield biased samples. In addition, the specific retrospective methodologies employed by Fowers and Olson and Larsen and Olson may have further distorted their samples by polarizing the outcomes. Fowers and Olson essentially asked clergy to identify notably good and poor marriages from their parishes. Similarly, Larsen and Olson included only the highest third and lowest third of their married couples on the dimension of marital satisfaction for their prediction analyses. Thus, the predictions in these two studies could have been enhanced because, rather than predicting across an entire dimension of marital quality, they were merely predicting between the extremes of the distribution. In an important analysis, Williams and Jurich tested out this possibility within their data set. When they selected only the extremes of marital satisfaction from their sample, their prediction accuracy rose significantly, thereby demonstrating that polarization of the sample can lead to inflated levels of prediction. In conclusion, although these retrospective studies provide some evidence that self-report variables have similar levels of predictive power to those found with behavioral variables, the methodologies employed limit their direct comparison to the behavioral studies.

The ability of self-report variables to predict marital outcome has also been studied with prospective designs. Hill and Peplau (1998) followed 65 marriages longitudinally from the initial stages of dating prior to marriage up to a 15-year follow-up. Prior to marriage, the couples were given 38-page questionnaires to fill out individually. Using different combinations of subscales derived from these questionnaires, Hill and Peplau were able to predict which couples would divorce or remain intact 15 years later with 95% accuracy. Despite the extraordinary length of the follow-up period, the rate of divorce within their sample was notably low, with only 15 divorces out of 65 marriages in those 15 years. Notwithstanding this limitation, Hill and Peplau (1998) were able to predict the divorces within their sample with a high degree of accuracy, thus demonstrating that self-report variables can have similar levels of predictive power to those found with objective behavioral data, even without extreme outcome groups.

In a similar prospective longitudinal study, Kelley and Conley (1987) used self-report data collected from engaged couples and from their close acquaintances to classify marital outcomes. In a discriminant analysis of the data from 168 couples who remained married over 50 years and the 39 couples who divorced within that time, personality variables such as neuroticism and impulse control weighed most heavily in distinguishing between the two outcome groups. The authors did not report the accuracy of prediction resulting from their discriminant analysis, but in a multiple regression with the predictor variables, Kelly and Conley found a multiple correlation of .50 between the predictor variables and the outcome or criterion variable. Although the accuracy of classification from this study is not available to be compared to previous studies, the results demonstrate that self-report variables taken just prior to marriage can account for a significant proportion of the variance in couples' outcomes 50 years later.

Finally, Kurdek (1993) followed a sample of 286 newlyweds through the first 5 years of marriage. Kurdek collected self-report data from a variety of domains including demographics, personality variables, and relationship values within the first year of marriage. Using that data in logistic regressions, a technique similar to discriminant analysis, the author was able to accurately classify 81% of the marital outcomes. Despite the fact that the overall level of accuracy achieved within this study is comparable to that found in previous studies, unlike the previous findings, the variables used in these analyses were not able to predict the two outcomes equally. Whereas the logistic regressions were able to predict 94% of the 222 stable marriages, they were able to predict only 39% of the 64 divorces. Thus, these analyses fall somewhat short in their ability to identify the couples who are at high risk for divorce. One possible explanation for this discrepancy with prior findings is that, in contrast to the previous studies, Kurdek did not include any measures of communication or problem solving within the study, focusing instead on variables involving personality and demographics. Consequently, although this study further demonstrates that self-report variables can accurately classify marital outcomes, the specific variables used within the analyses only weakly identified couples who ultimately divorced, thereby limiting their utility in identifying high-risk couples.

Prediction of Marital Stability With Interviewer Ratings

Buehlman, Gottman, and Katz (1992) examined the ability of a slightly different form of data, objective interviewer ratings, to classify marital outcomes within a prospective, longitudinal study. The researchers followed 54 married couples with a target child of from 4 to 5 years of age for 3 years. At the beginning of their study, Buehlman et al. (1992) interviewed the couples using an oral history interview. Based upon their answers and behavior during the interview, the interviewers rated the couples on six main dimensions: Affection, Negativity, Expansiveness, We-ness, Gender Stereotypy, and Coping Styles. Unlike the objective behavioral data described earlier, this coding system consists solely of macroanalytic codes and is based not only upon behavioral cues, but also upon the responses given to the interview questions. Thus, the interviewer ratings fall somewhere between pure self-report data and microanalytic behavioral data on the spectrum of objectivity. A discriminant analysis using the interviewer ratings to predict between married and divorced couples successfully predicted 94% of the outcomes. Despite a low rate of divorce (7 out of 54) in their sample, the results of Buehlman et al. suggest that objective interviewer ratings have levels of predictive power similar to those seen with both microanalytic behavioral data and self-report data. However, objective interviewer data comes with a cost similar to that associated with objective behavioral coding, in that teams of interviewers must be trained to make reliable ratings across couples, thereby limiting its practical application in identifying high-risk couples. These results must also be taken with the caveat that the couples in the sample were neither newlyweds nor necessarily at similar stages of marriage, because the only requirement for inclusion in the sample was that the couples each had a child of from 4 to 5 years of age. In studying older couples, the task of prediction may be facilitated by the fact that the predictor variables may simply be tapping the initial stages of divorce, thereby using an earlier stage of the outcome to predict the outcome. Thus, the levels of prediction seen within an older sample are not directly comparable to those found in a sample that has been followed either from engagement or from the period immediately following marriage.

☐ Summary of Research

Table 15.1 summarizes the prediction studies reviewed above. The studies as a group focus primarily on communication variables, problem solving variables, and management of affect as key predictors of marital outcomes. Thus, either by asking the couples how they interact or by directly observing their behavior during interactions, researchers were able to classify marital outcomes by closely measuring how couples navigate difficult situations with each other. In addition, all of the studies reviewed above dichotomized marital outcomes, collapsing the various outcomes into two groups when trying to predict them. This means that the married and dissatisfied couples would either be grouped with the divorced and separated (unstable) couples or they would be grouped with the married and satisfied couples. This was often necessary because of the small number of cases in the unstable groups or in the married but dissatisfied groups. Predicting between dichotomous outcomes, the studies reported rates of accuracy between 75% and 95%. Taken together, the results of these studies suggest that behavioral data and self-report data have the ability to accurately classify subsequent marital outcomes.

Methodological and Conceptual Refinements

Previous prediction studies have established a reasonably solid base of longitudinal results suggesting that many different forms of data can be used to efficiently identify couples at risk for divorce. However, in order to broaden the potential scope of the findings, it is important to examine some possible practical and conceptual refinements upon previous work.

The studies reviewed above raise five significant practical concerns. First, the studies mentioned above used both prospective and retrospective methods to obtain samples of couples. As noted earlier, purposefully selecting failed and successful marriages in a retrospective manner (Fowers & Olson, 1986; Larsen & Olson, 1989) can polarize the sample to extreme outcomes, thereby artificially inflating the levels of prediction achieved and limiting the generalizability of the findings (see Williams & Jurich, 1995). Second, several of the previous studies were designed to test premarital therapy outcomes and consequently provided counseling to all or part of their samples as a key feature of their research project (Fowers & Olson, 1986; Larsen & Olson, 1989; Williams & Jurich, 1995; Lindahl et al.,1998). The counseling the couples received could have altered the natural course of their marriages and therefore constrains interpretation of the prediction findings, further restricting the scope of those results.

A third practical concern with previous methods is that the prediction

(*text continues on page 341*)

TABLE 15.1. Summary of previous prediction studies

Study	Predictor variables	Time in Years	Attrition/Rate/ Avg Rate Per Year	# of Divorces/Rate/ Avg Rate Per Year	Outcome Groups	Prediction Rate (Overall/ Unstable)	Comments
Gottman et al. (1994) 90 newlywed couples	4 microanalytic behavioral variables (SPAFF)	2	—	5/6%/3%	Married vs. divorced	84%/80%	Low divorce rate; Short length of follow-up
Lindahl et al. (1998) 99 engaged couples	7 self-report and behavioral variables (CISS)	12	11/11%/0.9%	19/21%/1.75%	Married vs. divorced	80%/—	Intervention given to 25% of sample
Fowers and Olson (1986) 112 married couples	11 self-report variables (PREPARE)	3	a	31/20%/9%	Happily married vs. divorced/sep.	81%/81%	Retrospective; selected extremes; intervention given to all couples
Larsen and Olson (1989) 179 married couples	8 self-report variables (PREPARE)	2	a	36/27%/10%	Happily married vs. divorced/sep.	84%/81%	Retrospective; selected extremes; intervention given; to all couples
Williams and Jurich (1995) 207 married couples	14 self-report variables (FOCCUS)	5	a	8/4% 0.8%	High quality vs. low quality	80%/75%	Retrospective; low divorce rate; intervention given to all couples; some remarriages

(continued)

TABLE 15.1. *Continued*

Study	Predictor variables	Time in Years	Attrition/Rate/ Avg Rate Per Year	# of Divorces/Rate/ Avg Rate Per Year	Outcome Groups	Prediction Rate (Overall/ Unstable)	Comments
Hill and Peplau (1996) 231 college dating couples, 65 marriages	Numerous groups to 12 self-report variables	15	30/13%/0.9%	15/23%/1.53%	Married vs. divorced	95%/ —	Low divorce rate
Kelly and Conley (1987) 207 engaged couples	5 self-report and acquaintance-report variables	50	51/17%/0.3%	39/19%/0.38%	—	—	
Kurdek (1993) 286 newlywed couples	Numerous groups of self-report variables	5	218/43%/8.6%	65/22%/4.4%	Married vs. divorced	81%/48%	High attrition; no measure of communication; low prediction of divorce outcome; some remarriages
Buehlman et al. (1992) 54 married couples	9 objective interviewer ratings	3	4/7%/2.3%	7/13%/4.3%	Married vs. divorced	94%/100%	Older marriages; low divorce rate

[a]These studies used retrospective methods and consequently have no attrition. However, the authors did report response rates of 49% for Fowers and Olson (1986), 44% for Larson and Olson (1989), and 66% for Williams and Jurich (1995).

studies reviewed above did not exclusively study newlywed marriages, as some of the studies collected data from older marriages without attempting to control for the different stages of marriage within their samples (e.g., Buehlman et al., 1992). The use of such methods has three immediate implications for the interpretation of the findings: (a) The predictors of marital stability and satisfaction may change over time as the marriage develops, so that entirely different factors may be involved in predicting late divorces as opposed to early divorces. Such a dynamic would be obscured when using a sample of marriages at heterogeneous stages. (b) The study of older marriages, as opposed to newlywed marriages, makes it more likely that the predictor variables identified may simply represent initial stages of the ultimate outcome rather than underlying factors responsible for that outcome. (c) If a study begins with couples who have been married for more than four years, then that study will miss the largest fraction of couples who ultimately divorce.

A fourth practical concern with previous research is that the samples generally contained low levels of dissatisfaction and divorce (e.g., divorce rates were 6% in Gottman, 1994; 4% in Williams & Jurich, 1995; 13% in Buehlman et al., 1992). To fully understand the factors that lead to distress and divorce, it is important to obtain samples with representative levels of marital discord that can be analyzed. When samples contain unduly low levels of discord, then the analyses of that marital discord must be viewed with caution, as they may not be applicable to all distressed couples. The low rates of divorce in previous samples could be attributed to the high rates of attrition found in many of the studies, as distressed couples may drop out of research projects focused on marriage at a higher rate than nondistressed couples (see Karney & Bradbury, 1995). The low rates of divorce could also be attributed to the use of established couples, as samples of older marriages would lack those couples at high risk for early divorce. Regardless of their origins, the low rates of divorce seriously limit the general application of the findings.

Finally, all of the studies mentioned above dichotomized the outcomes that they were predicting. This means that the couples who were married but distressed at follow-up were either grouped with the divorced couples to create a "bad" marriage category or they were grouped with the married and satisfied couples to create a simple "married" category. The processes giving rise to marital stability and marital satisfaction may not be identical or even similar, with separate underlying variables and thus separate predictor variables. Dichotomizing outcomes results in marital outcomes being collapsed down to a single dimension, restricting subsequent researchers from exploring this possibility.

In addition to the aforementioned practical concerns, the previous prediction studies raise several conceptual issues as well. First, none of the studies reviewed above assembled a representative set of potential predictor variables in order to identify the variables that are most salient in the prediction of different marital outcomes. As a result, seemingly important variables like aggression were not tested as potential predictors within previous studies despite the fact that recent evidence suggests the presence of aggression in over half of all newlywed marriages (O'Leary, Barling, Arias, & Rosenbaum, 1989). Additionally, although the majority of previous studies have assessed marital communication and have demonstrated its importance in predicting marital outcomes, the current literature is rich with a wide variety of variables also implicated in predicting marital outcomes but impoverished when it comes to any replication or direct comparison of these additional predictor variables identified within different research projects. Without a direct comparison of the predictive validities of the various predictor variables within the same sample, it is difficult to determine the nature of the constructs that underlie the prediction of marital satisfaction and marital stability. Finally, the previous studies chose to use either behavioral or self-report measures of communication as potential predictors, but never directly compared the accuracy of prediction for these two different types of data within the same data set, leaving their relative value with respect to each other unclear.

Conclusion

Previous studies suggest that data collected early in marriage can be used to classify marital outcomes with a relatively high degree of accuracy. By focusing on variables such as communication and problem-solving skills, researchers have been able to predict dichotomous outcomes with levels of accuracy ranging from 75% to 95%. Although these studies represent an important first step in identifying risk factors associated with marital discord and divorce, the general application of their findings is limited by several practical and conceptual issues. We turn now to an example of research that was designed to extend previous work by engaging these issues.

☐ A Prospective Study of Newlywed Marriage: The UCLA Newlywed Project

Sixty newlywed couples were recruited from ads in newspapers across the Los Angeles metropolitan area to take part in a longitudinal study of newlywed marriage. This sample served as a pilot study within a larger project studying the longitudinal course of marriage (e.g., see Karney & Bradbury, 1997; Pasch & Bradbury, 1998; Sullivan & Bradbury, 1997; Karney et al., 1995). Several features of this study allow us to circumvent the problems associated with retrospective sampling, systematic counseling interventions, nonhomogeneous samples, low levels of divorce and discord, dichotomous outcome groupings, and nonsystematic variable selection. First, the prospective selection of couples ensured a sample free of potential retrospective selection biases. Thus, by recruiting subjects without prior knowledge of their ultimate marital outcomes, we avoided the confound of oversampling the extremes of the outcome distributions, enabling us to predict across a more representative distribution of outcomes. Second, although some of our subjects sought out premarital counseling prior to participating in our study (see Sullivan & Bradbury, 1997), no formal interventions were offered as part of our research project. Third, couples were allowed to participate provided that they had been married less than 6 months. This resulted in a sample with an average length of marriage of 12 weeks at the first point of data collection. To avoid the confounding effect of a previous, failed marriage, couples were only allowed to participate if this was the first marriage for both partners. These inclusion criteria ensured that the couples would be at a relatively uniform stage within their marriages, allowing us to track their progress through the initial high-risk period for divorce. Fourth, the UCLA Newlywed Project made use of regular contact and tracking information to keep attrition down to a minimum, with only 4 of 60 couples dropping out of the study by the eighth wave of data collection. The resulting levels of marital discord and divorce within the sample more closely approximated national norms, suggesting that the results obtained from that sample could be more appropriately generalized to the newlywed population. Fifth, the outcome of married-dissatisfied was treated as a distinct outcome from the outcomes of married-satisfied and divorced/separated in our analyses. This enabled us to determine if the dimensions of marital quality (satisfied vs. dissatisfied) and marital stability (married vs. divorced/separated) represented separate outcome dimensions with different predictor variables. Finally, a broad array of potential predictor variables was assessed in order to systematically compare their relative predictive abilities within the same sample. This put us in a position to synthesize an assortment of prediction findings into a parsimonious view of the key factors underlying marital dysfunction and instability. The husbands in the UCLA Newlywed Project averaged 25.5 years of age ($SD = 3.4$) and the wives 24.0 years of age ($SD = 2.9$). Husbands and wives had an average of 15.6 years of education ($SD = 2.2$ and 1.6, respectively). A majority of the subjects were White (75%) and most of the subjects were employed and/or in school (91%).[2]

Couples were assessed at eight time points, at 6-month intervals, dur-

---

[2]See Rogge and Bradbury (in press) for a complete presentation of this study.

ing the first 4 years of their marriages. During their first lab session, the couples completed the Marital Adjustment Test (MAT; Locke & Wallace, 1959), the Conflict Tactics Scale (CTS; Straus, 1979), the Multidimensional Anger Inventory (MAI; Siegel, 1986), the Communication Patterns Questionnaire, Constructive Communication subscale (CPQ-CC; Christensen & Sullaway, 1984), the Marital Coping Inventory (MCI; Bowman, 1990; see also Cohan & Bradbury, 1994), the Social Support Questionnaire, short form (SSQ; Sarason, Sarason, Shearin, & Pierce, 1987), the Divorce Attitudes Scale (Veroff, 1988), the Inventory of Marital Problems (Geiss & O'Leary, 1981), and the Marital Status Inventory (MSI; Weiss & Cerreto, 1980). These variables were chosen to approximate the measures that had proven to be most salient in the prediction of marital outcomes in previous studies. Additionally, the couples participated in a 15-minute conflict interaction in which they discussed a problem in their marriage, which they agreed upon mutually. The interactions were audiotaped and later coded for individual expressions of affect with the SPAFF (Gottman, 1988; see Gottman & Krokoff, 1989). At the eighth wave of data collection (3½ years after the first lab session and approximately 4 years into their marriages), 38 intact couples completed the MAT. For 16 of these 38 couples, one or both of the spouses scored in the distressed range on the MAT,[3] and so those couples were classified as dissatisfied couples. At this same time point, 18 couples had already separated or divorced and 4 couples had withdrawn from the study. This gave a final count of 22 married satisfied couples, 16 married dissatisfied couples, 18 divorced or separated couples, and 4 withdrawn couples. Only the data collected during the first lab session (at the first time point) were used as predictor variables in our analyses, while the couples' 4-year status was used as the dependent variable.

Prediction of Marital Outcomes

A discriminant function analysis was conducted to classify 4-year marital outcomes based on a broad array of self-report variables taken from both spouses shortly after marriage. Discriminant analysis (DA) creates factors similar to those obtained in factor analysis. However, the factors, or discriminant functions, created within discriminant analysis do not simply account for the largest amount of shared variance within a pool of independent variables, as they do in factor analysis. In DA, the discriminant functions correspond specifically to the factors underlying the indepen-

---

[3]Many studies have demonstrated the utility of using the MAT in distinguishing between distressed and nondistressed couples (O'Leary et al., 1989). MAT scores range from 2 to 158 and a cutoff score of 100 has been established as the threshold for identifying distressed couples.

dent variables that can optimally differentiate between the various groups in question. Thus, in DA, the factors created account for discriminating variance between groups as well as shared variance within groups. When the discriminating variables are assessed initially and the outcome groupings are based upon the status of the subjects at a later time point, discriminant analysis serves as a method of prediction. In such a paradigm, DA will generate discriminant functions corresponding to the factors that optimally separate the longitudinal outcome groups using initial data. As a result, those discriminant functions can also be used to optimally predict a subject's subsequent status from their initial data. When applied to the task of identifying couples at greatest risk for marital discord and divorce, the discriminant functions become clinical tools with which a couple's raw data on self-report measures can be transformed into a normative prediction of their subsequent marital outcomes.

Instead of collapsing the outcomes down to a single dimension with only two outcome groups, as has been done previously, the outcomes of married-satisfied, married-dissatisfied, and divorced/separated were predicted simultaneously with the same set of independent variables. This enabled us to determine if the outcome of married-dissatisfied was merely a point along a single dimension between married-satisfied and divorced or if it was in fact a unique outcome, with separate predictors, or risk factors. For our first analysis, we entered self-report measures of communication (CPQ-CC and MCI), measures of marital problem severity (Inventory of Marital Problems, IMP), measures of social support networks (SSQ), measures of divorce attitudes (Divorce Attitudes Scale), measures of commitment (MSI), measures of anger (MAI), and measures of physical violence (CTS, Violence subscale) as discriminating variables.

With this set of variables, the DA yielded two distinct discriminant functions, producing the scatter-plot seen in Figure 15.1. Each dot in the figure represents a couple and the shading of the dot indicates the couple's outcome status after 4 years of marriage. The group centroids shown in the scatter-plot are calculated by entering the group means for each independent variable into the discriminant functions. Thus, the group centroids represent the central tendencies for each outcome group on the two discriminant functions. As the scatter-plot indicates, the first discriminant function primarily separates the intact couples from the dissolved couples. In contrast, the second discriminant function discriminates between the married-satisfied and the married-dissatisfied couples but offers little help at identifying the divorced or separated couples. This suggests that the three outcome groups are not simply points along a single dimension, but that marital satisfaction and marital stability represent unique outcomes within the first 4 years of marriage.

To determine the nature of the factors that distinguish between the different outcomes, we examined the structural coefficients for the two

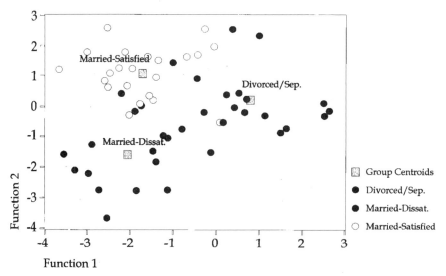

FIGURE 15.1.   Scatter-plot of the couples on the two discriminant functions derived from an extensive set of self-report variables including violence and communication.

discriminant functions (Table 15.2). Structural coefficients represent correlations between the independent variables and the resulting discriminant functions. The patterns seen in these correlations can begin to suggest the nature of the underlying factors involved in distinguishing outcomes. As shown in Table 15.2, although several variables show moderate correlations with the first discriminant function, the self-report variables measuring physical violence show the strongest correlations with this function. This suggests that initial reports of violence or aggression are most salient in predicting marital instability within the first 4 years of marriage. In contrast, measures of communication and severity of marital problems demonstrated the strongest correlations with the second discriminant function. This finding replicates previous results suggesting that initial measures of communication and problem solving predict subsequent marital satisfaction. Surprisingly, the measures of communication showed low to insignificant levels of correlation with the first discriminant function, suggesting that whereas poor communication could lead to low levels of marital satisfaction within the first 4 years of marriage, it does not appear to be as strong of a risk factor for divorce or separation within that initial high-risk period. This finding provides an important qualification to previous results, for although we replicated previous observations that communication is predictive of marital outcomes, our results help to delineate the boundaries of that effect, suggesting that the quality of communication is predictive of marital satisfaction but not necessarily marital stability within the first 4 years of marriage.

TABLE 15.2.   Discriminant analysis using self-report violence variables and an extensive set of self-report variables

Variable[a]	Structural Coefficients for Function 1	Structural Coefficients for Function 2
Violence: Husbands' reports of wives' (CTS)	.565**	-.214
Violence: Wives' reports of their own (CTS)	.281*	-.145
Positive Communication: Wives (CPQ)	-.272*	.237*
Social support: Available to husbands	-.261*	.002
Severity of marital problems: Wives reports	.196	-.057
Violence: Wives' reports of husbands' (CTS)	.163	-.082
Violence: Husbands' reports of their own (CTS)	.151	-.151
Attitudes toward divorce: wives'	.134	.129
Social support: Available to wives	-.069	-.004
Initial commitment: Wives' (MSI)[b]	.069	-.010
Anger: Wives' reports (MAI)	-.054	.036
Positive communication: Husbands' (CPQ)	-.223*	.431**
Severity of marital problems: Husbands' reports	-.007	-.358**
Conflict scale: Husbands' (MCI)	.007	-.318**
Attitudes toward divorce: Husbands'	-.033	.304**
Introspective self-blame scale: Husbands' (MCI)	-.055	-.290*
Introspective self-blame scale: Wives' (MCI)	.052	-.248*
Anger: Husbands' reports (MAI)	.028	-.232*
Conflict scale: Wives' (MCI)	.075	-.220*
Initial commitment: Husbands' (MSI)[b]	.081	-.184
Positive approach scale: Husbands' (MCI)	.059	.138
Positive approach scale: Wives' (MCI)	.047	.079

Note. Correlations between the independent variables used in the discriminant analysis and the resulting discriminant functions or factors.

[a] CTS = Conflict Tactics Scale, MAI = Multidimensional Anger Inventory, CPQ = Communication Patterns Questionnaire, MCI = Marital Coping Inventory, T1 MAT = Initial Marital Adjustment Test, and MSI = Marital Status Inventory.

[b] This scale is scored in such a way that a high value indicates low commitment.

*$p < .05$.

**$p < .01$.

Using the discriminant functions to calculate scores for each couple, it is possible to then predict group membership by determining which centroid they fall closest to on the scatter-plot and assigning them to that group outcome. By doing this with the 56 couples in our sample, we were able to classify the different couples with 84% accuracy (Table 15.3). In this particular analysis, the accuracy of classification was highest for the unstable group, as we were able to classify 89% of the divorced or separated couples correctly. Thus, both the overall level of accuracy as well as our ability to correctly identify those couples at greatest risk for

TABLE 15.3. Accuracy of classification using an extensive set of self-report variables including violence ratings

Actual Outcome Group	Number of Cases	Predicted Group Membership		
		Married-Satisfied	Married-Dissatisfied	Divorced or Separated
Married-Satisfied	22	18 (81.8%)	1	3
Married-Dissatisfied	16	3	13 (81.3%)	0
Divorced or Separated	18	2	0	16 (88.9%)

Percent of Outcomes Accurately Classified: 83.93%

Note. Discriminant scores are calculated for each couple by entering their data into the discriminant functions. Group membership is then predicted based upon where those discriminant scores place the couple with respect to the group centroids.

divorce compare favorably with previous studies. These results are even more striking given that our analyses were simultaneously predicting between three separate outcomes rather than between dichotomous outcome groups, thereby tripling the number of possible errors in prediction. Even with this increased chance for errors in prediction, the discriminant functions from this analysis predicted with comparable levels of accuracy.

A longitudinal study of aggression in early marriage (O'Leary, Malone, & Tyree, 1994) found that psychological aggression was the strongest predictor of physical aggression. In fact, their structural equation modeling results suggested that most of the other risk factors contributed to physical aggression through the construct of psychological aggression. This suggests that psychological aggression could simply represent an early stage of physical aggression. Thus, measures of psychological aggression could actually serve as more sensitive measures of low-level physical aggression. To test this hypothesis, we repeated the discriminant analysis with the comprehensive set of self-report variables using the couples' scores on the full CTS rather than just their scores on the physical violence items, thus including a measure of psychological aggression. Consistent with the hypotheses of O'Leary et al. (1994) we found that by using the more sensitive or complete measure of aggression, our levels of classification rose from 84% to 91% overall and from 89% to 100% for divorced or separated couples. This marked increase in accuracy of classification could result from an increased ability to identify couples who may not have been physically violent initially but will become violent as evidenced by their high levels of reported psychological violence.

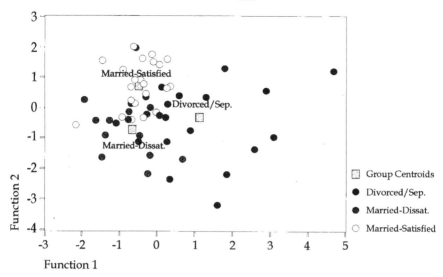

FIGURE 15.2. Scatter-plot of the couples on the two discriminant functions derived from core communication measures and violence ratings.

The foregoing discriminant analysis directly compared the predictive validities of an extensive set of predictor variables identified by previous work, suggesting that the variables of communication and aggression were most predictive of marital outcomes. To further analyze the predictive validities of these two constructs, a second discriminant analysis was performed using self-report measures of communication (CPQ-CC subscale; MCI, Conflict subscale) and aggression (CTS, Violence subscale; MAI) as the sole predictor variables. As seen in Figure 15.2, reducing the number of predictor variables by half resulted in less distinct separation between the various outcome groups. However, even with this reduced set of predictor variables, the groups form distinct clusters on the two discriminant functions, where the first discriminant function predicts stability while the second discriminant function predicts marital satisfaction. As in the prior analysis, the structural coefficients for these discriminant functions would suggest that measures of violence correlate most strongly with the first discriminant function, thus predicting marital stability (Table 15.4). In contrast, both husbands' and wives' reports of communication (CPQ-CC and MCI) correlate strongly with the second discriminant function, suggesting that measures of communication predict marital satisfaction within the first 4 years of marriage.

Using the discriminant functions resulting from this analysis to predict group membership within our sample, we were able to correctly classify 73% of the couples (Table 15.5). Whereas the discriminant analysis using

TABLE 15.4. Discriminant analysis using self-report variables measuring communication and violence

Variable[a]	Structural Coefficients for Function 1	Structural Coefficients for Function 2
Violence: Husbands' reports of wives' (CTS)	.757**	-.326**
Violence: Wives' reports of their own (CTS)	.359**	-.243*
Violence: Wives' reports of husbands' (CTS)	.205	-.123
Anger: Wives' reports (MAI)	-.053	.020
Positive communication: Husbands' (CPQ-CC)	-.091	.781**
Conflict scale: Husbands' (MCI)	-.069	-.592**
Positive communication: Wives (CPQ-CC)	-.293**	.443**
Conflict scale: Wives' (MCI)	-.009	-.415**
Anger: Husbands' reports (MAI)	-.102	-.402**
Violence: Husbands' reports (CTS)	.128	-.186

Note. Structural coefficients are correlations between the independent variables used in the discriminant analysis and the resulting discriminant functions or factors. The patterns of correlations in these coefficients help identify which factors best discriminate between the various outcome groups.

[a] CTS = Conflict Tactics Scale; MAI = Multidimensional Anger Inventory; CPQ-CC = Communication Patterns Questionnaire, Constructive Communication subscale; MCI = Marital Coping Inventory.

*p < .05.

**p < .01.

an extensive set of predictor variables gave an 84% overall level of accuracy, reducing the discriminant variables down to communication and aggression alone resulted in only a moderate loss of accuracy, still predicting nearly 3 in 4 of the outcomes correctly. This would suggest that the constructs of communication and aggression account for a majority of the variance in predicting marital outcomes.[4] Thus, these findings lend

---

[4]Initial marital satisfaction can also predict subsequent marital satisfaction. To examine its effect on our analyses we performed a second set of discriminant analyses entering initial marital satisfaction as an additional predictor variable. Initial marital satisfaction did in fact load on the discriminant functions predicting subsequent marital satisfaction. However, the pattern of structural coefficients for the other variables remained the same in both the DA using the extensive set of predictor variables and the DA using the communication and violence variables, suggesting that the factors of communication and violence were not merely artifacts of initial marital satisfaction. More importantly, the addition of initial marital satisfaction as a predictor variable did not produce any increase in the accuracy of prediction. This suggests that the outcome variance associated with initial marital satisfaction was already accounted for by our factors of communication and violence. Thus, our results seem to be independent of the contribution of initial marital satisfaction as a predictor variable (see Rogge & Bradbury, in press, for further discussion).

TABLE 15.5. Accuracy of classification using self-report variables measuring communication and violence

Actual Outcome Group	Number of Cases	Predicted Group Membership		
		Married-Satisfied	Married-Dissatisfied	Divorced or Separated
Married-Satisfied	22	17 (77.3%)	5	0
Married-Dissatisfied	16	3	12 (75.0%)	1
Divorced/Separated	18	3	3	12 (66.7%)
Percent of Outcomes Accurately Classified: 73.21%				

Note. Discriminant scores are calculated for each couple by entering their data into the discriminant functions. Group membership is then predicted based upon where those discriminant scores place the couple with respect to the group centroids.

additional support to the interpretation that communication and violence are key factors predicting marital satisfaction and marital stability, respectively.

To graphically depict the importance of violence in these analyses, Figure 15.3 illustrates the distributions observed for the different outcome groups when the scatter-plot is collapsed down to the communication axis, removing violence completely. While the outcomes of married-satisfied (white) and married-dissatisfied (striped) show clear separation on the communication axis, the couples who will later go on to separate or divorce (grey) are clearly distributed across the entire range of the communication function. Thus, some of the couples who will go on to divorce or separate actually appear to be very effective communicators. Without assessing for violence, it would be difficult if not impossible to identify these couples with communication measures alone.

In sum, the results of the discriminant analyses using self-report indices as predictor variables suggest that the constructs of aggression and communication account for the majority of the variance in prediction. This suggests that the broad array of predictor variables identified within previous studies can be simplified down to a parsimonious model in which violence predicts divorce within the first 4 years of marriage, whereas communication predicts marital satisfaction within that same period.

Having clarified the specific roles of aggression and communication in predicting marital outcomes, we turned next to the issue of measuring communication with objective ratings of problem-solving behavior as opposed to self-report questionnaires. To determine if there was any predictive advantage to the use of objective ratings of behavior, we performed

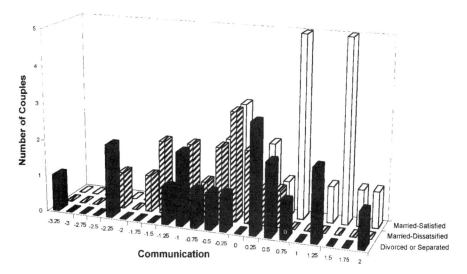

FIGURE 15.3.   Histogram showing distribution of outcome groups on communication function.

a discriminant analysis using measures of aggression (CTS, Violence subscale; MAI) and measures of expressed affect in problem-solving interactions (SPAFF), essentially replacing the self-report measures of communication with objective-behavioral measures. This discriminant analysis generated a scatter-plot virtually identical to the one obtained from the previous DA, where the first discriminant function separated stable from unstable marriages and the second discriminant function separated the married couples who were satisfied from those who were dissatisfied (Rogge & Bradbury, in press). Once again, the structural coefficients indicated that aggression was strongly correlated with the first discriminant function, suggesting that it is predictive of marital stability (Table 15.6) in contrast to the behavioral codes that correlated with the second discriminant function, predicting marital satisfaction. The pattern of structural coefficients generated by this discriminant analysis suggests that the SPAFF codes of expressed affect are accounting for the same predictive variance that the self-report measures of communication covered in the previous analyses. Thus, regardless of the method used to collect measures of communication and problem-solving behavior, the construct of communication appears to operate in a consistent manner in all of our analyses.

With this combination of self-report aggression measures and behavioral communication codes, we were able to classify outcomes with 73% accuracy (Table 15.7), giving the same level of accuracy found in the discriminant analysis using only self-report aggression and communication

TABLE 15.6.   Discriminant analysis using core behavioral and self-report violence variables

Variable[a]	Structural Coefficients for Function 1	Structural Coefficients for Function 2
Violence: Husbands' reports of wives' (CTS)	.825**	.077
Violence: Wives' reports of their own (CTS)	.430**	-.033
Violence: Wives' reports of husbands' (CTS)	.239*	-.007
Violence: Husbands' reports of their own (CTS)	-.197	-.090
Anger: Wives' reports (MAI)	-.056	-.008
Anger: Wives' expressions (SPAFF)	.390**	-.465**
Humor: Husbands' expressions (SPAFF)	-.101	.457**
Anger: Husbands' reports (MAI)	.085	-.361**
Contempt: Wives' expressions (SPAFF)	-.061	-.357**
Humor: Wives' expressions (SPAFF)	.055	.261*
Anger: Husbands' expressions (SPAFF)	.172	-.241*
Contempt: Husbands' expressions (SPAFF)	.116	-.237*

Note. Structural coefficients are correlations between the independent variables used in the discriminant analysis and the resulting discriminant functions or factors. The patterns of correlations in these coefficients help identify which factors best discriminate between the various outcome groups.

[a] CTS = Conflict Tactics Scale, MAI = Multidimensional Anger Inventory, SPAFF = Specific Affect Coding System.

*p < .05.

**p < .01.

measures. However, the ability to identify the couples at risk for divorce or separation within the sample was notably lower in this analysis (61%). This would suggest that objective-behavioral measures of communication do not offer a predictive advantage over self-report measures.[5]

☐ Summary and Conclusions

A discriminant analysis using an extensive set of self-report measures suggested a parsimonious model in which aggression predicts divorce

---

[5]When a larger number of SPAFF behavioral codes were entered into the discriminant analysis (including anger, contempt, whining, sadness, anxiety, humor, interest, and affection) the pattern of structural coefficients remained the same and the level of accuracy in the prediction rose to 86%, resembling the levels of accuracy attained with all of the self-report variables. Thus, when comparable numbers of either self-report or behavioral variables are used, similar levels of prediction are attained, indicating no relative predictive advantage for behavioral data.

TABLE 15.7. Accuracy of classification using core behavioral codes and self-report violence variables

Actual Outcome Group	Number of Cases	Predicted Group Membership		
		Married-Satisfied	Married-Dissatisfied	Divorced or Separated
Married-Satisfied	22	17 (86.4%)	2	1
Married-Dissatisfied	16	5	11 (68.8%)	0
Divorced/Separated	18	5	2	11 (61.1%)

Percent of Outcomes Accurately Classified: 73.21%

Note. Discriminant scores are calculated for each couple by entering their data into the discriminant functions. Group membership is then predicted based upon where those discriminant scores place the couple with respect to the group centroids.

within the first 4 years of marriage, whereas communication predicts marital satisfaction among the couples who remain married. When the discriminant analysis was repeated using only aggression and communication measures, a similar pattern of results was obtained. Furthermore, in reducing the number of predictor variables by more than half within the second discriminant analysis, the level of accuracy in prediction only fell from 84% to 73%, suggesting that violence and communication account for the majority of the outcome variance in these analyses. Finally, the discriminant analysis was repeated using behavioral measures of communication in place of self-report measures. The behavioral measures not only functioned in a manner identical to the self-report measures of communication, but the discriminant analysis using the behavioral data also gave comparable levels of prediction. Taken together, our results offer a coherent and simple synthesis and extension of previous findings in which aggression places couples at greatest risk for divorce in the first 4 years, whereas poor communication places couples who remain married at greatest risk for marital discord.

These findings suggest a number of practical recommendations for the task of preventing adverse marital outcomes and for the premarital intervention programs striving toward that end. First, our findings suggest that with only a small set of questionnaires it appears to be possible to identify couples at risk for marital discord and instability with reasonably high levels of accuracy. Thus, these discriminant analyses could be used as clinical tools for professionals working with couples planning marriage. A couple's raw data could be entered into the discriminant functions to generate a normative prediction of their 4-year outcome in comparison to the current sample. The couple's resulting discriminant scores could then be plotted within the scatter-plots generated by our sample to give the couple visual feedback. These discriminant functions would enable the professionals working with such a couple to determine both their level of risk for negative marital outcomes and their specific therapeutic needs (e.g., communication training or violence prevention). A number of limitations (see the next section) preclude our recommending this procedure at present, but applications of this sort are likely to emerge in the next several years. Second, by beginning with an extensive set of predictor variables and then directly measuring their predictive validities, our results were able to clarify the factors important for predicting marital outcomes from the diverse set of potential candidates offered by prior studies. When combined with the practical refinements over previous studies, this enables us to assert with greater certainty that poor communication and violence represent the two factors most salient in the prediction of marital discord and divorce, respectively. These findings would suggest that premarital interventions could focus on these two dimensions in determining risk and assessing couples' needs. Third, our results would suggest that it may be unnecessary to obtain behavioral measures of couples' communication to accurately predict their marital outcomes. In fact, the behavioral measures of communication failed to demonstrate any predictive advantage over self-report measures of communication, giving identical levels of accuracy in prediction. As behavioral data are typically expensive to collect, our results suggest that self-report measures of communication offer a comparable, low-cost alternative. Of course, behavioral observation will probably prove to be invaluable in identifying specific behavioral antecedents to marital dysfunction, in general and for any particular couple seeking to enhance their behavioral repertoire. Fourth, the discriminant analyses conducted with this sample suggest that marital quality and marital stability represent unique outcome dimensions with different risk factors. Previous studies made the implicit assumption that marital outcomes fell along a single dimension: A couple becomes dissatisfied and then gets divorced. Our results would suggest that growing unhappy within the first 4 years and getting divorced or separated may be two very different things. Although it is important for premarital interventions to work on improving and maintaining marital quality, it is equally important for them to address the factors leading to marital instability. Finally, our results suggest that the seeds of divorce and marital instability within the first 4 years of marriage lie predominantly within a couple's aggressive behavior toward one another and far less within any poor communication that might exist. Thus it would seem that in determining marital stability within that initial high-risk period, it matters more how the couple respond to one another in the heat of anger and less how they are able to communicate about their disagreements subsequently. This is exemplified by some of the divorced couples in our study, who initially reported both high-quality communication and high levels of violence and yet went on to divorce within the first 4 years. Accordingly, it seems appropriate to view communication and aggression as distinct dimensions with unique contributions to marital outcomes. We do not mean to imply that communication is not an important factor in marriage; however, our results would indicate that aggression, particularly physical violence, is far more damaging to the stability of a marriage than poor communication within this early high-risk period of 4 years. This would suggest that premarital intervention programs should both assess for violence using a standard measure like the CTS, and then add in a violence prevention module to their program in order to intervene with any couples who report current violence in their relationships.

Application to the Couple at Risk

Turning to the case of Ben and Alyssa, the summary presented in the introductory chapter of this book paints a picture of a couple who, despite their strong feelings for one another, are struggling with how to effectively discuss and resolve problems in their relationship. After 6 years of marriage, they find themselves confronted with the prospect of a second child after a difficult initial transition to parenthood, Ben's unspoken frustration and disappointment with work, and Alyssa's newfound religious life. Both Ben and Alyssa are reluctant to openly discuss these matters and share their true feelings and concerns, for fear of hurting each other or being hurt. However, by not sharing their feelings about these important topics, they are gradually growing apart and becoming strangers. Thus, Ben and Alyssa's seemingly strong marriage is gradually being eroded by their ineffective methods of handling problems that arise from naturally occurring differences of opinion.

This case helps to clarify the distinct roles of aggression and communication in marriage suggested by our analyses. If Ben and Alyssa had been participants in our study as newlyweds, they probably would have failed to demonstrate any significant risk for divorce within the first 4 years of marriage. They were not described as physically aggressive, nor were their discussions described as angry and hostile. However, Ben and Alyssa's tendencies to avoid discussing sensitive topics and their inexperience at handling sensitive issues would probably have come out on the self-report questionnaires and in the audiotaped problem discussions. There is a good chance that Ben and Alyssa would have elected to discuss Alyssa's parents in their problem discussion. This would most likely have sparked many of the feelings from the first 4-hour discussion of their wedding plans, and the discussion could easily have turned into a rather heated exchange. A discussion marked by negative emotions would have placed them at risk for growing dissatisfied over the first 4 years of marriage. Thus, Ben and Alyssa would have presented little risk for divorce in the early stages of marriage, but their poorly developed communication skills place them at a long-term risk for marital discord and possibly divorce. Our findings would suggest that the effects of aggression are relatively immediate and devastating. However, communication is more of a latent risk factor that does not threaten relationships until life confronts couples with struggles and challenges that they must navigate together.

Alternately, Ben and Alyssa may have demonstrated very little risk for any negative outcomes. Their communication deficits may have been subtle enough that we would not have been able to identify the risk that they would pose 6 years later. In order to be able to identify varying levels of risk, it may be necessary to include other factors in the analyses such as external interference (Alyssa's parents) and social support. It is also important to note that Ben and Alyssa may simply not fit in this model. The analyses presented focused on the central tendencies of the outcome groups and they provide information that is true for the majority of marriages, but not for all marriages.

Limitations of the Research

The findings presented here offer clear implications for the prevention of marital discord and divorce, yet it is important to also note a number of limitations within the present study. First, the sample used in these analyses was small, particularly for the type of multivariate analyses that were performed. Multivariate techniques like discriminant analysis capitalize on unique or unusual variance within a sample, automatically assuming that the variance is not spurious but in fact comes from some underlying factor. When working with large samples, this is a reasonable assumption. However, as the sample size gets smaller, it becomes easier for spurious, random variance to take on undue significance within these multivariate techniques, creating effects where none exist. Consequently, in this paper, we focused primarily on the general trends that could be observed across many different discriminant analyses, rather than on the intricate details of any single analysis in order to avoid analyzing what may be spurious fluctuations. Even with that precaution, the results presented here should be viewed as exploratory and require replication and cross-validation with a larger sample. Second, the objective behavioral variables used do not account for all of the behavioral variance within the couple's conflict interactions. As a result, the finding that the behavioral variables contained levels of predictive validity only comparable to those seen with self-report variables applies only to the constellation of behavioral variables tested. It could be argued that a behavioral coding system that accounts for a broader range of behavioral variance would yield higher levels of prediction. However, this argument is not unique to behavioral measures and could apply to the self-report measures of communication as well. Third, the prediction results made use of data exclusively from newlywed couples in their first marriages, and those analyses were only predicting marital outcomes in the first 4 years. It is possible that predictors of marital discord and divorce could change over time, so that the risk factors leading to divorce after 10 years could be very different from the risk factors that led to divorce within the first 4 years. This would suggest that our findings may only be valid for couples in the early stages of their marriages. Additionally, couples may systematically change the manner in which they respond to questionnaires regarding their relationship over the course of their marriage. If this were the case, it would be inappropriate to enter data from established couples into discriminant functions derived from newlywed data. Even data from a couple 1 year into their marriage may already be inappropriate to enter into discriminant functions developed with data from less than 6 months of marriage. Thus, although our results suggest that among newlyweds violence is a salient predictor of marital stability, this may not be the case for older couples. These arguments raise an additional caveat for applying the discriminant analyses to premarital couples, and we do not know how engaged couples who never marry would fit into our predictive model.

Directions for Future Research

The present study served to clarify the role of communication and violence in predicting marital satisfaction and stability. However, more work remains to be done in order to determine how to effectively prevent negative marital outcomes. To begin, the results of this study need to be replicated with a second sample of newlyweds in order to verify their true predictive validity. This work is currently underway in a separate cohort of 172 newlywed couples who are now 3 years into their marriages. In addition, although the present study focused on 4-year outcomes to determine factors underlying marital dysfunction within that initial high-risk period, it will be important to also study the later stages of marriage in order to determine which factors are most salient in long-term marital outcomes. Finally, although identifying risk factors represents an important first step in preventing negative outcomes, more research needs to be done in order to determine how best to address the various risk factors. For example, through the careful analysis of covariates of aggression in predicting marital outcomes, it would be possible not only to refine our predictions further, but also to identify the mechanisms through which it affects marital stability. Analyses of this sort would thereby suggest specific methods of intervention that would most directly address the needs of couples currently experiencing aggression. In conclusion, whereas the current analyses appear to provide an important step forward in understanding the antecedents of marital dysfunction, they clearly serve as a point of departure from which future studies can extend in order to determine how best to help these couples that can now be identified as at risk for discord or divorce.

☐ Contact References

Correspondence concerning this article should be addressed to Ronald D. Rogge or Thomas N. Bradbury, Department of Psychology, UCLA, 405 Hilgard Avenue, Los Angeles, CA 90095-1563. Electronic mail may be sent to ronrogge@ucla.edu or to bradbury@psych.ucla.edu. Information may also be obtained from the UCLA Newlywed Project website at http://www.psych.ucla.edu/resources/newed/

☐ References

Bowman, M. L. (1990). Coping efforts and marital satisfaction: Measuring marital coping and its correlates. *Journal of Marriage and the Family, 52,* 463–474.

Buehlman, K. T., Gottman, J. M., & Katz, L. F. (1992). How a couple views their past predicts their future: Predicting divorce from an oral history interview. *Journal of Family Psychology, 5,* 295–318.

Christensen, A., & Sullaway, M. (1984). *Communication patterns questionnaire.* Unpublished manuscript, University of California at Los Angeles.

Cohan, C. L., & Bradbury, T. N. (1994). Assessing responses to recurring problems in marriage: Evaluation of the Marital Coping Inventory. *Psychological Assessment, 6,* 191–200.

Fowers, B. J., & Olson, D. H. (1986). Predicting marital success with PREPARE: A predictive validity study. *Journal of Marital and Family Therapy, 12,* 403–413.

Geiss, S. K., & O'Leary, K. D. (1981). Therapist ratings of frequency and severity of marital problems: Implications for research. *Journal of Marital and Family Therapy, 7,* 515–520.

Gottman, J. M. (1994). *What predicts divorce? The relationship between marital processes and marital outcomes.* Hillsdale, NJ: Lawrence Erlbaum Associates.

Gottman, J. M. (1988). *Specific affect coding system.* Unpublished manuscript, University of Washington at Seattle.

Gottman, J. M., & Krokoff, L. J. (1989). Marital interaction and satisfaction: A longitudinal view. *Journal of Consulting and Clinical Psychology, 57,* 47–52.

Hill, C. T., & Peplau, L. A. (1998). Premarital predictors of relationship outcomes: A 15-

year follow-up of the Boston Couples Study. In T. N. Bradbury (Ed.), *The developmental course of marital dysfunction* (pp. 237–278). Cambridge, UK: Cambridge University Press.

Jacobson, N. S., & Addis, M. E. (1993). Research on couples and couple therapy: What do we know? Where are we going? Special Section: Couples and couple therapy. *Journal of Consulting and Clinical Psychology, 61,* 85–93.

Karney, B. R., & Bradbury, T. N. (1997). Neuroticism, marital interaction, and the trajectory of marital satisfaction. *Journal of Personality and Social Psychology, 72.*

Karney, B. R., & Bradbury, T. N. (1995). The longitudinal course of marital quality and stability: A review of theory, method, and research. *Psychological Bulletin, 118,* 3–34.

Karney, B. R., Davila, J., Cohan, C. L., Sullivan, K. T., Johnson, M. D., & Bradbury, T. N. (1995). An empirical investigation of sampling strategies in marital research. *Journal of Marriage and the Family, 57,* 909–920.

Kelly, E. L., & Conley, J. J. (1987). Personality and compatibility: A prospective analysis of marital stability and marital satisfaction. *Journal of Personality and Social Psychology, 52,* 27–40.

Kurdek, L. A. (1993). Predicting marital dissolution: A 5-year prospective longitudinal study of newlywed couples. *Journal of Personality and Social Psychology, 64,* 221–242.

Larsen, A. S., & Olson, D. H. (1989). Predicting marital satisfaction using PREPARE: A replication study. *Journal of Marital and Family Therapy, 15,* 311–322.

Lindahl, K., Clements, M., & Markman, H. (1998). The development of marriage: A nine-year perspective. In T. N. Bradbury (Ed.), *The developmental course of marital dysfunction* (pp. 205–236). Cambridge, UK: Cambridge University Press.

Locke, H. J., & Wallace, K. M. (1959). Short marital adjustment and prediction tests: Their reliability and validity. *Marriage and Family Living, 21,* 251–255.

National Center for Health Statistics. (1987). Advance Report of Final Marriage Statistics, 1987. *Monthly Vital Statistics Report, 38,* Supplement. Hyattsville, MD: Author.

O'Leary, K. D., Barling, J., Arias, I., & Rosenbaum, A. (1989). Prevalence and stability of physical aggression between spouses: A longitudinal analysis. *Journal of Consulting and Clinical Psychology, 57,* 263–268.

O'Leary, K. D., Malone, J., & Tyree, A. (1994). Physical aggression in early marriage: Prerelationship and relationship effects. *Journal of Consulting and Clinical Psychology, 62,* 594–602.

Pasch, L. A., & Bradbury, T. N. (1998). Social support, conflict, and the development of marital dysfunction. *Journal of Consulting and Clinical Psychology, 66,* 219–230.

Rogge, R. D., & Bradbury, T. N. (in press). Till violence does us part: The differing roles of communication and aggression in predicting adverse marital outcomes. *Journal of Consulting and Clinical Psychology, 67.*

Sarason, I. G., Sarason, B. R., Shearin, E. N., & Pierce, G. R. (1987). A brief measure of social support: Practical and theoretical implications. *Journal of Social and Personal Relationships, 4,* 497–510.

Siegel, J. M. (1986). The Multidimensional Anger Inventory. *Journal of Personality & Social Psychology, 51,* 191–200.

Straus, M. A. (1979). Measuring intrafamily conflict and violence: The Conflict Tactics (CT) scales. *Journal of Marriage and the Family, 41,* 75–86.

Sullivan, K. T., & Bradbury, T. N. (1997). Are premarital prevention programs reaching couples at risk for marital dysfunction? *Journal of Consulting and Clinical Psychology, 65,* 24–30.

Veroff, J. (1988). *Divorce Attitudes Scale.* Unpublished Measure. Ann Arbor: University of Michigan.

Weiss, R. L., & Cerreto, M. C. (1980). The marital status inventory: Development of a measure of dissolution potential. *American Journal of Family Therapy, 8,* 80–85.

Williams, L., & Jurich, J. (1995). Predicting marital success after five years: Assessing the predictive validity of FOCCUS. *Journal of Marital and Family Therapy, 21,* 141–153.

16

CHAPTER

Adrian B. Kelly, M.Clin.Psych.
Frank D. Fincham, Ph.D.

Preventing Marital Distress: What Does Research Offer?

☐ Introduction

Divorce rates in Western countries have focused attention on the need to support couples experiencing marital problems. Unfortunately, only about half the couples who receive marital therapy benefit from it and few experience long-term improvement in their relationship (Jacobson & Addis, 1993). But even if success rates improved dramatically, the ubiquity of marital discord makes it unlikely that marital therapy will ever be able to meet the need for services. Largely in response to these problems, a variety of marital prevention and enrichment programs have been developed. The goal of such programs is to prepare couples for future problems and resolve any existing marital problems before they become significant (Coie et. al, 1993; Muehrer, Moscicki, & Koretz, 1993).

In view of their significance for public health, it is important to evaluate the effectiveness of programs designed to prevent marital problems. This can only be done by systematic research. However, the contribution of research to the area of prevention is not limited to program evaluation. Research findings on marriage can also inform the content and delivery of prevention programs. For example, research on the longitudinal development of marital relationships can be used to ensure that programs target characteristics of marriage that influence long-term outcome. Incorporating research findings into prevention programs is clearly a continual process of monitoring the empirical marital literature and refining prevention programs to best represent what we know about marriage.

The aim of this chapter is to illustrate the contribution of research to the prevention of marital problems. The chapter is divided into two parts. In the first, we identify programs that have been subject to empirical study and evaluate their efficacy. The second part examines the extent to which the content and evaluation of existing programs are informed by current knowledge of marriage and then offers a broader perspective on prevention programs informed by research that has had little impact on the prevention literature. We end with a summary of the main themes of the chapter.

☐ The Efficacy of Prevention Programs

A variety of providers and approaches have been used in attempts to prevent marital problems. The clergy and church-affiliated organizations are perhaps the most extensive providers of marriage preparation courses (Markman, Floyd, Stanley, & Lewis, 1986). Such services are typically limited to educating couples about the importance of maintaining religious practices in the home, and providing guidance and advice about current problems or anticipated future problems as expressed by the couple. While such services are the most widely available, they vary widely in program content, duration (from one to several sessions), and format (one couple vs. group interventions), and there is little empirical evaluation of these programs beyond their immediate effects (Giblin, Sprenkle, & Sheehan, 1985).

Other programs are more closely linked to the professional literature on marriage. For example, Relationship Enhancement interventions (Guerney, Brock, & Coufal, 1986) are a form of intervention that has been effectively used with newlywed couples (Avery, Ridley, Leslie, & Milholland, 1980) and in established marriages (e.g., Brock & Joanning, 1983). These interventions focus on enhancing the positive aspects of relationships, rather than removing or preventing marital pathology (Guerney et al., 1986). Such programs probably serve to prevent marital distress indirectly, through enhancing marital quality, and so are not strictly preventive approaches.

The most widely studied programs with an exclusive preventive focus are those based on behavioral marital theory. The essential principle of this approach is that spouses respond to their partners according to the contingencies experienced; happy relationships are assumed to occur when interactions are experienced as rewarding overall, and unhappy relationships are assumed to result from a history of interactions experienced as aversive. Behaviorally based programs therefore aim to maximize the likelihood that marital interactions will stay positively reinforcing and minimally aversive.

A prototypical example of behavioral approaches is the Premarital Relationship Enhancement Program (PREP; Markman et al., 1986). PREP is based on the idea that there are several developmental tasks that couples need to achieve together (Markman et al., 1986), including the need to (a) develop and engage in constructive communication and conflict resolution skills, (b) develop realistic attitudes and expectations regarding marriage, (c) develop interactions that satisfy the basic emotional and psychological needs of each partner, (d) become primary sources of gratification and anxiety reduction, (e) develop constructive mechanisms for regulating enmeshment and independence, and (f) develop skills of adaptation to changes within the relationship. The essential theme is that couples need to develop skills to manage problems that may erode marital quality. In practice, PREP therefore consists of therapy techniques such as training in speaker and listener skills, expressing negative feelings and managing conflict, problem solving, identifying and changing unrealistic expectations and relationship beliefs, and sexual enhancement.

The emphasis of PREP is on the future of the relationship, rather than directly addressing current problems. It therefore differs in an important way from a behavioral analysis of marriage which emphasizes the learning history of spouses prior to and during the relationship. PREP minimizes attention to learned history prior to the relationship, as it does not emphasize the differences between people entering marriage that potentially cause problems, but the way these differences are handled. Markman's PREP program therefore represents a rather specialized form of the potential range of behaviorally based prevention program content.

Short-Term Efficacy of Marriage Preparation Programs

Many studies have evaluated the short-term benefits of preparation programs. Giblin et al. (1986) conducted a meta-analysis of 85 prevention and enrichment programs that varied across a range of dimensions, such as content (e.g., provision of manuals, activities), format (group vs. individual couple), duration (from 2 to 36 hours contact time), orientation (e.g., communication focused, discussion based, religious programs, behavior exchange focused), subject characteristics (e.g., mild marital distress or happy), outcome measures (observed behavior vs. self-report) and follow-up (from 2 to 52 weeks postintervention). Because of this variability, it is difficult to delineate clearly effects associated with dependent variables of interest.

Across all studies, the average participant improved from pretest to posttest more than did 67% of those in corresponding control groups (average effect size of .44, with a 95% confidence interval ranging from .79 to .48). This result indicates a modest increase of 17% improvement compared to an ineffective treatment (where the average participant is better off than 50% of the controls). For premarital couples the average effect size across 23 program types (assessed in 43 studies) was .53. When comparing these effects to the average of .85 found for psychotherapy studies (Smith, Glass, & Miller, 1980), the impact of these programs appears modest.

In this meta-analysis, a closer examination of different types of programs revealed that Relationship Enhancement programs demonstrated the largest effect sizes, couple communication programs and marriage encounter groups showed intermediate effect sizes, and attention placebo and discussion groups showed the smallest effect sizes. This meta-analysis includes studies using couples who were mildly maritally distressed. Because maritally distressed couples may show more significant short-term change (given that there is more room for immediate change), and higher percentages of maritally distressed couples were present in Relationship Enhancement studies, it is unclear whether overall effect sizes were inflated in Relationship Enhancement programs. Another finding of this meta-analysis was that stronger effects were observed for measures which used behavioral observation compared to self-report measures.

Consistent with Giblin et al.'s (1986) findings, Markman and colleagues show that PREP leads to short-term treatment gains. Although no significant differences were found immediately following the program, a 1-year follow-up showed that PREP couples exhibited more positive and fewer negative communication skills and higher marital satisfaction (Markman, Jamieson, & Floyd, 1983) than couples who had not completed the program.

Even though they used the same format and experimental design as Markman and colleagues (1983), Van Widenfelt, Hosman, Schaap, and Van Der Staak (1996) found no significant short-term gains using a Dutch version of PREP that included an additional session on family-of-origin issues. An important difference that may account for this disparity in findings was the selection of couples who were currently mildly maritally distressed and included at least one partner who had experienced parental divorce (two risk factors for marital difficulties identified by Karney & Bradbury, 1995). Postintervention effects were first assessed approximately 6 months after completing the intervention, and no significant differences in overall marital quality between treatment and control groups were observed at this time or at a later follow-up 2 years after beginning the intervention. In fact, at the first follow-up, couples who had participated in the program had higher ratings of problem intensity than control couples, a greater number of negative psychological symptoms, and higher dissatisfaction with life.

The different findings obtained in Markman et al.'s (1983) and Van Widenfelt et al.'s (1996) research may also be due to the differences in outcome measures used. Markman and colleagues utilized observational measures, whereas Van Widenfelt and colleagues relied on self-report measures of outcome (observations were conducted before the intervention, but no observational data is presented). Perhaps observational data are more sensitive to change in couples where marital distress is generally not present, a hypothesis supported by Giblin et al.'s (1985) meta-analytic study (see a later section for a discussion of outcome measures).

Long-Term Efficacy of Marriage Preparation Programs

More important than short-term outcome is whether prevention programs produce lasting effects. The only study that has evaluated long-term benefits focuses on PREP. Markman, Floyd, Stanley, and Storaasli, (1988) have shown that at a 3-year follow-up, couples receiving PREP reported significantly higher sexual satisfaction, less intense marital problems, and higher relationship satisfaction than control couples. Five years after the intervention, couples receiving treatment reported more positive and fewer negative communication skills and less marital violence than control couples (Markman, Renick, Floyd, Stanley, & Clements, 1993). Detailed 12-year follow-up results are forthcoming, but preliminary analyses show that the PREP group had lower rates of divorce and separation than control groups, though the difference in rates was not statistically significant (19% for PREP couples, 28% for controls; Stanley, Markman, St. Peters, & Leber, 1995).

What degree of confidence can we have in the conclusion that these sorts of preparative interventions impact skills important to the maintenance of satisfying relationships? Unfortunately, the above PREP evaluations lacked an attention-only control condition, making it unclear whether the interventions used were responsible for the effects, or whether the effects were due to some general attention factor. Nevertheless, preliminary findings suggest that PREP programs result in added postintervention gain compared to premarital interventions commonly offered by religious institutions (Renick, Blumberg, & Markman, 1992; Blumberg, 1991) and to information-only control groups (Behrens & Halford, 1994). Replication using longer follow-ups and larger samples is needed before firm conclusions about the added efficacy of PREP can be made. Also, several researchers have raised questions about the selection biases that occur in these programs, and question whether they reach couples at high risk of marital deterioration. Perhaps such couples would have had successful marriages regardless of their participation in a prevention program (Sullivan & Bradbury, 1996).

Unfortunately, there is little evidence to suggest that the samples used in Markman et al.'s (1993) study were at risk. In fact, recent evidence suggests that the consumers of prevention programs may be couples who are likely to have successful marriages even without an early marital intervention. Sullivan and Bradbury (1996) compared community samples of newlywed couples who received premarital counseling with those who did not and found that participating couples were not at greater risk for marital difficulties. In some cases, participating husbands were at significantly lower risk for marital difficulties than husbands who did not participate. It appears that the treatment effects of evaluated prevention programs are confounded by the inclusion of both low- and high-risk couples in samples.

Should we expect short marriage preparation courses to have such long-lasting effects? Markman and colleagues (1993) report that the effects of PREP appeared to be weakening by five years after the intervention. Long-term effects make several assumptions about how couples retain and implement preventive strategies. Uncovering these assumptions and subjecting them to empirical evaluation is critical to improving the efficacy of prevention programs, and we therefore briefly discuss processes assumed to produce durable treatment changes.

Uncovering Processes Assumed to Produce Durable Treatment Effects

Couples are likely to experience changes in their circumstances over time (children are born, careers and social networks are likely to change, and so on). When spouses need to implement the skills taught in marital prevention programs, they may be experiencing stressors that were not present when the skills were initially acquired. Do the skills learned in a short marriage preparation course produce lasting changes to couple interactions? If so, there are several unresolved issues regarding how couples utilize the skills and information from such programs.

We might hypothesize that partners consciously retrieve and implement strategies taught in marital preparation courses. Alternatively, we might assume that they do not consciously retrieve earlier learned strategies because once these strategies replace ineffective skills, they become overlearned and continue, not so much because they result in external reinforcement, but because they are more effective and efficient. From this perspective, couples acquire skills during marital preparation that are naturally reinforced and become part of their behavioral repertoire for dealing with stress or problems. So, by the time long-term follow-ups occur, couples may no longer consciously retrieve strategies initiated through marriage preparation. It would be helpful to examine the retrieval of course content in evaluating the long-term impact of marriage preparation. If the later use of skills depends on retrieval of program content, then steps can be taken to enhance the memorability of program material (e.g., through the use of mnemonics). However, if skill use is not associated with recall, greater emphasis might be placed on practicing skills during the course so that they become overlearned.

The mechanism that accounts for the durability of effects also has implications for booster sessions, an addition suggested for future prevention programs (Markman et al., 1993). If the use of skills depends on recall of prevention course material, such sessions may be more valuable than if skill use is maintained by natural reinforcers and does not require recall. In any event, 1 year after completing the intervention, Van Widenfelt and colleagues (1996) offered a booster session that reviewed the intervention and aspects of their relationship the couple had identified as problematic. As noted, however, there were no intervention effects 2 years after its implementation. Any impact of booster sessions may be increased through offering them just prior to important developmental life transitions, such as parenthood (e.g., a single session exploring the practical problems and stressors of pregnancy, birth, and caring for an infant, and the effects these events may have on marital quality). At these times, generalization of skills to new content areas may be important and couples may be most receptive to interventions, as the perceived need for them may be high.

Summary

There is comparatively little data on how preparation programs affect long-term marital quality. Behaviorally based programs appear to result in improved sexual satisfaction, more positive communication skills, less dysfunctional communication, higher relationship satisfaction, and less marital violence in participants than in control couples in the long term. A fundamental and as yet largely unresolved issue is the type of couple that volunteers for and remains in such programs. Preliminary evidence suggests that these couples may not be at risk of marital problems, and in couples who are at risk, there is no clear evidence that marriage preparation courses are beneficial. However, these conclusions are based on limited evidence. Clearly, there is a need to replicate long-term outcomes of marriage preparation programs, and that is currently being addressed (e.g., the AUSSIE PREP program; Halford, Sanders, & Behrens, 1996).

☐ Towards More Empirically Informed Prevention Programs

Given the status of data on prevention efficacy, it is timely to consider how research might contribute to the improvement of prevention programs and their evaluation. Towards this end, we consider three issues. First, we evaluate the empirical foundations for current program content for the PREP program as a representative example of published behaviorally based prevention programs. Second, we evaluate the outcome measures used to evaluate prevention programs. Finally, we offer a broader perspective on prevention and outline how research on marriage can extend the boundaries of prevention programs and their evaluation.

Empirical Foundations of Program Content

It is widely assumed that communication problems and patterns of destructive arguing erode love, sexual attraction, friendship, trust, and commitment, and place couples at risk for significant marital distress (Stanley et al., 1995). Consequently, PREP focuses on four main areas (Markman et al., 1986), using good communication to address problem issues (Sessions 1, 2, and 3), expectations about relationships (Session 4), and sexual enhancement and prevention of problems (Session 5). Do empirical data support the emphasis placed on these variables?

Communication Skills

Good communication skills appear to be critical to long-term marital quality. Negative interactional behavior is now well established as a predictor of future marital problems. In a recent meta-analysis on 115 longitudinal studies on marital quality (Karney & Bradbury, 1995), negative behavior and negative reciprocity were strong predictors of decreases in marital quality over time (aggregate effect sizes between -.30 and -.42). Does such data justify the focus on doing all that we can to prevent negative behaviors from occurring? Aren't occasional arguments (even severe ones) present in most marriages? In fact, there is some evidence that it is not so much the frequency of negative behaviors that is related to marital quality, but the ratio of negative to positive behaviors that is important. Gottman's (1993) study suggests that negative affect is not necessarily dysfunctional. He reliably classified three types of stable couples (validators, volatiles, avoiders) and two types of unstable couples (hostile and hostile/detached), and the ratio of positive to negative affect observed during interaction discriminated stable from unstable couples. When discussing events of the day, and a pleasant topic, the ratio of positive to negative affect was nearly 5 to 1 for stable couples, and was less than 1 for unstable couples. For a conflict discussion, wives in the hostile group had a higher ratio of positive to negative affects than wives in the hostile/detached group.

An interesting finding was that different types of couples achieved a ratio of 5 to 1 by mixing different amounts of positive and negative affect. Volatile couples mixed a lot of positive with a lot of negative affect; validators mixed a moderate amount of each; and avoiders mixed a small amount of each. So, despite evidencing different overall frequencies of positive and negative affect, the ratio remained similar across different types of stable couples. Negativity appeared to be dysfunctional only when it was not balanced with about 5 times the positivity, and when there were high levels of complaining, criticizing, defensiveness, contempt, and disgust. This study is limited by its focus on predicting marital stability, rather than marital quality. It is well known that many stable marriages are not necessarily high in marital quality.

However, the findings are similar to two other studies that do examine marital satisfaction. In a study that tends to be overlooked by marital researchers, Howard and Dawes (1976) found that marital satisfaction was related to the arithmetic difference between rates of sexual intercourse and arguments. In a similar vein, Veroff, Sutherland, Chadha, and Ortega (1993) found in conflicting interactions in mutual storytelling that the ratio of husbands' and wives' positive and negative responses were significantly related to marital strength. In neither study were the individual measures alone significantly related to marital satisfaction.

Behavioral analyses of marriage traditionally view the validating couple as ideal, with therapists attempting to increase empathic listening and we-ness while attempting to minimize combativeness and avoidance. The notion that a distressed couple confronted with a problem should empathically listen, summarize their spouse's statements, generate solutions, and negotiate a compromise, has seemed curious to many critics of behavior therapy. Do happy couples do this? Gottman's (1993) data suggest that some couples do, but that for other stable couples, avoidance may be functional.

In summary, a focus on negative communication patterns appears justified. However, there is some evidence that it is the ratio of positive to negative behaviors that determines marital stability and satisfaction, as well as certain specific dysfunctional behaviors. However, some behaviors previously thought of as negative are not necessarily dysfunctional and consequently may not need to be prevented from occurring. Interestingly, prevention programs have placed much more weight on preventing negative behaviors, rather than placing equal emphasis on fostering the development of positive behaviors.

Expectations

PREP contains interventions designed to alter irrational relationship beliefs and destructive attributions that are commonly associated with marital distress (e.g., Eidelson & Epstein, 1982; Fincham, 1994). In particular, PREP encourages participants to attribute problems to lack of communication skills rather than to intrinsic characteristics of the partner. In the delivery of expectation-related interventions, the focus remains on communication. Expectations are presumed to have negative relationship effects because they are not expressed clearly and not understood adequately. Differences in expectations are also raised in order to practice communication skills on emotionally charged issues. What evidence is there that good communication skills can be used to circumvent dysfunctional differences in expectations?

Therapy outcome studies suggest that expectations are sensitive to behavioral marital therapy techniques which do not address expectations as the primary intervention target. However, adding cognitive interventions to standard behavioral marital therapy does not appear to improve marital therapy outcome (Baucom & Lester, 1986; Baucom, Sayers, & Sher, 1990). It is therefore possible that changes in expectations may not be related to later prevention outcome. A longitudinal study supports this view, as unrealistic relationship beliefs did not predict satisfaction 12 months later (Fincham & Bradbury, 1987). In contrast, spousal attributions predict later satisfaction in newlywed husbands (over 12 months, Fincham, Beach, Harold, & Osborne, 1997) and in established marriages (over 12 and 18 months, Fincham & Bradbury, 1987, 1993; Fincham, Harold, Osborne, & Gano-Phillips, 1996). Whether the attention to expectations produces attributional changes important to the outcome of prevention programs is unknown. Data are needed to determine whether attention to expectations is critical to the efficacy of prevention programs.

Sex

Because couples often receive little guidance on sex, PREP includes education about the sexual response and associated gender differences, sexual dysfunction, birth control, and sensate-focusing exercises. These interventions appear to improve knowledge of human sexual functioning and decrease misconceptions. As with expectations, however, the view is taken that sexual problems within marriage are probably best resolved through good communication, and hence the principles learned in earlier sessions on communication are assumed to be critical to the prevention of sex-related problems. Interestingly, in their analysis of longitudinal studies on marital quality, Karney and Bradbury (1995) found insufficient longitudinal data available on sex to warrant its inclusion in their meta-analysis. The importance of the sexual relationship as a predictor of marital quality remains unresolved.

☐ Outcome Measures Used to Assess Program Efficacy

We next turn to the measures used to evaluate outcome and ask whether they measure adequately the constructs targeted in behaviorally based programs. In order to address this question, we need to identify what constitutes a favorable outcome, an issue that has not received the attention it deserves in the prevention literature. Is a favorable outcome one in which a couple remain together? Is it one where both spouses report high marital quality? These two questions are frequently assessed in outcome studies, and we therefore begin our discussion by examining the constructs of marital stability and marital quality.

Marital Stability

Although marital stability has long been used as an outcome measure, it is not without problems. Imagine a couple who experience a couple of years of satisfied marriage, but who thereafter experience increasing marital distress, negotiate a relatively conflict-free separation, and experience improved psychological and physical health as a consequence. If this couple participated in a marital preparation program would the program be a failure for them? After all, it may have been responsible for their 2 years of happy marriage. In contrast, imagine a couple who become distressed after a year but who remain together, experiencing low life satisfaction and physical and psychological health consequences. Is this couple an example of a successful outcome? Perhaps failure occurs when a couple remain together in the face of chronic marital distress that resists all reasonable attempts to be resolved. Clearly, marital stability is a central outcome measure, but it is not necessarily correlated with marital quality.

Marital Quality

The most widely used measures of marital quality are the Dyadic Adjustment Scale (DAS; Spanier, 1976) and the Marital Adjustment Test (MAT; Locke & Wallace, 1959). Markman and colleagues (1993), for example, report MAT data as the primary indicator of marital quality at 4- to 5-year follow-up. Marital quality in these measures is conceived of as unidimensional, ranging from the divorcing couple to the blissfully married couple. Spanier (1979) wrote:

> Marital quality, then, has been defined as a subjective evaluation of a married couple's relationship, with the range of evaluations constituting a continuum reflecting numerous characteristics of marital interaction and marital functioning. A couple can be placed on a continuum ranging from high to low quality rather than being considered fixed in a discreet category of high or low quality. (p. 290)

What do these measures tell us about longitudinal changes in marital quality? Unfortunately, not a lot, owing to conceptual and methodological problems associated with such measures. To illustrate, the measures contain a mixture of differentially weighted items, ranging from reports of specific behaviors that occur in marriage to evaluative inferences regarding the marriage as a whole. For example, on the MAT, items include ratings of disagreement on 8 issues (most, but not all, of which are scored from 0 to 5), and questions like "Do you ever wish you had not married?" (scored as 0, 1, 8, or 10 depending on responses). The inclusion of behavioral and subjective categories and the number and weighting of items used to assess each category varies across measures of marital quality, making it unclear what these tools actually measure. Consequently, such omnibus measures may be useful in identifying distressed and nondistressed couples but they do little to enlighten us as to the nature and critical components of marital quality.

Some researchers have questioned the assumption that marital quality is continuous and unidimensional (e.g., Beach & O'Leary, 1985; Fincham, Beach, & Kemp-Fincham, 1997; Snyder, 1981), as several phenomena are difficult to explain from this perspective. For example, couples with the same score on the DAS may be ambivalent (both very positive and very negative), or indifferent (neither positive or negative) about the marriage. Also, some couples show high variability in their daily satisfaction with the marriage, whereas others do not. Conventional measures of marital quality fail to capture ambivalence, indifference, and variability in marital quality.

Marital theorists have argued that conceptual understanding of marital quality is enhanced by reconceptualizing it as multidimensional. For example, Fincham, Beach, and Kemp-Fincham (1997) advocate a bidimensional approach in which marital quality is conceived of in terms of positive and negative components and have offered data to show that these components provide nonredundant information about relationship quality (e.g., Fincham, Beach, & Kemp-Fincham, 1997; Fincham & Linfield, 1997). In a similar vein, Snyder (1981) developed the Marital Satisfaction Inventory, a psychometrically sophisticated instrument that offers a profile of marital quality much like the Minnesota Multiphasic Personality Inventory (MMPI) offers a profile of individual functioning and, like the MMPI, offers actuarial data to assist in its interpretation. Although promising for understanding marital quality, such tools have been underutilized in comparison to the DAS or the MAT.

Viewing marital quality as multidimensional does fit with findings regarding the orthogonality of positive and negative dimensions of marital interactions and quality over the lifespan. Using cross-sectional studies of age cohorts, researchers have compared the moment-by-moment interactions of younger and older couples. Couples have been found to vary in the overall level of interactional positivity and negativity as years of marriage increase. Two studies have found that behavioral negativity tends to decrease as couples age together (Guilford & Bengston, 1979; Levenson, Carstenson, & Gottman, 1994). Interestingly, Guilford and Bengston found that negative sentiment may act independently of global relationship satisfaction in older, happily married couples. Levenson, Carstensen, and Gottman (1994) found higher reports of positive affect during marital interaction in older couples than in younger couples, and older couples found discussion of difficult issues less physiologically arousing, even after controlling for overall greater positivity.

The degree to which the findings of cross-sectional studies represent how relationships develop longitudinally is questionable. Given high divorce rates, it is likely that a highly select sample of couples will still be married in older age. Also, differences in the correlates of satisfaction in older couples may reflect historical factors (for example, cohort effects such as the exposure of many older couples to the Second World War may have systematically changed aspects of marriage). Longitudinal studies are the most effective way of avoiding these methodological problems. Nevertheless, these results provide tentative evidence that positive and negative dimensions of marital quality are likely to exist independently, and current unidimensional measures of marital quality commonly used in prevention research fail to capture the richness of changes in marital quality.

Demonstrating that prevention programs have a systematic effect on marital quality and stability is, however, a rather inadequate test of the hypothesis that a focus on preventing dysfunctional communication skills is efficacious. It is critical that changes in communication skills also be demonstrated. In the ensuing paragraphs, we therefore narrow our focus to the measurement of communication patterns.

Assessing Communication

Because destructive patterns of communication are thought to be central to understanding declines in marital quality, empirically evaluated programs have included measures of constructive and destructive interactional behaviors in outcome assessment batteries. Typically, these are self-report measures, such as the Conflict Tactics Scale (CTS; Straus, 1979), which measures reasoning, verbal aggression, and physical violence. Van Widenfelt and colleagues (1996) also used the conflict subscale of the Family Environment Scale (FES; Moos & Moos, 1983), which consists of 11 items such as "We fight a lot in our family" and "Family members sometimes hit each other."

Self-report measures, however, have several limitations. Interspousal agreement is often low, and a range of biases are likely to apply, particularly in questionnaires that measure the occurrence of violent and aggressive behavior. Another method extensively used in the marital literature is to observe couples interacting.

It is therefore noteworthy that some program evaluations include observation of communication between spouses. Typically, couples complete a 10- to 15-minute structured discussion task that is videotaped and coded for specific microbehaviors or interactional processes. An extensive body of research shows that such methods reliably discriminate distressed from nondistressed couples, that couples are unable to "turn off" certain domains of behavioral responses, that couples report these interactions as representative of their typical interactions, and that observed verbal and nonverbal behavior predicts future marital quality (for a review, see Weiss & Heyman, 1990).

Coding systems vary widely in the types of coding units that are used, the level of inference used, and the relative independence of behavioral codes (Floyd, 1989). In the prevention area, macroanalytic (or "molar") behavioral coding systems have been used. These molar systems are characterized by large coding units, nonindependent dimensions of behavior, and higher levels of inference required by the coder, when compared to microanalytic systems. The primary advantage of these coding systems is that they reduce coding time. A disadvantage is that, unlike microanalytic systems, which use small coding units, sequential analysis of chains of behavioral responses cannot be derived. For example, coding of turns at speaking facilitates the examination of the impact of each communication on the partner using sequential analysis techniques. These sorts of statistical procedures cannot be applied to data coded through molar coding systems (for an excellent discussion of macro- versus microcoding, see Bell & Bell, 1989; Floyd, 1989).

Markman and colleagues (1993) used the Interactional Dimensions Coding System (IDCS; Julien, Markman, & Lindahl, 1989) to evaluate PREP. The IDCS assesses five negative dimensions (conflict, dominance, withdrawal, denial, negative affect), and four positive dimensions (communication skills, support-validation, problem solving, positive affect). Two dyadic dimensions are also included, negative and positive escalation. For the nine individual dimensions, the coding unit is obtained by dividing the interaction into three equal segments of thought units (e.g., verbal phrases grammatically separated by conjunctions, question marks, or periods), or by equal overall discussion time intervals. For the two dyadic dimensions, the whole interaction is the coding unit. Observers view the relevant section of the interaction and make a single global rating for each partner, taking into account affect and content cues as required by coding definitions.

Julien et al. (1989) found that IDCS negative and positive escalation dimensions were modest predictors of marital satisfaction at 4 years postassessment, and IDCS codes were significantly correlated with males' reports of marital quality. Molar coding systems are in their early stages of development, and further refinement of behavioral codes to increase inter-rater agreement, and validation using samples more variable in marital distress is needed. But even if programs are shown to reliably reduce negative communication patterns and successfully help couples to anticipate stressful events, is this necessary and sufficient to ensure high, long-term marital quality? Although the answer to this question is critical to understanding communication-based prevention programs, existing research also points to ways in which current prevention programs can be broadened.

☐ A Broader Perspective on Marriage Preparation Programs

In this section we argue that the current content of empirically evaluated marriage preparation programs and the criteria used to assess their outcome are unnecessarily limited. Existing knowledge of the nature and development of high-quality marriage suggests two broad areas for improvement. First, current prevention programs should be expanded to include additional factors known to affect marital quality. Second, outcome criteria need to be expanded to more fully capture marital health.

Content

Several lines of evidence suggest that the limited focus of current programs is insufficient to produce high, long-term marital quality. First, as already noted, available evidence on the intermediate-term effect of preparation programs is mixed. There is also the need to demonstrate that prevention has a replicable effect with homogeneous groups. Second, removing destructive communication patterns in couples who are maritally distressed does not work particularly well in producing high marital quality.

Behavioral marital therapy (BMT), which has traditionally focused on extinguishing destructive interactional patterns, has limited long-term efficacy. Numerous empirical reviews have evaluated over 20 controlled trials of BMT containing combinations of behavior exchange, communication, and problem solving training (e.g., Hahlweg & Markman, 1988; Jacobson & Addis, 1993). BMT is clearly more effective than either no treatment or nondirective counseling (Hahlweg & Markman, 1988). However, a significant proportion of couples (25% to 30%) do not evidence any improvement at the end of therapy, and only about half are no longer maritally distressed (Halford, Sanders, & Behrens, 1993; Jacobson et al., 1984). For those couples that do show improvements in marital satisfaction, there is substantial relapse, with less than half of presenting couples maintaining clinically significant gains longer than 2 years after therapy (Jacobson, 1989; Snyder, Willis, & Grady-Fletcher, 1991). Behavioral marital interventions designed to rectify or prevent such problems have modest effects in producing long-term high marital quality.

There are, of course, some limitations when we draw parallels between removing negatives in distressed couples and preventing negatives in happy couples. For example, in distressed couples there is the possibility that relatively immutable factors, such as memories of physical abuse, may result in sustained marital distress even if dysfunctional communication patterns are extinguished. Nevertheless, there is some evidence that negative communication patterns alone do not determine marital quality.

The tertiary intervention literature suggests that there are likely to be a variety of necessary characteristics and skills associated with high marital quality, including good communication skills, ability to successfully and mutually anticipate and resolve problem issues, anticipation of and preparation for future marital stressors, and maintaining a high ratio of positive to negative interactional behaviors. There is not convincing evidence to suggest that these characteristics are sufficient to produce high marital quality. A similar argument may hold for behaviorally based prevention programs. Perhaps current intervention foci are not sufficient to maintain marital quality.

Longitudinal research on marriage can be used to identify other potentially important areas for intervention. Karney and Bradbury (1995) consolidate the huge variety of individual and interpersonal research findings in this area by proposing a vulnerability-stress-adaptation framework which they believe best fits with what we currently know about the longitudinal development of marital satisfaction and stability. Interactive processes are viewed in the context of risk factors or vulnerabilities that couples bring to their relationship, stressful events that occur during marriage, and the ways that couples adapt to stressful events.

Enduring Vulnerabilities

Karney and Bradbury (1995) found considerable evidence that individual characteristics brought into a relationship have a strong impact on marital quality and stability. For example, neurotic personality traits and unhappy childhood experiences are predictive of marital quality and stability. Parental divorce also predicts marital stability and, to a lesser extent, marital quality. With the exception of Van Widenfelt et al.'s PREP program (which included a session on parental divorce issues), these personality traits and historical factors are not clearly addressed in existing behaviorally based prevention programs.

What sorts of interventions might be included in prevention programs to address enduring vulnerabilities? The answer to this question depends, in part, on where in the developmental stage of a relationship the prevention program is initiated. For example, if prevention programs begin before the relationship develops (for example, as part of school curricula), then interventions which address issues that place individuals at risk (for example, parental divorce, high conflict in the home), current expectations regarding marriage (myths about marriage, e.g., good marriages come naturally and effortlessly), processes in mate selection, norms regarding marital relationships, and danger signs for marital distress (for example, dating violence, sexual coercion, heavy alcohol consumption) may be efficacious.

Positive Interactional Behavior

While negative behavior is clearly a critical variable in marital outcomes, there is considerable evidence that positive interactional behaviors are important determinants of marital quality and stability (Karney & Bradbury, 1995). Despite the discriminant and predictive validity of positive interactional behavior, behaviorally based marital intervention and prevention programs have placed relatively little emphasis on addressing positive behaviors in couples.

The emphasis appears to be shifting as marital theorists begin to focus on such positive dimensions as tolerance and acceptance (Hayes, Jacobson, Follete, & Dougher, 1994), and preliminary evidence suggests that intimacy enhancement interventions are as effective as behavioral marital interventions (Johnson & Greenberg, 1985). The discriminant and predictive validity of positive dimensions of marital interactions, combined with the effectiveness of intimacy enhancement interventions for couples who are distressed, suggests that the content of prevention programs may be enhanced with the addition of interventions which aim to boost and maintain positive dimensions of marital quality.

What does empirical data offer regarding the positive dimensions of marital quality and interactions that could be targeted in prevention programs? Compared to distressed couples, short interactions on problem issues in nondistressed couples show more positive behaviors, such as agreement (Margolin & Wampold, 1981; Revensdorf, Hahlweg, Schindler, & Vogel, 1984), empathy (Birchler, Clopton, & Adams, 1984), pinpointing and verbalizing problems in a noncritical way (Margolin & Wampold, 1981), and generation of solutions to problems (Birchler et al., 1984; Floyd, O'Farrell, & Goldberg, 1987; Margolin, Burman, & John, 1989). It is likely that rewarding and intimate verbal interactions and activities are critical components of happy couple relationships. Happy couples report that spending positive shared time together is a major reason for the rewarding nature of their relationship (Osgarby & Halford, 1996), and partners in happy couples also actively share and build on experiences communicated by their mate (Osgarby & Halford).

The social psychological literature has much to contribute here also. Such constructs as love, perceptual idealization, and commitment have received attention in the social psychological literature, but have yet to be applied in the marital therapy literature. These are important self-reported characteristics of happy couples married 20 years or more (Fenell, 1993), and it is often the waning of these qualities that are the primary presenting problem of distressed couples (Margolin, 1983). Monitoring changes in these qualities in responders and nonresponders to prevention would be a good place to start in determining their importance for sustained marital quality.

Ironically, the marital literature offers little when it comes to models of marital health. For the most part, it appears that marital health is assumed to be the opposite of marital dysfunction. Kelly and Fincham (in press) have therefore attempted to provide a more complete account of marital health.

Stress

Behaviorally oriented marriage preparation programs have a focus on anticipating and preparing for future problems, and this focus is supported by several empirical findings. First, stressful events do impact negatively on marital quality. For example, unemployment (e.g., Aubry, Tefft, & Kingsbury, 1990) and work stress (e.g., Halford, Gravestock, Lowe, & Scheldt, 1992) are common stressors associated with decreases in marital quality and increases in negative interactional behavior. Developmental transitions such as parenthood are often associated with stress and declines in marital satisfaction (e.g., Belsky & Pensky, 1988). Finally, some couples experience stress outside the norm of marital experience, such as infertility, having a child with a physical or intellectual handicap, or illness or injury that may profoundly influence marital quality (Revenson, 1994). The need to begin documenting stressors in examining the outcome of marital preparation programs appears self-evident.

Adaptation

It also appears that the spouse is the most significant source of social support available to most married people, especially men, when stressful events occur. The spouse is frequently the first person from whom support is sought during crises (e.g., Beach, Martin, Blum, & Roman, 1993), and support from other sources cannot compensate for a lack of intimate or marital support (Coyne & DeLongis, 1986; for a review, see Cutrona, 1996).

Spousal support can reduce the impact of individual problems and stressors. In the alcohol area, for example, Moos and colleagues (e.g., Billings & Moos, 1981, 1983) found that family support (reflected by such measures as cohesiveness and lack of conflict), assessed following discharge from treatment, is predictive of both short-term (6 months) and long-term (2 years) treatment outcome. Rosenberg (1983) also found that recovered alcoholics reported higher levels of support from family and friends and more people that they could turn to for assistance than relapsed alcoholics. Booth, Russell, Soucek, and Laughlin (1992), while controlling for the history of prior treatment failure, found that reassurance of worth from family and friends significantly predicted the time to readmission in participants in an inpatient alcohol treatment program.

Current prevention programs address the issue of dealing with stressful events through the development of communication skills. However, being able to resolve problems using effective communication skills is only one aspect of handling stressful events. A related adaptive aspect of marital quality is the provision of effective spousal support. While mutually supportive partners probably show good communication, it is not necessarily true that a couple who show good communication skills, particularly in a structured observation session, are high in their support of each other. To make this point, we explore a definition of social support within marriage.

The term "social support" has been used to refer to the mechanisms by which interpersonal relationships buffer one against a stressful environment (Sells, 1970). While the topography of "supportive" behaviors is vast, a recent theoretical analysis analyzed the forms and functions of social support that assist in coping with specific types of stressors (Cutrona & Russell, 1990). On the basis of Weiss's (1974) theory of social provisions, Cutrona and Russell conceptualized two basic forms of social support within marriage: assistance-related social provision (including guidance, for example, giving the partner in need advice and or information, and reliable alliance, where the partner of the spouse in need can be depended on for tangible assistance if required) and nonassistance-related social support (including reassurance of worth or feeling esteemed or valued by others, opportunity for nurturance or providing assistance to others, attachment or a strong emotional bond with at least one other person, and social integration or having other people who share interests).

This brief examination of the theoretical components of social support leads to two observations. First, the behavioral element of social support is not fully addressed by communication-oriented interventions. Providing problem-focused coping strategies aimed at managing or eliminating the source of stress (such as providing information about coping options, planning coping strategies, providing instrumental assistance) as well as providing emotional support (such as providing opportunities to debrief, responding with unconditional regard to distress, and physical affection) are all potential examples of supportive acts within the marital context (Revenson, 1994). It appears that only some of these behavioral elements receive attention in current prevention programs. An essential element of social support is the sense of being supported, or "perceived support" (Cutrona, Suhr, & MacFarlane, 1990). This is not well captured in purely behavioral analyses of social support (Cutrona et al., 1990; Vinokur, Schul, & Caplan, 1987). Fincham and Bradbury (1990) argue that the reason inferred for a partner behavior is likely to be a major factor in determining whether it is perceived as supportive. For example, if a spouse in need perceives a partner's positive behavior as something that was involuntary, unlikely to occur again, and selfishly motivated, perceived support may be low or absent. Conversely, if the same behavior was perceived as freely and unselfishly performed, perceived support may be high. It is reasonable to hypothesize that perceived support (i.e., behavior independently coded as supportive, as well as attributions about the behavior) is likely to covary with marital satisfaction and facilitate successful adaptation to stress.

Finally, it is worth noting that a couples' capacity to provide support in the event of stress may not be readily evident until stress arises. For example, marital satisfaction may be high, but partners' resources for coping with stress and providing support may be poor when significant stress occurs. This observation serves to underscore our earlier emphasis on the need to assess stressors in research on the prevention of marital distress.

Outcome Assessment

Prevention research fails to capture the wider definition of spousal support outlined above. Observed behavior is necessarily limited in what it can tell us about social support, given that the construct includes intrapersonal elements such as cognition and emotion. Also, discussion tasks used in prevention research are not conducive to the occurrence of partner support behaviors. Recent observational studies have begun to investigate couples discussing personal issues or problems that are not associated with marital conflict (e.g., Cutrona & Suhr, 1994). Ongoing research by Bradbury and colleagues has spouses make ratings of the anticipated levels of partner support before a videotaped discussion, and after the discussion spouses make a second rating of how supported they felt during the discussion. Such a task has the potential to document more fully the various elements of social support.

Outcome assessment also needs to be informed by research on the interaction of marital and individual well-being. There is growing evidence that a functional and healthy marital relationship is one that contributes to individual well-being for both partners. In contrast, an unhealthy relationship is one that detracts from or impedes individual well-being in one or both partners. It has been argued that individual well-being is an important index of marital quality that, until the present, has been underutilized in prevention research.

As regards psychological health, a large body of research links marital quality to psychopathology (Gotlib & McCabe, 1990). For example, depressive symptoms and marital quality are strongly related, with longitudinal studies suggesting that marital quality and interactional behavior may have a causal role in the etiology and maintenance of depressive symptoms (for reviews, see Beach, Sandeen, & O'Leary, 1990; Beach, Smith, & Fincham, 1994; Gotlib & Hammen, 1992). For example, Beach and colleagues, using a randomly recruited community sample of married women, found that marital satisfaction predicted depressive symptomatology 1 year later (Beach et al., 1995). However, Fincham, Beach, Harold, and Osborne (1997) found an interesting sex difference, in that marital quality predicted depressive symptoms 18 months later only for women, whereas depressive symptoms predicted later marital quality for men.

There is also evidence that marital quality may be associated with prolonged and dependent use of alcohol. People presenting for marital therapy report high levels of substance abuse (Halford & Osgarby, 1993), and people presenting for alcohol dependency treatment report high levels of marital distress (Blankfield & Maritz, 1990). Marital distress is often reported as a precipitant of problem drinking (Maisto, O'Farrell, Connors, McKay, & Pelcovits, 1988), and is associated with increased likelihood of relapse in recently treated alcohol-dependent women (Haver, 1986).

Despite such research we still know relatively little about how marital distress and mental health problems evolve over time. Prevention research could potentially address this lacuna by using measures of mental health in outcome evaluations of prevention programs. In any event, the inclusion of such measures is appropriate to gain a more complete picture of outcome efficacy.

As regards physical health, there is also growing evidence that marital quality influences partner outcomes, either directly or through the mediation of psychological or behavioral processes (Burman & Margolin, 1992). One mechanism by which marital quality impacts on health is through persistent alterations to cardiovascular and endocrine functioning (O'Dorisio, Wood, & O'Dorisio, 1985; Pert, Ruff, Weber, & Herkenham, 1985). Individuals with consistently more pronounced, frequent, or enduring increases in blood pressure or heart rate in response to stressors (e.g., marital discord) are more likely to develop cardiovascular diseases (Brown & Smith, 1992).

What evidence is there that marital quality is associated with deleterious biological responses and the subsequent development of illness? Kiecolt-Glaser and colleagues found a positive correlation between marital distress, conflict and marital termination, and biological indices of stress and physical health problems. For example, Kiecolt-Glaser et al. (1987) examined the association of marital quality (poor, high, or separated or divorced) with physiological indices of stress and psychological functioning among women. Poorer marital quality was associated with greater depression and a poorer response on measures of immune function. Women who had been separated for a year or less had poorer immune functioning than their matched married counterparts. In their most recent study, Kiecolt-Glaser and colleagues showed a significant positive association between conflict behavior and stress-responsive hormones in women (Kiecolt-Glaser et al., 1996). They also demonstrated that these elevations in stress-responsive hormones were maintained for several hours longer than the usual half-life of these hormones. Such findings suggest that repeated marital conflict may result in sustained elevations in stress-responsive hormones.

Other studies give us a clearer picture of exactly what sorts of marital interactions are associated with elevations in biological indices of ill health. Brown and Smith (1992) examined the effects of exerting social influence or control within marital interactions on cardiovascular response. This study found that, compared to female partners, male partners attempting to influence or persuade their wives displayed higher systolic blood pressure before and during the interaction. These physiological effects were associated with increases in anger and a more hostile interpersonal style. Female partners who engaged in social control behaviors did not show these elevations in systolic blood pressure.

In a related study that used far more sophisticated measures of marital conflict, expression, and physiological stress responses, Ewart, Taylor, Kraemer, and Agras (1991) measured blood pressure changes in maritally distressed hypertensive patients while they attempted to resolve a disagreement with their spouse. Blood pressure increased dramatically during hostile exchanges but was little affected by expressions of affection or support. A gender effect was also observed. In female partners, blood pressure changes were related to the emotional quality of dyadic exchanges and were correlated with marital satisfaction. For male partners, blood pressure increased when speech rate increased and the male partner dominated the discussion. This gender effect of "nasty versus nice" interactional behavior on blood pressure has been replicated (Kiecolt-Glaser, et al., 1993).

An important point regarding marital interaction and its effect on physiological indicators of stress and health outcomes is that arousal and stress responses are unlikely to be unidimensional. Different negative emotions may produce different patterns of physiological arousal. For example, Ekman, Levenson, and Friesen (1983) found that facial configurations associated with different negative emotions produce different patterns of autonomic nervous system (ANS) activity. ANS activity is likely to vary according to the type of emotive response (anxiety, anger, depression), physical activity, and different perceptual and cognitive states (Gottman & Levenson, 1986).

Also, there may be systematic differences in how marital conflict affects men and women physiologically. Gottman and Levenson (1988) argue that men experience greater physiological arousal during marital conflict than women and that men are slower to return to baseline after conflict. However, Kiecolt-Glaser and colleagues found that women showed more physiological arousal using indices of stress hormones (Kiecolt-Glaser et al., 1996). If we are to employ physiological indices of stress responses, more research is needed on gender differences in profiles of physiological arousal.

The likely variation in profiles of indices of emotion (i.e., physiological responses to different types of emotions, gender differences in physiological indices) makes it advisable to employ markers from a range of domains. Unfortunately, this makes measurement of physiological indices impractical for most researchers with limited resources. In the face of limited resources, maximum heart rate may be the best dependent measure of physiological arousal, given that this measure was found to be the best physiological predictor of marital distress (Levenson & Gottman, 1983, 1985), and is also significantly higher in maritally distressed couples (Gottman & Levenson, 1992). Clearly, the links among marital quality, interactional behavior, physiological arousal, immune functioning, and the development of physical health problems are in need of replication with larger samples across different laboratories.

The research on marital quality and physical well-being points to some exciting areas for expansion of outcome evaluations in prevention research. While biological indices are no doubt expensive and difficult to implement, longitudinal evaluations of prevention programs that incorporate such measures would provide additional data on the public health significance of prevention programs.

Summary

Our analysis suggests that the focus on adaptive communication patterns in marital preparation programs needs to be expanded to include attention to factors associated with long-term marital outcomes (e.g., what spouses bring to the relationship; Karney & Bradbury, 1995) as well as factors identified as important for marital health (e.g., positive behaviors, see Kelly & Fincham, in press). In addition, measuring psychological and physical health and combining these measures with biological indices of stress, such as blood pressure and stress-related hormones, would provide a more complete picture of the public health significance of prevention programs.

☐ Conclusions

The goal of this chapter was to explore how research can better inform marital prevention programs. Towards this end, we evaluated the efficacy of current programs and the empirical foundations for the content they cover. The attention given to communication skills in these programs has strong empirical support, but this limited focus may be insufficient to sustain marital quality over time. Until we conduct longer term studies of prevention programs that control for risk of marital distress, the issue of whether a communication skills focus is enough will remain unresolved.

In addition, we pointed to the need to identify the mechanisms that mediate intervention outcomes if we are to maximize program impact.

We also explored the broader marital literature for factors other than those already incorporated into prevention programs that may have an impact on marital quality. Drawing on Karney and Bradbury's (1995) meta-analysis, we reviewed the importance of vulnerabilities, stressors, and adaptive processes in enhancing prevention efforts. Although good communication may do much to resolve individual differences and facilitate adaptation to stress, in some couples this may be treating behavioral manifestations of underlying individual characteristics that are resistant to change. Interventions addressing these areas are likely to enhance the efficacy of prevention programs.

Finally, our analysis of the outcome measures commonly used in prevention research (and indeed in much therapy research as well) showed that they are unnecessarily limited. Current outcome measures focus on marital stability, marital quality, observed communication, and self-reports of aggression and violent behavior. These outcome measures are theoretically justified, although in the case of marital quality, we noted several conceptual inadequacies in conventional measures of marital quality. We argued that outcome measures could profitably be expanded to include positive and negative dimensions of marital quality, spousal support, and measures of psychological and physical well-being.

Our analysis of the role of research in prevention efforts is illustrative rather than exhaustive. However, we hope to have convinced you that the contribution of research is not limited to evaluating the efficacy of prevention programs. Basic research on marriage can inform virtually every aspect of our prevention efforts. However, if it is to do so, we need to pay attention to developments in research and be prepared to revise even our most cherished beliefs and practices relating to the prevention of marital problems.

☐ References

Aubry, T., Tefft, B., & Kingsbury, N. (1990). Behavioral and psychological consequences of unemployment in blue-collar couples. *Journal of Community Psychology, 18,* 99–109.

Avery, A. W., Ridley, C. A., Leslie, L. A., & Milholland, T. (1980). Relationship enhancement with premarital dyads: A six month follow-up. *American Journal of Family Therapy, 8,* 23–30.

Baucom, D. H., & Lester, G. W. (1986). The usefulness of cognitive restructuring as an adjunct to behavioral marital therapy. *Behavior Therapy, 17,* 385–403.

Baucom, D. H., Sayers, S. L., & Sher, T. G. (1990). Supplementing behavioral marital therapy with cognitive restructuring and emotional expressiveness training: An outcome investigation. *Journal of Consulting and Clinical Psychology, 58,* 636–645.

Beach, S. R. H., Harwood, E. M., Horan, P. M., Katz, J., Blum, T. C., Martin, J. K., & Roman, P. M. (1995, November). *Marital effects on depression: Measuring the longitudinal relationship.* Paper presented at the 29th Annual Convention of the Association for the Advancement of Behavior Therapy, Washington, DC.

Beach, S. R. H., Martin, J. K., Blum, T. C., & Roman, P. M. (1993). Effects of marital and coworker relationships on negative affect: Testing the central role of marriage. *American Journal of Family Therapy, 21,* 312–322.

Beach, S. R. H., & O'Leary, K. D. (1985). Current status of outcome research in marital therapy. In L'Abate (Ed.), *Handbook of family psychology and therapy* (Vol. 2, pp. 1035–1072). Homewood, IL: Dorsey.

Beach, S. R. H., Sandeen, E. E., & O'Leary, K. D. (1990). *Depression in marriage: A model for etiology and treatment.* New York: Guilford.

Beach, S. R. H., Smith, D. A., & Fincham, F. D. (1994). Marital interventions for depression: Empirical foundation and future prospects. *Applied and Preventive Psychology, 3,* 233–250.

Behrens, B. C., & Halford, W. K. (1994, October). *Advances in the prevention and treatment of marital distress.* Paper presented at the Helping Families Change Conference, University of Queensland, Brisbane, Australia.

Bell, D. C., & Bell, L. G. (1989). Micro and macro measurement of family systems concepts. *Journal of Family Psychology, 3,* 137–157.

Belsky, J., & Pensky, E. (1988). Marital change across the transition to parenthood. *Marriage and the Family, 52,* 5–19.

Billings, A. G., & Moos, R. H. (1981). The role of coping responses and social resources in attenuating the stress of life events. *Journal of Behavioral Medicine, 4,* 139–157.

Billings, A. G., & Moos, R. H. (1983). Psychosocial processes of recovery among alcoholics and their families: Implications for clinicians and program evaluators. *Addictive Behavior, 8,* 205–218.

Birchler, G. R., Clopton, P. L., & Adams, N. L. (1984). Marital conflict resolution: Factors influencing concordance between partners and trained coders. *American Journal of Family Therapy, 12,* 15–28.

Blankfield, A., & Maritz, J. S. (1990). Female alcoholics. IV. Admission problems and patterns. *Acta Psychiatrica Scandinavica, 82,* 445–450.

Blumburg, S. L. (1991). *Premarital intervention programs: A comparison study.* Unpublished doctoral dissertation, University of Denver, Colorado.

Booth, B. M., Russell, D. W., Soucek, S., & Laughlin, P. R. (1992). Social support and outcome of alcoholism treatment: An exploratory analysis. *American Journal of Drug and Alcohol Abuse, 18,* 87–101.

Brock, G. W., & Joanning, H. (1983). A comparison of the Relationship Enhancement program and the Minnesota Couple Communication program. *Journal of Marital and Family Therapy, 9,* 413–421.

Brown, P. C., & Smith, T. W. (1992). Social influence, marriage, and the heart: Cardiovascular consequences of interpersonal control in husbands and wives. *Health Psychology, 11,* 88–96.

Burman, B., & Margolin, G. (1992). Analysis of the association between marital relationships and health problems: An interactional perspective. *Psychological Bulletin, 112,* 39–63.

Coie, J., Watt, N., West, S. G., Hawkins, J. D., Asarnow, J. R., Markman, H. J., Ramey, S. L., Shure, M. B., & Long, B. (1993). The science of prevention: A conceptual framework and some directions for a national research program. *American Psychologist, 48,* 1013–1022.

Coyne, J. C., & DeLongis, A. (1986). Going beyond social support: The role of social relations in adaptation. *Journal of Consulting and Clinical Psychology, 54,* 454–460.

Cutrona, C. E. (1996). *Social support in couples.* Beverly Hills, CA: Sage.

Cutrona, C. E., & Russell, D. (1990). Types of social support and specific stress: Toward a theory of optimal matching. In I. G. Sarason, B. R. Sarason, & G. Pierce (Eds.), *Social support: An interactional view* (pp. 319–366). New York: Wiley.

Cutrona, C. E., & Suhr, J. A. (1994). Social support communication in the context of marriage: An analysis of couples' supportive interactions. In B. B. Burleson, T. L. Albrecht, & I. Sarason (Eds.), *Communication of social support: Messages, relationships, and community* (pp. 113–135). Beverly Hills, CA: Sage.

Cutrona, C. E., Suhr, J. A., & MacFarlane, R. (1990). Interpersonal transactions and the psychological sense of support. In S. Duck & R. Silver (Eds.), *Personal relationships and social support* (pp. 30–45). London: Sage.

Eidelson, R. J., & Epstein, N. (1982). Cognition and relationship maladjustment: Development of a measure of dysfunctional relationship beliefs. *Journal of Consulting and Clinical Psychology, 50,* 715–720.

Ekman, P., Levenson, R. W., & Friesen, W. V. (1983). Autonomic nervous system activity distinguishes among emotions. *Science, 221,* 1208–1210.

Ewart, C. K., Taylor, C. B., Kraemer, H. C., & Agras, W. S. (1991). High blood pressure and marital discord: Not being nasty matters more than being nice. *Health Psychology, 10,* 155–163.

Fenell, D. (1993). Characteristics of long-term first marriages. *Journal of Mental Health Counseling, 15,* 446–460.

Fincham, F. D. (1994). Cognition in marriage: Current status and future challenges. *Applied and Preventive Psychology: Current Scientific Perspectives, 3,* 185–198.

Fincham, F. D., Beach, S. R. H., Harold, G. T., & Osborne, L. N. (1997). Marital satisfaction and depression: Different causal relationships for men and women? *Psychological Science, 8,* 351–357.

Fincham, F. D., Beach, S. R. H., & Kemp-Fincham, S. I. (1997). Marital quality: A new theoretical perspective. In R. J. Sternberg & M. Hojjat (Eds.), *Satisfaction in close relationships* (pp. 275–304). New York: Guilford.

Fincham, F. D., & Bradbury, T. N. (1987). The impact of attributions in marriage: A longitudinal analysis. *Journal of Personality and Social Psychology, 53,* 481–489.

Fincham, F. D., & Bradbury, T. N. (1990). Social support in marriage: The role of social cognition. *Journal of Social and Clinical Psychology, 9,* 31–42.

Fincham, F. D., & Bradbury, T. N. (1993). Marital satisfaction, depression, and attributions: A longitudinal analysis. *Journal of Personality and Social Psychology, 64,* 442–452.

Fincham, F. D., Bradbury, T. N., Arias, I., Byrne, C. A., & Karney, B. R. (1997). Marital violence, marital distress and attributions. *Journal of Family Psychology, 11,* 367–372.

Fincham, F. D., Harold, G. T., Osborne, L. N., & Gano-Phillips, S. (1996). *Longitudinal and concurrent effects between attributions and marital satisfaction: Are they bi-directional?* Manuscript submitted for publication.

Fincham, F. D., & Linfield, K. (1997). A new look at marital quality: Can spouses feel positive and negative about their marriage? *Journal of Family Psychology, 11,* 489–502.

Floyd, F. (1989). Segmenting interactions: Coding units for assessing marital and family behaviors. *Behavioral Assessment, 11,* 13–29.

Floyd, F. J., O'Farrell, T. J., & Goldberg, M. (1987). Comparison of marital observational measures: The Marital Interaction Coding System and the Communication Skills Test. *Journal of Consulting and Clinical Psychology, 55,* 423–429.

Giblin, P., Sprenkle, D. H., & Sheehan, R. (1985). Enrichment outcome research: A meta-analysis of premarital, marital and family interventions. *Journal of Marital and Family Therapy, 11,* 257–271.

Gotlib, I. H., & Hammen, C. L. (1992). *Psychological aspects of depression: Toward a cognitive-interpersonal integration.* New York: Wiley.

Gotlib, I. H., & McCabe, S. B. (1990). Marriage and psychopathology. In F.D. Fincham & T.N. Bradbury (Eds.), *The psychology of marriage: Basic issues and applications* (pp. 226–257). New York: Guilford.

Gottman, J. M. (1993). The roles of conflict engagement, escalation, and avoidance in marital interaction: A longitudinal view of five types of couples. *Journal of Consulting and Clinical Psychology, 61,* 6–15.

Gottman, J. M., & Levenson, R. W. (1986). Assessing the role of emotion in marriage. *Behavioral Assessment, 8,* 31–48.

Gottman, J. M., & Levenson, R. W. (1988). The social psychophysiology of marriage. In P. Noller & M. A. Fitzpatrick (Eds.), *Perspectives on marital interaction* (pp. 182–199). Clevedon, England: Multilingual Matters.

Gottman, J. M., & Levenson, R. W. (1992). Marital processes predictive of later dissolution: Behavior, physiology, and health. *Journal of Personality and Social Psychology, 63,* 221–233.

Guerney, B., Brock, G., & Coufal, J. (1986). Integrating marital therapy and enrichment: The relationship enhancement approach. In N. S. Jacobson & A. S. Gurman (Eds.), *Clinical handbook of marital therapy* (pp. 151–172). New York: Guilford.

Guilford, R., & Bengston, V. (1979). Measuring marital satisfaction in three generations: Positive and negative dimensions. *Journal of Marriage and the Family, 52,* 818–831.

Hahlweg, K., & Markman, H. J. (1988). The effectiveness of behavioral marital therapy: Empirical Status of behavioral techniques in preventing and alleviating marital distress. *Journal of Consulting and Clinical Psychology, 56,* 440–447.

Halford, W. K., Gravestock, F. M., Lowe, R., & Scheldt, S. (1992). Toward a behavioral ecology of stressful marital interactions. *Behavioral Assessment, 14,* 199–217.

Halford, W. K., & Osgarby, S. (1993). Alcohol abuse in clients presenting with marital problems. *Journal of Family Psychology, 6,* 1–11.

Halford, W. K., Sanders, M. R., & Behrens, B. C. (1993). A comparison of the generalization of behavioral marital therapy and enhanced behavioral marital therapy. *Journal of Consulting and Clinical Psychology, 61,* 51–60.

Halford, W. K., Sanders, M. R., & Behrens, B. C. (1996). *The Australian Premarital Relationship Enhancement Program.* Department of Psychiatry, University of Queensland, Australia.

Haver, B. (1986). Female alcoholics. II. Factors associated with psycho-social outcome 3-10 years after treatment. *Acta Psychiatrica Scandinavica, 74,* 597–604.

Hayes, S. C., Jacobson, N. S., Follete, V. M., Dougher, M. J. (1994). *Acceptance and Change: Content and context in psychotherapy.* New York: Context Press.

Howard, J. W., & Dawes, R. M. (1976). Linear prediction of marital happiness. *Personality and Social Psychology Bulletin, 2,* 478–480.

Jacobson, N. S. (1989). The maintenance of treatment gains following social learning-based marital therapy. *Behavior Therapy, 20,* 325–336.

Jacobson, N. S., & Addis, M. E. (1993). Research on couples and couple therapy: What do we know, where are we going? *Journal of Consulting and Clinical Psychology, 61,* 85–93.

Jacobson, N. S., Follette, W. C., Revensdorf, D., Baucom, D. H., Hahlweg, K., & Margolin, G. (1984). Variability in outcome and clinical significance of behavioral marital therapy: Analysis of outcome data. *Journal of Consulting and Clinical Psychology, 52,* 497–504.

Johnson, S. M., & Greenberg, L. S. (1985). Differential effects of experiential and problem-solving interventions in resolving marital conflict. *Journal of Consulting and Clinical Psychology, 53,* 175–184.

Julien, D., Markman, H. J., & Lindahl, K. M. (1989). A comparison of a global and a microanalytic coding system: Implications for future trends in studying interactions. *Behavioral Assessment, 11,* 81–100.

Karney, B. R., & Bradbury, T. N. (1995). The longitudinal course of marital quality and stability: A review of theory, method, and research. *Psychological Bulletin, 118,* 3–34.

Kelly, A. B., & Fincham, F. D. (in press). *Marital health: Towards a more complete account of functional and satisfying couple relationships.* Encyclopedia of Mental Health. New York: Academic Press.

Kiecolt-Glaser, J. K., Fisher, L. D., Ogrocki, P., Stout, J. C., Speicher, C. E., & Glaser, R. (1987). Marital quality, marital disruption, and immune function. *Psychosomatic Medicine, 49,* 13–34.

Kiecolt-Glaser, J. K., Malarkey, W. B., Chee, M. A., Newton, T., Cacioppo, J. T., Mao, Y., & Glaser,

R. (1993). Negative behavior during marital conflict is associated with immunological down-regulation. *Psychosomatic Medicine, 55,* 395–409.

Kiecolt-Glaser, J. K., Newton, T., Cacioppo, J. T., MacCallum, R. C., Glaser, R., & Malarkey, W. B. (1996). Marital conflict and endocrine function: Are men really more physiologically affected than women? *Journal of Consulting and Clinical Psychology, 64,* 324–332.

Levenson, R. W., Cartensen, L. L., & Gottman, J. M. (1994). The influence of age and gender on affect, physiology, and their interrelations: A study of long-term marriages. *Journal of Personality and Social Psychology, 67,* 56–68.

Levenson, R. W., & Gottman, J. M. (1983). Marital interaction: Physiological linkage and affective exchange. *Journal of Personality and Social Psychology, 45,* 587–597.

Levenson, R. W., & Gottman, J. M. (1985). Physiological and affective predictors of change in relationship satisfaction. *Journal of Personality and Social Psychology, 49,* 85–94.

Locke, H. J., & Wallace, K. M. (1959). Short marital adjustment prediction tests: Their reliability and validity. *Marriage and Family Living, 21,* 251–255.

Maisto, S. A., O'Farrell, T. J., Connors, G. J., McKay, J. R., & Pelcovits, M. (1988). Alcoholics attributions of factors affecting their relapse to drinking and reasons for terminating relapse episodes. *Addictive Behaviors, 13,* 79–82.

Margolin, G. (1983). Behavioral marital therapy: Is there a place for passion, play, and other non-negotiable dimensions? *Behavior Therapist, 6,* 65–68.

Margolin, G., Burman, B., & John, R. S. (1989). Home observations of married couples reenacting naturalistic conflicts. *Behavioral Assessment, 11,* 101–118.

Margolin, G., & Wampold, B. E. (1981). Sequential analysis of conflict and accord in distressed and nondistressed marital partners. *Journal of Consulting and Clinical Psychology, 49,* 554–67.

Markman, H. M., Floyd, F., Stanley, S., & Lewis, H. (1986). Prevention. In N. Jacobson & A. Gurman (Eds.), *Clinical handbook of marital therapy* (pp. 173–195). New York: Guilford.

Markman, H. J., Floyd, F. J., Stanley, S. M., & Storaasli, R. D. (1988). Prevention of marital distress: A longitudinal investigation. *Journal of Consulting and Clinical Psychology, 56,* 210–217.

Markman, H. J., Jamieson, K., & Floyd, F. (1983). The assessment and modification of premarital relationships: Preliminary findings on the etiology and prevention of marital and family distress. *Advances in Family Intervention, 3,* 41–90.

Markman, H. J., Renick, M. J., Floyd, F. J., Stanley, S. M., & Clements, M. (1993). Preventing marital distress through communication and conflict management training: A 4- and 5-year followup. *Journal of Consulting and Clinical Psychology, 61,* 70–77.

Moos, R. H., & Moos, B. S. (1983). Clinical applications of the Family Environment Scale. In E. E. Filsinger (Ed.), *Marriage and family assessment: A sourcebook for family therapy* (pp. 253–274). London: Sage.

Muehrer, P., Moscicki, E. K., & Koretz, D. S. (1993). Prevention as psychological intervention research. *NIMH Psychotherapy and Rehabilitation Research Bulletin, 2*(3), 16.

O'Dorisio, M. S., Wood, C. L., & O'Dorisio, T. M. (1985). Vasoactive intestinal peptide and neuropeptide modulation of the immune response. *Journal of Immunology, 135,* 792–796.

Osgarby, S., & Halford, W. K. (1996). *Behaviour, affect and cognition in happy and unhappy couples during problem solving and positive reminiscence.* Unpublished manuscript, Griffith University, Brisbane, Australia.

Pert, C. B., Ruff, M. R., Weber, R. J., & Herkenham, M. (1985). Neuropeptides and their receptors: A psychosomatic network. *Journal of Immunology, 135,* 820–826.

Renick, M. J., Blumberg, S., & Markman, H. J. (1992). The prevention and relationship enhancement program (PREP): An empirically based preventive intervention program for couples. *Family Relations, 44,* 392–401.

Revensdorf, D., Hahlweg, K., Schindler L., & Vogel, B. (1984). Interaction analysis of marital conflict. In K. Hahlweg & N. S. Jacobson (Eds.), *Marital interaction: Analysis and modification* (pp. 159–181). New York: Guilford.

Revenson, T. A. (1994). Social support and marital coping with chronic illness. *Annals of Behavioral Medicine, 16,* 122–130.

Rosenberg, H. (1983). Relapsed versus non-relapsed alcohol abusers: Coping skills, life events, and social support. *Addictive Behavior, 8,* 183–186.

Sells, S. B. (1970). On the nature of stress. In J. E. McGrath (Ed.), *Social and psychological factors in stress* (pp. 9–33). New York: Holt.

Smith, M., Glass, G., & Miller, T. (1980). *Benefits of psychotherapy.* Baltimore: The John Hopkins University Press.

Snyder, D. K. (1981). *Marital Satisfaction Inventory.* Los Angeles: Western Psychological Association.

Snyder, D. K., Willis, R. M., & Grady-Fletcher, A. (1991). Long-term effectiveness of behavioral versus insight-oriented marital therapy. *Journal of Consulting and Clinical Psychology, 59,* 138–141.

Spanier, G. B. (1976). Measuring dyadic adjustment: New scales for assessing the quality of marriage and similar dyads. *Journal of Marriage and the Family, 38,* 15–28.

Spanier, G. B. (1979). The measurement of marital quality. *Journal of Sex and Marital Therapy, 5,* 289–300.

Stanley, S. M., Markman, H. J., St. Peters, M., & Leber, D. B. (1995). Strengthening marriages and preventing divorce: New directions in prevention research. *Family Relations, 44,* 392–401.

Straus, M. (1979). Measuring intrafamily conflict and violence: The Conflict Tactics (CT) scales. *Journal of Marriage and the Family, 41,* 75–88.

Sullivan, K. Y., & Bradbury, T. N. (1996). Preventing marital dysfunction: The primacy of secondary strategies. *The Behavior Therapist, 19,* 33–36.

Sullivan, K. T., & Bradbury, T. N. (1997). Are premarital prevention programs reaching couples at risk for marital dysfunction? *Journal of Consulting and Clinical Psychology, 65,* 24–30.

Van Widenfelt, B., Hosman, C., Schaap, C., & Van Der Staak, C. (1996). The prevention of relationship distress for couples at risk: A controlled evaluation with nine-month and two-year follow-ups. *Family Relations, 45,* 156–165.

Veroff, J., Sutherland, L., Chadha, L. A., & Ortega, R. M. (1993). Predicting marital quality with narrative assessments of marital experience. *Journal of Marriage and the Family, 55,* 326–337.

Vinokur, A. D., Schul, Y., & Caplan, R. D. (1987). Determinants of perceived social support: Interpersonal transactions, personal outlook, and transient affective states. *Journal of Personality and Social Psychology, 53,* 1137–1145.

Weiss, R. S. (1974). The provisions of social relationships. In Z. Rubin (Ed.), *Doing unto others* (pp. 23–45). Englewood Cliffs, NJ: Prentice Hall.

Weiss, R. L., & Heyman, R. (1990). Observation of marital interaction. In F. D. Fincham & T. N. Bradbury (Eds.), *The psychology of marriage: Basic issues and applications* (pp. 87–117). New York: Guilford.

Rony Berger, Psy.D.
Rita DeMaria, Ph.D.

Epilogue: The Future of Preventive Interventions With Couples

The goals of this chapter are to provide a recap of the field of prevention of couple distress, to compare programs along important dimensions, and to identify issues needing further exploration. We start with a brief review of the history and founding programs of this field and proceed with a critical evaluation of the different preventive programs presented in the text. Next, we delineate future trends by addressing professional, sociopolitical, and research dilemmas. We conclude with recommendations for clinical practice and future research.

☐ Historical Roots of Preventive Interventions With Couples

Before outlining the historical background of the field, we would like to point out how difficult it is to differentiate between social change and professional reform, due to the reciprocal and circular relationship shared by these two forces. Thus, unraveling the sources of influence in the development of preventive interventions is not an easy task.

Despite its having its own trajectory, the history of preventive interventions with couples parallels those of contemporary marital interventions and of the general prevention movement in the mental health field. The underlying philosophy and practice of prevention can be traced back to its theoretical, professional, and empirical roots as well as to political and sociocultural trends in Western society. Perhaps more than any other, the enrichment/encounter movement influenced the emergence of preventive interventions with couples (Hof & Miller, 1981; Hunt, Hof, & DeMaria, 1998; L'Abate, 1977). However, the family life education movement should also be credited for strengthening the development and transmission of preventive programs.

Although there is no universally accepted metatheory guiding the development of marital interventions, several unified theories have contributed to our understanding of marital distress and the improvement of marital relationships (see, for example, Stuart's, 1980, social-learning approach). Many recently developed marital therapies are eclectic, focusing on diverse aspects of marital interaction, including the behavioral, emotional, and cognitive components. Likewise, prevention, with its focus on multiple aspects of marital relating, such as empathy, communication skills, bonding, and the use of group process, represents an integration of diverse theoretical perspectives.

An Historical Overview of Marital Interventions

Marital interventions surfaced in the 1930s, when marriage counselors shifted away from their initial focus on sexual difficulties to provide counseling for marital distress. Eventually, marriage counseling emerged as a professional specialty. Throughout the 1940s, psychoanalysts conducted concurrent analyses of marital partners. Hollis (1949), who was influential in the development of social work practice theory, reinforced the psychoanalytic approach of individual treatment for marital problems. During this period, conjoint treatment for couples was considered heretical; individual psychodynamics and pathology were considered the source of marital dysfunction (Eisenstein, 1956).

Professional views of family relations changed considerably during the 1950s. In particular, general systems theories were being applied to the study of family relationships. Communication styles and processes between spouses were closely examined. Ackerman's classic paper, "Diagnosis of Neurotic Marital Interaction" (1954), advanced the notion that the marital relationship was an entity in and of itself.

With the emergence of family therapy approaches in the late 1960s, conjoint marital therapy, as it is known today, began to be practiced (Lederer & Jackson, 1968). The 1960s witnessed as well a growing recognition of the interdisciplinary nature of marital and family therapies. With the formation of the American Association for Marriage Counseling (now known as the American Association for Marriage and Family Therapy; AAMFT), marriage counseling became a formal profession. By the end of the 1960s, behavioral methods were included in the repertoire of marital interventions (Ard & Ard, 1969). Eventually, an integrative model based on psychodynamic theory, behavioral theory, and sexuality, as advocated by Kaplan (1974), became the hallmark of marital therapy practice. However, there was a concurrent proliferation of marital therapy approaches derived from the various models of individual and family therapy (O'Leary & Turkewitz, 1978; Weiss, 1978).

An Historical Overview of the Marriage Enrichment/Encounter Movement

While the marriage enrichment/encounter movement almost dovetailed with the development of marital counseling, it was the enrichment/encounter movement that most directly influenced the emergence of preventive programs for couples' distress. The roots of marriage enrichment are diverse, springing from the fields of family sociology, human sexuality, conflict resolution, small group dynamics, affective education, programmed instruction, social skills training, humanistic psychology, and communication theory (Leight, Loewen, & Lester,1986).

The major figure in the enrichment movement was undoubtedly David Mace, who in 1943 opened the first marriage counseling clinic in England. After returning to the United States in 1949, Mace and his wife, Vera, became convinced that "preventive services" were needed to supplement what they considered "remedial services" for couples. In 1962, the Maces led their first marriage enrichment program for married couples wishing to enhance their relationship. However, the Maces also influenced the marital counseling field and, from 1960 to 1967, served as the executive directors of the American Association of Marriage Counselors (now AAMFT). Coincidentally, that same year, Father Gabriel Calvo, a Catholic priest in Spain, started a weekend retreat that evolved into the Marriage Encounter movement. By the late 1970s, Marriage Encounter was reaching over 250,000 couples a year. The Marriage Encounter movement spread beyond the Catholic community into other religious denominations and now consists of three separate groups: National, International, and Worldwide Marriage Encounter. The Maces and the early leaders of Marriage Encounter were thus the pioneers of what would eventually become the marriage enrichment movement.

The 1970s and 1980s, in particular, were years of expansion for marriage enrichment, being marked by a proliferation of marital enrichment programs. In 1973, the Maces founded the Association for Couples in Marriage Enrichment (A.C.M.E.); a few years later, they united many of the national enrichment groups into the Council of Affiliated Marriage

Enrichment Organizations (CAMEO). The majority of programs had been spurred by religious organizations (for a review of specific programs, see L'Abate, 1977), although there were a number of secular programs. Miller, Nunnally, and Wackman (1975) laid the foundation for the Minnesota Couple Communication Program. Guerney (1977) published *Relationship Enhancement*. Gottman detailed the early framework of his Marriage Lab (Gottman, 1979). Olson and his associates (Fournier, Olson, & Druckman, 1983) were developing a premarital assessment tool that would be reliable, valid, and clinically useful. Among the more prominent secular enrichment programs were the More Joy in Your Marriage program (Otto & Otto, 1976), Marriage Renewal Retreats (Schmitt & Schmitt, 1976), A.C.M.E.'s Enrichment Programs (Mace & Mace, 1975); the Behavioral-Exchange Program (Stuart, 1980), and L'Abate's (1977) Structured Enrichment (SE) Programs.

In the mid-1980s, a new generation of prevention programs began to gain precedence. In contrast to the religious roots of many earlier programs, this new wave was developed by social workers, psychologists, and family therapists who used couple-process models (see Gottman, Coan, Carrere, & Swanson, 1998) and updated research. The growing interest in these programs among mental health professionals as well as educators and politicians was demonstrated by the eventual emergence of the Coalition for Marriage, Couple, and Family Education (CMCFE), which hosted the major leaders in the marital intervention field at its first annual conference in 1997.

☐ Theoretical and Professional Roots

The evolution of alternative theoretical viewpoints stemmed from the counterreaction to the dominant psychoanalytic model. In the 1950s and 1960s, behaviorism emerged, and then, in the 1970s, humanism. Despite their divergent philosophical perspectives, these approaches shared a rejection of the medical-disease model, advocating instead a more optimistic, growth-oriented model. Through the prisms of these theories, human nature was no longer chained by early developmental experiences, necessitating treatment by experts; rather, people were capable of gaining self-control and changing their fates. The preventive model was consistent with such thinking. Clinical applications of behaviorism and learning theories led to the development of social skills training (SST), a major component of most preventive programs for couples. The spirit of humanism, on the other hand, with its therapeutic tributaries (client-centered therapy, psychodrama, Gestalt therapy, etc.) provided the ideological framework for the human potential movement. This movement, which encompassed T-groups, sensitivity groups, and self-help groups, incorporated the focus of primary prevention in its use of psychoeducational and experiential group activities.

The emergence of the preventive model in the mental health field was influenced by two major professional trends: the establishment of the child-guidance clinics in the 1930s, followed by the emergence of community mental health clinics in the 1960s (L'Abate,1990; Levant,1986). These two movements exemplified the theoretical and professional paradigm shifts in the field.

☐ Political and Sociocultural Trends

The social and political milieus of the 1960s and the 1970s challenged traditional family structure and roles. Particularly during the early 1970s, significant social changes, such as the shrinking of family size, an increase in the divorce rate, the growing acceptance of nontraditional families (single-parent, blended, etc.), the sexual revolution, and feminism dramatically changed the landscape of the American family. Consequently, couples and families, faced with new and often conflicting needs, were subjected to growing levels of stress. Preventive strategies were designed in part to address such issues.

The mid-1980s witnessed the debate over family values. Both conservative and liberal politicians recognized the alarming socioeconomic impact of the breakdown of the American family. A consensus emerged regarding the need for methods of preventing marital dissolution and other types of family discord. The Clinton administration, with its focus on the reformation of the national health care system, facilitated the prevention movement. Even managed care organizations began to show interest in incorporating preventive programs into their array of services.

Likewise, divorce reform during the 1990s led to a renewed emphasis on prevention as a component of the larger sphere of marital interventions. Given the growing body of empirical data on the deleterious effects of divorce, it was not surprising that grassroots movements like the Promise Keepers and Marriage Savers achieved widespread popularity. Some states chose to adopt the option of the "covenant marriage," with its stricter proscriptions against divorce.

☐ Comparative Review of Preventive Programs

Any responsible overview of preventive programs should include an evaluation of the dimensions related to program effectiveness. Earlier evaluations of preventive programs have, in fact, cast doubt regarding their effectiveness (Bagarozzi & Rauen, 1981; Fournier & Olson, 1986; Guerney & Maxson, 1990; Gurman & Kniskern, 1977; Hof & Miller,1981). Nevertheless, we believe that the number and variety of preventive approaches for couples, as manifested by this volume, attests to the compelling need for such interventions.

The most comprehensive assessment of preventive programs, performed by the American Psychological Association's (APA's) Task Force on Promotion, Prevention, and Intervention Alternatives (Price, Cowen, Lorion, Ramos-McKay, 1989), used 11 criteria for evaluating program effectiveness. To those criteria we added 3 more, and we now use the resulting 14 dimensions in an evaluative overview of the programs presented in this handbook.

The 14 dimensions are:

- coherence and consistency of theoretical framework;
- consistency between intervention model and theory;
- clear and realistic program goals;
- clear, step-by-step description of program;
- incorporation of both risk factors and protective factors;
- adequacy of process for selecting participants;
- generalizability to different settings and populations;
- competence of program leaders and adequacy of training;
- provision for follow-up or booster sessions;
- utilization of effective strategies;
- solid empirical evidence for efficacy of program;
- empirical evidence regarding long-term effects of program;
- satisfaction of program's participants; and
- program's cost-effectiveness.

Coherence and Consistency of Theoretical Framework

All programs for preventing distress in couples are in some way informed by an underlying theory regarding interpersonal relationships, one that is either generic (as in Relationship Enhancement [RE], for example) or specific (e.g., Imago Relationship Therapy [IRT]) to committed intimate relationships. Such a theoretical framework, we believe, is the foundation on which the entire preventive program ought to be constructed. Without a clear, focused, and consistent theory, even those programs using otherwise effective interventions may have limited efficacy in the long run.

Couple therapy was once characterized as "a technique in search of a theory" (Manus, 1966). We wish to circumvent a similar description of the couple distress prevention field. Therefore, we evaluated the theoretical frameworks of the programs described in this volume according to: (a) the clarity with which the theory is articulated and (b) internal consistency, that is, consistency across the various assumptions and hypotheses of the theory.

Our examination of the programs' underlying theories revealed, for most, a high degree of clarity. Two exceptions were Marriage Encounter (ME) and the Caring Couples Network (CCN), whose theoretical bases we found less clear. The ME movement, as presented in chapter 3 by Elin, uses vague concepts like "a divine energy of love" to describe the core construct of intimate relationships. This construct was not clearly defined in Elin's chapter. The CCN model is admittedly "more about implementing existing theory than about creating new theory" (Hunt & Hunt, p. 258, this volume). CCN espouses a variety of models of marital enrichment, with its own guiding principle of "mentoring couples" being an expansion of A.C.M.E.'s notion. We also found the TIME model, with its concept of "the purpose of the symptom which keeps the marriage from being enriched" (Carlson & Dinkmeyer, p. 151, this volume), along with its Adlerian foundations, in need of clarification and expansion. In contrast, SE and Distance Writing (DW), which also borrow from existing models, utilize a comprehensive interpersonal competence theory.

Examination of the consistency of the programs' theoretical frameworks reveals what appears to be a correlation between the specificity of the model and its internal consistency. Empirically based programs (Prevention and Relationship Enhancement Program [PREP], Marriage Survival Kit [MSK], PREPARE/ENRICH, SE & DW) seem more internally consistent than more eclectic programs (A.C.M.E., IRT, Practical Application of Intimate Relationship Skills [PAIRS]). Although eclectic approaches have the advantage of presenting a wide variety of interventions, eclectically based programs can be limited by a failure to carefully prioritize those interventions.

Consistency Between Intervention Model and Theory

Likewise, the more concise the program's underlying theoretical framework, the greater the consistency between the theory and the intervention model. Indeed, programs based on empirical data, particularly those rooted in learning theory, are very much in accord with their intervention models. However, we noted that some programs using eclectic theories and complex intervention models demonstrated similarly high consistency. RE, Couple Communication (CC), Saving Your Marriage Before It Starts (SYMBIS), and Training in Marriage Enrichment (TIME), each of which integrate humanistic, interpersonal, systems, communications, and cognitive-behavioral theories, provide excellent examples. To a lesser extent, PAIRS, IRT, ME, and A.C.M.E. have successfully translated their eclectic theoretical frameworks into comprehensive and relatively consistent intervention models.

Clear and Realistic Program Goals

A program that realistically delineates its goals is likely to be more effective in achieving those goals. Although the programs in this book use different terminology to describe their goals, we found the commonality among program goals to be far greater than the differences. Most programs focus on increasing participants' awareness, whether of their own emotional needs, their personal expectations, their partner's needs, their mutual commitment as a couple, their communication skills, their conflict resolution skills, or their ability to nurture and please their partner.

The programs did vary, however, in the clarity and the ambitiousness of their goals. We judged the clearest goals to be those of PREPARE/ENRICH, CC, RE, PREP, SE & DW, MSK, SYMBIS, PAIRS, and A.C.M.E. Less clearly articulated were the goals of TIME, IRT, CCN, and ME. The empirically driven programs, such as SE & DW, PREP, MSK, and PREPARE/ENRICH, hold the most realistic program goals, although at the expense of being somewhat narrow. Some of the more eclectic programs, like A.C.M.E., SYMBIS, TIME, and CCN, also outline fairly realistic goals. PAIRS and IRT share many goals which, due to their breadth, seem overly ambitious, particularly for a preventive program. When considering, for instance, the goal of "identifying your needs and getting them met," as proposed by PAIRS, or the goal of mutual healing of childhood wounds and repair of developmental arrests, as suggested by IRT, one might question whether those objectives are likely to be achieved over the average duration of couples therapy, not to mention within the time-frame of a preventive program. Although the goals of ME appear realistic, the program itself portrays romantic relationships in what some would consider a glorified and unrealistic manner.

Clear, Step-by-Step Description of Program

To allow implementation by practitioners and investigation by researchers, a clear, step-by-step description of the program is necessary. Naturally, there is some correspondence between the program's degree of structure (see Table 1.1 in the introductory chapter) and the clarity of its description. However, we found that even programs with less structure, such as A.C.M.E. and CCN, could be described in satisfactory detail.

Two exceptions are the MSK and RE programs, which do not provide any sequential descriptions of their programs. It is unclear whether this omission reflects flexibility of structure or is simply an oversight by our contributors.

Incorporation of Both Risk Factors and Protective Factors

As suggested in the Introduction (chapter 1), most preventive programs for couples address both risk factors and protective factors, as defined by Coie et al. (1993). Because preventive programs in the mental health field have traditionally been risk oriented, we expected the balance to tip in the direction of eliminating dysfunctional behaviors. In fact, this was somewhat the case, but not as much as we expected. In our opinion, prevention programs should provide a relatively equal balance as far as addressing the two types of factors. Therefore, we attempted to evaluate the degree of balance within each program as described by the contributor, recognizing that this might not be an accurate reflection of the program as it is actually applied in the field.

Two programs that stress the importance of protective factors without neglecting risk factors are PREP and MSK. A good balance between risk and protective factors was demonstrated also by RE, TIME, PREPARE/ENRICH, PAIRS, and IRT. CC and SYMBIS place greater focus on risk factors while not ignoring protective factors. A.C.M.E. and ME, on the other hand, tip toward the protective side, although they do not ignore risk factors. Finally, the balance between risk and protective factors in CCN and SE & DW cannot be assessed without knowing which particular intervention associated with those programs is being utilized.

Adequacy of Process for Selecting Participants

Prevention experts generally agree that a primary requirement of participants is the ability to actively participate in group and educational activities. There remains some question, however, about the advisability of imposing additional selection criteria.

For instance, the common wisdom and practice among prevention programmers has been to exclude distressed couples, referring them instead to remedial interventions. This practice was based on the assumption that preventive programs are not useful for, and in some cases can be damaging to, dysfunctional couples. In actuality, many distressed couples self-select into preventive programs (DeMaria, 1998; Giblin, Sprenkle, & Sheehan, 1995; Markman, Floyd, Stanley, & Lewis, 1986) and experience benefits similar to those of nondistressed couples.

Each of the programs described is the handbook use one of three differ-ent approaches to screening participants: preprogram screening, postprogram screening, and no screening. Two programs use preprogram screening. CCN's rather innovative approach has a multidisciplinary team performing an "intake-like" process based on the couple's desires and needs. When appropriate, referrals are made to various preventive, en-richment, or remedial services. SE & DW determine the needs of the couple based on the combination of a questionnaire and assessments tools. RE recommends some form of intake (the nature of which is unclear) to assign participants to the various formats offered by this approach. Some PAIRS practitioners prescreen participants, although this does not appear to be required. The contributors for PREPARE/ENRICH, MSK, PREP, and, to some extent, IRT acknowledge the special needs of some couples (e.g., "conflicted" and "devitalized" couples, partners with severe individual psychopathology, those who exhibit "fundamental violations of the marital contract," abusive partners, "early-wounded" couples). However, none of these programs exclude such couples from their programs; rather, they are referred to additional services after the program is over. Other pro-grams, including A.C.M.E., TIME, PAIRS, SYMBIS, and ME either do not report any screening of participants or reject such a concept based on the humanistic theories to which they subscribe. Finally, several contributors note the appearance of a self-selection process in virtually all the pro-grams, one based on the availability, accessibility, and financial demands of the program.

Generalizability to Different Settings and Populations

The programs presented in this handbook are generic, although some of them are geared to specific types of couples, such as premarital, engaged, newlywed, or married for various lengths of time. However, most pro-grams assume that they are applicable in different settings with varied popula-tions without significant modifications being made. This might in fact be the case; we maintain, however, that this notion needs empirical validation.

We evaluated the degree of applicability based on information provided by our contributors. For some programs, data are not yet available (MSK and PREPARE/ENRICH).

RE is the program that has been the most widely applied across diverse settings and different populations. According to Cavedo and Guerney (see chapter 4 of this volume), the program was successfully applied in set-tings ranging from private organizations and academic institutions to public agencies and clinics and religious organizations. RE was also used in ma-jor urban centers as well as in rural areas. It has been taken by premarital couples, newlyweds, and both distressed and nondistressed couples from various racial, ethnic, and cultural backgrounds. It has been tested on couples with a variety of problems and individual psychopathologies. Particularly impressive is the fact that RE is one of the only programs that has been applied to minority couples.

CC has been successfully applied with premarital and marital couples of various ages and socioeconomic backgrounds in diverse settings. Although studies indicate that CC has been used with both distressed and nondistressed couples, this approach shows better results with more functional couples. Research suggests that CC has positive effects with less educated couples, but there is no evidence of its having been applied with racially and culturally diverse populations.

A.C.M.E. has been used primarily with married couples and newlywed couples. Although this program has attempted to reach couples from a wide range of socioeconomic backgrounds, the vast majority of the participants are White, educated, middle-class couples. Additionally, A.C.M.E. has been used with couples from diverse cultures around the world, including in Canada, Thailand, Taiwan, and countries in Central and South America.

ME and CCN, like A.C.M.E., are primarily aimed at married couples, drawing most of their participants from religious organizations. Unlike A.C.M.E., however, they have been applied with couples from a variety of socioeconomic backgrounds. ME reported its programs having been applied successfully in correctional facilities and in various countries around the world. TIME, as well, has been applied to married couples and seems to be popular among religious groups.

IRT, PAIRS, and SYMBIS have been applied in a wide variety of settings; however, these programs, like many others, serve primarily White, highly educated, middle- to upper middle-class couples. There have been some attempts to apply these programs with couples from different socioeconomic levels and varied ethnic and racial backgrounds; however, no data regarding effectiveness with these groups were provided. IRT and PAIRS have been adapted for use in a variety of countries with cultures similar to that of the United States. It should be noted that IRT is the only program, in our awareness, that has been adapted to serve the needs of homosexual couples.

SE and DW have been used with premarital and marital couples with a range of problems and varying degrees of psychopathology.

Competence of Program Leaders and Adequacy of Training

All of the contributors stressed the importance of the leader or facilitator to the success of the program. There appear to be two perspectives regarding facilitator qualifications. The first view maintains that a high level of maturity and personal integrity and good interpersonal skills, coupled with basic training in administering the program, are sufficient qualifications. The other view requires, in addition, that the facilitator demonstrate professional- or paraprofessional-level knowledge regarding human behavior, couple relationships, or group processes or, alternatively, intensive training in those areas coupled with professional supervision.

The majority of the programs use paraprofessionals and lay people. ME and CCN do not require training but operate in the context of teams which include professionals or clergy. SE and DW also use paraprofessionals but require direct supervision by qualified therapists. Other programs, like A.C.M.E., RE, and CC, provide leader training and also demand demonstration of knowledge via written tests or apprenticeship periods for certification.

On the other hand, there are programs that require their leaders to have obtained graduate training in one of the helping professions before undergoing rigorous leader training. Perhaps the most demanding programs are IRT and PAIRS, both of which require a graduate degree in a mental health field as well as many hours of training and apprenticeship. PREP and SYMBIS also require their facilitators to be professionals, but their training is less time consuming.

Provision for Follow-up or Booster Sessions

Despite several recent studies suggesting sustained or even improved gains at follow-up (Markman, Floyd, Stanley, & Storaasli, 1988; Markman & Hahlweg, 1993; Zimpher,1988), research generally indicates declines of positive program effects over time (Giblin, 1986; Markman and Hahlweg, 1993; Wampler, 1990). To counteract this problem of durability of effects, some prevention experts (e.g., Floyd, Markman, Kelly, Blumberg, & Stanley, 1995) have recommended that programs employ follow-up assessments and periodic booster sessions. This is particularly important for programs that use a brief and condensed retreat format. For instance, ME and A.C.M.E., both of which have used intensive weekend retreats as their trademark, have moved toward stressing ongoing small-group experiences. These programs encourage their participants to attend a variety of follow-up activities, including monthly programs, anniversary meetings, and other voluntary activities. CCN and RE offer participants individualized preventive or remedial services. CCN encourages couples to be mentored by a matched couple. However, no formal follow-up assessments were reported by those two programs. MSK, the only program reported to use rigorous follow-up procedures, includes a 6-month booster workshop and a regular 3-month assessment using questionnaires. SYMBIS schedules a follow-up session but does not conduct evaluation at follow-up. Several programs, including CC, IRT, TIME, PREP, and PAIRS provide participants with audiovisual and written materials that support the concepts and skills. Participants are encouraged to use these materials to complete special maintenance assignments.

Utilization of Effective Strategies

This criterion is a crucial one that determines the overall effectiveness of the program. A review of the various strategies used by the programs reveals more commonalities than differences across the programs. For example, most programs teach couples communication, problem-solving, negotiation, and conflict resolution skills. Almost all programs address issues of expectations, common values, and mutual commitment. Yet there are also some differences: Only a subset of programs uses strategies to enhance spouses' awareness of self and of intergenerational dynamics, processes that promote bonding and intimacy, or those that encourage expressive and emotive exercises. Unfortunately, there are almost no studies on the relative effectiveness of specific strategies, and none have evaluated the effectiveness of the interactions among such strategies. Hence, at this point we forgo any comparison of the relative effectiveness of strategies offered by the programs.

Solid Empirical Evidence for Short-Term Effectiveness of Program

Like the previous factor, this one is undoubtedly one of the most pertinent in evaluating any intervention, whether remedial or preventive. The focus here is not merely on empirical data but on solid empirical evidence. Anecdotal evidence and poorly designed studies may suggest intriguing trends but do not constitute persuasive evidence.

The three most thoroughly researched preventive programs are RE, CC, and PREP. Studies for the past two decades have consistently demonstrated the effectiveness of RE programs as compared with no-treatment groups, attendance-placebo groups, and several other preventive programs (see Cavedo & Guerney, chapter 4 of this volume). RE was shown to be successful in improving communication and problem solving in distressed and nondistressed couples, in promoting couple adjustment and relationship satisfaction, and in increasing relationship stability.

The most impressive outcome was revealed in a meta-analysis of 85 studies analyzing 14 preventive and enrichment programs attended by nearly 4,000 couples and families (Giblin et al., 1985; Giblin, 1986). While the average effect size for the preventive programs studied in the analysis was .44 (that is, the average person who participated in a preventive program improved more than did 67% of the controls), the effect size for RE was .96 (meaning that the average person attending RE improved more than did 83% of the controls). This result is particularly striking in light of the fact that the next highest effect size for any particular preventive program was only 0.45. It should be mentioned that RE was not compared to the majority of programs presented in this handbook.

Despite this excellent track record, some degree of caution, particularly in terms of comparing the effectiveness of RE with other programs, has been recommended (Wampler, 1990). Several methodological concerns, including problems related to the utilization of appropriate control groups, random assignment of subjects to groups, the particular outcome measures used, and the fact that a great deal of the empirical data is generated by the program's developers also cast some doubt on the results.

CC also is a well-researched program, with over 40 empirical outcome studies, along with 25 master's theses and one meta-analysis having been performed. These studies suggest that CC is effective for changing marital interactions of both nondistressed and distressed couples, as measured by level of satisfaction, quality of communication, and ability to resolve problems. The research revealed improvements in overall relationship quality and in individual functioning (self-esteem) as well. On the other hand, Giblin et al.'s (1985) large meta-analysis found CC's effect size to be relatively small. Despite this finding and the methodological limitations of the studies mentioned above, findings on the short- and moderate-term effectiveness of CC in changing communication patterns and the overall relationship satisfaction of marital couples are promising.

While RE and CC both have long histories, it is the relatively new program, PREP, which appears to use the best research methodology of all the programs. Several carefully designed studies on premarital couples showed significant changes in negative communication patterns and in conflict management skills from pre- to posttest. PREP couples also exhibited more positive interaction patterns and higher levels of relationship and sexual satisfaction, as compared with matched control couples. These results were maintained and sometimes even improved long after the program had been administered. Further, the divorce rate of PREP couples was found to be significantly lower than that of matched control couples.

Outcome research on the PAIRS program also offers promising indicators of the short-term effectiveness of this program. Although previous outcome studies showed positive effects in terms of individual dynamics and relationship adjustment and satisfaction, poor experimental design and the use of small samples prohibited firm conclusions regarding the effectiveness of the program. Recent studies using much improved research designs suggest short-term positive effects in terms of marital adjustment and marital satisfaction. Nonetheless, some experimental flaws, notably subject selection and a lack of matched controls, render even these promising results inconclusive.

SE & DW have been studied primarily with students. These studies showed short-term positive outcomes for couples in terms of the skills taught by specific programs, as compared with control groups. These studies, although encouraging, must be considered cautiously due to methodological flaws. Documentation of the effectiveness of SE & DW in improving couples' overall satisfaction and stability would require further research.

Research on A.C.M.E. and ME has shown positive outcomes on broad categories of factors, such as values regarding marriage and level of intimacy; however, the studies lacked the basic experimental requirements needed to draw conclusions regarding effectiveness. Several other programs, such as TIME, IRT, and SYMBIS, also show positive indications in recent studies, but the research is either too sparse or too preliminary to draw any conclusions.

Finally, there are a few new programs, such as MSK, PREPARE/ENRICH, and CCN, which have not yet been empirically tested. MSK is currently being tested using an interesting experimental design ("proximal change experiments"), which hopefully will assess not only the efficacy of the entire program but also the effectiveness of its various components.

The PREPARE/ENRICH program, although based on reliable and valid instruments, has not yet been tested. Likewise, no outcome studies were performed on the overall CCN package, although CCN incorporates components of programs cited above.

Empirical Evidence Regarding Long-Term Effects of Programs

Preventive programs are, by definition, future-oriented interventions. Hence, assessment of their long-term effects is the single most important criterion regarding their effectiveness. Since recent reviews of preventive and enrichment programs (Giblin et al., 1985; Markman & Hahlweg, 1993; Wampler, 1990) clearly indicate that most program effects dissipate over time, we agree with Bradbury and Fincham's (1990) assertion that "lack of long-term longitudinal data is incongruent with the purpose of prevention" (p. 387). Unfortunately, most programs presented in this volume have yet to demonstrate their long-term effectiveness empirically.

PREP, as suggested before, is not only the best-researched preventive program for couple distress, but has also conducted the longest term follow-up tests. PREP couples have been followed up at the University of Denver since 1988. These subjects have shown maintenance of gains in relationship and sexual satisfaction and in lowering problem intensity at 1, 3 and 5 years postintervention. The PREP researchers plan to continue to follow these subjects (Floyd et al., 1995). Similar long-term effects were seen in a study of PREP in Germany. Even more interesting is the finding that, on some measures (for example, negative communication patterns), the gap between the PREP group and a matched control group actually increased 4 years postintervention. In one study, PREP couples also reported increased relationship satisfaction at 3-year follow-up. In addition, significantly lower divorce rates were found up to 5 years postintervention for premarital couples who took the PREP program. These impressive results demonstrate the durability of PREP in promoting couple satisfaction and stability.

The substantial body of outcome research on RE and CC cited above lacks long-term follow-ups. Giblin et al. (1985) found that the average follow-up period for the 85 studies they reviewed was 12 weeks, with many studies not employing any follow-up tests. Wampler (1990), reviewing the CC research, indicated that no study conducted follow-ups at longer than 4 months poststudy. Further, in studies that did employ follow-ups, there was evidence of decay of positive effects. An exception was a study by Huppert (1984), who showed positive effects at the 3-year follow-up, although the results were compromised by the high attrition rate. Hence, assessing the long-term effects of even well-researched program like RE and CC demands further investigation.

Despite the sparsity of longitudinal studies of preventive programs, a shift away from this trend is evident in recent studies and in studies in progress. One good example is the examination of long-term effectiveness of the PAIRS program. Durana (1996c) found that positive effects in marital adjustment, marital satisfaction, conflict, and level of intimacy had endured at 6- and 8-month follow-ups for both distressed and nondistressed PAIRS couples. Although improvements in experimental design and longer term follow-up is still needed, these results are encouraging. SYMBIS and IRT also report current involvement in longitudinal outcome studies.

Satisfaction of Program Participants

The extent to which participants are satisfied with a particular program does not necessarily correspond to the program's effectiveness in improving relationship satisfaction or couple stability. However, satisfaction may affect participants' motivation to use the knowledge and skills imparted by the program as well as contribute to the popularity of the program among consumers. Participant satisfaction is, therefore, an important criterion on which to compare the programs.

A relatively high degree of satisfaction is reported by the majority of preventive programs, with A.C.M.E., ME, TIME, IRT, and PAIRS, in particular, reporting that vast proportions of participants (between 90% and 99%) rank their experience as highly satisfactory. Because standardized tools were not used to evaluate participant satisfaction, conclusions cannot be drawn regarding differences in participant satisfaction with the various programs. Furthermore, there is a lack of data concerning dropout rates, percentages of participants who did not complete the evaluations, and the attrition rates at follow-up.

Program's Cost-Effectiveness

In this era of quality assurance and managed care, all interventions need to pass the litmus test of cost-effectiveness. Indeed, this factor is perhaps the most crucial in determining whether or not a preventive program will become widely used. Unfortunately, calculating the cost-effectiveness of a single program is a complicated task, not to mention comparing the cost-effectiveness of many diverse programs. Furthermore, our evaluation is compromised by limited comparability of program goals, formats, training costs, etc., as well as by gaps in the information provided by some of our contributors.

Despite the aforementioned difficulty, we attempted to compare the programs by using a formula that combines each program's effectiveness rating (on a five-point likert scale) with the ranking of its estimated costs (using the same five-point scale). Our effectiveness and cost ratings, although made subjectively, are based on data provided by the contributors. For instance, we rated program effectiveness based on the quality and quantity of studies that document the program's significant and durable positive effects on relationship quality, couple stability, and couple satisfaction. In assessing program cost, we focused not on market value but rather on factors like length of time, application format, and use of paraprofessionals. Programs having several different formats were compared using their shortest group format. For a number of programs, cost-effectiveness could not be calculated because we did not have enough data to assess effectiveness or cost.

The highest ratings for cost-effectiveness were those of three programs: PREP, RE, and CC. The next highest set included ME, A.C.M.E., and TIME, and perhaps SE & DW. The ratings of these programs were significantly lower due to the lack of empirical data on their effectiveness. Despite their widespread popularity, PAIRS and IRT scored lower on cost effectiveness, due primarily to their high cost. However, these models emerged from clinical work with couples and may have greater applicability with severely distressed couples. Other programs could not be evaluated.

Summary

We have attempted to evaluate program effectiveness based on fourteen criteria. Our findings can be summarized as follows:

1. Most of the programs are based on coherent and consistent theoretical frameworks. Many programs successfully integrate various theoretical approaches.
2. We found consistency between theoretical approaches and intervention models for these programs.
3. Some differences were noted between programs in the clarity of their goals and the degree to which their goals appear to be realistic. Goals of "empirically driven programs" seem clearer and more realistic than "theoretically driven" programs.
4. Clear, sequential program descriptions or guidelines were provided by almost all programs.
5. The programs addressed both risk and protective factors; however, there were differences between programs in terms of the emphasis given to these two groups of factors.
6. The effectiveness of specific program strategies could not be determined due to a lack of empirical data, which is badly needed.
7. Self-selection was the primary method for selecting participants. Better methods were used by CCN, SE & DW, and RE, and further exploration in this area also is needed.
8. By and large, participants in most programs are Caucasian, educated, middle-class couples. Many programs reported applying their programs with both functional and dysfunctional couples. Among the programs, RE has been most frequently applied to different populations and settings.
9. Considerable variability in the background and training of program leaders and facilitators was noted. Studies examining the relative effectiveness of facilitator types are needed.
10. Most programs attempt to distribute their training effects over a period of time, using, for example, follow-up groups or mentoring couples for program graduates. However, only a few programs, with

MSK being the best example, have integrated systematic follow-up assessments and booster sessions into their program structure.

11. Many programs have not yet provided solid evidence to document their short-term effectiveness. Exceptions are RE, CC, and PREP, which are the most thoroughly researched preventive programs. Several programs, PAIRS, for example, reported positive short-term effects either in recent studies or in studies in progress.

12. Most programs also have not yet empirically demonstrated the durability of positive effects. PREP is the only program that provided solid evidence for effects up to 5 years postintervention. Programs such as RE, CC, and PAIRS provided some evidence for their long-term effects, although more studies are needed.

13. A high level of participant satisfaction was reported by most programs.

14. Based on the material provided by our contributors, PREP, RE, and CC are the most cost-effective programs. However, our conclusions should be viewed with caution due to a lack of empirical evidence, particularly data on the relative effectiveness and generalizability of the programs.

☐ Future Trends in the Field of Prevention of Couples' Distress

Having uncovered the historical roots of the field and having surveyed its current parameters, as represented by the programs in this handbook, we consider ourselves well equipped to explore its horizons. We will now address the central issues relevant to the "new generation" of preventive programs by focusing on theoretical, methodological, applied, sociopolitical, and ethical considerations. Although, for the purpose of clarity, we present these issues separately, it will become obvious that they are intricately interrelated.

Theoretical Issues

Blurring Between Preventive and Remedial Intervention

The program models presented in this handbook and their various formats of application highlight what we alluded to in the Introduction (chapter 1) as a trend toward blurring the differences between preventive and remedial interventions. This tendency is manifested not only in the way interventions are practiced (see review by Hof and Miller, 1981), but also in the way relationship theories are constructed. This is particularly true when a theory does not qualitatively differentiate between functional and dysfunctional couples, instead seeing them as resting on the same continuum.

Consequently, these programs offer a similar intervention model for distressed and nondistressed couples. Based on the recently developed programs, which have integrated marriage enrichment, marriage education, and couples therapy within their models, this trend appears to be gaining precedence.

Adopting an Eclectic Orientation

Another common trend in this field is the integration of diverse theoretical frameworks within an intervention model. Unlike models of couples therapy, where theoretical boundaries are more clearly delineated (see Jacobson & Gurman, 1986, 1995), preventive approaches focus on diverse aspects of couple functioning, leading to a borrowing of interventions from several theoretical perspectives (see Table 1.1 of chapter 1). Although programs differ in terms of their emphasis on behavior versus affect or cognition, a shared eclectic orientation is likely to continue.

Balance Between Risk and Protective Factors

An additional issue that has brought controversy to the field relates to the definition of prevention (for further discussion, see chapter 1). While some preventionists address risk factors by focusing on dysfunctional interactions, others stress protective factors by promoting positive interactional patterns and enhancing relationship quality. In the past, these differing foci brought some divergence between enrichment/enhancement approaches and those designed to remediate couples' distress. However, judging from the programs in this volume, the trend seems to be toward integration and equal focus on risk factors and protective factors.

Expanding the Theoretical Framework

Finally, the most significant theoretical development in the area relates to a push to enlarge the theoretical scope through which we view the causes of couple dysfunction. Best exemplified by Bradbury and Fincham's (1990) recommendations, such proposals challenge the "narrow" and often exclusive focus of current preventive theories on interpersonal factors (particularly on dysfunctional or functional interaction patterns). Bradbury and Fincham call instead for the inclusion of intrapersonal factors (for example, personality characteristics and vulnerabilities) as well as of contextual and circumstantial factors (such as financial difficulties, chronic illness, unemployment, racism). This new perspective may help us to better understand the multiple contributors to couples' distress and, even more importantly, may broaden the intervention model and provide a more comprehensive programs to address those issues.

An outstanding proposal for such a theoretical framework was presented by Karney and Bradbury (1995) in their vulnerability-stress-adaptation model. Based on their meta-analysis, these researchers constructed a sophisticated model that explores the mechanisms of change in the marital relationship, taking into account stressful circumstances, personal vulnerabilities, and adaptive styles. Different pathways that lead to marital stability and relationship quality are explored in the context of interactions between those factors. L'Abate (1990), in his developmental theory of interpersonal competence, also proposed an interesting multilevel model that is far more inclusive than previous theories. These theoretical frameworks appear to be the prototypes of the next generation of theories, which will probably lead to the development of more comprehensive and effective preventive programs.

Application Issues

Tailoring Programs to the Needs of Specific Populations

Although noted in all overviews about prevention with couples, there have been few attempts to systematically match couples' characteristics with specific preventive interventions. An exception is the work by L'Abate and colleagues using their laboratory method (see chapter 5 of this volume). Utilizing methods for classifying preventive programs and couples, methods that are rooted within a theoretical framework (L'Abate, 1990), these practitioners designed tailor-made SE and DW programs. Unfortunately, this unique work has not been popular either among couples therapists, who find it too structured and goal oriented, or among prevention experts, who view it as too individualized and too therapeutic.

Other ways of dealing with the specificity issue are through modifying existing preventive models or creating special programs based on the particular needs of a group, for example, high-risk couples. Prevention experts have suggested targeting couples in critical transitional stages, such as upon first marrying or upon the birth of the first child (Cowan & Cowan, 1995; Markman et al., 1986) Other special-needs groups include couples dealing with destructive behaviors such as violence or alcoholism (O'Leary, Malone, & Tyree, 1994) or couples struggling with difficult socioeconomic conditions (Bradbury & Fincham, 1990; Albee, 1996). Efforts to address such circumstances have recently begun to surface. For instance, the PREP model has been adapted for use with first-time parents (S. Stanley, personal communication, October 1997), with violent couples (Holzworth-Munroe et al., 1995), and with couples who experienced divorce in their family of origin (Van Widenfelt, Hosman, Schaap, & van der Staak, 1996). Several programs have also been modified to fit the needs of religious organizations (see Hunt & Hunt, chapter 12 of this volume; Stanley, Blumberg, & Markman, chapter 13 of this volume). On the other hand, specifically designed programs addressing select populations show promising results. Among them are the Becoming Family Project (Cowan & Cowan, 1992), which works with couples making the transition to parenthood, and the Counseling for Alcoholics Marriages (CALM) program, for couples with an alcoholic partner in rehabilitation (Rotunda & O'Farrell, 1997).

Utilization of Programs by Distressed Couples

Preventive approaches were developed initially to supplement remedial approaches and were geared primarily for nondistressed couples. The assumptions that have prevailed among clinicians are that these programs are not effective for clinical populations or that exposure to such programs poses the risk of exacerbating the couple's problems. Recently, this view has been challenged by several preventionists, who cite findings (DeMaria, 1998; Durana, 1996c; Giblin et al., 1985; Guerney, Brock, & Confal, 1986; Hawley & Olson, 1995) that preventive and enrichment programs are effective with dysfunctional couples (sometimes even more so than for nondistressed couples). Furthermore, according to this research, there is no evidence for relationship deterioration due to exposure to these programs. A number of studies suggest that a sizable proportion of prevention participants are, in fact, distressed (DeMaria, 1998; Krug & Ahadi, 1986; Powell & Wampler, 1982; Zimpher, 1988).

Despite the historical reluctance among clinicians to use preventive approaches with distressed couples (Arcus, 1995; Lebow, 1997; Riehlmedle & Willi, 1993), these recent data (DeMaria, 1998) suggest that distressed couples are utilizing these programs.

Underutilization of Programs by Underprivileged Couples

One of the most problematic areas in the field has been the underutilization of preventive programs by lower socioeconomic status (SES) couples and by minority and ethnically diverse populations. This is particularly disturbing in light of the fact that many of these couples are at high risk for marital distress. Despite the recommendations of many prevention experts (Bradbury & Fincham, 1990; Floyd et al., 1995; L'Abate, 1977; Mace,

1976), only a few studies have been conducted to demonstrate the successful application of enrichment and preventive programs with these populations (Allan, 1997; Burnham, 1984; Van Widenfelt & Schaap, 1991). However, there appears to be a growing recognition of the need to understand and ameliorate the reasons for underutilization of preventive programs by minority and ethnically diverse couples. Floyd et al. (1995) suggested that this situation is due to the special circumstances these groups face and challenged preventive programs to show greater sensitivity to their unique needs. Additional discussion of the appropriateness of enrichment and preventive programs for different populations and of the adequacy of recruitment strategies for these groups is warranted.

Delivery Issues

As the field moves into its "consolidation phase," the effectiveness of programs is being examined from a practical perspective. A myriad of questions regarding delivery methods are pertinent here: What format should be used to deliver the information and skills contained in the program? What support system can be put in place after the intervention to enhance the efficacy of the program? Can the program be delivered effectively by nonprofessionals? In addition, in light of the blurring between preventive, enrichment, and therapeutic models, there appears to be a pressing need to explore how these various services can best be delivered to couples.

As far as format and duration are concerned, based on a review of the programs in this volume, the trend is toward increasing program duration and spreading the program content over longer periods of time. Although there are no empirical data on the relative efficacy of intensive formats as opposed to prolonged formats, preliminary evidence suggests a positive correlation between program length and efficacy (Giblin et al., 1985; Seligman, 1995).

The difference between the effectiveness of programs delivered under the leadership of professionals and that of programs facilitated by nonprofessionals has not yet been empirically tested. Nevertheless, programs using professionals report no significant difference in the quality of their programs as compared with programs that use nonprofessionals. Finally, a considerable number of programs report using posttreatment interventions, such as structured homework assignments, audiovisual materials, computer-based programs, booster sessions, couples' support groups, and a variety of mentoring systems. Although there are also no data regarding the efficacy of those postprogram services, preventionists are beginning to recognize the need to move from "a strictly inoculation model to a more long-term maintenance model" (Floyd et al., 1995, p. 222).

Another question concerns how to design a prevention program, given the various potential levels of intervention as well as the different types of services. Hof and Miller (1981) concluded in their review of enrichment programs that preventive services can be employed either concurrently with the beginning, middle, or ending phases of therapy or subsequent to therapy. L'Abate (1990), on the other hand, suggested a bidirectional delivery system he called the "Successive Sieves" model, which moves couples from primary prevention to secondary prevention and then tertiary prevention, or in the other direction, depending on their ability to benefit from these services.

In view of the blurring of differences between preventive, enrichment, and therapeutic models, these proposals deserve further consideration.

Marketing Issues

Because preventive programs have not been part of the mainstream of couples interventions and have thus been underutilized by couples therapists, both the marketing and delivery of preventive programs are outside the normal venues. Attempts to incorporate programs into managed care markets have been sparse and, in general, poorly received. There are isolated instances of prevention programs being offered through either government or privately funded agencies.

Thus far, preventionists have used primarily grass roots marketing approaches to make their programs known. Many have been marketed, with varying degrees of success, by clergy and religious organizations. With prevention being an "invisible product" still lacking product recognition, marketing is one of preventionists' greater challenges. Despite enjoying recent media attention, prevention programs will continue to need creative marketing methods to reach the many segments of the population that have not previously been consumers of these services.

Methodological Issues

Methodological problems are not unique to the field of prevention of couple distress; these difficulties are prevalent in research on psychotherapy in general and couple therapy in particular (Jacobson & Addis, 1993). Although there has been significant improvement during the last decade in the quantity and quality of the research on preventive programs, much more progress is needed to unequivocally demonstrate the effectiveness of these approaches. Since cost-effectiveness is one of the more formidable criteria for the widespread adoption of preventive technology (for further discussion, see chapter 1), this field, unlike the field of couples therapy, cannot afford to overlook the task of documenting cost-effectiveness. Guerney & Maxson (1990), summarizing their review of the last decade of research on marital and family enrichment, conclude that the most pertinent question to be answered is, "Which programs work best for what populations, what makes them best, and how they— and new programs—can be made more efficient and less costly and be better marketed" (p. 1133).

We will first attempt to deal with each issue raised by Guerney and Maxson and will then try to address other important methodological dilemmas.

Which Programs Work Best for Which Populations?

After two decades of calls by preventionists for information necessary to answer this question, few answers have emerged. We are not aware of any study of differential effects of various programs with different populations. However, prospective outcome studies comparing different preventive programs and retrospective meta-analyses comparing programs' effect sizes would shed light on this issue.

As we suggested above in our comparison, there are considerable difficulties, both practical (in terms of organization and expense) and methodological (in terms of controlling confounding variables resulting from differences between programs' goals, formats, duration, and so on), associated with conducting a meaningful comparative study. Despite those difficulties, recently some progress has been noted. A good example is a study by Hawley and Olson (1995), who compared three preventive programs for newlywed couples (two of these programs, TIME and A.C.M.E., are presented in this volume). Although not all subjects were randomly assigned to programs, this study offered significant improvements over earlier research: It was conducted by experimenters with no affiliation with any of the programs, the samples were demographically homogeneous, and the same psychometrically sound outcome measure was administered to all subjects.

Another improvement would be through the use of meta-analysis, such as that conducted by Giblin and his colleagues (Giblin et al., 1985). For instance, based on this method, one would be able to conclude that RE programs are more effective for distressed couples than CC or ME, although other interpretations might be equally plausible. As suggested by Guerney and Maxson (1990), an update of Giblin et al.'s (1985) meta-analytic study is needed, especially in light of the many new programs described in this volume. However, the lack of details regarding subjects' characteristics may prohibit inferences about the relative efficacy of programs.[1]

What Makes a Preventive Program "The Best?"

Another question posed by Guerney and Maxson (1990) is, "What makes them [the programs] best?" In other words, what are the effective ingredients of these programs? Methodologically, there are several ways to address this complicated issue: comparative outcome research on various programs, basic research on couple relationships, and research on specific program ingredients. With the exception of RE, comparative outcome research for most programs presented in this handbook has so far been extremely limited. An example of a relatively good comparison study was the Hawley and Olson (1995) research mentioned above, which found no statistically significant differences between three preventive programs for newlyweds.

Another way to examine the effects of specific active ingredients of preventive programs is to conduct basic research on dysfunctional and functional couple interactions. The work of Gottman and his colleagues (Gottman, 1994; Gottman, 1979; Gottman, Gonso, Notarius, & Markman, 1978; Gottman et al., 1998) has been invaluable in elucidating the processes involved in couples' interactions. Further exploration of these processes would inform preventionists regarding relevant program contents, thus making programs more efficient (for more discussion, see chapter 16, by Kelly & Fincham, in this volume).

The most effective approach would be to conduct studies on the efficacy of specific program components. As we indicated in our comparison, there is almost no existing research in this area. However, a few explorations have recently begun. For example, Gordon and Durana (see chapter 10 in this volume), in a series of outcome studies on the PAIRS program, demonstrated the efficacy of a particular component of this program in changing marital adjustment. Gottman and Gottman (see chapter 14 of this volume) also reported plans to evaluate each component of their MSK program through a series of eight proximal change studies. These studies and similar ones in the future will enable preventionists to modify preventive programs, weed out ineffective from effective strategies, and hopefully make the programs more cost-effective.

---

[1]Originally, Paul Giblin planned to contribute an update of his meta-analysis to this volume, but had to withdraw due to technical difficulties.

Long-Term Outcome Studies

Practitioners have long been urged to conduct long-term outcome studies to demonstrate the durability of the effects of their programs (Bradbury & Fincham, 1990; Guerney & Maxson, 1990; Gurman & Kniskern, 1977; Hof & Miller, 1981; L'Abate, 1981; Mace & Mace, 1975). One compelling reason for conducting longitudinal studies is the growing body of evidence suggesting the presence of delayed positive effects up to as long as 5 years postintervention (Bader & Remmel 1981; Markman et al., 1988; Zimpher, 1988). Unfortunately, there is still a paucity of research on durability of positive effects for most of the programs. Practical issues, such as time constraints and funding, as well as research problems, such as attrition rates, often deter preventionists from conducting such studies.

Measurement Issues

Recently, outcome researchers have been grappling with two major research dilemmas: Which criteria should be used to determine the efficacy of programs, and how should these criteria be measured? As is evident in this handbook, outcome studies use both marital/relationship quality and marital/couple stability as criteria for program success. The underlying assumption here is that these two constructs are strongly correlated and that one leads to the other. However, it is entirely possible that a program that is successful in averting relationship breakup may leave individuals dissatisfied with their relationship. If such is the case, then in the long run, this scenario could deny some couples the opportunity of allowing their relationship to "fail" (and be dissolved by mutual consensus), which would in turn liberate the spouses to find happiness with a new partner. Although there is no doubt that relationship satisfaction and stability are related, the precise nature of their relationship is not fully understood (for further discussion, see Karney and Bradbury, 1995). Indeed, in a recent study of newlywed couples, Rogge and Bradbury (see chapter 15 of this volume) suggested the presence of different mechanisms that influence marital quality and marital stability during the first 4 years of marriage.

A related issue is the notion that marital quality may not be a continuous unidimensional concept (Beach & O'Leary,1985; Karney & Bradbury, 1995). Kelly and Fincham (chapter 16) suggest a bidimensional conceptualization in which marital quality is viewed as a combination of negative and positive elements. Other suggestions regarding this issue include the recommendation to use instruments that measure variability of marital quality over time.

Another measurement issue concerns the use of self-report measures as opposed to behavioral observation in assessing program efficacy. Giblin et al. (1985) reported significantly larger effect size for programs when using behavioral instruments, as opposed to self-report instruments. Several interpretations of these results have been proposed, including sensitivity of behavioral measures, experimental bias favoring observational instruments, and response-shift bias against self-report instruments (for additional discussion, see chapter 16, by Kelly & Fincham, and chapter 15, by Rogge & Bradbury, in this volume). Some researchers (Giblin et al., 1985; Shoham-Salomon & Hannah, 1991; Stanley, 1997), noting interactions between individual and couple variables, recommend using methods that account for such effects in analyzing the outcomes of interventions.

Generalizability Issues

By their very nature, and in their attempts to reach a wide audience, preventive programs cast a wide net. Indeed, the contributors to this volume describe "universal" programs which, by definition, are presented as applicable to a variety of populations. To provide an empirical basis for this claim, however, program outcome studies need to be based on large representative samples. Unfortunately, most studies fail to meet this requirement; rather, research subjects are usually selected from the programmer's natural constituency group, typically, Caucasian, educated, middle-class persons with a religious affiliation. Thus, the results of these studies cannot be generalized to the greater population, particularly to low SES couples and minority couples, especially those at high risk.

A related issue was raised in a series of studies by Sullivan and Bradbury (1996, 1997), who suggested that couples who participate in preventive programs may differ from nonparticipating couples in that participants are more amenable to change in the first place, even without any intervention. In other words, these researchers raised the possibility that prevention and enrichment subjects comprise a subgroup that is lower in risk relative to the population of couples in the general population; therefore, results found on participants should not be generalized to other groups.

Finally, it remains to be seen whether programs developed in a laboratory setting or effectively administered in a university setting can be successfully transferred into the community. Because outcome studies conducted in experimental settings often demonstrate more powerful effects than do studies run in naturalistic settings (Hahlweg & Klann, 1997; Renick, Blumberg, & Markman, 1992), one cannot assume that programs demonstrated to be effective in the laboratory will automatically be effective when applied in more naturalistic settings.

Clinical Significance Versus Statistical Significance

Although traditionally this issue has been raised within the context of remedial interventions, some researchers suggest examining it in relation to preventive programs (Berger & Hannah, 1997; Jacobson & Addis, 1993). As Jacobson and Traux (1991) indicated, most clinicians are interested in promoting meaningful change in clients' lives and are not concerned with statistically significant changes demonstrated in outcome studies. The question remains, however, concerning the determination of clinical significance. For instance, if a particular program results in statistically significant changes in both spouses' Marital Adjustment Test scores, but their scores nonetheless remain within the distressed level, should we consider the program effective? Consensus regarding this and related questions has not been reached.

Sociopolitical Issues

The Antidivorce Legislation

A recent trend in the field is political advocacy by some prevention experts and religious groups against "no-fault" divorce laws. Citing studies which suggest that legal reforms in the 1970s contributed to the sharp increase in divorce rate (Levant, 1986; Norton & Glick, 1976), these groups advocate repealing no-fault divorce laws, replacing them with the option of "covenant marriage," and imposing mandatory premarital preparatory programs. Although virtually all prevention advocates share in the intentions of seriously preparing couples for marriage and preventing unnecessary divorces, many object to the imposition of what they view as coercive methods to accomplish these objectives. Further, the success of the campaign against the current divorce laws (several states have passed covenant marriage bills) has brought sharp criticism from women's groups, who warn against what they see as a backlash against women (see Pollit, 1997). We maintain that the advocacy by some in the prevention movement for antidivorce laws needs to be carefully thought through, and we believe that other, less legalistic ways of promoting marital stability are preferable.

Politicizing of the Field

As indicated above, the costly socioeconomic impacts of the breakdown of the American family brought together liberals and conservatives in a joint effort to combat this decline. However, in the euphoria of joining forces against the evil of divorce, basic ideological differences were shoved aside. This phenomenon was well captured in an article entitled "No Joy in Splitsville" (Levy, 1997), which reported on the first meeting of the Coalition of Marriage, Family, and Couples Education in June 1997. Although the article perhaps overemphasized the differences between the various approaches within the field, it also suggested that deep ideological differences cannot, and perhaps should not, be ignored. Les Parrott is quoted as saying, "We believe in the traditional value of marriage; the religious aspect is a priority, but I really don't emphasize it. I don't want to alienate anybody." Unfortunately, such a respectful position is not shared by all preventionists. For instance, Mike McManus, the force behind Marriage Savers, is quoted as stating, "The liberal approach—any sex, anywhere, anytime—has obviously been a gross failure." He goes on to discuss his objections to assisting gay couples, observing that "Homosexual sex is promiscuous, uncommitted, shameful and degrading." Such abject prejudice, in our opinion, sabotages the preventive agenda by presenting as gospel the position of a minority of ultraconservative and religious groups that have promoted ideologically driven preventive strategies. Although these groups share with other prevention experts the goal of promoting couple satisfaction and stability, their philosophy and methodology are the antithesis of the humanistic bedrock of the prevention movement.

It is therefore not surprising that, although many prominent couple therapists and researchers have supported the prevention movement, there are others, particularly those espousing liberal and feminist values, who have been reluctant to join the coalition. The challenge of adopting social values and policies that enhance couples' and families' relationships, yet simultaneously are tolerant of a diversity of couples, still remains unmet.

Ethical Issues

Despite having received minimal attention thus far, ethical issues are of vital importance to the field of prevention. With the growing popularity of prevention among the public and policy makers, along with the recent proliferation of preventive programs for couples' distress, ethical concerns are becoming even more pressing. We decided to address this issue by focusing on three areas: the potentially deleterious effects of programs, the use of nonprofessionals, and the overselling of preventive programs.

Potential Deleterious Effects

Outcome research in the fields of prevention and psychotherapy rarely addresses the possibility of undesirable effects of interventions, although most clinicians are aware of this phenomenon. Several practitioners (for example, Gurman, 1980) have raised concerns over the potential delete-rious effects of preventive programs; such issues, however, were rejected on the basis of a lack of empirical support (Markman et al., 1986). Still, Doherty and his colleagues (Doherty & Walker, 1982; Doherty, Lester, & Leigh, 1986) demonstrated that some couples who participated in ME experienced negative effects in the form of increased conflict, which lingered subsequent to the program. Although, to the best of our knowledge, these results were not replicated, the possibility that preventive programs may yield negative effects cannot be ruled out.

Use of Nonprofessionals

The use of nonprofessionals (paraprofessionals or quasiprofessionals) in prevention services is based on both philosophical and pragmatic rationales. Although preventive and enrichment programs originally were designed for relatively functional couples (Mace, 1983; L'Abate, 1977), the burgeoning use of these programs by significantly distressed couples (Wampler, 1982; Zimpher, 1988) has raised concerns about the ability of nonprofessionals to perform competently as program leaders and facilitators. Although some data exist regarding the efficacy of using trained paraprofessionals in prevention work (Durlak, 1979; Most & Guerney, 1983), more research is needed, particularly to answer the following questions: Can we adequately select and train nonprofessionals to serve as group leaders for preventive programs? Can preventive groups run by non-professionals with minimal training pose potential risk to some participants? In response to such questions, our chapter contributors proposed various solutions, which ranged from excluding leaders without adequate academic backgrounds, professional training, or experiences to requiring ongoing training and supervision of leaders by professionals. Although at this juncture we remain unaware of any incidents of inappropriate or incompetent leadership by nonprofessionals, this issue begs further exploration.

A related and equally challenging issue is the overlapping of the numerous roles in which preventionists find themselves. Those who attempt to integrate couples therapy, preventive interventions, and educational programs fulfill a variety of roles in their interactions with participants. Although family therapists have long been confronted with these issues, individually oriented therapists now working in the prevention field may find this intermingling of roles complicated and confusing.

Overselling Preventive Programs

Another, perhaps more disturbing, ethical issue is the tendency among some preventionists to oversell their programs (L'Abate, 1981; Levant,

1986; Smith, Shofnner, & Scoot, 1979). As Markman et al. (1986) aptly pointed out, there is a need to strike a balance between motivating couples to participate in preventive programs and "oversell[ing] a generally untested product" (p. 191).

Despite this caveat, some practitioners are still promoting their programs in a less than responsible manner. For instance, we recently saw an advertisement for a couples workshop claiming to be "a program based on a proven method for long-lasting happiness in your marriage." Incidentally, there are no existing outcome studies of that particular method. Such advertisements, along with possibly being unethical, are counterproductive in that they raise unrealistic expectations among participants.

☐ Summary and Recommendation

In this chapter we have taken you on a journey across the terrain of preventive interventions for couples' distress, beginning with their early inception through current major approaches and into the future. Based on our review of the milestones, programs, and central issues of the movement, the field can be conceptualized as being in transition from its "building phase" to a "consolidation phase." In paying attention to the developmental tasks of establishing a firm identity and proving one's competency, the preventive models presented in this volume are typical of programs in the building phase.

As the field enters the next phase, different tasks, such as setting boundaries and recognizing limitations, will take precedence. We expect prevention experts to gradually shift away from modifying and refining their programs to work instead on honing them to fit the specific needs of various populations. Signs of this trend are already evident in the way practitioners are urging prevention experts to concentrate on improving their own programs, rather than focusing on proving the legitimacy of the entire field (Floyd et. al. 1995; Guerney & Maxson, 1990; Hahlweg & Markman,1988; L'Abate, 1990).

While we support collaboration among diverse preventionists working in the field, we are concerned about ideologically oriented approaches that espouse a particular style of couplehood as the ideal form of intimacy. We call for attitudes, practices, and policies that are tolerant and respectful of the diversity of couples. We would like also to draw the attention of preventionists to the ethical issues relevant to their field, and we propose the establishment of an ethics committee to develop an ethics code similar to that of other professional organizations.

In the coming years, we anticipate significant developments in theory, research, and practice. In the area of theory development, we believe that there is much promise in expanding the scope of current theoretical frameworks by incorporating multilevel and multisystemic variables. On the other hand, developing more refined and empirically based process models (Gottman et al., 1998) which explain the underlying mechanisms of dysfunctional and, even more importantly, functional couples would also be invaluable. In terms of practice, we believe that progress has been made, as is attested to by the proliferation of preventive programs and by their popularity among the public and policy makers. We expect prevention experts to gradually shift their attention to the tasks of tailoring programs to fit the needs of specific populations, improving recruitment and delivery methods, and making programs more cost-effective.

Although significant progress in theory building and practice in the field of preventive interventions for couples has been noted, forward movement in the research arena has been painfully slow. Hence, the research area is a top priority.

Perhaps the most pressing research issue is the need to identify which program, in which format, and delivered in which setting and by whom, works best for which type of couple at which risk level. Answering this complex question would require a thorough examination of a multitude of interacting variables; these involve, first, program variables, such as the type of change processes tapped by the program (e.g., personal awareness and knowledge regarding self and partner's intergenerational patterns); the skills and competencies addressed in the program, such as communication skills and conflict resolution skills; and the format and length of the program (e.g., a weekend marathon or a limited number of 2-hour sessions). Couples variables would include individual variables like demographic characteristics (age, sex, race, ethnic background, education, SES), personality characteristics, such as degree of competency and pathology, and couple characteristics, like level of distress, interaction pattern (such as that identified by topologies like Gottman's, 1994), and stage of couple development. Also important to assess are early risk factors, such as parental divorce, history of childhood abuse, and substance abuse or psychiatric history in family of origin, and whether there is a current violation of major relationship ground rules, like infidelity, physical abuse, or alcoholism. The roles of external stressors, like financial and legal difficulties, of delivery variables, like the type of setting in which the program is held, and of the nature of the contact between facilitator and client (e.g., direct vs. indirect contact) must be taken into consideration. Finally, preventionist variables, including preventionists' skills and characteristics (e.g., teaching ability, mastery of the material, warmth, genuineness, nondefensiveness, sense of humor) and whether professionals or paraprofessionals are used as facilitators contribute part of the answer, as well.

Another important methodological issue relates to the use of outcome measures. We suggest making independent measurements of marital quality and marital stability, using a multidimensional approach to measurement, which should include behavioral observations and self-reports, employing individual measures of adjustment and well-being, and analyzing the differences within the couple on outcome measures.

Research should also address generalizability issues by focusing on sampling effects. We recommend that researchers utilize large, demographically representative samples and pay close attention to the recruitment procedures being used for the study. Alternatively, sampling specific homogeneous groups (e.g., low SES couples) might shed light on the particular issues relevant to such groups. Additionally, outcome studies should compare the relative efficacy of programs in the laboratory setting and those same programs when applied in naturalistic settings. Effects related to a lack of randomized assignment or differential attrition may bias the results of a study. Thus, researchers need to analyze subjects who drop out at various stages of the project.

Outcome studies should employ measures that tap clinical as well as statistical significance. The lack of longitudinal studies and of long-term follow-ups have been major barriers to demonstrating the usefulness of these services. We suggest, therefore, that research programs commit themselves to at least 1 to 2 years of follow-up assessments.

The above summary reflects the complexity of the task faced by researchers of preventive programs for couples. As in other fields, methodological dilemmas have thus far dampened the persuasiveness of findings on these programs. However, as we hope our overview has elucidated, researchers are clearly headed in the right direction.

☐ References

Ackerman, N. (1954). Diagnosis of neurotic marital interaction. *Social Casework, 34,* 139–146.

Albee, G. W. (1996). Revolutions and counterrevolutions in prevention. *American Psychologist, 51,* 1130–1133.

Allan, W. (1997) *Replication of five types of married couples based on ENRICH.* Unpublished doctoral dissertation, University of Minnesota, St. Paul.

Allen, W. D. (1996). *Five types of African-American marriages based on ENRICH: A Replication study.* Doctoral dissertation submitted to University of Minnesota, St. Paul.

Arcus, M. (1995). Advances in family life education—Past, present, and future. *Family Relations, 44,* 336–344.

Ard, B., & Ard, C. (1969). *Handbook of marriage counseling.* Palo Alto, CA: Science and Behavior Books.

Bader E., & Remmel, A. (1987). *Learning to live together.* Toronto: University of Toronto.

Bader, E., Microys, G., Sinclair, C., Willett, E., & Conway, B. (1980). Do marriage preparation programs really work? A Canadian experiment. *Journal of Marital and Family Therapy, 6*(2), 171–179.

Bagarozzi, D. A., & Rauen, P. I. (1981). Premarital counseling: Appraisal and status. *The American Journal of Family Therapy, 9*(3), 13–27.

Beach, S. R. H., & O'Leary, K. D. (1985). Current status of outcome research in marital therapy. In L. L'Abate (Ed.), *Handbook of family psychology and therapy, Vol. 2* (pp. 1035–1072). Homewood, IL: Dorsey.

Berger, R., & Hannah, M. T. (1996, October). *What can clinicians learn from research?* Paper presented at the annual convention of the Association for Imago Relationship Therapy, Philadelphia, PA.

Bradbury, T. N., & Fincham, F. D. (1990). Preventing marital dysfunction: Review and analysis. In F. D. Fincham & T. N. Bradbury (Eds.), *The psychology of marriage: Basic issues and applications* (pp. 375–401). New York: Guilford.

Burnham, R. A. (1984). Effects of the Couple Communication Program on the marital and family communications of high and low socioeconomic status couples (Doctoral dissertation, University of Notre Dame, 1984). *Dissertation Abstracts International, 45,* 1006B–1007B. (University Microfilms No. 84-14128)

Coie, J., Watt, N., Ewst, S., Hawkins, J., Asarnow, J., Markman, H., Ramey, S., Shure, S., & Long, B. (1993). The science of prevention: A conceptual framework and some directions for a national research program. *American Psychologist, 48*(10), 1013–1022.

Cowan, C. P., & Cowan, P. A. (1992). *When partners become parents.* New York: Basic Books.

Cowan, C. P., & Cowan, P. A. (1995). Interventions to ease the transition to parenthood: Why they are needed and what they can do. *Family Relations, 44,* 412–423.

DeMaria, R. (1998). *A national survey of married couples who participate in marriage enrichment.* Ann Arbor, MI: UMI Dissertation Services, No. 983-3080.

Doherty, W. J., & Walker, B. J. (1982). Marriage Encounter casualties: A preliminary investigation. *American Journal of Family Therapy, 10,* 15–25.

Doherty, W. J., Lester, M. E., & Leigh, G. (1986). Marriage Encounter weekends: Couples who win and couples who lose. *Journal of Marital and Family Therapy, 12,* 49–61.

Durana, C. (1996a). Bonding and emotional re-education of couples in the PAIRS training: Part I. *The American Journal of Family Therapy, 24*(3), 269–280.

Durana, C. (1996b). Bonding and emotional re-education of couples in the PAIRS training: Part II. *The American Journal of Family Therapy, 24*(4), 315–328.

Durana., C. (1996c). A longitudinal evaluation of the effectiveness of the PAIRS psychoeducational program for couples. *Family Therapy, 23*(1), 11–36.

Durlak, J. A. (1979). Comparative effectiveness of paraprofessional and professional helpers. *Psychological Bulletin, 86,* 80–92.

Elliot, S. S., & Saunders, B. E. (1982). The Systems Marriage Enrichment Program: An alternative model based on systems theory. *Family Relations, 31,* 53–60.

Eisenstein, V. W. (1956). *Neurotic interaction in marriage.* New York: Basic Books.

Floyd, F., Markman, H., Kelly, S., Blumberg, S. L., & Stanley, S. (1995). Preventive intervention and relationship enhancement. In N. S. Jacobson & A. S. Gurman (Eds.), *Clinical handbook of couple therapy* (pp. 212–226). New York: Guilford.

Fournier, D. G., Olson, D. H., & Druckman, J. M. (1983). Assessing marital and premarital relationships: The PREPARE-ENRICH inventories. In E. E. Filsinger (Ed.), *Marriage and family assessment* (pp. 229–250). Beverly Hills, CA: Sage.

Fournier, D. G., & Olson, D. H. (1986). Programs for premarital and newlywed couples. In R. F. Levant (Ed.), *Psychoeducational approaches to family therapy and counseling* (pp. 194–231). New York: Springer-Verlag.

Giblin, P. (1986). Research and assessment in marriage and family enrichment: A meta-analysis study. *Journal of Psychotherapy and the Family, 2,* 79–86.

Giblin, P., Sprenkle, D. H., & Sheehan, R. (1985). Enrichment outcome research: A meta-analysis of premarital, marital, and family interventions. *Journal of Marital and Family Therapy, 11*(3), 257–271.

Gottman, J. M. (1979). *Marital interaction: Experimental investigations.* New York: Academic Press.

Gottman, J. M. (1994). *Why marriages succeed or fail.* New York: Simon & Schuster.

Gottman, J. M., Coan, J., Carrere, S., & Swanson, C. (1998). Predicting marital happiness and stability from newlywed interactions. *Journal of Marriage and the Family, 60,* 5–22.

Gottman, J. M., Gonso, J., Notarius, C., & Markman, H. (1978). *A couple's guide to communication.* IL: Research Press.

Guerney, B. G. (1977). *Relationship enhancement.* San Francisco: Jossey-Bass.

Guerney, B. G., Jr., Brock, G., & Coufal, J. (1986). Integrating marital therapy and enrichment: The relationship enhancement approach. In N. S. Jacobson & A. S. Gurman (Eds.), *Clinical handbook of marital therapy* (pp. 151–172). New York: Guilford.

Guerney, B. G., & Maxson, P. (1990). Marital and family enrichment research: A decade review and look ahead. *Journal of Marriage and the Family, 52,* 1127–1135.

Gurman, A. S. (1980). Behavioral marriage therapy in the 1980's: The challenge of integration. *American Journal of Family Therapy, 8,* 86–96.

Gurman, A. S., & Kniskern, D. P. (1977). Enriching research on marital enrichment programs. *Journal of Marriage and Family Counseling, 3*(2), 3–11.

Halhweg, K., & Klann, N. (1997). The effectiveness of marital counseling in Germany: A contribution to health services research. *Journal of Family Psychology, 11*(4), 410–421.

Hahlweg, K., & Markman, H. J. (1988). The effectiveness of behavioral marital therapy: Empirical status of behavioral techniques in preventing and alleviating marital distress. *Journal of Consulting and Clinical Psychology, 56,* 440–447.

Hawley, D. R., & Olson, D. H. (1995). Enriching newlyweds: An evaluation of three enrichment programs. *The American Journal of Family Therapy, 23*(2), 129–147.

Hof, L., & Miller, W. R. (1981). *Marriage enrichment: Philosophy, process and program.* Bowie, MD: Robert J. Brady.

Hollis, F. (1949). *Women in marital conflict.* New York: Family Service Association of America.

Holtzworth-Munroe, A., Markman, H. J., O'Leary, D. K., Neidig, P., Leber, D., Heyman, R. E., Hulbert, D., & Smutzler, N. (1995). The need for marital violence prevention efforts: A behavioral-cognitive secondary prevention program for engaged and newly-married couples. *Applied and Preventive Psychology, 4,* 77–88.

Hunt, R. A., Hof, L., & DeMaria, R. (1998). *Marriage enrichment: Preparation, outreach, and mentoring.* Philadelphia: Brunner/Mazel.

Huppert, N. M. (1984). Communicating for better or for worse. *Australian Journal for Sex, Marriage and Family, 5,* 25–35.

Jacobson, N. S. & Addis, M. E. (1993). Research on couples and couple therapy: What do we know? *Journal of Consulting and Clinical Psychology, 61,* 85–93

Jacobson, N. S., & Gurman, A. S. (Eds.). (1986). *Clinical handbook of marital therapy.* New York: Guilford.

Jacoboson, N. S., & Gurman, A. S. (Eds.). (1995). *Clinical handbook of couple therapy.* New York: Guilford.

Jacobson, N. S., & Truax, P. (1991). Clinical significance: A statistical approach to defining meaningful change in psychotherapy research. *Journal of Consulting and Clinical Psychology, 57,* 138–147.

Kaplan, H. S. (1974). *The new sex therapy.* New York: Brunner/Mazel.

Karney, B. R., & Bradbury, T. N. (1995). The longitudinal course of marital quality and stability: A review of theory, method, and research. *Psychological Bulletin, 118*(1), 3–34.

Krug, S. E., & Ahadi, S. A. (1986). Personality characteristics of wives and husbands participating in marriage enrichment. *Multivariate Experimental Clinical Research, 8,* 149–159.

L'Abate, L. (1977). *Enrichment: Structured interventions with couples, families, and groups.* Washington, DC: University Press of America.

L'Abate, L. (1981). Skill training programs for couples and families. In A. S. Gurman & D. P. Kniskern (Eds.), *Handbook of family therapy* (pp.631–661). New York: Brunner/Mazel.

L'Abate, L. (1990). *Building family competence: Primary and secondary prevention strategies.* Newbury Park, CA: Sage.

L'Abate, L., Wildman, R. W., O'Callaghan, J. B., Simon, S. J., Allison, M., Kahn, G., & Rainwater, N. (1975). The laboratory evaluation and enrichment of couples: Applications and some preliminary results. *Journal of Marriage and Family Counseling, 1,* 351–358.

Lebow, J. (1997). *Is couples therapy obsolete? The Networker, 21*(5), 81–88.

Lederer, W. J., & Jackson, D. D. (1968). *The mirages of marriage.* New York: W. W. Norton.

Leight, G. K., Loewen, I. R., & Lester, M. D. (1986). Caveat emptor: Values and ethics in family life education and enrichment. *Family Relations. Journal of Applied Family and Child Studies, 35*(4) 573–580.

Levant, R. F. (Ed.). (1986). *Psychoeducational approaches to family therapy and counseling.* New York: Springer-Verlag.

Levy, A. (1997, May 12). *No joy in splitsville.* New York Magazine.

Mace, D. R. (1976). The couple dialogue—where it all begins. *Marriage Enrichment, 3*(2), 10–11.

Mace, D. (Ed.). (1983). *Prevention in family services: Approaches to family wellness.* Beverly Hills, CA: Sage.

Mace, D., & Mace, V. (1975). Marriage enrichment—Wave of the future? *The Family Coordinator, 24,* 171–173.

Manus, G. I. (1966). Marriage counseling: A technique in search for a theory. *Journal of Marriage and the Family, 28,* 449–453.

Markman, H. J., Floyd, F. J., Stanley, S. M., & Lewis, H. (1986). Prevention. In N. Jacobson & A. Gurman (Eds.), *Clinical handbook of marital therapy* (pp. 173–195). New York: Guilford

Markman, H. J., Floyd, F. J., Stanley, S. M., & Storaasli, R. D. (1988). Prevention of marital distress: A longitudinal investigation. *Journal of Consulting and Clinical Psychology, 56,* 210–217.

Markman H. J., & Hahlweg, K. (1993). The prediction and prevention of marital distress: An international perspective. *Clinical Psychology Review, 13,* 29–43.

Miller, S., Nunnally, E. M., & Wackman, D. B. (1975). *Alive and aware: Improving communication in relationships.* Minneapolis, MN: Interpersonal Communications Program.

Most, R. K., & Guerney, B. G., Jr. (1983). An empirical evaluation of the training of volunteer lay leaders for premarital relationship enhancement. *Family Relations, 32,* 239–251.

Munoz, R. F., Mrazek, P. J., & Haggerty, R. J. (1996). Institute of Medicine report on prevention of mental disorders. *American Psychologist, 51,* 1116–1122.

Nakonezny, P. A., Schull, R. D., & Rodgers., J. L. (1995). The effect of no-fault divorce law on the divorce rate across the 50 states and its relation to income, education, and religiosity. *Journal of Marriage and the Family, 57,* 477–488.

Norton, A. J., & Glick, P. C. (1976). Marital instability: Present, past, and future. *Journal of Social Issues, 32*(1), 5–20.

O'Leary, K. D., Malone, J., & Tyree, A. (1994). Physical aggression in early marriage: Prerelationship and relationship effects. *Journal of Consulting and Clinical Psychology, 62,* 594–602.

O'Leary, K. D., & Turkewitz, H. (1978). Marital therapy from a behavioral perspective. In. T. J. Paolino & B. S. McCrady (Eds.), *Marriage and marital therapy: Psychoanalytic, behavioral, and systems theory perspectives.* New York: Brunner/Mazel.

Otto, H., & Otto, R. (1976). The more joy to your marriage program. In H. A. Otto (Ed.), *Marriage and family enrichment: New perspectives and programs.* Nashville, TN: Abingdon.

Pollit, K. (1997, June 27). What's right about divorce. *The New York Times,* Op-Ed page.

Powell, G. W., & Wampler, K. (1982). Marriage enrichment participants: Levels of marital satisfaction. *Family Relations, July,* 389–393.

Price, R. H., Cowen, E. L., Lorion, R. P., & Ramos-McKay, J. (1989). The search for effective prevention programs: What we learned along the way. *American Journal of Orthopsychiatry, 59*(1), 49–58.

Renick, M. J., Blumberg, S., & Markman, H. J. (1992). The Prevention and Relationship Enhancement Program (PREP): An empirically-based preventive intervention program for couples. *Family Relations, 41*(2), 141–147.

Riehlmede, A., & Willi, J. (1993). Ambivalence of psychotherapists towards the prevention of marital conflicts. *System Familie-Forchung Und Therapie, 6*(2), 79–88.

Rotunda, R. J., & O'Farrell, T. J. (1997). Bridging the gap between research and practice. *Professional Psychology: Research and Practice, 28*(3), 246–252.

Schmitt, A., & Schmitt, D. (1976). Marriage renewal retreats. In H. A. Otto (Ed.), *Marriage and family enrichment: New perspective and programs* (pp. 110–120). Nashville, TN: Abingdon.

Seligman, M. E. P. (1995). The effectiveness of psychotherapy: The Consumer Reports study. *American Psychologist, 50,* 965–974.

Shadish, W. R., Montomery, L. M., Wilson, P., Wilson, M. R., Bright, I., & Okwumabua, T. (1993). Effects of family and marital psychotherapies: A meta-analysis. *Journal of Consulting and Clinical Psychology, 61,* 992–1002.

Shoham-Salomon, V., & Hannah, M. (1991). Client-treatment interactions in the study of differential change processes. *Journal of Consulting and Clinical Psychology, 5*(9), 217–225.

Smith, R. M., Shofnner, S. M., & Scoot, J. P. (1979). Marriage and family enrichment: A new professional area. *The Family Coordinator, 28,* 87–93.

Stanley, S. M. (1997). *Acting on what we know: The hope of prevention.* Paper presented at Family Impact Seminar, Washington DC.

Stanley, S., Trathen, D., McCain, S., & Bryan, M. (1998). *A lasting promise: A Christian guide to Fighting for Your Marriage.* San Francisco: Jossey-Bass.

Stuart, R. (1980). *Helping couples change.* New York: Guilford.

Sullivan, K. T., & Bradbury, T. N. (1996). Preventing marital dysfunction: The primacy of secondary strategies. *The Behavior Therapist, 19,* 33–35.

Sullivan, K. T., & Bradbury, T. N. (1997). Are premarital prevention programs reaching couples at risk for marital dysfunction? *Journal of Consulting and Clinical Psychologist, 65,* 24–30.

Van Widenfelt, B., Hosman, C., Schaap, C., van der Staak, C. (1996). The prevention of relationship distress for couples at risk: A controlled evaluation with nine-month and two-year follow-ups. *Family Relations, 45,* 156–165.

Van Widenfelt, B., & Schapp, C. (1991, November). *Preventing marital distress and divorce in a risk group in the Netherlands.* Presented at the Convention of the Association for the Advancement of Behavior Therapy, New York.

Wampler, K. S. (1982). Bringing the review of literature into the age of quantification: Meta-analysis as a strategy for integrating research findings in family studies. *Journal of Marriage and the Family, 44,* 1009–1023.

Wampler, K. S. (1990). An update on research on the Couple Communication Program. *Family Science Review, 3,* 21–40.

Weiss, R. L. (1978). The conceptualization of marriage from a behavioral perspective. In T. J. Paolino & B. S. McCrady (Eds.), *Marriage and Marital Therapy: Psychoanalytic, behavioral and systems theory perspectives* (pp. 165–239). New York: Brunner/Mazel.

Zimpher, D. G. (1988). Reviews and developments: Marriage enrichment programs: A review. *Journal for Specialists in Group Work, 13,* 44–53.

INDEX

('f' indicates a figure; 'n' indicates a note; 't' indicates a table)